D1234579

the complete guide to
cocktails
and drinks

the complete guide to
cocktails
and drinks

how to create fantastic drinks using
spirits, liqueurs, wine, beer and mixers

stuart walton

LORENZ BOOKS

This edition is published by Lorenz Books

Lorenz Books is an imprint of Anness Publishing Ltd
Hermes House, 88–89 Blackfriars Road, London SE1 8HA
tel. 020 7401 2077; fax 020 7633 9499
www.lorenzbooks.com; info@anness.com

© Anness Publishing Ltd 2003

This edition distributed in the UK by The Manning Partnership Ltd, 6 The Old Dairy
Melcombe Road, Bath BA2 3LR; tel. 01225 478 444; fax 01225 478 440
sales@manning-partnership.co.uk

This edition distributed in the USA and Canada by National Book Network 4720 Boston Way
Lanham, MD 20706; tel. 301 459 3366; fax 301 459 1705; www.nbnbooks.com

This edition distributed in Australia by Pan Macmillan Australia, Level 18, St Martins Tower
31 Market St, Sydney, NSW 2000; tel. 1300 135 113; fax 1300 135 103
customer.service@macmillan.com.au

This edition distributed in New Zealand by David Bateman Ltd, 30 Tarndale Grove
Off Bush Road, Albany, Auckland; tel. (09) 415 7664; fax (09) 415 8892

A CIP catalogue record for this book is available from the British Library.

Publisher: Joanna Lorenz
Managing editor: Judith Simons
Project editor: Felicity Forster
Photographers: Frank Adam, Steve Baxter and Janine Hosegood
Designer: Nigel Partridge
Copy editor: Kate Humby
Editorial reader: Jay Thundercliffe
Production controller: Steve Lang

1 3 5 7 9 10 8 6 4 2

NOTES

Bracketed terms are intended for American readers.

For all recipes, quantities are given in both metric and imperial measures. Where appropriate, standard bar measures are
used, alongside the imperial spoon equivalents. Follow one set, but not a mixture, because they are not interchangeable.

Standard spoon and bar measures are level.
1 tsp = 5ml, 1 tbsp = 15ml

American readers should note that the mixer known as Club soda is referred to throughout as soda or soda water.

CONTENTS

INTRODUCTION

At what point in history someone first used an alcoholic substance to fulfil what would become its time-honoured role as intoxicant is a question that may never be answered. What is certain is that the first such use arose from the discovery of the effects of fermentation on either fruit, honey or sticky-sweet palm sap.

First alcohol

The ancient Egyptians used fermented grains for making prototype forms of beer. These grains also enabled them to refine the techniques for producing raised breads. They found that adding beer sediment – which was still full of live yeasts – was the quickest and easiest method of encouraging the start of fermentation in a new batch of dough.

Below: This Egyptian figure dates from c.2450–2290 BC, and shows a woman at a mixing tub making beer.

Wine came after beer, but was to become of crucial cultural and religious importance to the civilizations of Egypt, and classical Greece and Rome. It was used as a sacrament in orgiastic celebrations of the festivals of Dionysos, the Greek god of nature (Bacchus to the Romans). From such ancient rituals, the first public performances recognizable as drama are said to have evolved.

In addition to its ceremonial and cultural role, wine was also used for culinary purposes. Not only was it capable of making tough meat more supple, but wine marinades would have removed excess salt from meats that had been encrusted with salt, or soaked in brine, for preservation. Wine vinegar, its alcohol lost to acetic acid, may have been the first recourse, but wine itself appears in sauce recipes in the historically important late Roman cookbook of Apicius (3rd century AD). The wine itself was commonly infused with spices to mask the rank flavours of oxidation or acetification.

Distillation

The next important step was the discovery of the art of distilling. Distillation (from the Latin *destillare*; to drip) is the extraction of higher alcohols from fermented drinks, which uses the action of heat to vaporize them. Compared to fermentation, distillation is a remarkably simple process, largely because it is much easier to control. Whereas freshly pressed grape juice needs the right ambient temperature to begin the process of turning into wine, a spirit can be produced from wine simply by applying heat to it.

Alcohol has a lower boiling point than water (about 78°C/172°F, compared to 100°C/212°F), so it vaporizes into steam some time before the water content in the wine starts to boil. When the alcohol-laden steam hits a cool surface, it forms a dripping condensation, and reverts to a liquid with a much higher proportion of alcohol than the wine. Boil that liquid

up again, and the same procedure will yield an even higher alcohol, and so on.

Much academic debate has been generated in the last 30 years or so as to when and where distillation was first discovered. The Greek philosopher Aristotle, who lived in the 4th century BC, writes of distillation as a way of purifying seawater to make it drinkable. He comments in passing that the same treatment can be given to wine, which is reduced thereby to a sort of "water". He was tantalizingly close to a breakthrough, but his experiment did no more than prove that wine is just a form of modified water, and that a liquid can only derive flavour from whatever happens to be mixed with the water that forms its base.

The documented beginnings of systematic and scientifically founded distillation, at least in Europe, come from the celebrated medical school at Salerno around AD 1100. Wine itself was held to have a range of medicinal properties (a view that found favour again in the 1990s), and the extraction of what was held to be the soul or spirit of the wine, through distillation, is what led to the naming of distillates as "spirits".

Alcohol and alchemy

Alcohol was believed to be the active ingredient in the healing powers of wine. Up to that time, the word "alcohol" was applied as a generic term to any product derived through vaporization and condensation. Its origin from the Arabic word *al-kuhl* refers to the Arab practice of producing a black powder by condensing a vapour of the metal antimony. The powder was then used as eye make-up, which is why eye-liner is still occasionally known as kohl. It was not until some time during the 16th century that "alcohol" was used specifically in reference to distilled spirits.

Not only medicine but the ancient practice of alchemy were involved in the European origins of distillation. Alchemy was a respected branch of the physical

Above: A vase painting from c.460–450 BC, showing Greeks sharing a drink at a banquet. Note the flat drinking vessel.

sciences, and was chiefly concerned with finding a means of transforming ordinary metals into gold. People wholeheartedly believed that if such a process could be discovered, it might well be possible to apply it to the human body and extract the essential life force from its mortal shell, thus guaranteeing eternal youth. With the realization that alcohol could be repeatedly distilled to ever-greater levels of purity, people came to believe that spirits could be the Holy Grail.

It can't have taken long for the Salerno doctors to ascertain that, whatever other remarkable properties distilled spirit had, the power to confer everlasting life wasn't one of them. However, the medical applications of spirits were to endure for hundreds of years. It was Arnaldo de Vilanova, a Catalan physician of the 13th century,

Right: This 15th-century English illustration shows scientists preparing for an alchemical experiment.

who first coined the Latin term *aqua vitae*, "water of life", for distilled spirits, indicating that they were associated with the promotion of vitality and health. (That term lives on in the Scandinavian *aquavit* and the French *eau de vie*, as well as the names of various other spirits.)

First distillates

Undoubtedly, the earliest distillates were of wine, since it had a more salubrious and exalted image than beer; grain

distillation to produce the first whiskies and neutral spirits followed in the Middle Ages. Many of these prototypes contained herb and spice extracts, or were flavoured with fruit, in order to enhance the medicinal properties of the preparation. The additives also conveniently masked what must have been the fairly raw taste and off-putting aroma of the unadulterated liquor.

Anyone who has smelt and tasted clear spirit dripping off the still in a brandy distillery (or, for that matter, has had a brush with illicit Irish poteen or American moonshine) will know how far removed untreated spirit is from the welcoming smoothness of five-star cognac or single malt Scotch. The infused distillates were the antecedents of many of the traditional aromatic liqueurs and flavoured vodkas of today.

Such, for centuries, was the official account of the birth of distilled spirits. In 1961, however, an Indian food historian, O. Prakash, argued that there was evidence that distillation of rice and barley beer was practised in India as early as 800 BC. Others have argued that, if this was so, then distillation probably arrived there from China even

Above: This late 14th-century Italian manuscript shows people enjoying their wine in an upper room, with the cellarman hard at work in the wine cellar below.

earlier. Thus, current theory cautiously credits the Chinese as the discoverers of the art.

It seems unusual that distilled alcohol was not remarked on or, apparently even encountered by soldiers engaged in the European invasion of India, led by Alexander the Great in 327 BC. His campaign is reliably credited with having brought rice back to Europe, but any rice spirit appears to have been overlooked. Perhaps, if it was drunk at all by the invaders, it was in a diluted form, and was therefore not perceived to be any higher in alcohol than the grape wine with which they were familiar. Then again, it may just have been rejected as smelling or looking unclean. Whatever the explanation, if the Chinese or Indians did practise distillation as long ago as is claimed, the expertise they had stumbled on centuries before the Europeans remained specific to that part of the world. Thus did the course of history remain tantalizingly unchanged.

Distillation methods

The original and widespread distillation vessel, still used in the Cognac region of France and by the whisky distillers of Scotland, is the pot still. It consists of the only three elements absolutely essential to the process: a pot in which the fermented product (malted grains, wine, cider, etc.) is heated; the alembic, or tube, through which the alcohol vapour driven off is sucked up; and the condenser, where the steam is cooled and reliquefied. To obtain a better quality product, spirits are generally distilled at least twice for greater refinement, so the still has to be started up again.

Not all the condensed vapour is suitable for use in fine liquor. The first and last of it to pass through (known as the "heads" and "tails") are generally discarded, because of the relatively high level of impurities they contain. The invention of the continuous still in the early 19th century, in which the process carries on to a second distillation uninterrupted, made spirit production more economical and easier to control. This is the method used in France's other classic brandy, armagnac, and the continuous still is now the preferred apparatus for the production of most spirits worldwide.

Below: Distillation in Strasburg, Germany, during the 16th century.

Spirits

Probably the first spirit to be taken seriously as an object of connoisseurship, as distinct from being purely medicinal or just a method of using up surplus grape or grain production, was the brandy of the Cognac region of western France. People noticed that the superior, mellower spirit produced by the light wines of Cognac responded particularly well to ageing in oak casks. The casks were traditionally fashioned out of wood from the Limousin forests of the region.

Cask-aged spirits derive every aspect of their final character – from the precise shade of tawny in the colour to their richness and roundness of flavour – from the maturation period they undergo in wood. They will not continue to develop in the bottle. The complex classification system in operation today for cognac is based on the length of time the spirit has been aged. It is testimony to a reputation for painstaking quality that dates back to around the end of the 17th century.

Scottish and Irish whiskies rose to similar prominence soon after this date. Their differing production processes resulted in quite distinct regional styles, depending on the quantities of peat used in the kilns where the malted grain is dried, on the quality of the spring water used in the mash and, some have claimed, on the shape of the still. Varieties of whisky are made across the world these days, from North America to Japan, but all attempts to replicate the precise taste of great Scotch – despite the use of identical ingredients and procedures – have somehow inexplicably foundered.

Liqueurs

Where a distilled drink stops being a spirit and turns into a liqueur is something of an elusive question. The one constant is that, to be a liqueur, a drink should have some obvious aromatizing element (perhaps even a hundred or more in the case of certain celebrated products). This doesn't mean that all flavoured distillates are liqueurs – flavoured vodkas are still vodka – but there are no neutral liqueurs. Some of these products have histories at least as venerable as those of cognac and Scotch. The most notable are those produced by the old French monastic orders. Bénédictine, the cognac-based, herb-scented potion that originated at the monastery in Fécamp, in Normandy, can convincingly lay claim to a lineage that rolls back to the beginning of the 16th century.

The first and greatest cocktail era, which arrived with the advent of the Jazz Age in the 1920s, rescued many of the traditional liqueurs from the niches of obscurity into which they had been relegated by popular taste. The Benedictine monks may have been a little shocked to hear that their revered creation was being mixed with English gin, American applejack, apricot brandy and maple syrup, and then shaken to within an inch of its life and renamed

Below: Cognac ageing in barrels at Courvoisier in Jarnac.

Right: Modern whisky stills at the Glenfiddich distillery in Scotland.

the Mule's Hind Leg, but at least it was drunk – as were the giggling flappers after recklessly knocking back three or four of them.

How to use this book

In this book, we shall look first at the histories and compositions of all the categories of alcoholic drink: spirits, liqueurs, wine, beer and cider. After a brief tour of the non-alcoholic ingredients with which they are mixed, we will look, in the second part of the book, at what equipment is needed and what techniques should be learned in home bartending. Whether you are throwing a cocktail party, or whether you just want to know how to make cocktails as good as – if not better than – those you have tasted in the cocktail bar, all the information you need is here.

Finally, getting down to business, the third part of the book consists of over 500 cocktail recipes, arranged by type,

so that you can happily expand your repertoire. That drink after work or on Saturday night need no longer be the same old bottle of beer, glass of wine or G&T. The drinking world is your oyster. Do it wisely, and have fun.

Types of drinks

We begin our tour of the drinking world with spirits, which were the last of all the basic types of alcohol to be invented. They are the products of distillation, made by heating fermented liquids until their vapours condense and form a much stronger alcohol. Following that, we delve into the weird and wonderful world of liqueurs, investigating their history and flavours, and suggesting some culinary uses along the way. A brief overview of wines (including champagne and fortified wines) comes next, and is followed by the other fermented drinks: beer and cider. We conclude the section with a comprehensive guide to the non-alcoholic ingredients used in mixed drinks.

SPIRITS

The earliest spirits were almost certainly fairly straightforward, rough-and-ready distillations of ordinary wine. For centuries, a form of distillation had been practised, using herbs and flowers infused in water, then cooked and condensed. The resulting essence was used medicinally, in cooking or just as a perfume. As we saw in the Introduction, the discovery in Europe of the art of distilling alcohol arose as a result of alchemical experiments designed to find the "elixir of life". The powerful brew that was created by distilling was thought to contain the "soul" or "spirit" of the wine.

When people realized that anything that had been fermented to produce alcohol could in turn be distilled into spirit, they began to ferment materials specifically for distillation. So, in regions that lacked the climate for winemaking, mashed malted grains were responsible for the first drinks definable as whiskies.

Below: Filling the mash tun at a single malt distillery in Dufftown, Scotland. Here, the two essential ingredients of malt whisky are brought together: finely ground malted barley and natural Highland spring water.

As wine itself was held in high esteem, and was imported in great quantity by the cooler countries of northern Europe, such as England and the Netherlands, the spirit produced from wine was the first to receive true acclaim. Traders on ships that arrived at La Rochelle and other ports in the Charente region of western France had no particular taste for the acidic, flavourless wines of the area, but the strong spirit made from these wines

Above: The Scottish Highlands at Lochnagar, north of Dundee.

was considered a lot better than other such distillates found elsewhere. Thus did cognac first come to prominence.

A memory of the alchemical quest to find the magic elixir was preserved in the Latin name first given to the product of distillation: *aqua vitae*, or water of life. That phrase has remained inseparable from spirits terminology: the French call their spirit *eau de vie*, the Scandinavians *aquavit*, and the Celts *uisge beatha*, which was eventually corrupted by non-Gaelic speakers into "whisky". In Russian, it became, more humbly, "little water" or vodka. The alternative medieval Latin name was *aqua ardens*, "burning water", for reasons that are not hard to fathom. The association with fieriness, both in the method used to extract the alcohol and in the sensation that drinking it produced, lived on in the naming of distilled wine *Gebranntwein* ("burnt wine") in German, *brandewijn* in Dutch, and eventually "brandy" in English.

Despite being highly prized at the time, these early spirits would not have tasted particularly pleasant to us. They would only have been distilled once and would therefore have contained

Right: The discovery of distillation provided the basis for all the classic spirits commonly in use today.

high concentrations of fusel oil, a group of compounds known in scientific parlance as the "higher alcohols", the "higher" referring to their greater acidity. It was only in 1800 that a physicist named Edouard Adam discovered the benefits of redistillation, or rectification. This dispensed with a large proportion, though not all, of the raw-tasting higher alcohols and resulted in a purer spirit. However, it also stripped away a lot of the positive by-products of distillation that gave the drink its character, and so for a while the infusions of herbs, spices and fruit extracts that had originally been used to disguise the roughness of the alcohol were reintroduced to give it flavour.

Eventually, the correct balance was struck. The products that needed some distillation character – brandies and

Below: Glenfiddich is distilled twice in traditionally shaped copper pot stills that are built and maintained by their own coppersmiths. The stills are unusually small, and have not changed size or shape since the distillery first started in 1887.

whiskies – retained it (undergoing a double distillation) and had it enhanced by ageing in wooden casks, while those that were intended to be as neutral as possible, such as vodka and gin, were subject to repeated redistillation. (In the case of gin and similar products, a neutral spirit base is created by prolonged rectification, so that the aromatic ingredients that are added can stand out more boldly.) Most commercial spirits produced today have been thoroughly rectified, which is not necessarily a blessing; for example, some brands of white rum can be extremely bland. The trend owes much to the fact that most of the white spirits are drunk with mixers these days.

When tasting a fine spirit – aged cognac, single malt whisky, sour-mash bourbon or old demerara rum, for example – the procedure that is used for tasting wine clearly won't do. Try rolling a liquid with 40% alcohol around your mouth and you'll soon wish you hadn't. Some tasters judge them on the nose alone; others add a similar quantity of water, which many feel emphasizes their aromatic subtleties. I prefer to be brave and taste them undiluted. If you adopt this technique, the trick is to take in only a very small amount of liquid, keep it at the front of

the mouth just behind the lips by lowering the head after sipping, draw some air over it quickly and spit it out before it starts burning. The whole exercise is much brisker than tasting a mouthful of wine.

Below: Classic cocktail recipes represent a fine way of bringing out the best in distilled spirits. In this drink – Paddy – Irish whiskey is mixed with sweet red vermouth and Angostura bitters.

Gin

Of the six essential spirits, gin is the only one that really has a reputation to live down. Over the years it has been the calamitous curse of the urban poor, the Mother's Ruin by which girls in trouble tried to induce miscarriages, the bathtub brew that rotted guts during American Prohibition, and the first resort of the miserable as the storm clouds of depression gathered. It was all so different in the beginning.

Although the English often claim to be the true progenitors of gin, its origins in fact go back to 16th-century Holland. Like many other distilled drinks, it was firstly medicinal. The blend of herbs and aromatics it contained was believed to guard against all the ills to which flesh was heir. Principal among these aromatics was the dark-berried plant

juniper, the Dutch word for which – genever – is the linguistic root of the English word "gin".

The dark little fruits of the juniper tree contribute to the characteristic, strong perfume of gin. They are prized medicinally as a diuretic. Despite the predominance of juniper in the aroma and flavour of gin, however, there are other ingredients. Precise recipes vary according to the individual distiller, but other common components include angelica, liquorice, orris-root, dried citrus peel, caraway and coriander seeds, and many others.

It was probably British soldiers returning home from the Thirty Years War who first brought the taste for Dutch genever across the North Sea. In any case, a form of gin was being distilled in London by the 17th century, using the basic beer ingredients – hops and barley – and the essential juniper berries.

The rise in gin's popularity in Britain had two main causes. First, periodic hostilities with the French led to the application of punitive tariffs to their exports and, just as port came to be the wine of patriotic choice among the elite, so gin replaced cognac. To compound that, reform of the excise system resulted in beer being subjected to a much stricter levy than before, so that gin was

Left: The company of Booth's Finest was established during the ban on gin in the UK.

actually cheaper. Not surprisingly, it became the staple drink of the poorest classes, who consumed it in much the same quantities as they had beer. Gin shops were born, and public drunkenness and alcohol-related illness soared.

So began gin's long association with gloom (which still persists today in the enduring myth that gin is more of a depressant than the other spirits). The purveyors of gin sold their wares in terms that no advertiser today could get away with: "*Drunk for a penny. Dead drunk for tuppence. Clean straw for nothing.*" In 1736, the purchase of small quantities was made illegal by Act of Parliament, but the law was hastily reversed six years later after it was predictably discovered that the contraband stuff then being drunk was considerably more toxic than the official spirit had been.

Far left: Belgravia London dry gin is one of the lesser-known London brands.

Left: Beefeater is one of the most famous London gins.

HOW TO SERVE

The age-old mixer for gin is, of course, Schweppes tonic, the production of which is almost exclusively sustained by gin drinkers. A gin and tonic is usually offered as a long drink with a slice of lemon and plenty of ice, but equal measures are a more sensitive way of treating the gin. Gin rubs along with any old mixer, though: orange juice, bitter lemon, ginger beer, whatever. (It isn't very nice with cola perhaps, but then few things are.)

In 1750, the artist William Hogarth produced his famous engraving *Gin Lane*, depicting the degradation that was being wrought by the widespread consumption of gin. It was only in the late Victorian period that it began to regain a more dignified reputation, being seen as a usefully ladylike alternative to whisky and cognac. Finally, the gin and tonic, the world's favourite aperitif, was born, and a new era in gin's fortunes was ushered in. Gin has recently lost a lot of ground to vodka in the youth market, as its peculiar perfume is something of an acquired taste to untutored palates. Chic new brands may just reverse that trend.

Right: Dutch genever is the prototype for London gin.

Right: Bombay Sapphire is a more delicately aromatic gin than the commercial norm.

Far right: Gordon's is the brand leader among London gins.

Types of gin
English Gin There are two types. London dry gin is by far the more commonly known, although it doesn't have to be distilled in the capital. It is an intensely perfumed spirit, and varies greatly in quality between producers. Gordon's, Booth's and Beefeater are the most famous names. Speciality brands include Tanqueray and Bombay Sapphire in the pale blue, tinted bottle.

The other type is Plymouth gin, of which there is only one distiller, at the Blackfriars distillery not far from the city's waterfront. Plymouth gin is distinctly drier than the big London brands, and the aromatics used somehow give it a subtler bouquet than most gin-drinkers may be used to.

A very small amount of gin is cask-aged; this is referred to as golden gin, after the colour it leaches out of the wood.

Dutch Genever This is quite different from English gin, owing to the more pungently flavoured grain mash from which it is made. The mixture of barley, rye and corn (or maize) is often heavily malted, giving older spirits a lightly beery tinge. There are basically two grades: *oude* (old) or *jonge* (young), the latter looking more like the English article. They frequently come in an opaque "stone" bottle, and have a more rustic flavour.

How it is made
Gin is an extremely simple drink, almost as elementary as vodka. A grain spirit is produced from rye and barley, although corn is commonly used in Dutch genever and American gin. For the English style, it is ruthlessly rectified through successive distillations until all the higher alcohols are driven off. After the aromatization process, which is carried out either by macerating the dry herbs, berries and spices in the alcohol or by running the spirit through them, the finished product is bottled for immediate release.

Tastes good with
The oily texture of gin complements the oiliness of certain fish reasonably well. Sip it with marinated herring covered in chopped raw onion – real Amsterdam street food. Even in this context, though, you may find its pungency easier to cope with if slightly diluted.

Vodka

In one sense, vodka is the closest thing to perfection ever conceived in the history of spirits. Had it been invented in the era of alcopops and ice beers, it would have been hailed as a supremely adept piece of marketing wizardry. Nobody, other than a confirmed teetotaller, could possibly dislike it, for the simple reason that it tastes of nothing whatsoever. It is pure, unadulterated, uncomplicated alcohol. At least, most of it is.

The word "vodka" is a Russian endearment meaning "little water", from their word for water, *voda*. That in turn derives from the widespread European practice of referring to all distillates originally as a form of water (as in *aqua vitae* or *eau de vie*).

Precisely because it is such a simple drink, it is almost impossible to pinpoint the origins of vodka. A potent spirit

Below: Blue label Absolut (left) is the unflavoured version. Absolut Kurant (middle) is solidly fruity and flavoured with blackcurrants. Absolut Citron (right) has a musky lemony tinge.

distilled from various grains has been made in Poland, Russia and the Baltic states since the very early days of distillation in Europe. But as to where a drink specifically recognizable as vodka first arose is a matter for the Poles and the Russians to sort out between themselves. (Most outsiders now tend to come down on the Polish side.) What is certain is that, by the time home distillation had become a favoured way of passing the long winters in Poland, peasant families were producing their own domestic vodkas extensively.

Rectification techniques having only been discovered at the beginning of the 19th century, these early distillates would have tasted fairly unclean. Any herbs, seeds or berries that were to hand would be steeped in the spirit to mask its rankness. So the first vodkas were not the

Left: This smooth Stolichnaya vodka should be sipped appreciatively.

anonymous products preferred today, but the true ancestors of the flavoured vodkas.

Nonetheless, it was the neutral, ultra-purified grain vodka – made from wheat or rye – that came to prominence in the West. So prevalent is it now, particularly among younger drinkers who have yet to appreciate the taste of unrectified spirits such as whisky and cognac, that it is hard to believe that barely anyone in western Europe or America had heard of it until the late 1940s. That all changed with the first stirrings of interest in California, during the period of the Beat Generation.

Vodka was seen as a provocatively dissident drink in the era of the onset of the Cold War. It was the

HOW TO SERVE

When serving vodka, everything should be almost painfully cold to the touch. The bottle should be kept in the freezer and the glasses should also be iced. If there isn't a heavy mist of condensation on the outside of the glass, it isn't cold enough. Some vodka shots are thrown back like schnapps, owing to an old folk belief that if you inhale the fumes for more than a split second, you will get too drunk too quickly. The aged vodkas, and specialities such as Zubrowka, are more often sipped slowly and appreciatively. A little shot glass is traditional, but in some homes a rather larger, narrow tumbler, or even something like a goblet wine glass, is used.

consumed may raise eyebrows in our Western unit-counting culture, but a vodka hangover is very rare, owing to the purity of the drink.

Perhaps the most celebrated flavoured product is Zubrowka, bison-grass vodka, which is generally sold with a blade of grass in the bottle, bison grass being the gourmet preference of the wild bison that roam the forests of eastern Poland.

Wisniowka (cherries), Limonnaya (lemon) and the Swedish Absolut company's Kurant (blackcurrant) are all appetizing drinks. Pieprzowka is infused with chilli peppers, and has a burning, spicy finish. Russia's Okhotnichya – "Hunter's Vodka" – is impregnated with orange rind, ginger root, coffee beans, juniper berries and even a drop of white port.

Neutral vodkas are produced all over the world now, although most grades are only intended to be served in mixed drinks. Russian Stolichnaya, particularly the Cristall bottling, is an honourable, silky-smooth exception. Smirnoff makes three types, in red, blue and black labels to denote varying strength. Scandinavian vodkas such as Finlandia and Absolut have their deserved followings, while most British vodka tends to be little more than patent alcohol. Also seen on the export markets is Polish Pure Spirit, bottled at around 70% ABV.

How it is made

Although potatoes and other vegetables have been used to make vodka at various times in its history, nowadays it is made virtually exclusively from grains, principally rye. A basic mash is made by malting the grains, and encouraging them to ferment with cultured yeasts. The resulting brew is then continuously distilled in a column still to increasing degrees of alcoholic strength, driving off nearly all of the higher alcohols. As a final insurance against flavour,

the spirit is filtered through a layer of charcoal, which strips it of any remaining character. It is then bottled at an average of 37.5% ABV.

In the case of flavoured vodkas, the aromatizing elements are added to the new spirit after rectification, and left to infuse over long periods – sometimes three years or more. Occasionally, a speciality vodka will be aged in cask and take on a tinge of colour; others derive their exotic hues from spices, flowers or nuts.

Tastes good with

Cold vodka is the classic accompaniment to Russian caviar, itself served on heaps of ice. In the Scandinavian countries, it is drunk, like aquavit, with marinated and smoked fish such as herring, mackerel and even salmon.

Below: This Pieprzowka vodka (left) has been coloured and flavoured with chillies. Cherry vodka (right) has a lustrous, deep red colour and is intensely fruity.

Above: Smirnoff, with its basic red label (left), is the market leader in vodka. Blue label (right) is a higher-strength version.

favoured "hooch" of the Soviet bloc, and in the witch-hunting atmosphere of 50s America, nothing was more guaranteed to inflame bourbon-drinking patriots than young folks gleefully imbibing the spirit of communism. The late Alexis Lichine, drink historian, attributes the start of vodka's meteoric rise in the West to the purchase by a US company of a recipe from a Russian refugee called Smirnoff, on the eve of the Second World War. The rest is history.

Vodka is still very much the drink of gastronomic choice in its native lands, drunk as aperitif, digestif and even as an accompaniment to food. It is nearly always taken icy-cold, preceded in Polish homes by the ritual wishing of good health – *na zdrowie* – to one's family and friends. The quantities

Rum

Probably the least understood of the five main spirits, rum is actually, in its white version, one of the biggest-selling of them all. Indeed, it is debatable whether many of those knocking back Bacardi-and-Cokes realize they are drinking some form of rum at all. To many, rum is inextricably associated with a rather antiquated pantomime idea of "Jolly Jack Tars" and a life on the ocean wave.

There is some uncertainty over the origin of the spirit's name, but the favourite theory is that it is a shortening of an old West Country English word "rumbullion", itself of unknown origin, but generally denoting any hard liquor.

The invention of rum dates from not long after the foundation of the sugar plantations in the West Indies, in the early 16th century. Until the voyages of Christopher Columbus, sugar was a luxury product, and much sought after in southern Europe, having originally

HOW TO SERVE

The best dark rums, and aged rums in particular, should be served straight, unchilled, as digestifs. They make stimulating alternatives to malt whisky or cognac. Premium white rums from the independent producers are also best enjoyed neat, but they should be served cold, with a twist of lime.

Left: Lamb's is one of the leading brands of dark rum.

been brought into Venice from India. When the Spanish explorers landed in Hispaniola and the neighbouring Caribbean islands, they saw promising environments for cultivating sugar cane for themselves. If yeasts need to feed on sugar in order to produce alcohol, then the sugar plant was always going to be an obvious candidate for distillation. When first pressed, cane juice is a murky, greenish colour and full of impurities. Boiled down, it crystallizes into sucrose and a sticky brown by-product, molasses, that would have fermented readily in tropical conditions. Rum is the result of distilling the fermented molasses.

Sugar soon became a widespread everyday product in Europe. The astronomical demand for it was serviced by the most notorious episode in European colonial history – the slave trade, in which rum played a crucial role. Settlers in New England financed their trips to West Africa by selling rum. A consignment of African slaves would be delivered to the

Right: Wood's 100 is a particularly rich naval-strength dark rum.

Far right: Captain Morgan is the leading brand of dark rum.

West Indies and sold for molasses, which would then be shipped back to New England to be turned into more rum, in a self-perpetuating cycle.

The association of rum with the British Navy arises from the fact that rum was provided to ordinary sailors as a daily ration from the 18th century. That tradition endured, basically because rum could withstand hot weather more sturdily than beer could. The initial allowance was a fairly rollicking half-pint a day, watered down eventually into the despised "grog", and then mixed with lemon juice to prevent scurvy. It was only in 1970 that the rum ration was abolished.

Today, rum is produced all over the West Indies and eastern South America, to a lesser extent in the Indian Ocean area – the Philippines and

Above left: Bacardi is the world's favourite white spirit brand.

Above right: Mount Gay Barbados is a major Caribbean brand of golden rum.

Mauritius – and in smaller quantities still in the USA and Australia. Inevitably, much of it is a by-product of the sugar-refining industry, but the best grades are made by smaller, independent companies growing sugar cane specifically for distillation.

Some rum is made from the pressed cane juice itself, but most is made from fermented molasses. In the former French colonies in particular, there is a distinguished tradition of *rhum agricole*, speciality products made on small sugar farms, produced with different strains of yeast.

Both methods of distillation are practised in the making of rum: the premium versions are double-distilled in a copper pot still, whereas continuous distillation and thorough rectification are used mainly by the bulk producers, particularly for the neutral-tasting white rums. Freshly distilled spirit from the pot still method is very high in impurities and must be allowed to mellow through a period of cask-ageing, which gives colour to the darker rums.

After white rum, dark rum is the next most important category commercially, and is certainly where the superior products are found. Leading brands are Captain Morgan and Lamb's. Some high-quality dark rums are bottled at the original naval strength of more than 50% ABV (Wood's Navy Rum, for example, is 57%); the traditional name for such strengths was "overproof". The everyday dark rums are a more standard 40%, while Bacardi is adjusted down to 37.5%, equivalent to the other white spirits.

Between the two styles is the increasingly popular golden or light rum, which is a particular speciality of Cuba and Puerto Rico, aged for less time in the barrel. The darkest and heaviest rums, some not far from the colour of black treacle, traditionally come from Jamaica. Good white rum, such as the white Rhum St James of Martinique, is full of burnt-sugar richness. Some exporters make a virtue of selling rums with 30 or 40 years of cask age, and there is even a tiny production of vintage-dated rum for the true connoisseur.

How it is made

Juice from the sugar cane is pressed and either fermented straight or boiled down to extract the molasses, which itself forms the basis of the ferment. It is either continuously distilled or, for speciality products, double-distilled in a pot still. For a headier product, some of the residue of the first distillation – known as "dunder" – may be added to the molasses during fermentation. Commercial white rums are rectified and bottled immediately. Coloured rums

are cask-aged, sometimes for decades, before they are bottled. The longer they are aged, the deeper the colour.

Tastes good with

More than any other basic spirit, rum makes an excellent accompaniment to fruits of all kinds. A "salad" of orange segments in golden rum was already a favoured dessert in the 18th century. Rum can be added to the syrup of all fruit salads, however, and works especially well with pineapple and banana. It is excellent for adding an enriching note to sponge-based desserts such as charlottes, as well as the famous rum baba – a soft rum-soaked sponge filled with raisins. Rum has a great natural affinity with that other celebrated Caribbean product, chocolate. Add dark or golden rum to the mixture for chocolate truffles, or the *ganache* mixture with which a chocolate gâteau may be glued together. In the Caribbean, they like a rum-based mixed drink with fish and meat dishes.

Whisky

One of the world's leading spirits, whisky (or whiskey, depending on where it hails from) boasts a history every bit as distinguished as that of cognac. Like the classic brandies of France, its spread around the world from its first home – the Scottish Highlands – has been a true testament to the genius of its conception. Tennessee sour mash may bear about as much relation in taste to single malt Scotch as Spanish brandy does to cognac, but the fact that they are all

Below left: Laphroaig is one of the richest of the peaty styles of Scotch produced in Islay.

Below right: This Glenlivet is a ten-year-old Speyside malt from the Scottish Highlands.

great products demonstrates the versatility of each basic formula.

Today, whiskies are produced all over the world. As the name is not a geographically specific one, all of these products may legitimately call themselves whisk(e)y. The five major producing countries are Scotland, the United States, Ireland, Canada and Japan.

The name "whisky" is yet another variant of the phrase "water of life". In translation, the Latin *aqua vitae* became *uisge beatha* in the Scots branch of Gaelic and *usquebaugh* in the Irish. The half-Anglicized "whisky" was in official use by the mid-18th century.

In countries that lacked the warm climate for producing fermented drinks from grapes, beer was always the staple brew and, just as brandy was the obvious first distillate in southern Europe, so malted grains provided the starting point for domestic production further north. Unlike brandy, however, which starts life as wine, whisky doesn't have to be made from something that would be recognizable as beer.

Left: Whyte & Mackay whisky is re-blended for a second period of maturation.

Before the Act of Union of 1707, Scotch was hardly known in England. Gin was the national drink south of the border. Once the English laid their administrative hands on Scotland, they set about bringing whisky distillation under statutory control. Whisky-makers within striking distance of the border fled northwards with their stills into the Highlands, but by the 1870s, the number of convictions for illegal distilling was down to six (compared to nearly 700 only 40 years earlier).

In the early years of the 20th century, a Royal Commission was set up to determine the parameters for Scotch whisky production, i.e. the methods of distillation, rules on blending, minimum maturation times and, of course, the fact that Scotch could only be distilled and aged in Scotland, rather than anywhere south

SCOTLAND

Home distillation in Scotland can be traced back to the 15th century, when the practice of distilling surplus grain to make a potent drink for clan chieftains was established.

Initially, the drink was valued for its medicinal powers, and early examples were no doubt infusions of herbs and berries rather than the pure grain product we know today. Although at first other cereals would have been used, malted barley became pre-eminent relatively early on.

HOW TO SERVE

The finest whiskies are not necessarily drunk neat. It is widely believed that taming some of the spirit's fire helps to bring up the array of complicated scents and flavours. A dose of water should be added, ideally the same spring water that goes into the whisky itself, otherwise any pure, non-chlorinated water. Half-and-half are the preferred proportions in Scotland and Ireland, while in Tennessee and Kentucky they add a little less than half.

Above left: The Famous Grouse is one of the leading brands of blended Scotch whisky.

Above right: J&B is a blended whisky that is popular in the American market; J&B stands for Justerini & Brooks.

of the border. These parameters remain in force today as the legal textbook for an industry that is a central part of the Scottish economy.

Types of Scotch

The most highly prized of Scotch whiskies are the single malts, which are produced entirely from malted barley, double-distilled, and made at a single one (hence the terminology) of Scotland's 100 or so working distilleries. Some of these products are aged for many years. Twenty-five-year-old Scotch will be shot through with all sorts of profoundly complex flavours and perfumes, from the cask and perhaps from the sea air that wafts around the coastal distilleries.

Some malts are the blended produce of several single malts, in which case they are known as vatted malts. Whiskies made from corn or unmalted barley are known as grain whiskies, and are always considerably lighter in style than malts. They could be described as beginner's Scotch, since they have far fewer of the aromatic components that account for the pedigree of great malt, although they should not be seen as worthless imitations.

Blended Scotch is made from a mixture of malt and grain spirits. This is the market-leading category, occupied by virtually all of the big brand names, such as Bell's, J&B, Johnnie Walker, Ballantine's, Whyte & Mackay, The Famous Grouse, White Horse and Teacher's. Most of these have fairly low concentrations of malt in the blend, although Teacher's and Johnnie Walker's Black Label are notable exceptions.

Scotch whisky is mostly retailed at the standard dark spirit strength of 40% ABV. A small proportion of the best grades are bottled from the barrel undiluted. These are known as "cask-strength" whiskies. You are not intended to drink them neat, but they should be diluted with water to the level of potency you prefer.

Areas of production

For the purposes of whisky production, Scotland is divided up into four broad regions: the Lowlands; Campbeltown; Islay and the Western Isles, including Jura, Mull and Skye; and the expansive Highlands region.

Lowland whiskies are generally the gentlest and sweetest styles of Scotch, while Campbeltown's are fresh and ozoney. Islay produces an instantly recognizable pungent spirit, full of seaweed and peat, while many Highland malts have a soft smokiness to them.

How it is made

In the case of malts, the grains of barley are soaked in water to encourage them to germinate. Soon after they have begun sprouting, the process is arrested by heating them in a kiln, in which variable quantities of peat will be added to the fuel, depending on the intended final flavour of the whisky. After kilning, the grain is mashed and drained and then poured into large tanks to begin fermentation, either with natural or cultured yeasts. The resulting brew is double-distilled in the traditional copper pot still.

The other factor in determining the character of a whisky is the maturation vessel. Scotch was traditionally aged in casks that had previously been used for shipping sherry, and some still is, but used bourbon casks from Kentucky are now quite common. In both cases, the wood is American oak, capable of imparting great richness to a whisky.

Tastes good with

Scotch is naturally the only accompaniment to the ceremonial haggis on Burns Night (January 25). Un-iced Scotch is also great with hearty soups, such as thick, barley-based Scotch broth or cock-a-leekie.

Right: Wild Turkey bourbon, which is aged in cask for eight years, comes from Lawrenceburg, Kentucky.

Above left: In Maker's Mark, small-volume production is allied to top quality.

Above right: Jim Beam is a particularly popular bourbon.

UNITED STATES

In North America, where whiskey is mostly spelled with an "e" as it is in Ireland, production of the drink dates back to the 18th century, in the era leading up to Independence. Before that, the staple spirit in America was dark rum. It was British and Irish settlers, bringing their own whisky with them from the old countries, who provided the impetus for the development of America's national spirit.

The first American whiskeys were made with malted barley and rye. Soon, however, a group of distillers in Bourbon County, Kentucky, began producing pure corn whiskey. By happy chance, from 1794 onwards their communities were infiltrated by droves of tax refugees who were fleeing from revenue officers in Pennsylvania. Suddenly, the Kentuckians had a ready-made new

market for their own product and, before too long, bourbon had established an illustrious reputation.

Rye whiskey is still made in Pennsylvania, Maryland and Virginia, but in ever-decreasing quantities.

Bourbon

Nowadays, most bourbon distilleries are concentrated not in Bourbon County, but around the towns of Louisville, Bardstown and Frankfort. Whiskeys from Kentucky are the only ones allowed to use the state name, alongside "bourbon", on the label.

Bourbon is not a straight corn whiskey, but is made from a mixture of not less than 51% corn with malted barley. Some may contain a little rye. The chief distinguishing taste of bourbon, however, derives from the barrels it matures in. These are made of new American oak, charred on the insides, which allows the spirit freer access to the vanillin and tannins in the wood.

There are two styles of bourbon: sweet mash and sour mash. The differences arise at the fermentation stage. For sweet mash, the yeasts are allowed to perform their work over a couple of days, while for sour mash, some yeast from the preceding batch augments the brew. This doubles the length of the fermentation and ensures that more of the sugars in the grain are consumed.

Most bourbon is labelled "Kentucky Straight Bourbon", which means it is made from at least 51% corn and is aged for a minimum of two years in charred new barrels.

The leading brand is Jim Beam, made at Bardstown. Other brands include Wild Turkey, Evan Williams, Early Times, Old Grand-Dad and Maker's Mark.

Tennessee

South of Kentucky, in Tennessee, a different but equally distinctive style of whiskey is made. Tennessee sour mash is represented by just two distilleries – Jack Daniel's in Lynchburg, and George Dickel in Tullahoma.

Whereas bourbon is matured in charred barrels, Tennessee takes the principle a stage further by actually filtering the newly-made spirit through a mass of charcoal. In the yards behind the distilleries, they burn great stacks of sugar maple down to ash, and then grind it all to powder. This is piled to a depth of around three metres or ten feet into so-called mellowing vats. The whiskey drips at a painfully slow rate from a gridwork of copper pipes above the vats, filtering gradually through the charcoal bed, prior to its period of cask maturation.

Jack Daniel's is one of the world's best-loved whiskey brands, led by its flagship Old No. 7 in the famous square bottle. Dickel (which spells its product "whisky" in the Scottish way), matures its No. 12 brand for several years longer, and the results are evident in a mellower nose and deeper colour. It is bottled at 45% ABV.

Tastes good with

There is a cultural affinity between bourbon and Tennessee whiskeys and the huge flame-grilled carpetbag steaks of Bardstown and Nashville. Add a little spring water to the spirit.

Left: Jack Daniel's is by far the bigger brand of the two Tennessee whiskeys.

Right: Paddy whiskey is distilled at Midleton, just outside the city of Cork in Ireland.

IRELAND

The origins of distillation in the Emerald Isle are lost in swathes of Irish mist, but are certainly of great antiquity. Irish whiskey once enjoyed an unrivalled reputation as a more approachable style of spirit than Scotch. It was only when blended Scotch began to be made on any significant scale towards the end of the 19th century that Irish whiskey was overshadowed.

The mellowness of Irish whiskey derives from its production process. No peat is used in the kilns, and Irish distillers use a mixture of malted and unmalted grain in their mash. It was a blended product long before today's standard Scotch blends were invented. It is then triple-distilled in a copper pot still, which results in a product with a softer palate that still retains all its complexity. The whiskey

Below: Crown Royal is a Canadian brand owned by Seagram's.

must then be cask-aged for a minimum of three years, although in practice most varieties are aged for two to three times longer. It is usually bottled at 40% ABV.

The brand leader on the export markets is Jameson's. Others include Bushmills, John Power, Murphy's, Paddy, Dunphy's and Tullamore Dew. All but one are made in the Irish Republic, the exception being Bushmills, which is made in County Antrim in the North.

CANADA

Canada's whiskies are made from blends of different grains, combining rye, corn and malted barley. They nearly always contain some spirit that is produced entirely from the heavier-tasting rye, but it usually accounts for less than a tenth of the final blend. As a result, they have the reputation of being among the lightest classic whiskies of all.

Distillation is by the continuous process, in gigantic column stills. Different spirits produced from different

Left: Suntory's 12-year-old Yamazaki is a kind of Japanese single malt.

mashes, or fermented from different yeast strains, are painstakingly blended by the distiller. All whiskies must spend at least three years in new barrels, but some are aged for 10, 12, even 18 years. The standard blends are sold at 40% ABV, but speciality aged bottlings may be stronger.

A curiosity of Canadian whisky is that the regulations permit the addition of a tiny quantity of other products, such as sherry or wine made from grapes or other fruits. While this may only account for 1% of the finished product, it makes its presence felt in the fleeting suggestion of fruitiness in some whiskies.

Most of the Canadian distilleries are situated in the eastern provinces of Ontario and Quebec. The leading label is Hiram Walker's Canadian Club, first blended in the 1880s, and is supported by the Burke's and Wiser's ranges from Corby's, McGuinness's Silk Tassel, Alberta Springs and Seagram's Crown Royal.

JAPAN

Of the leading five producers, Japan has by far the youngest whisky industry. The first distillery was established in 1923, and it is only in the last 30 years or so that its products have become known elsewhere.

The model for Japan's whiskies is single malt Scotch. They are made from a mash of malted barley, dried in kilns fired with a little peat. Distillation is by the pot still method. Some of the brands are aged in used sherry or bourbon casks, and others in heavily charred new American oak. The premium brands are generally bottled at around 43% ABV.

The giant drinks company Suntory is the biggest producer of Japanese whisky, accounting for 75% of the country's output. Behind Suntory comes the Nikka company, followed by the smaller producers Sanraku Ocean and Seagram's.

Tequila

Tequila is the national spirit of Mexico. It is one stage further down the road to refinement than its fellow cactus-based spirit, mescal, but several leagues ahead in terms of drinking pleasure. It starts life as *pulque*, the fermented

beer-like juice of the agave plant, and is distilled twice before being aged in cask. It comes in two versions: silver is clear like vodka, and gold (or Oro) spends a longer period in contact with the barrels. Virtually unknown in Europe until comparatively recently, it made its first inroads into the world's drinks cabinet by travelling northwards to the USA, and it is now something of a cult drink in the youth market.

The name, tequila, is echoed in the full botanical name of the plant from which it is sourced: *Agave tequilana*. Perhaps what put everybody else off trying it for so long was the thought of a spirit made from cacti, and indeed even the finest grades don't actually smell particularly inviting. It has a sweaty, slightly muggy quality that must have come as something of a jolt at first to tastebuds honed on squeaky-clean vodka.

In recognition of its cultural importance, the production of tequila has been strictly delimited within Mexico. It may be distilled in only a handful of towns, including Tequila itself, and in the area immediately surrounding Guadalajara. Two of the brands most commonly encountered on the export markets are Cuervo and Montezuma, the latter usually in an engraved bottle.

HOW TO SERVE

Your drink is served to you cold and straight in a small shot glass. You then season your tongue with citrus and salt, by squeezing a wedge of lime (lemon for wimps) and pouring salt on to the back of the hand and then licking them up. To be anatomically precise, the hand should be held at a 45° angle away from the body, with the thumb extended downwards, and the juice and salt deposited along the groove between the bases of the thumb and forefinger. The tequila is then thrown back in one gulp like schnapps, carrying the seasonings with it. Repeat *ad infinitum*. Believe it or not, this really is how tequila is widely drunk on its native territory. If it sounds like a fiddly and indescribably messy procedure, the answer is that it is, but long practice induces a sort of head-tossing, devil-may-care sanguineness in experienced users.

Above left: Golden Montezuma is a gold tequila that has aged in cask for longer than the white variety.

Above right: Cuervo tequila is the white version of Mexico's national spirit.

How it is made

Like mescal, tequila is distilled from the chopped, pressed and fermented hearts of agave plants. The juice is quite high in acidity, which lends even the refined spirit a certain piquancy. It is distilled a second time in a pot still, and then matured in wooden casks, briefly for the silver version, and up to five years for the gold.

Tastes good with

The sharpness of the flavour of tequila is somehow appetizingly emphasized by the addition of salt, which is why tequila cocktails are often served in salt-rimmed glasses. In Mexico, they feel that their highly spiced food overwhelms the taste of most wines, so tequila is seen as a gastronomic drink. Otherwise, assuming you are not drinking a salted cocktail, or performing the salt-licking ritual, a tequila-based mixed drink is best accompanied by highly seasoned nibbles, such as salted nuts, marinated olives or Spanish-style tapas, including the likes of cured ham and brined cheeses. This is especially so if you have resorted to drinking Tequila Slammers.

Brandy

Strictly speaking, the term brandy applies to any grape-based spirit distilled from wine. There are "brandies" made from other fruits, but we shall deal with these under their own headings. The English name is a corruption of the Dutch *brandewijn*, meaning "burnt wine", an apt term for the product of distillation.

The most famous of all true brandies is cognac, named after a town in the Charente region of western France. It was to here that traders from northern Europe came in the 17th century, putting in at the port of La Rochelle to take delivery of consignments of salt. They inevitably took some of the region's thin, acidic wine with them as

Below left: The basic Rémy Martin is a VSOP grade of cognac.

Below right: Martell, the oldest house in Cognac, is still a brand leader.

well. Because of tax regulations, and to save space in the ships, the wines were boiled to reduce their volume and then reconstituted with water on arrival. It came to be noticed that the Charente wines positively benefited from the reduction process, and it was a short step from this to actual distillation.

Such was the fame and the premium paid for the distilled wines of the Charente that they came to have many imitators. None, however, could match the precise local conditions in which cognac is made. The chalky soils, maritime climate and ageing in barrels of Limousin oak were what gave it the pre-eminence it still enjoys.

France's other brandy of note, armagnac, is made in the south-west. Although not as widely known as cognac, it has its own special cachet, and is preferred by many as the better digestif.

There are grape brandies produced all over Europe and the Americas, the best of which are generally made by pot-still distillation.

Cognac

The Cognac region covers two *départements* in western France: inland Charente, and coastal Charente-Maritime. Cognac is a small town close to the border between the two. The vineyards are sub-divided into six areas, the best being Grande Champagne and Petite Champagne.

First among Cognac's entrepreneurs was Jean Martell, a Jersey-born

Left: Hennessy XO is a premium cognac in a singularly shaped decorative bottle.

opportunist who, in 1715, turned away from a life of crime (smuggling) in order to found the house that still bears his name. Other leading brands are Hennessy, Courvoisier, Hine, Otard and Rémy Martin.

The relative qualities of cognacs depend on the length of time they have been aged. No *appellation contrôlée* cognac may be blended from spirits less than two years old. At the bottom rung of the classification is VS (designated by three stars on the label), which may contain brandies as young as three years old. ➤

HOW TO SERVE BRANDY

The finest, oldest brandies should not be mixed. Younger products mix reasonably well with soda; the vogue for brandy-and-tonic being assiduously promoted in Cognac, of all places, is not one that finds favour with the author. In the Far East, brandy is mixed with plenty of iced water and consumed in this denatured form with food.

HOW TO SERVE COGNAC

Fine cognac should be drunk just as it comes, without mixers and/or ice. It is traditionally served in balloon glasses that allow room for swirling. In fact, the aromas are better appreciated in something resembling a large liqueur glass, which mutes the prickle of the spirit. The bouquet is also encouraged by a gentle warming of the glass in the hand (for which the balloon was indisputably better designed), but not – as in former times – over a flame.

The next stage up is VSOP, Very Special (or Superior) Old Pale, a 19th-century British term. This is five-star cognac because the youngest spirit it contains has spent at least five years in wood.

Those cognacs blended from minimum six-year-old spirits may be entitled XO, or given one of the producers' own designations: Réserve, Extra, Cordon Bleu, Paradis or, classically, Napoléon – so named because the bottles once contained brandies aged since Bonaparte's day. The oldest cognacs generally come in something that looks like a giant

Right: The term "Hors d'Age" on an armagnac label denotes very long cask-ageing.

perfume bottle, fashioned in cut crystal and presented in a silk-lined box.

Armagnac

Once seen merely as France's "other brandy", armagnac is made in Gascony in the south-west. Of the three sub-regions – Bas-Armagnac, Ténarèze and Haut-Armagnac – the first is considered the best. Armagnac is a more venerable product than cognac, distillation in the region having been reliably dated back to the 1400s. While cognac is made largely from the Ugni Blanc grape, armagnac's base wine is made from a blend of several varieties. A local black oak (as distinct from Limousin) is used for the maturation, and the continuous still is widely used to distil the spirit.

So inextricably linked with armagnac was the continuous still that, for a long time, it was the only authorized apparatus. It yields a spirit rich in the aromatic impurities that promote character, which is why armagnac is noticeably more fragrant – biscuity, or even violetty – than cognac. The flavour tends to be drier because, unlike cognac, armagnac isn't adjusted with sugar, and the absence of caramel as a colouring matter leaves it paler.

The labelling system of armagnac (VS, VSOP, XO) is the

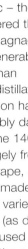

Left: Lepanto is Spain's leading brandy, made by Gonzalez Byass of sherry fame.

same as that of cognac, except that the very youngest armagnacs may be released after two years in cask rather than three. Vintage-dated armagnac – the unblended produce of a single year's harvest – has always been a local peculiarity (although vintage labelling has recently been relegalized in Cognac). If the label on, say, a 1959 armagnac looks suspiciously new, remember that it is because it has probably only recently been bottled. The ageing can only take place in wood, not glass. Prices for even the top armagnacs are considerably gentler than cognac.

Other European brandies

Spain The most significant producer of grape brandy outside France is Spain. There, premium products are accorded the same care as France's finest and, as a result, are comparable in quality.

Brandy production is concentrated in the southern, sherry-producing region of Jerez. Indeed, most Spanish brandy is distilled by the sherry houses. The grapes generally come from the huge central plain of La Mancha, but the wines are distilled and aged in Jerez. Look for "Brandy de Jerez" on the label, as it is a dependable indicator of quality.

Maturation is by a process known as fractional blending, or the *solera* system, which is also used for the finest sherries. The new spirit enters the top row of a stack of barrels and, at intervals of several months, a quantity of it is drawn off and added to the next row down, where it displaces a similar quantity into the row below, and so on. The bottom row contains the oldest brandies, which are drawn off in fractions for bottling. The brandy therefore gains greater age characteristics than it would if it were matured in the same barrel.

Top brands of Spanish brandy include Lepanto, made by Gonzalez Byass, Sanchez Romate's Cardinal Mendoza and Osborne's Conde d'Osborne, which comes in a bottle designed by Salvador Dali. The brand leader is Domecq's commendable Fundador. In Catalonia, the Torres winery makes its own excellent brandies.

Germany The best German offering seen on export markets is Uralt, an aged product made by Asbach in the Rheingau. It receives a maturation period of around 18 months.

Others Italy's brandies are fairly basic commercial spirits. Portugal makes a handful of good brandies, but its industry is heavily geared to supplying grape spirit for the port shippers. Cyprus makes some rough-and-ready brandies too.

Metaxa

Among Greek brandies, the abidingly popular Metaxa deserves a special mention. Despite the brouhaha with which it is treated in Greece itself, and a distinctly specious system of age-labelling, it is a fairly basic industrial product. The grape varieties that go into it are not generally held to be of sufficiently high acidity to produce a suitable base wine.

There are three grades of Metaxa, ascending in quality from three stars to seven. It is relatively pale in colour and much sweeter on the palate than cognac, with a highly moreish toffee flavour making it taste deceptively light.

American brandies

USA Brandy has been made in the United States since the days of the pioneers, mostly in California. At one

Left: Metaxa is the holidaymaker's favourite brandy.

time, brandy production was simply a convenient means of using up sub-standard grapes, but in the last 30 years or so, some finer aged spirits have been produced, and a number of these are capable of giving VSOP cognac a run for its money. Not all are made in the image of cognac; some are discernibly more Spanish in style. They are matured in American oak, which gives a more pronounced aroma to the spirit, accentuated by the charred inner surfaces of the barrels, and a great richness and complexity on the palate. Star names include Germain-Robin and RMS (the latter owned by Rémy Martin).

Latin America There is a long tradition of fiery spirits all over Central and South America, in which grape brandy plays its part – particularly in the areas where Spanish colonists first planted vines. Mexico is the most important producer. Its flagship is a big-selling global brand called Presidente, made in the light, simple style of basic Spanish brandy.

The peculiarly South American offering, however, is pisco. There is still much dispute over whether it originated in Peru or Chile, the two main centres of production. I shall forbear to come down on either side, except to say that the Pisco valley and its eponymous seaport are in Peru, although the Chileans simply insist that the port was one of the principal export destinations for their spirit, and that consequently the name just stuck.

Despite receiving some cask-ageing, pisco is always colourless because

the barrels it matures in are so ancient that they can't tint the spirit. In Chile, the longer the maturation, the lower the dilution before bottling, so the finest grades (Gran Pisco is the best) are the strongest. Owing to widespread use of the Muscat grape, nearly all types and nationalities of pisco are marked by unabashed fruitiness.

Although it is technically a brandy, pisco should be treated more like the other white spirits – fine vodka and silver tequila. That is to say, it should be mixed, classically as a Pisco Sour, but also with any kind of fruit juice, and served over ice. I have tried it neat at room temperature, but it wasn't a particularly successful experiment.

Below left: Carneros Alambic comes from the Napa Valley, California.

Below right: This top-quality pisco hails from Peru.

Bitters

The term "bitters" refers to any of a number of spirits flavoured with bitter herbs or roots, which are generally held to have medicinal properties. They range from products such as Campari, which can be drunk in whole measures like any other spirit, to those that are so bitter that they are only added in drops to season another drink.

Bitterness is the last of the four main taste sensations (the others being sweetness, saltiness and sourness) that

Below left: Campari is Italy's most famous bitter aperitif. It also comes as a pre-mix, bottled with a crown cap.

Below right: The Italian bitter Fernet Branca is much prized as a hangover cure, and actually seems to work.

Left: Underberg is a pungent digestive bitter from Germany.

developing tastebuds learn to appreciate. A fondness for bitter flavours is often thought to be a sign of the palate having reached its true maturity.

The link between bitterness and health is evident in the fact that tonic water was originally conceived as an all-purpose pick-me-up containing the stimulant quinine, rather than as a mixer for gin, although these days its flavour tends to be drowned with artificial sweetening. The other unquestionably effective medicinal role of bitters is as an aid to digestion.

The origins of bitters lie in the flavouring elements that were commonly added to the very earliest spirits. These elixirs were taken as restoratives and remedies for a number of conditions, ranging from poor digestion to painful joints. The apothecaries who concocted them drew on the collected wisdom of herbal medicine, and added extracts of bark, roots, fruit peels, herbs and spices to enhance the healing powers of the drink.

Bitters are made all over the world. Perhaps the most famous of all is Angostura. An infusion of gentian root with herbs on a strong rum base, Angostura was invented in the 19th century by a German medic who was personal doctor to the South American revolutionary hero Simón Bolívar. It is named after a town in Venezuela, although today it is made exclusively in Trinidad, albeit still by the company founded by its inventor. Angostura is one of the few such medicinal drinks that can legitimately claim to have been formulated by a doctor.

In Europe the two major centres of production of bitters are Italy and France. Italy has Campari – a bright red

HOW TO SERVE
Campari is classically served with soda water and a twist of lemon peel, but don't drown it.

aperitif of uncompromising bitterness, made in Milan – and also Fernet Branca. Like Germany's Underberg, the latter is sold in little bottles as a hangover cure. France's bitters include Amer Picon (invented as an anti-malarial remedy by an army officer serving in Algeria). English fruit bitters, such as orange and peach, were widely used in the 1920s. Hungary's runner is Unicum, while the Latvians have their own treacle-dark dry tonic, Melnais Balzams (Black Balsam).

Below left: Angostura is the most widely used bitter in the cocktail repertoire.

Right: Unicum is a deeply coloured bitter speciality of Hungary.

Calvados

In areas where wine grapes could not be grown, other fruits were used in making distilled drinks. The most important as a source of alcohol, after grapes, is the apple. Apple trees are capable of fruiting in much more wintry conditions than the vine, and since many varieties of apple are too tart or bitter to be eaten, cider became an adjunct to beer in the cooler northern climates.

The distillation of cider is quite as old as the practice of distilling wine for grape brandy. In its heartland of Normandy in northern France, the earliest reference to an apple distillate dates from 1553, and the practice is probably older than that.

Calvados received *appellation contrôlée* status in 1942, soon after the introduction of the AC system. At the heart of the region is a particularly fine area called the Pays d'Auge, with its own designation. Both pot-still and

Left: The best calvados comes from the Pays d'Auge in Normandy, France.

continuous distillation are used, but the esteemed calvados of the Pays d'Auge area may only use the former.

Bitter-sweet apple varieties make up most of the blend in a typical calvados. After distillation, the spirit matures in French oak. The younger the calvados, the more likely it is to smell of apples; older ones take on the vanilla and spice tones of oak.

Age indications are similar to those of grape brandy. Three-star calvados spends a minimum of two years in cask; Vieux or Réserve three years; and Vieille Réserve or VSOP four years. Those aged for six or more years may be labelled "Hors d'Age" (beyond age!) If a calvados label describes it as, say, an eight-year-old product, the reference applies to the youngest spirit in it, rather than being the average. A small amount of vintage-dated calvados is made.

In the USA, an apple spirit has been made ever since the first British settlers found that apple trees proved hardier than grain crops in New England. Applejack is made in much the same way as calvados, starting with good cider, which is distilled twice in a pot still. It is then oak-aged for anything up to five years. The younger stuff is pretty abrasive, but on the eastern seaboard – as in

Right: Apple brandy is a fine, powerful apple spirit from Somerset, England.

Far right: Applejack is America's answer to calvados.

Normandy – they like it that way. Laird's is one of the bigger-selling brands, and gives a reliable introduction to this singular product.

Apple brandy, or cider brandy, is now being revived in the west of England, where Somerset is considered by many to produce the world's best ciders. Properly aged, such brandy can be quite impressive, although calvados aficionados would be unlikely to be fooled by it.

How it is made
Apples are harvested from September to December, depending on the variety. A blend of juices from different types is fermented into cider at about 5–6% alcohol. This is subjected to a double distillation (or continuous distillation, except in the Pays d'Auge). The spirit is then aged in cask for anything up to 40 years, and bottled at 40–45% ABV.

HOW TO SERVE

Younger calvados works surprisingly well with tonic, as long as you don't drown it. Varieties that have aged for longer, such as those labelled Hors d'Age, must be drunk unmixed.

Eau de vie

Eau de vie is the French phrase for the Latin *aqua vitae*, meaning "water of life". Strictly speaking, the term refers to all spirits distilled from fermented fruits, starting with wine-based cognac and armagnac. By the same token, calvados could therefore be considered an eau de vie of cider. Since the names of these individual spirits are legally protected by France's geographical *appellation contrôlée* regulations, they

Below left: Fraise is a popular eau de vie made from strawberries.

Below middle: Poire-Williams is an eau de vie flavoured with Williams pears.

Below right: Framboise Sauvage is an eau de vie intensely flavoured with wild raspberries.

have come to be known by those names instead of being referred to as eaux de vie.

Spirits can be produced from many other fruits as well as grapes or apples, however, and these are much less precisely defined. The term eau de vie, therefore, tends now to be reserved for these other fruit brandies. Apart from their basic ingredients, the main attribute that distinguishes eaux de vie from cognac and armagnac is that they are colourless because they haven't been aged in wood like their more famous cousins. The theory is that they develop in glass, which rather flies in the face of what is scientifically known about spirits – namely, that development stops once they are in the bottle.

Of the range of fruits used, the most often encountered – and those producing the most delicious eaux de vie – are the various soft summer berries. Alsace, a wine region of north-east France that has lurched from French to German domination and back again since

the late 19th century, is a particularly rich source of these spirits, although they are also made in Switzerland and Germany. Some of them are made by winemakers, others by specialist distillers. What they have in common is high alcohol (sometimes around 45% ABV), absence of colour and a clear, pure scent and flavour of the fruit from which they are made. They are not sweetened, and should not be confused with the syrupy liqueurs of the same flavours, which tend to be coloured anyway.

Tastes good with

Served very cold in small measures, eaux de vie can work well with certain desserts, particularly frangipane-based tarts topped with the same fruit as that used to make the spirit.

Left: Pascall makes the celebrated plum eau de vie, La Vielle Prune.

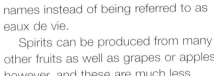

Kirsch

Kirsch is the original cherry spirit. It is a colourless pure distillate made from cherries, and has traditionally been seen as a distinctive product from the other fruit eaux de vie. It is principally made in the Alsace and Franche-Comté regions of eastern France, as well as in the Black Forest region of Bavaria in western Germany, its name being the German word for "cherry". It is also made in Switzerland and Austria.

When the cherry juice is pressed for the initial fermentation, the stones are ground up too and left to infuse in it, imparting a slightly bitter note to the spirit. It is generally given a short period of ageing in large earthenware vats. The true kirsch cherry is the black morello, but these days red varieties are often used instead.

Tastes good with

Use kirsch to add a touch of alcoholic richness to sweet desserts, whether for soaking the sponge base for a mousse, or moistening fresh fruit such as pineapple.

Left: Kirsch is a cherry eau de vie with an identity all of its own.

Slivovitz

True slivovitz is the local fruit brandy, or eau de vie, of Serbia and Bosnia-Herzegovina. The ravages of the war in the early 1990s in the former Yugoslavia, of which those countries were once part, put paid to a lot of the production capacity of the distilleries. A little did continue to be made, however, and with peace, production has risen once more.

At its best, slivovitz is one of the most distinguished eaux de vie made anywhere in Europe. The base fruit is a particular variety of black plum called Madjarka, which imparts a richly heady scent to the spirit. For the best grades, the spirit is cask-aged, and steeped in yet more whole fresh fruit during maturation to emphasize the flavour.

It comes in a variety of weirdly shaped bottles, some tall and thin, some round and flask-shaped with bevelled edges, still others of faceted glass.

Slivovitz has always been made and drunk elsewhere in eastern and central Europe, notably in Bulgaria, Hungary, Germany, Austria and Italy. In the Balkans, it may also go by its other name of rakija. This name denotes its origin as one of the European fruit versions of the arak that originally came from the Far East.

How it is made

Black plums are crushed along with their stones and fermented very slowly over a period of around three months. A double distillation is carried out, and then the new spirit is aged in great casks of Slovenian oak. Sometimes, whole plums are thrown in to macerate in the spirit while it ages, further intensifying its ripe, musky flavour. It is generally bottled at about five years old and at 35–40% ABV.

Tastes good with

A little slivovitz added to stewed plums, or even to a traditional Christmas pudding, will enrich the dish no end.

Below: Sljivovica is a Croatian slivovitz in a flask-shaped bottle.

Marc

In European vineyards, winemakers have long had to accustom themselves to the precarious existence that nature imposes. A bumper harvest of healthy grapes means a reasonable income, but in the lean years, a by-product proves a valuable stand-by.

For many winemakers, marc is the answer. After grapes have been pressed for fermentation, a mass of skins and pips, itself capable of fermentation, is left. Marc is the distillate of this residue. In France, the most celebrated marc is made in Burgundy and Champagne, frequently by producers enthusiastic enough to buy other growers' leftovers, but it is also made in Alsace, Provence and the Jura.

In Italy, marc is known as grappa, and such is the connoisseurship surrounding it that varietal grappa, from the skins of single grape varieties, has become something of a fad. An indication of its trendiness is that several California producers (whose climate is sufficiently benign not to need such a stand-by) are making versions of grappa too. In all regions, the finer spirits may be treated to oak maturation, resulting in a golden colour, but most marc or grappa is clear.

Tastes good with

I once ate a sorbet in Reims that had been made with Marc de Champagne and anointed with yet more of it. It was acutely, if intriguingly, horrible. More palatable is the use of Marc de Bourgogne for marinating the rind of the pungently powerful soft cow's-milk cheese, Chambertin. It adds to the complexity of flavour of a mature specimen.

Left: This Marc de Champagne is made by the champagne giants Moët & Chandon.

> **HOW TO SERVE**
> Their strong tannins make marcs unsuitable for mixing. They are intended to be drunk neat, though their profoundly earthy flavour may come as a shock to the uninitiated. On the calvados principle that a strong spirit aids digestion, the Burgundians value them as after-dinner drinks.

Arak

Although the discovery of distillation is still hotly disputed, it is possible that some form of arak, or raki, was the very first spirit. There are even claims that it might have been made in India around 800 BC.

Arak is not really one drink, but a generic name for a group of clear distillates, for which the base material and method of production vary according to the region of origin. In Indonesia, the fermented juice of sugar cane provides the base, but there are also rice versions. The sap of palm trees is popular as a source of arak in India.

The drink came to the Middle East and the Mediterranean with the Arab spice trade; its name comes from the Arabic word for juice or sap, *araq*. Other easily fermentable products such as dates and figs were used, and still are in parts of North Africa and the Middle East. Finally, grape and raisin wine came to be used in the old winemaking cultures of Greece and Cyprus.

In the West today, arak is most commonly encountered in the form of raki, the aniseed-tasting spirit of Greece and Turkey. Some coloured, cask-aged raki is very fine, but most is a colourless and pretty raw-tasting spirit that can be anything up to 50% ABV.

Raki is an everyday product made virtually throughout all of the Balkan countries of south-east Europe.

Right: This simple Turkish raki has not been cask-aged.

> **HOW TO SERVE**
> Arak should be drunk fairly abstemiously. Owing to its rough potency, it isn't generally served chilled, and should be sipped slowly rather than downed in one.

Aquavit

Among the spirits whose names are derived from the phrase "water of life", Scandinavian aquavit or akvavit has a particularly ancient history. It is known to have been distilled in northern Europe since medieval times, and its use as a drink dates back as far as the 15th century.

Production is very similar to that of flavoured vodkas. Its base is a neutral grain and/or potato spirit, which is rectified to a high degree of purity and then aromatized, usually with spices. Scandinavia and Germany are the main production centres. Its alternative name, schnapps, derives from an old Nordic verb *snappen*, meaning to snatch or seize, denoting the way it is traditionally drunk – snatched down the throat in a single gulp.

How it is made

Potatoes are boiled in a contraption rather like a huge pressure cooker, and the resulting starchy mass is then mixed with malted grains. After fermentation with yeasts, it is double-distilled to obtain a neutral spirit. Dilution reduces it to a drinkable strength, and contact with charcoal, together with the approved flavouring elements, gives it its final character.

Right: Aalborg is a premium high-strength aquavit from Denmark.

Far right: Peach County Schnapps is a fruit-flavoured commercial "schnapps".

> **HOW TO SERVE**
> Aquavit should be served like good vodka – that is, ice-cold and neat from a receptacle no bigger than a shot glass. The bottle should be kept in the freezer prior to serving. It makes a superb winter aperitif.

Mescal

Mescal, or mezcal, is one of Mexico's indigenous drinks. It is a pale, yellowish spirit made from the juice of the agave cactus, like tequila.

It would be fair to say that mescal doesn't have a very salubrious image. It is the rapacious firewater drunk by the British Consul in Malcolm Lowry's alcohol-saturated novel, *Under the Volcano*. In the past, it was considered to be capable of inducing hallucinations, a feature Lowry's novel reports, but it is hard to account for this since the agave cactus is not one of the hallucinogenic species.

Mescal is often sold with a pickled white agave worm in the bottle. It is genuine, and is intended to be eaten as the last of the drink is poured out. Supposedly, ingestion of the worm encourages great heroism in those already brave enough to swallow it. Do try this at home.

How it is made

The unattractive agave plant has an enormous core, the shape of a pine cone, which is surrounded by great, spiny, fat leaves. This is hacked away and the expressed bitter, milky-white juice is fermented into pulque beer at around 5–6%. Mescal is the first rough distillation of this. It may be given a short period of wood-ageing.

Right: A little white worm lurks at the bottom of a mescal bottle.

> **HOW TO SERVE**
> If you want to tame its fire, mix mescal with a little lime juice and top it up with soda or tonic. In Mexico, they knock it back neat.

LIQUEURS

Since we are clearly distinguishing between spirits and liqueurs, it would be useful to arrive at a working definition of what constitutes a liqueur. Why is kirsch a spirit, for example, but cherry brandy a liqueur?

The distinction lies in the way that the various flavours of these drinks are obtained. Essentially, a liqueur is any spirit-based drink to which flavouring elements have been added, usually by infusion, and – in the vast majority of cases – enhanced by sweetening. Sometimes the flavourings are themselves subjected to distillation; sometimes they are merely soaked or macerated in an alcohol base. Although there are flavoured spirits, such as lemon vodka (or, for that matter, gin) there are no unflavoured liqueurs.

Below: Liqueurs play an indispensable part in the cocktail repertoire, usually sandwiched between one of the basic spirits and a non-alcoholic mixer or two.

Kirsch is a spirit because it is a straight, unsweetened distillate of cherries, whereas cherry brandy is a neutral spirit from other sources to which a cherry flavour is added by infusion of the fruit.

Liqueurs have their origins in the practice of adding aromatic ingredients, such as herbs, fruit extracts, seeds, spices, nuts, roots and flowers, to the earliest distilled spirits. This was done both to mask the unappealing flavour of the impurities that remained after rectification, and to endow the resulting potions with medicinal value. As long as basic spirits were available, a liqueur could and often would be concocted in a domestic kitchen for use in cooking as well as for drinking. As various proprietary liqueurs came on the market during the 19th century, so home liqueur-making declined.

When the science of distillation was still in its infancy in Europe, the Catalan physician Arnaldo de Vilanova advanced the theory that steeping

certain medicinal herbs in alcohol extracted the beneficial qualities. This was a logical progression of the non-alcoholic distillation of essential oils that had been practised in ancient Egypt and classical Greece. As an offshoot of the alchemical arts, distillation was intimately bound up with the doomed enterprise of attempting to turn base metals to gold, and so gold itself came to play a part in the formulation of alcohol-based remedies. (Arnaldo was saved from the Spanish Inquisition, it is said, because he had cured the Pope of a life-threatening illness by means of a tonic containing flakes of gold.) The tradition lives on today in the form of a drink called Goldwasser. Shake the bottle and it is suddenly alive with sparkling petals of gold leaf, like a child's snowstorm toy.

It was in the religious orders that many of the traditional liqueurs were first formulated, since the medicinal ingredients used were often grown in

Above: The Grand Monastery of Chartreuse in France, where the famous Chartreuse liqueurs are made.

the monastery gardens. By the late Middle Ages, the Italians had become the most celebrated practitioners of the art of liqueur-making. In 1533, the marriage of Catherine de Medici to the future French King Henri II brought a wave of Italians into France, and they brought their expertise with them. Some of the more notable products, such as Bénédictine, were made by French monastic orders until relatively recently. Chartreuse still is.

In the 19th century, liqueurs had an aura of being soothingly palatable after-dinner digestifs for people, essentially women, who were not fond of the stronger alternatives, such as cognac. Liqueurs were seen as more ladylike drinks altogether, an image enhanced by the introduction of the tiny glasses that are still depressingly enough seen as their appropriate receptacles. By now, they had shed most of their health-giving claims and become

honest-to-goodness drinks, although it was still popularly believed by imbibers that they had prophylactic properties.

The cocktail era of the 1920s and 30s that had doggedly to contend with universal prohibition in the USA, but suffered no such constraints in London, Paris, Berlin and Venice, freed liqueurs from the straitjacket of cultured politeness in which the Victorian period had imprisoned them. At a stroke, the era transformed the old slings and fizzes, fixes, sours, punches, cups and smashes into drinks worthy of their names. A mixture of gin with lemon juice, sugar and soda may have been a pleasant way of taking gin, but with a slug of cherry brandy added, it became an altogether more exciting and hazardous proposition. That sense of playing with fire is inscribed in many of the most colourful names of the great cocktail recipes of the 1920s, in their evocations of gambling (Casino), sex (Maiden's Blush), spiritual danger (Hell, Little Devil) and even First World War munitions (Whizzbang, Depth Bomb, Artillery).

No drinking culture was ever happier or more heedless than that of the original and greatest cocktail era, and it couldn't have happened without the liqueurs. The following pages are a taster's tour of the famous and the not-so-famous.

Below: The blue curaçao in this cocktail certainly makes its presence felt.

Cointreau

One of the most popular branded liqueurs of all, Cointreau is, properly speaking, a variety of curaçao. This means it is a brandy-based spirit that has been flavoured with the rind of bitter oranges. When it was launched in 1849 by the Cointreau brothers, Edouard-Jean and Adolphe, it was sold under the brand name Triple Sec White Curaçao, but so many other proprietary curaçaos began to be sold as triple sec that the family decided to give it their own name instead.

The centre of operations, as well as a distillery, are located in the French town of Angers, in the Loire valley, although Cointreau is also made in the Americas. A variety of different bottlings is available at different strengths, including a cream version, but the best-loved Cointreau is the one that comes in a square, dark-brown bottle at 40% ABV.

Despite its spirit strength, Cointreau tastes deliciously innocuous. It is sugar-sweet and colourless, but has a

powerful fume of fresh oranges, with an underlying, vaguely herbal note too. The oranges used are a clever blend of bitter, green, Seville-style varieties from the Caribbean (the island of Curaçao itself is close to Venezuela) and sweeter types from the south of France.

How it is made

Cointreau is a double distillation of grape brandy, infused with orange rind, and then sweetened and further aromatized with other secret plant ingredients.

Tastes good with

If the balance of other seasonings is right, Cointreau works admirably in the orange sauce that is classically served with duck. It is excellent in a range of desserts, particularly rich chocolate mousse.

Left: Cointreau is one of the best-loved liqueurs, and was one of the first of the orange-flavoured ones to achieve fame.

HOW TO SERVE

Absolutely everyone's favourite way of serving Cointreau is either on the rocks or frappé, depending on whether you like your ice in chunks or crystals. The cold then mitigates some of the sweetness of the liqueur, while the pure citrus flavour is exquisitely refreshing.

Cointreau can be mixed with virtually any spirit (except perhaps whisky) and a quantity of lemon juice, and shaken with ice. This is a Sidecar, made with cognac, Cointreau and lemon juice, one of the classic recipes of the original cocktail era.

Mix Cointreau with cognac, white rum and lemon juice to make another variation, Between the Sheets, a powerful, sharply flavoured cocktail from the 1920s. Whatever the formula, the pure orange flavour of the liqueur comes singing through.

Grand Marnier

Grand Marnier is another of the world's most popular orange-flavoured liqueurs. The original product is a little younger than Cointreau, its big French rival, but the style is quite different. In the sense that the oranges used in it are bitter varieties from the Caribbean, it may be classed as another type of curaçao, but it is a distinctly finer product than most ordinary curaçao.

The house that owns it was founded in 1827 by a family called Lapostolle. Louis-Alexandre Marnier later married into the family business and it was he who, in 1880, first conceived the liqueur that bears his name. Encountering the bitter oranges of Haiti on a grand tour, he hit upon the idea of blending their flavour with that of finest cognac, and then giving it a period of barrel-ageing that basic grades of curaçao never get.

Today, the production of the liqueur is split between two centres, one at Château de Bourg in the Cognac region, and the other at Neauphle-le-Château, near Paris. The initial blending is carried out at the former site, the ageing at the latter. What results is a highly refined, mellow, full-strength spirit that has a warm, amber colour and an intense, festive scent of ripe oranges.

It is sweet, but the distinction of the Fine Champagne cognac on which it is based prevents it from being in any way cloying when served straight.

The Marnier-Lapostolle company also tried cashing in on the mania for cream liqueurs that has arisen over the last 20 years by launching a Crème de Grand Marnier at a much lower strength, which I can't find it in my heart to recommend. On the plus side, it also makes a Cherry Marnier, from the *griotte* black cherry variety, naturally coloured a deep red and deeply delicious too.

How it is made
The distilled juice of Caribbean oranges is blended with top-quality cognac. After full amalgamation of the flavours, it is then re-distilled, sweetened and given a period of cask-ageing.

Tastes good with
Grand Marnier is the classic ingredient used in duck à l'orange.

Right: Grand Marnier is the equal of cognac.

HOW TO MIX
Grand Marnier is mixed with curaçao, grenadine and lemon juice to make a Gloom Chaser.

The top layer of the pousse-café cocktail B52 is Grand Marnier.

Orange and coffee make a surprisingly successful combination in this Café à l'Orange.

Curaçao

First invented by the Dutch, curaçao was a white, rum-based liqueur flavoured with the peel of bitter green oranges found by the settlers on the Caribbean island of the same name, not far off the coast of Venezuela. Despite its geographically specific name, the liqueur has never been subject to anything like appellation regulations. It is made by many different companies in a number of countries, where brandy is used as the starter spirit instead.

A variant name in common use was triple sec, the most famous example being Cointreau, although confusingly curaçao is not at all *sec* (dry) but always sweet. The bitterness of the oranges – which are green simply because they are not quite ripe, not because they are some notably exotic variety – balances the sweetness, however, to the extent that drinkers may have been prepared to consider it relatively dry.

Curaçao comes in a range of colours in addition to the clear version. The orange curaçao, such as that made by Bols, is often particularly bitter, its colour a deep, burnished, tawny orange. Curaçao also comes in bright blue, dark green, red and yellow versions for novelty value, but the flavour is always of orange. The strength is generally somewhere between 25–30% ABV.

Below: All curaçao is flavoured with bitter oranges.

Below: The term triple sec tends to be used for the colourless curaçao.

The name of the island is not, of course, Dutch but Portuguese, after the original discoverers. There is more confusion over the correct way to pronounce "curaçao" than over the name of any other liqueur. It should properly be "coorashow" (to rhyme with "miaow"), but is corrupted by English speakers into something like "cura-say-oh".

These days it is probably the blue version that is most commercially popular, largely because it was for years the only blue alcoholic drink available. It added an unearthly hue to many cocktails, although the flavour – reassuringly enough – was only slightly bitter orange.

HOW TO SERVE
The bitterness of the fruit mixes well with other bitter flavours, so orange curaçao and tonic makes a particularly appealing long drink. Alternatively, use a not-too-sweet sparkling lemonade, if you can find one. Curaçao also works well when mixed in equal measures with either dry or sweet vermouth. It is not especially attractive taken neat.

How it is made
The blossom and dried peel of wild oranges are steeped in grape brandy or even neutral spirit, and the resulting infusion is sweetened, clarified and coloured according to style.

Tastes good with
Curaçao is indispensable in the classic crêpe suzette. In the recipe created by the great French chef Auguste Escoffier, pancake batter is flavoured with tangerine juice and curaçao, and the cooked crêpe sauced with butter, sugar and tangerine zests. These days, it is generally Grand Marnier that is used in this enduringly popular dessert, probably because it is a ritzier product.

Mandarine Napoléon

Mandarine is another type of curaçao, this time made with the skins of tangerines as opposed to bitter Caribbean oranges. By far the most famous brand is Mandarine Napoléon, the origins of which really do derive from the drinking preferences of the Emperor Napoleon I. The key figure in its history is a French chemist, Antoine-François de Fourcroy, who rose to prominence as a key figure in public administration after the French Revolution. Following the demise of the Jacobin regime, de Fourcroy found favour with Napoleon Bonaparte and was made a member of his Imperial State Council.

Left: Mandarine Napoléon is a French invention, which is now exclusively made in the Belgian capital, Brussels.

When the tangerine first arrived in Europe from China (hence its synonym, mandarin) at the end of the 18th century, there was something of a craze for it. The fashion was to steep the peel in cognac after eating the fruit, and Antoine-François records in his diary that many was the night he was called on to share such a convivial tot with Napoleon.

Mandarine Napoléon was launched in 1892 by a Belgian distiller, Louis Schmidt, who stumbled on the recipe in de Fourcroy's correspondence. It was only after the Second World War, when the distillery was relocated from Belgium to France, that the de Fourcroy family once again became involved with the liqueur, eventually taking on the worldwide distribution of Schmidt's preparation. As it became ever more successful, they moved the production back to Brussels, where it remains to this day – the primary Belgian liqueur.

The tangerines used in Mandarine Napoléon come exclusively from Sicily. Other companies make versions of tangerine liqueurs – Italians themselves make one from their Sicilian crop – but Mandarine Napoléon remains justifiably the pre-eminent example. Italian versions are named mandarinetto.

Van der Hum

Van der Hum is South Africa's equivalent of curaçao, made by several producers in the Cape, including the giant national wine consortium KWV. The whimsical name literally translates as "What's-his-name". Its base is Cape brandy, and the citrus fruit used is a tangerine-like orange variety locally known as *naartjies*. The rinds of the orange are infused in the brandy (as for Mandarine Napoléon) and supplemented with a herb or spice element, which generally includes nutmeg.

Like Mandarine Napoléon, the drink derives from the practice of steeping citrus rinds in the local brandy. It is a reliable and attractive liqueur, pale gold in colour and with a pronounced, bitter orange scent. The bottled strength is generally 25%-plus. Different brands have varying degrees of concentration.

Left: Van der Hum is South Africa's answer to orange curaçao.

Aurum

The name Aurum is Latin for "gold". Made in the Abruzzi mountains, on the Adriatic coast of Italy, Aurum is a brandy-based proprietary liqueur in which a mixture of orange rind and whole oranges is infused, its lustrous golden intensity enhanced by saffron. The basic formula is said to be of great antiquity. Aurum was given its name by the Italian writer Gabriele d'Annunzio.

The name hints that it may at one time have contained particles of genuine gold, harking back to the alchemical origins of distillation, and it has logically been argued that Aurum was the true forerunner of Goldwasser.

Left: Golden Aurum comes from Abruzzo, in eastern Italy.

How it is made

The brandy in Aurum is distilled by the makers from vintage Italian wines, and the distillate is cask-aged for around four years to take up colour. The oranges (and other citrus fruits) are infused separately in more brandy, and then the infusion is triple-distilled. This, and the first brandy, are then blended and allowed another period of oak maturation. The result is an impressively smooth liqueur, with a deceptive 40% alcohol.

Liqueur brandies

Some fruit liqueurs have traditionally been referred to as "brandies", even though they are properly nothing of the sort, in the sense that we now understand the term. There are essentially three fruit "brandies" – cherry, apricot and peach – and, although they are occasionally known by other names, it is as cherry brandy, etc. that drinkers know them best.

Strictly speaking, these products belong to the same large category as those liqueurs prefixed with the phrase "crème de", in that they are sweetened, coloured drinks, based on simple grape brandy that has been flavoured with the relevant fruits, as opposed to being primary distillates of those fruits themselves. The maceration of the fruit usually includes the stones or pips as well, for the bitter flavour they impart and, in the case of apricot kernels especially, the distinctive flavour of toasted almonds.

Of the three fruit brandies, the apricot variant has probably travelled the furthest. There are true apricot distillates made in eastern Europe, of which the Hungarian Barak Pálinka is

Right: Cusenier's liqueurs all come in distinctive bottles, such as this apricot brandy.

the most renowned, but they are dry like the fruit brandies of France. Good examples of sweet apricot liqueurs are Bols Apricot Brandy, Cusenier, and Apry, which is made by the Marie Brizard company of Bordeaux.

Cherry brandy is one of the few liqueurs that may have been invented by the English; the role of creator was claimed by one Thomas Grant of Kent. The original version was made with black morellos, although other cherry varieties may be used in modern products, depending on what is locally available. English cherry brandy contributed to the downfall of the dissolute King George IV, who consumed it in ruinous quantities, perhaps to get over the memory of his doomed affair with Mrs Fitzherbert in Brighton.

Among the more famous cherry liqueur brands are Cherry Heering, now properly known as Peter Heering Cherry Liqueur, which was first formulated in the mid-19th century by a Danish distiller of that name. The Heering company grows its own cherries to make this product, which is cask-aged. Others include Cherry Rocher, De Kuyper, Garnier and Bols, and there are brands produced in Germany and Switzerland.

Peach brandy is the one least frequently seen, its most famous manifestation probably being the one marketed by Bols. Its flavour is not quite as distinctive as the apricot.

HOW TO SERVE
The best of these liqueur brandies make wonderful digestifs served in small quantities, provided they are not the very sweetest styles.

Above right: Cherry brandy is crucial in the making of a Singapore Sling.

How they are made
The pressed juice and stones of the respective fruits are generally mixed with a neutral grape spirit (more rarely a grain spirit), sweetened with sugar syrup and macerated until the take-up of flavour is complete. If the fruit juice itself has a fairly high natural sweetness, correspondingly less syrup will be added. In some cases, the liqueurs may be treated to a period of cask-ageing, followed by adjustment of the colour with vegetable dyes. They are generally bottled at the standard liqueur strength of between 24% and 28% ABV.

Crème liqueurs

Liqueurs that use the prefix "crème de" may be bracketed together here. They are nothing at all to do with cream liqueurs, despite the terminology. They nearly always consist of one dominant flavour, which is indicated in the name. This is often, but not always, a fruit, and the liqueurs are usually appropriately coloured. In the main, they are bottled at 25–30% ABV, and may be considered among the more useful building-blocks of the cocktail-mixer's repertoire.

Originally, the term "crème" was used to indicate that these were sweetened liqueurs, as distinct from

Below left: Crème de Banane contains banana, a versatile flavour.

Below right: Crème de Cassis is a speciality of Burgundy.

dry spirits such as cognac or calvados. They were mainly French in origin, such as those produced by the 19th-century Bordeaux company Marie Brizard, but production soon spread to other specialist liqueur manufacturers such as Bols and De Kuyper of Holland.

Before the widespread availability of such products, the sweetening element in a cocktail used to be pure sugar, or perhaps a sugar syrup. The crème liqueurs had the advantage not only of providing that sweetness, but also of introducing another flavour into the cocktail mixture.

Most of these products are based on a neutral-tasting, un-aged grape brandy, and the various flavouring ingredients are either infused or macerated in the spirit rather than being subject to distillation themselves. The difference, essentially, between infusion and maceration is that the former involves some gentle heating action, while the latter is just a cold soaking of the flavouring element in the spirit. Maceration is obviously a considerably slower process than infusion. In both cases, the ingredient has to be rendered water-soluble.

Since they are intended to be rich but simple products, with one overriding flavour, crème liqueurs are not generally treated to ageing in wood. Oak maturation would interfere with the often bold primary flavours of the drinks.

How they are made

After the infusion or maceration, the aromatized spirit may then be strained to remove any solid particles caused by making the flavouring agent water-soluble. It is

HOW TO SERVE
These drinks were originally intended to be drunk as pleasant aids to digestion at the end of a grand dinner. As such, they are best served *frappé* (poured over shaved ice) rather than neat, to mitigate some of their sweetness.

then sweetened, usually by means of sugar solution. Unless it is possible to achieve a striking colour naturally (which is in fact quite rare), the colour is then created by the addition of vegetable-based colouring matter such as carotene or beetroot. Red colourings are often created by adding cochineal. The liqueur is then subjected to a heavy filtration to ensure a bright, crystal-clear product of unvarying consistency.

Tastes good with

The most obvious way to use crème liqueurs based on fruit is in desserts that are flavoured with the same principal ingredient. Enliven your strawberry mousse with crème de fraise, or your blackberry cheesecake with crème de mûre. Add crème de framboise to desserts based on raspberries, and crème de cassis to those made with blackcurrants. The flowery crème liqueurs, such as crème de violette and crème de roses, make exotic additions to the syrup for a simple fruit salad.

Maraschino

The original maraschino (which should be pronounced with a "sk" sound in the middle, not "sh") was a distilled liquor of some antiquity made from a sour red cherry variety called Marasca, which grew only on the Dalmatian coast.

When the Italian-speaking enclave of Dalmatia was incorporated into the then Yugoslavia, Italian production of maraschino was continued in the Veneto region of Italy.

Maraschino is a clear liqueur derived from an infusion of pressed cherry skins in a cherry-stone distillate. After further distillation to obtain a pure, clear spirit, it is aged, ideally for several years. It always remains colourless, and should have a pronounced aroma.

A number of Italian firms are especially associated with the production of maraschino, notably Luxardo, which traditionally sells its product in straw-covered flasks.

How it is made

The pomace of pressed cherries is infused over gentle heat in a cherry distillate for several months. It is then rectified and transferred to neutral maturation vessels to finish its ageing.

Left: Luxardo's fine maraschino is traditionally sold in straw-covered bottles.

HOW TO SERVE

The best grades of maraschino should be smooth enough to drink on their own, but the sweeter it is, the more recourse to the ice-bucket you will need.

Poire William

Poire William is not to be confused with true pear brandy, also known as eau de vie de poire. Instead, it is a sweet, pear-flavoured liqueur, traditionally lightly coloured and made by the usual method of infusing crushed fruit in neutral grape spirit. The big liqueur companies nearly all make a version. Some may have a brief period of cask-ageing, but most don't.

Pear-flavoured liqueurs are made in France (about the best brand is Marie Brizard), Italy (which has Pera Segnana), Germany and Switzerland. A novelty product is Poire Prisonnière,

which comes with a whole pear in the bottle. The pears are grown in the bottles, which are attached to the tree, so that each fruit has its own private greenhouse. Before the bottles are filled with the liqueur, the pears are pricked in order to release their juices.

Right: Poire William is a delicately flavoured, French pear liqueur.

HOW TO SERVE

Served well chilled, or perhaps with a single piece of ice, it makes a good aperitif. Alternatively, Poire William is delicious with a splash of lemonade.

Tastes good with

Poire William is excellent poured over certain fresh fruits, notably pink grapefruit segments, pineapple and, of course, pear, when it subtly enhances the flavours.

Sloe gin

Sloe gin, and its French equivalent prunelle, are derived from a small, bitter-tasting plum, the fruit of a shrub called the blackthorn. English sloe gin is nothing more than sweetened gin in which sloes have been steeped and then strained out once they have stained it a deep red. The drink has a strong, rather medicinal taste.

Prunelle, from the French word for the fruit, is not red but green, and is made by macerating the fruit kernels in a grape spirit base. Although colour may be added, it does reflect the greenish flesh of the fruit. In Burgundy and Alsace, sloes are also used to make eau de vie.

Sloe gin is still made domestically in country areas of England, but only with commercial gin, of course. The picked fruits are left to macerate for several months.

Left: This sloe gin is made by one of the big names in gin.

HOW TO SERVE

Sloe gin is best served neat at room temperature. Alternatively, add ¼–½ measure/1–2 tsp to a glass of sparkling wine.

Midori

An instant hit when it was launched in 1978, Midori was another product from the giant Japanese drinks group, Suntory. It aimed for a slice of the cocktail action with this bright green liqueur in an idiosyncratic little bottle of textured glass. Originally a Japanese product, it is now made in Mexico.

The flavouring agent is melons, not a particularly common taste in the liqueur world, but the drink's vivid green colour is achieved by means of a dye. Indeed, its greenness is its principal sales pitch, since *midori* is the Japanese word for "green". The colour is perhaps intended to

Left: Bright green Midori has cornered the market in melon liqueurs.

evoke the skins of certain melon varieties, such as Canteloupe or Galia, as opposed to the flesh that is actually used to flavour it. Its aroma is in fact much closer to banana. It is sweet and syrupy, and at the lower end of standard alcoholic strength for liqueurs: 20%.

Tastes good with

Midori was seized on by adventurous chefs for use in desserts that involve tropical fruit. Salads of mango, pineapple, melon, passion fruit and other tropical fruits are perfect choices, although the problem of the drink's unapologetic colour remains.

HOW TO SERVE

Midori is much better mixed than served straight, when its flavour quickly cloys. It blends beautifully with iced fruit juices, notably orange, except that the resulting colour is fairly lurid.

Midori can be treated in much the same way as the basic spirits to make a Sour, mixed with lemon juice and a dash of sugar syrup. It is always better shaken rather than stirred.

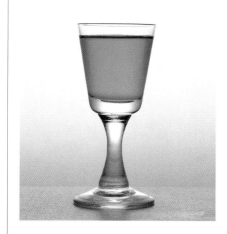

Pisang Ambon

An Indonesian liqueur made by the Dutch drinks company Bols, Pisang Ambon deserves its own separate entry. Ambon is the name of one of the many islands of Indonesia, in whose language *pisang* is the word for "banana". More than just another

HOW TO SERVE

Pisang Ambon is excellent topped up with good, sharply flavoured sparkling lemonade.

type of crème de banane, however, Pisang is made of green bananas and other tropical fruits, with a mixture of herbs thrown in for good measure. The formula is evidently based on an old local recipe.

The drink is a pronounced, deepish green colour, but nowhere near as vivid as Midori, and it is naturally very sweet. However, in comparison with the simplicity of other banana liqueurs, Pisang has an attractive savoury note of

cooked banana, making it a rather more versatile cocktail ingredient than a simple crème liqueur.

Tastes good with

It can be used to flavour desserts and pastries that use exotic fruits, including, of course, bananas.

Left: Pisang Ambon, Indonesia's contribution to the world of classic liqueurs.

Southern Comfort

The foremost American liqueur is Southern Comfort. Naturally, American whiskey is used as its starting point. The exact composition of Southern Comfort is of course a closely guarded secret, but what we do know is that the fruit flavouring it contains is peach, a fruit that grows in great quantities in the southern states.

The origins of Southern Comfort probably lie in the mixing of bourbon with peach juice as a traditional cocktail in the southern states. Down in Louisiana, close to New Orleans (as the song goes), there was once a mixed drink

Right: Southern Comfort is a fruity whiskey liqueur of the Deep South.

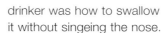

called Sazerac. It consists of a shot of rye whiskey, with a sprinkling of peach bitters, a lump of sugar and a dash of absinthe. So traditional is it that a New Orleans company has been producing a pre-mixed version of it since around the middle of the 19th century.

The Southern Comfort distillery is located in St Louis, Missouri. The drink comes in two strengths, 40% and 50% ABV, both of which have an appealing, fruity roundness of flavour and a mellow finish.

Tastes good with
Southern Comfort makes a good substitute for bourbon, poured over the traditional light fruitcake at Thanksgiving or Christmas. Quantities should be extremely generous.

HOW TO SERVE
Southern Comfort is intended to be meditatively sipped, like other fine American whiskeys, but you could try taming its fire and emphasizing its fruitiness with a mixer of peach nectar. It's also fine with orange juice on the rocks.

Sambuca

An Italian liqueur that became quite fashionable beyond its home region of Rome in the 1970s, Sambuca Romana is a clear, moderately sweet, quite fiery drink, flavoured with elderberries and aniseed. Its name is derived from the botanical name for elderberry, *Sambucus nigra*. Although it also contains many other herbs and roots, these are the two predominant flavours.

In the days when every drink had to be dignified with its own particular serving ritual, it was decreed that Sambuca was to be garnished with coffee beans and set alight. Aficionados of the custom differed quite sharply as to whether the correct number of beans was two or three. Such detail scarcely mattered, since what mostly preoccupied the

drinker was how to swallow it without singeing the nose.

To earn your Sambuca stripes, you have to blow out the flame on a glassful and then swallow the drink in one. In Rome, they will ask you whether you want it *con la mosca*, which literally means "with the fly" (i.e. with the coffee beans). There, they are not merely for garnish. If you say *si*, you will be expected to crunch the beans up as you drink.

Tastes good with
A chilled glass of Sambuca makes a good accompaniment to a genuine Italian torta, one of those heavenly sticky cakes of dried fruits, almonds and lemon rind.

Left: Sambuca is a fiery liqueur in more ways than one.

HOW TO SERVE
If you are going to try the flaming Sambuca trick, it helps to serve the liqueur in a narrow glass like an old-fashioned sherry schooner, because the flame will take more easily on a smaller surface.

Ratafia

Centuries ago, the term "ratafia" was used to describe fruits or nuts that were steeped in a sweetened spirit base. The term has now come to be applied mainly to a type of aperitif made in the brandy-producing areas of France. The brandy is mixed with fresh fruit juice.

Ratafia's name is not a geographical one. It derives from the old French practice of concluding any formal agreement, such a legal contract or business transaction, with a shared drink – a "ratifier", if you like. The original phrase is Latin: *rata fiat* (let the deal be settled).

There are also ratafias made in winemaking areas – particularly Burgundy and Champagne, in which the naturally sweet grape juice is mixed with some of the regional wine. The most celebrated ratafia, however, is Pineau des Charentes, made in the

Cognac region from grape juice fortified with cognac. It can't be considered a fortified wine, though, because the grape juice has not undergone fermentation. It comes in white and rosé versions, and always has the sweetness of ripe grape juice about it.

In Armagnac, not to be outdone, they make their own version of this drink by exactly the same method. Called Floc de Gascogne, its production, like that of armagnac itself, is on a much more modest commercial footing than its Charentais counterpart.

There is also a variant of this type of ratafia made in the Calvados region of Normandy, in which fresh apple juice is fortified with apple brandy. It is called pommeau, and is a considerably more palatable proposition (to the author's taste at least) than either Pineau or Floc.

Lesser-known variants of ratafia are made in most of the old wine-producing countries, wherever a grape spirit is produced. The Spanish drink, Moscatel de Valencia, should technically also be considered a type of ratafia, as it consists of grape spirit added to an unfermented, naturally sweet Moscatel grape juice.

How it is made
Grape brandy is added to unfermented grape juice, or apple brandy to apple juice. In each case the product is made to an average bottled strength of around 17% ABV, the same as a fortified wine.

Above left: Pineau des Charentes is the ratafia of the Cognac region.

Above right: Pommeau is an apple ratafia from Normandy.

Tastes good with
Ratafia works quite well, or at least better than most wine, as an accompaniment to a slice of aromatic melon. Because these drinks are all naturally sweet, they don't immediately appeal to all tastes as obvious aperitifs, where the preference is usually for something dry. They may work better as dessert wines for many, with fruit tarts, or a slice of sumptuously rich cake.

HOW TO SERVE
These drinks should be served, vigorously chilled, in wine glass quantities as aperitifs. In Armagnac, they mix the Floc with sparkling wine and call it a pousse-rapière (literally "rapier-pusher").

Amaretto

Of all the liqueurs that rely on almonds for their principal flavouring, amaretto is the most famous. It has become widely associated in people's minds with one particular Italian brand, Disaronno Originale, made by a company called Illva, although there are other liqueurs that may properly be called amarettos. The famous amaretto comes in a rectangular bottle, with a label in the form of an old scroll and a disproportionately large, square screw-top. The flavour is not entirely derived from almonds but from the stones of apricots too. Resembling a kind of liquid marzipan, the taste is strong and sweet and is quite assertive, even when mixed in a cocktail.

Legend has it that the recipe was given to an Italian painter of Leonardo da Vinci's school, Bernardino Luini, in 1525 by a young innkeeper. She had sat as the model for the Virgin Mary in his wall-painting of the Nativity at

Left: Disaronno is the most famous brand of Italian amaretto.

Right: Casoni amaretto's flavour is like marzipan in a bottle.

Saronno, and taken rather a shine to him. Whether or not there is much truth in the tale, the original domestic concoction was probably grape brandy in which apricot kernels, with their strongly almondy flavour, had been left to infuse.

How it is made

Almond extracts, along with apricot kernels and seeds, are steeped in brandy, and the resulting drink is sweetened with sugar syrup and coloured to a deep brown.

Tastes good with

Just as a frangipane mixture, full of ground almonds, makes a good base for almost any fruit tart, so amaretto works well in the syrup for a fruit salad, or added to whipped cream or ice cream for most fruit-based desserts.

HOW TO SERVE

The flavour of Disaronno Originale amaretto is quite complex enough for it to be enjoyable on its own, although it works better chilled. Serving it *frappé* (poured over crushed ice) is highly refreshing.

In a cocktail, amaretto mixes well with dry spirits such as cognac and gin, with perhaps some pure citrus juice (orange or lemon) to mitigate its sweetness.

It also marries deliciously with chocolate in the super-rich *pot au chocolat*. It is excellent in a liqueur coffee, and perhaps with cognac too. It pays to use the liqueur sparingly though, even in these culinary contexts, as its flavour is unignorably powerful. A little goes a long way.

Malibu

With the growth of tourism in the Caribbean islands, it was only a matter of time before liqueurs flavoured with coconut began to make their presence felt on the international market. Of these, the most famous is Malibu, made in Jamaica. Presented in an opaque white bottle, with a depiction of a tropical sunset on the front, it is a relatively low-strength (24% ABV) blend of rectified Barbados white rum with coconut extracts. The flavour is pleasingly not too sweet. Malibu was a better product than most of the liqueur concoctions with tropical names that bombarded the market during the cocktail renaissance of the early 1980s.

Another reasonably good product was Batida de Coco, a coconut-flavoured neutral spirit made in Brazil that was also exported in quantity to the holiday islands of the Caribbean. Cocoribe was similar.

All of these products are colourless, with an alcohol level slightly higher than that of fortified wine. Encouraged by the success of these proprietary products, some of the famous Dutch and French liqueur manufacturers have also marketed variants of crème de coco, although they aren't as good.

How they are made

Most of the coconut liqueurs are based on ultra-refined white rum, although one or two are made with a neutral grain alcohol. The dried pulp and milk of the coconut are used to flavour the spirit, which is then sweetened and filtered.

Tastes good with

A splash of coconut liqueur may productively be added to the sauces in Cajun or Far Eastern dishes, particularly those of Thai or Indonesian cuisine, where coconut itself figures strongly. Otherwise, it is splendid as a flavouring in a richly creamy ice cream, or poured over a salad of exotically flavoured tropical fruits.

Far left: Malibu is perhaps the best of the coconut liqueurs.

Left: Batida de Coco is Brazil's contribution to the coconut collection.

HOW TO SERVE

These drinks are not great on their own, but make excellent mixes with ice and fruit juices, which is how they were originally intended to be served. Orange, grapefruit and pineapple are the best.

Bearing their tropical origins in mind, coconut rums mix well with other fruit-flavoured liqueurs from the hot regions. Crème de banane is an especially good partner for it.

Nut liqueurs

Liqueurs based on hazelnut, walnut and almond deserve to be considered separately, since they form quite a large sub-group.

In their French manifestations, hazelnut and walnut liqueurs are straightforward enough. They are named noisette and crème de noix, after the French words for hazelnut and walnut respectively. In the case of almonds, it all becomes a little more complicated, because the stones of certain fruit, such as apricots and cherries, have an almond-like taste. A liqueur that contains almonds themselves is called crème d'amandes. However, a liqueur called crème de noyau – *noyau* being the French term for the stone in which the almond-like kernel of a fruit is encased – will contain no

Left: Nocino is a strong walnut liqueur from Italy.

actual almonds, only an approximation of the flavour.

All nut liqueurs are brandy-based drinks in which the chopped nuts are steeped in a clear grape spirit and the resulting liqueur is clarified and bottled in a colourless state. The exception is crème de noyau, which more often than not has a faint, pinkish hue if it has been made from cherry stones. All of these liqueurs are sweet, with fairly syrupy textures, and make invaluable additions to the cocktail repertoire.

Italy produces a range of nut-based liqueurs, too. In addition to the distinctive almond-flavoured Disaronno Originale, there is also a walnut liqueur called Nocino. In the 1980s, a product called Frangelico was released. It was a delicate, straw-coloured liqueur flavoured with hazelnuts and herbs, dressed up initially in a faintly ridiculous, dark brown bottle designed to look like a monk. The large, brown, plastic top represented his cowl, and around the gathered-in waist, a length of white cord was knotted. It looked like a particularly embarrassing tourist souvenir, but the liqueur itself turned out to be delicious; it was not too sweet, and had an intriguing range of flavours.

How they are made
The nuts are crumbled up and left to infuse with the base spirit before sweetening and filtration. The liqueurs are bottled at the average liqueur strength, around 25%. In the case of the crème de noix of Gascony, the walnuts

are beaten off the trees while still green, and the spirit is sweetened with honey before being subjected to a further distillation. For crème de noyau, fruit stones are the infusion agent. They are usually either cherry or apricot, but peach and even plum may also be used, to much the same effect.

Taste good with
Nut liqueurs work well with nutty desserts, such as those containing almond paste or praline, but are also good in a chocolate mousse, or drunk alongside a piece of rich, dark fruitcake. Served chilled, Frangelico makes an unlikely table-fellow for a piece of mature Stilton.

Below left: Frangelico is a branded liqueur dressed up to look like a monk.

Below right: Eau de Noix is a rare French walnut liqueur.

HOW TO SERVE
These drinks are quite commonly taken with crushed ice as a digestif in France. Alternatively, they may be iced, slightly watered (using about the same amount of water as liqueur) and drunk as aperitifs.

Tia Maria

Jamaica's contribution to the world of liqueurs, Tia Maria has turned into one of the best-loved of all such products in both America and Europe. It is a suave, deep brown coffee-flavoured drink, based on a recipe around three centuries old, that proves itself highly versatile on the cocktail circuit as well as for after-dinner sipping.

It is based, not surprisingly, on good, dark Jamaican rum of at least five-year-old standard and flavoured with the beans of the highly prized coffee variety, Blue Mountain. In addition to the coffee, the palate is further deepened by the addition of local

Right: Tia Maria is the world's most famous and best-loved coffee liqueur.

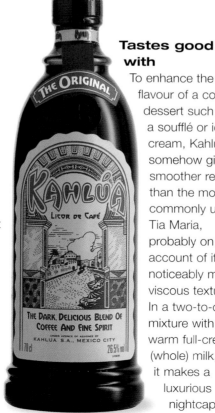

spices, including vanilla. Although the liqueur is sweet, the aromatic components in it prevent it from being cloying. This makes it one of the few such drinks that is actually quite acceptable to savour on its own.

One reason for the popularity of Tia Maria in Europe was the craze for the cocktail Black Russian, usually made with cola. Here, it provides a luxurious note of richness in what is otherwise a fairly prosaic mix.

How it is made

Coffee beans and various spices are infused in a base of cask-aged rum, which is then lightly sweetened. It is bottled at just under 27% ABV.

HOW TO SERVE
A pleasant way to enjoy Tia Maria as a digestif is to serve it on the rocks. Otherwise, it is one of the few liqueurs to make a successful mix with cola. Some people like it with orange juice, but the resulting colour is a little muddy.

Tastes good with
Tia Maria is brilliant for lacing chocolate desserts, and of course makes a good liqueur coffee – particularly when the coffee used is Blue Mountain. Although it isn't a strictly canonical ingredient in the original recipe, it also works well in the Italian dessert tiramisu, which is flavoured with coffee anyway. The essential alcohol ingredient of it is marsala, but a good slug of Tia Maria adds an extra-special kick.

Kahlúa

The only liqueur of any note to have been conceived in Mexico, Kahlúa is a dark brown, coffee-flavoured essence packaged in a round-shouldered, opaque bottle with a colourful label. Although some of it is still made in Mexico using home-grown arabica coffee beans, it is also made under licence in Europe. It is inevitably often compared to the other, more famous coffee liqueur, Tia Maria, but it is slightly thicker in texture and somewhat less sweet than its Jamaican counterpart. In addition to that, it has a more complex range of spice notes, including vanilla and nutmeg. The spirit base of the drink is a white cane rum, as opposed to the cask-aged base of Tia Maria, but the final strength is the same.

Right: Kahlúa is a liqueur with the stimulant properties of strong coffee.

Tastes good with
To enhance the flavour of a coffee dessert such as a soufflé or ice cream, Kahlúa somehow gives a smoother result than the more commonly used Tia Maria, probably on account of its noticeably more viscous texture. In a two-to-one mixture with warm full-cream (whole) milk, it makes a luxurious nightcap.

HOW TO SERVE
Kahlúa makes a very good chilled alternative to a liqueur coffee. Pour the Kahlúa over crushed ice in a tall glass and float some thick cream on top. Alternatively, add it to hot black coffee, top it with cream and a dusting of ground cinnamon.

Crème de cacao

Endlessly useful in the cocktail repertoire, the world of chocolate-flavoured liqueurs begins with simple crème de cacao, which comes in two versions, brown or dark (which may also contain some vanilla flavouring) and white (which tends to be considerably sweeter). If the designation "Chouao" appears on the label, then the cocoa beans used have come from that particular district of the Venezuelan capital, Caracas.

Tastes good with

Use crème de cacao to boost the richness of your most chocolatey desserts, or add it to a cup of hot, strong coffee on a cold day.

HOW TO SERVE
Crème de cacao mixes well with coconut cream in a cocktail.

Right: Brown and white crème de cacao.

Sabra

This is Israel's entry in the liqueur stakes: a svelte concoction, flavoured with a clever mélange of Jaffa orange and chocolate, bottled at 26% ABV. Despite the gentle bitterness contributed by the orange peels, the resulting drink is exceptionally sweet. Try mixing it with cognac and ice to throw it into relief. The same company also makes a coffee liqueur called Sabra Café, which is a tiny bit less sweet.

Left: Sabra is a very sweet, but luscious, orange-chocolate liqueur from Israel.

Tastes good with

Sabra is an instant treat if poured over vanilla or chocolate ice cream, or it can be added to a chocolate mousse or ganache mixture for a particularly sumptuous dessert.

HOW TO SERVE
Sabra can be served as it comes, as its flavours are so indulgent.

Tuaca

An Italian liqueur reputed to be based on a 16th-century recipe created for Lorenzo de Medici, Tuaca is made by the resourceful Tuoni liqueur family of Livorno. It made its international debut in the 1950s after American servicemen stationed in Italy during the Second World War demanded that their local bars back home start stocking it. Its flavour is a beguiling mixture of orange essence and vanilla on a base of Italian brandy. Because it is not excessively sweet and is bottled at almost spirit strength (35% ABV), it is

Right: Tuaca has become deservedly popular in recent years.

one of those liqueurs that makes an excellent single shot taken neat, as well being a good blending partner in the cocktail bar.

Tastes good with

Tuaca can be used to flavour desserts based on orange or chocolate, and is brilliant as an enriching ingredient in a chocolate sauce.

Cream liqueurs

Cream liqueurs are an ever-expanding category in the contemporary market. Whether the makers acknowledge it or not, cream liqueurs all owe something of their inspiration and appeal to the archetypal brand, Bailey's Irish Cream, made in Dublin. The manufacturers tend to push them particularly at Christmas, where they occupy a niche as the soft option for those who feel they need a spoonful of sugar and a dollop of cream to help the alcohol dose go down.

Bailey's itself is a blend of Irish whiskey and cream flavoured with cocoa, bottled at 17% ABV. It became suddenly chic after its invention in 1974, but was quickly saddled with the image of the kind of soft, svelte drink that unscrupulous boys plied unsuspecting girls with in nightclubs.

Left: Cadbury's Cream Liqueur can be substituted as a ready-made Brandy Alexander, at a pinch.

Right: Bailey's is the daddy of all cream liqueurs.

Since then, cream liqueurs have gone on relentlessly multiplying. Coffee and chocolate flavourings are particularly common, and indeed some cream liqueurs are made by confectionery companies, such as Cadbury's and Terry's. Then again, some of the more reputable liqueur-makers have produced cream versions of their own top products (such as Crème de Grand Marnier) in order to grab a share of this evidently lucrative market.

I have to say I decline to take these products seriously. At best, they are substitutes for real cream cocktails, but they are always sweeter and less powerful than the genuine home-made article, and many of them contain an artificial stabilizer to stop the cream from separating. In any case, why rely on somebody else's formula when you can follow your own specifications? Once you have made your own Brandy Alexanders, you won't want chocolate cream liqueur.

The extreme was reached when another Irish drinks company launched a product called Sheridan's Liqueur in 1993. It came in a bifurcated bottle with two tops, one half-filled with a dark chocolate and coffee liqueur, the other with thick, white, vanilla cream spirit. The idea was that you poured first from one side of the bottle and then from the other in order to simulate the appearance of a liqueur coffee. An even sweeter product is Dooley's, launched in 1999, a toffee-flavoured cream creation containing vodka, sugar, milk and cream, and with a quite

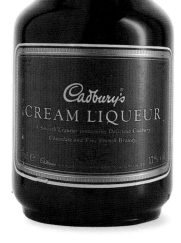

HOW TO SERVE
Both the sweetness and the texture of these products need the mitigating influence of ice to make them attractive. A brandy glass is the best receptacle.

A Brandy Alexander (equal measures of cognac, crème de cacao and thick cream) is the prototype cocktail upon which many of the cream liqueurs are based, and still manages to rise head and shoulders above them.

exceptionally cloying flavour. Some claim to find it intensely moreish and delicious, which only goes to show there's no accounting for taste.

Advocaat

Advocaat is a Dutch speciality. It is essentially a customized version of the humble egg-nog, without the milk: a mixture of simple grape brandy with egg yolks and sugar, as thick and as yellow as tinned custard. Most of it is sold in this natural form, although it is possible in the Netherlands to buy vanilla- and fruit-flavoured versions. As a result of its velvety texture and bland wholesomeness, advocaat is often thought of as a drink for the elderly, and is commonly added to mugs of hot chocolate or strong coffee.

The drink originated among Dutch settlers in South America, where its original main ingredient was the thick, fatty flesh of the avocado, hence its name. Attempting to replicate the recipe back home, the Dutch substituted egg yolk for the fruit.

There are a few widely available brands of advocaat on the market: the red-labelled Warninks is probably the most familiar, but Fockinks, and the liqueur specialists, Bols and De Kuyper, also make it. The standard bottled strength of around 17% ABV is quite low for a liqueur, and is about the same strength as the average fortified wine.

As well as the basic egg-and-sugar version, other variants of advocaat produced by the Dutch include orange, lemon and cherry versions. It isn't entirely surprising that these haven't much caught on among foreigners, as their sweetly fruity, eggy richness seems almost like too much of a good thing.

How it is made

Commercial grape spirit is sweetened with sugar syrup. Only the yolks of the eggs are added, along with an emulsifying agent to prevent the mixture from separating.

Tastes good with

As the ready-made basis of an egg-nog, advocaat can be made into a long drink by topping it up with full-cream (whole) milk and a sprinkling of nutmeg.

Below left: Warninks is probably the most famous advocaat brand.

Below right: Advocaat is the only manufactured drink in this book to contain egg yolk.

HOW TO SERVE

In the Netherlands, advocaat is drunk both as aperitif and digestif. Unmixed, its texture is such that it is often consumed with a teaspoon. Taken in a hot beverage, it makes a comforting enough bedtime drink.

The Snowball cocktail, in which a good measure of advocaat is topped up with sparkling lemonade, is about the only form in which that liqueur is commonly drunk now outside the Netherlands.

Absinthe and Pastis

Pastis is one of the most important traditional drinks of Europe, despite having only minority status in Britain and the other northern countries. Around the Mediterranean fringe of Europe, from south-east France to the Greek islands, pastis, in its various forms, functions as an everyday thirst-quencher, much as beer does in the northern European countries.

Drinkers the world over have, on first contact with pastis, usually been fascinated by its most famous property: it clouds up when mixed with water. This attribute is what gives the drink its name, "pastis" being a corruption of the French word *pastiche*, meaning a mixture.

The principal flavouring element in pastis is either liquorice or aniseed – more often the former – but there are other herbal

ingredients in it as well. Aniseed has been known as a digestive aid in medicine since the time of the Egyptians, and is still in use today.

The most famous pastis of them all is absinthe, the only category of alcohol (apart from home distillates) ever to have been made illegal; since the 1990s, however, it has happily been restored to us. What originally doomed it was that it contained wormwood in concentrations held responsible for corroding the brain. During the late 19th century, it was the house drink of decadent Parisian artists and others, many of whom died the kinds of squalid deaths associated with laudanum use during the English Romantic period.

Although absinthe is being made in France again, it is still offically *persona non grata* there, and much is made in eastern Europe, especially the Czech Republic. Its flavour is hauntingly dense and concentrated, backed up by an incredible alcohol strength: it is at least 55% ABV, and more usually 65–70%. For the truly suicidal, there is even a Bulgarian product bottled at just a heartbeat under 90%.

When absinthe was given its marching orders in France by a governmental decree of 1915, other countries followed suit. One of its chief manufacturers, the firm of Henri-Louis Pernod, which had been making it for over a century, then turned to making a similar product without wormwood at a lower alcoholic strength. In effect, Pernod was the sanitized version of absinthe. The other main quality French brand, Ricard, is now part of the same group, although they are made at opposite ends of France.

Far left: Ricard is the famous pastis of southern France.

Left: Absinth made in eastern Europe is spelt without the "e".

The Spanish equivalent is *ojen* (pronounced "oh-hen"), named after the town where it is made, and sold in two versions, sweet and dry. Greece has ouzo, much beloved of holidaymakers on the Peloponnese and the islands. Its flavouring agent is anise and, like pastis, the drink turns milky-white when water is added. The bottled strength is around 35–40% ABV, which is similar to Pernod, but less than Ricard.

How they are made

The various herbs and plants are usually infused in a straight, highly purified vegetable spirit base, and essence of anise or liquorice is added. Further blending with rectified alcohol is followed by sweetening.

HOW TO SERVE

Absinthe should ideally be served in a small, thick-based glass with as much water as you feel you need. The water should be very cold, so as to obviate the need for ice. Those with slightly sweeter tastes may add sugar to it, classically by balancing a perforated spoon or metal tea-strainer with a sugar-cube on it across the top of the glass and then pouring the water over it.

Ouzo should be served cold in a small glass, either neat, with the equivalent amount of water, or with an ice cube or two.

Anis

Confusion reigns as to the precise differences between anis and pastis, and indeed whether there are any meaningful differences at all. They are both flavoured either with the berries of the aniseed plant, originally native to North Africa, or with Far Eastern star anise, and are popular all around the Mediterranean. They both turn cloudy when watered, and are both claimed as the respectable successor to the outlawed absinthe.

One august authority claims that pastis should be flavoured with liquorice rather than aniseed, although the two are very close in taste. Another claims that anis is simply one of the types of pastis. Still another claims that, whereas anis is a product of the maceration of aniseed or liquorice in spirit, pastis should properly be seen as a distillation from either of the two ingredients themselves.

These claims can't all be right of course, but for what it's worth, I incline to accept the last definition. For one thing, anis tends to be lower in alcohol than pastis, having the strength of a liqueur rather than a spirit. The one thing we can be sure of is that pastis is always French, whereas anis – particularly with that spelling – can also be Spanish. In Spain, there are sweet and dry varieties, whereas French anise tends mainly to be dry.

Ever since the days of the medical school of Salerno, and probably earlier, extract of anis has been seen as a valuable weapon in the apothecary's armoury. It is thought to be especially good for ailments of the stomach.

Anisette

Quite definitely a liqueur, anisette is French, sweetened, and usually somewhat stronger than anis. The most famous brand is Marie Brizard, from the firm named after the Bordelaise woman who, in the mid-18th century, was given the recipe by a West Indian sailor whom she had kindly nursed through a fever. The aromatizers in it include angelica, cloves, coriander and of course aniseed.

Far left: Dry and sweet, anis is made in Spain as well as in France.

Left: Anisette is a sweet liqueur form of anis, typified by this famed Marie Brizard version.

HOW TO SERVE
The only true way to serve anis is to take it ice-cold in a little, thick-based tumbler. The addition of a small amount of water – usually about as much again – turns it milky but with a faint greenish tinge. It is considered a great appetite-whetter.

Enhance the anise flavour in a cocktail in which either anis or anisette has been used by dropping in a whole star anise, the Far Eastern spice much used in Chinese and Thai cooking.

Chartreuse

Unlike Bénédictine, Chartreuse really is still made by monks, who make it at Voiron, near Grenoble, not far from the site of their Carthusian monastery, La Grande Chartreuse. Expelled from France at the time of the French Revolution, the order was allowed back into the mother country after the defeat of Napoleon, only to be kicked out again in 1903. It was then that a second branch of the operation was founded at Tarragona, in eastern Spain, and it continued as Chartreuse's second address until 1991, long after the production was finally re-established in France in 1932.

The Carthusians are a silent order, which has no doubt helped to keep the recipe a secret; like its Norman counterpart, it is known only to a lucky trio at any one time. Proceeds from the worldwide sales of Chartreuse are ploughed back into the order's funds, which pay for all kinds of charitable works.

There is a premium version of Chartreuse (the original recipe is said to date from 1605) called Elixir Végétal, which is sold in miniature bottles at a fearsome 71% ABV, but it is principally sold in two incarnations today: green (55%) and yellow (40%). The latter is a deep greenish-yellow hue, and is sweet, honeyed and slightly minty in flavour, while the green Chartreuse is a leafy colour, has a pungent herbal scent and is distinctly less viscous.

Additionally, the order produces a rare higher

Right: Green Chartreuse is intensely powerful and aromatic.

Far right: Yellow Chartreuse is sweeter than green Chartreuse and of normal spirit strength.

grade of each colour, labelled VEP, for *vieillissement exceptionnellement prolongé* (exceptionally long ageing).

How it is made

By varying processes of distillation, infusion and maceration, over 130 herbs and plants are used to flavour a base of grape brandy. They were all once gathered from the mountains surrounding the monastery, but some are now imported from Italy, Switzerland and further afield. Chartreuse is aged in casks for up to five years, except for the VEP, which is aged for at least eight.

Tastes good with

The French sometimes fortify their hot chocolate with a reviving splash of the green Chartreuse. The yellow is thought to be more suitable for coffee.

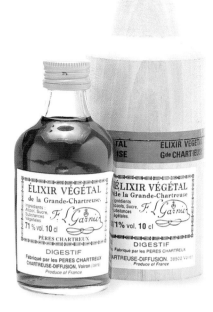

Above: Elixir Végétal is the original Carthusian elixir, bottled at very high strength: 71%.

HOW TO SERVE

If you find the flavour of Chartreuse overwhelming on its own, do as the French do and serve it mixed as a long drink with tonic or soda and plenty of ice. Alternatively, it mixes well (the yellow version especially) with gin in a cocktail, as below.

Bénédictine

"Deo optimo maximo" (To God, most good, most great), exclaimed the Benedictine monk, Dom Bernardo, who formulated the liqueur that now bears his order's name, on first tasting the results. Or so the story goes. It reputedly happened in 1510, so it isn't easy to verify. What is certain is that Dom Bernardo's monastery at Fécamp, in the Normandy region of northern France, produced this cognac-based herbal liqueur until the time of the French Revolution in 1789, when the monasteries were forcibly closed and production banned.

Bénédictine was officially extinct until the 1860s, when it was revived by a descendant of the monastery's lawyers, Alexandre Le Grand. On finding the secret recipe among a bundle of yellowing papers, he was inspired to build an extraordinary new distillery in the high Gothic style at Fécamp, and the now secularized liqueur, which was first christened Bénédictine by Le Grand, lived to fight another day.

Bénédictine is a bright golden potion of honeyed, spicy sweetness, containing a herbalist's pantheon of medicinal plants and spices. The exact formula is known only to three people at any given time, like Chartreuse, but it is thought to contain as many as 56 aromatizing ingredients. Its strength is 40% ABV.

While its flavour seems all honey at first, it develops very cleverly on the palate, and on the finish it is interesting to see how many of those herbs and spices you can correctly identify.

How it is made
The various herbs, spices, citrus peels etc. are left to infuse in a base of cognac, and then the resulting potion is re-distilled to concentrate the flavour.

Tastes good with
Because of its complex flavours, Bénédictine is not especially versatile in the culinary repertoire. It could perhaps be included in the syrup for a salad of citrus segments, and its honeyed roundness should work reasonably well with a honey-flavoured ice cream.

Left: Bénédictine is one of the old monastic liqueurs, still produced to a formula that reputedly dates back to the early 16th century. Its complex flavours result from a mixture of herbs, medicinal plants, spices and citrus fruit peels.

HOW TO SERVE
Bénédictine should ideally be served straight in a large liqueur glass at the end of a meal, but its makers clearly have no qualms about its use as a mixing ingredient by those who find the sweetness of classic liqueurs too much to take *au naturel*. Alternatively, try it with a dash of lemon juice and hot water, a comforting formula invented by English squaddies serving in wartime Normandy.

In cocktails, it rubs along nicely with the herbal fortified wine, vermouth, or with the other similarly flavoured liqueurs, such as Scotch-based Glayva or Drambuie (see entries on facing page).

Drambuie

Drambuie is Scotland's (and, for that matter, Britain's) pre-eminent contribution to the world's classic liqueurs. Hugely popular in the United States, it is a unique and inimitable concoction of Scotch whisky, heather honey and herbs. The story goes that the recipe was given as a reward to one Captain John Mackinnon in 1746, after the defeat at Culloden, by Charles Edward Stuart, or Bonnie Prince Charlie, as the pretender to the English throne became better known. The lad that was born to be king was of course ferried to Skye, and from thence to France, away from the clutches of the nefarious English. Captain Mackinnon was his protector.

That story has inevitably since been debunked by meticulous historians. The truth is almost certainly the other way round. It was the Mackinnons who revived the spirits of the fugitive Prince with their own Scotch-based home concoction, which was very much a typical blend of the period, an unrefined spirit disguised with sweet and aromatic herbal additives.

Today, the spirit is anything but unrefined, being a mixture of fine aged malt and straight grain whiskies, to which the flavourings are added. It is bottled at 40% ABV. The Mackinnon family still makes it, though near Edinburgh now rather than on Skye. They registered its name (from the Gaelic *an dram buidheach*, "the drink that satisfies") in 1892, but it was only launched commercially in 1906, with spectacular success.

Tastes good with

A hunk of rich Dundee cake doused in Drambuie is a sumptuous cold-weather treat. It is also very good added to whipped cream and lemon zest to make a very grown-up syllabub.

Left: Drambuie is perhaps Britain's greatest contribution to the liqueur world.

HOW TO SERVE

Serve Drambuie as it comes, over ice, or mixed with plain Scotch as a Rusty Nail.

Glayva

Like Drambuie, Glayva is a Scotch whisky-based liqueur made near Edinburgh, but it is of much more recent provenance. The drink was first formulated in 1947, its name a corruption of the Gaelic *glemhath*, or "very good". Its aromatizers are quite similar to those of Drambuie, although its flavour is intriguingly different. Heather honey and various herbs are used, and so is a quantity of orange peel, resulting in a noticeably fruitier attack on the palate. The strength is also slightly lower, at 35%.

The noble Scot commemorated in the case of Glayva is one

Right: The original formula for Glayva is much older than the product itself.

Master Borthwick, the phlegmatic 16-year-old credited with carrying Robert the Bruce's heart back to Scotland after the King's defeat at the hands of the Saracens. Not content with rescuing the regal heart, the indomitable lad cut off the head of a Saracen chieftain he had killed, impaled it on a spear, and brought that back too just to keep his spirits up. All those pubs named the Saracen's Head recall the event, as did the Moorish head once depicted on the Glayva label.

Tastes good with

Glayva is particularly good added to honey or orange ice cream.

HOW TO SERVE

Glayva should be served just as it is, in a standard whisky tumbler. Its fruitiness makes it slightly better for chilling than Drambuie, but don't overdo it. Alternatively, a dash of lemon juice and a squirt of soda won't go amiss.

Goldwasser

Goldwasser, or Danziger Goldwasser to give it its archetypal name, recalls the great Catalan physician Arnaldo de Vilanova who, in the 13th century, is reputed to have cured the Pope of a dangerous illness by giving him a herbal elixir containing specks of gold. In so doing, he also saved his own skin from the Inquisition.

The commercial prototype of the drink was first made in the Baltic port city of Danzig (now Gdańsk in Poland). Based on the drink kümmel, it is flavoured

Right: All Goldwasser originally came from Gdańsk, like this one.

with both aniseed and caraway seeds, is colourless, less sweet than many liqueurs, and it really does have a shower of golden particles added to it, in memory of Arnaldo. (There was also for a time a silver version, called Silberwasser.) Liqueur d'Or was a now-extinct French version of the same thing. Some brands also had a citric fruit flavour, which was sometimes lemon, sometimes orange.

Tastes good with

Soufflé Rothschild is a classic, hot dessert soufflé made from crème patissière and crystallized fruits that have been liberally macerated in Danziger Goldwasser.

HOW TO SERVE
The prettiness can be enhanced by serving Goldwasser in a little cut-crystal liqueur glass.

Galliano

One of Italy's liqueur specialities, golden-yellow Galliano is chiefly known on the international cocktail scene for its matchless role of livening up a vodka and orange in the Harvey Wallbanger cocktail, and for its tall, conical bottle.

It was invented in 1896 by one Arturo Vaccari, a Tuscan distiller who named his new creation in honour of an Italian soldier, Major Giuseppe Galliano. The previous year, Galliano had held out under siege at Fort Enda in Ethiopia for 44 days against vastly superior Abyssinian forces under the command of Haile Selassie's fearsome nephew.

The formula, as we are accustomed to hear in the world of liqueurs, is a jealously guarded secret, but is said to be based on over 30 herbs, roots, berries and flowers from the alpine

slopes to the north of Italy. Among its flavours is a strong presence of anise, and there is a pronounced scent of vanilla. It is also naturally very sweet. Despite the complexity of its tastes, it is a valuable addition to the bartender's battery, where it happily rubs shoulders with all of the white spirits, and is on nodding terms with cognac and even whisky as well.

How it is made

The various flavouring ingredients are steeped in a mixture of neutral spirit and water and then distilled; the resulting potion is then blended with refined spirits. It is bottled at 35% ABV.

Left: Galliano is an Italian classic that comes in a distinctive, conical bottle.

HOW TO SERVE
Galliano isn't particularly agreeable on its own, but makes a versatile cocktail ingredient, most notably with vodka and orange juice in the classic Harvey Wallbanger.

Kümmel

All we know of kümmel, one of the more ancient liqueurs, is that it originated somewhere in northern Europe, but precisely where isn't certain. The best guess is Holland, but the Germans have a respectable enough claim on the patent as well. Certainly, it was being made in Holland in the 16th century, and it very much fits the image of such drinks of the time, in that it would have been an unrefined grain spirit masked by an aromatic ingredient.

The ingredient in this case is caraway seeds. A certain amount of needless confusion is created by the fact that the name looks as though it has something to do with the more pungent cumin. This is only because, in certain European languages, caraway is often referred to as a sort of cumin. They have nothing to do with each other, the misleading nomenclature only arising because the seeds are supposed to look vaguely similar.

Left: Wolfschmidt is the leading brand of kümmel.

A key episode in kümmel's history occurred at the end of the 17th century, during Peter the Great's sojourn in Holland. He took the formula for the drink back home, and kümmel came to be thought of as a Russian product, or at least a Baltic one. The Baltic port of Riga, now capital of Latvia, was its chief centre of production throughout the 19th century, and some was also made in Danzig (now Gdańsk), where they eventually came to add flecks of gold to it and call it Goldwasser.

Versions of kümmel are today made not just in Latvia but also in Poland, Germany, Holland, Denmark and even the United States. One property of caraway, valued since Egyptian times, is its ability to counteract flatulence, which is why it was one of the traditional ingredients of gripe water for babies.

How it is made

The base is a pure grain distillate, effectively a type of vodka, in which the seeds are infused. Most brands are fairly heavily sweetened but they are always left colourless.

Tastes good with

Try adding kümmel to the mixture for old English seed cake, which is made with caraway seeds.

HOW TO SERVE

Kümmel is nearly always served on the rocks in its countries of origin.

Strega

The name Strega, a popular proprietary liqueur produced in Italy by the Alberti family since 1860, is Italian for "witch". It is so called because it is supposedly based on a witches' brew, an aphrodisiac love-potion guaranteed to unite in eternal togetherness any pair of lovers who drink it with each other. You have been warned.

It is a bright yellow concoction full of all sorts of complex flavours. The fruit base is a citrus blend and it reputedly also contains around six dozen

Right: Strega is an Italian liqueur that is full of complex flavours.

different botanical herbs, making it not dissimilar in style to the yellow version of Chartreuse. It has the same kind of syrupy texture, too, and is likewise considered an especially good digestif.

Although the colour resembles that of Galliano, Strega's flavour is quite different, more obviously herbal and minty, and with a stronger citrus element. It is also slightly stronger in alcohol, at 40% ABV. To my tastes at least, it is a more versatile mixing ingredient than Galliano, as its flavours blend more subtly with other drinks and mixers to create a pleasingly harmonious result.

How it is made

It is the product of a pot-still distillation, with the various aromatizers added separately before blending, after which it is aged in casks.

Tastes good with

Strega works particularly well as an accompaniment to freshly cracked nuts at the end of a meal, in particular walnuts and hazelnuts.

HOW TO SERVE

Strega is more appealing served frappé, on crushed ice, which takes the edge off its sweetness, than served on its own.

Parfait Amour

The long association of drinking and seduction is celebrated in the name of purple Parfait Amour, "perfect love". In the 18th century, particularly, the use of alcohol in amorous pursuits had less to do with getting your intended too stupefied to know what they were doing, than with stimulating the erotic impulses with artful concoctions of spices and flowers, mixed with alcohol.

Parfait Amour liqueur is really the only surviving link to that tradition. It is almost certainly Dutch in origin, a more exotic species of curaçao. Its name, as with all such potions, is French because that was considered the romantic language *par excellence*. As its (added) colour would lead you to expect, it is subtly scented with violets, but the flavour owes more to fruits and spices than to flowers, which marks it out quite distinctly from the colourless crème de violette. The main components are citrus fruits (usually lemons) and a mixture of cloves and other spices, including vanilla.

The drink enjoyed great popularity during the cocktail boom in the 1920s. Apart from anything else, no other liqueur is quite the same colour. There was once a red version of it too. Today, Parfait Amour is made not only by the Dutch liqueur specialists Bols, but by certain French companies as well. It has an average strength of around 30% ABV.

How it is made
The various aromatizing elements are macerated in grape spirit, which may then be re-distilled, and the purple colour is achieved by means of a vegetable dye.

Tastes good with
What else should be eaten with this purple liqueur but a box of violet creams?

Left: Parfait Amour is indelibly associated with romance on account of its singularly attractive colour, as well as the name.

> ### HOW TO SERVE
> It is best to serve Parfait Amour unmixed, or blended with something colourless such as lemonade, in order not to interfere with your beloved's enjoyment of the colour. It tastes better chilled.

Punsch

Although punsch is more familiarly known in English-speaking countries as Swedish punch, even then it isn't a drink many people have come across. Its lineage can be traced back to the 18th century, when Sweden's ocean-going trading vessels began doing business in the East Indies. Among the commodities they brought back was the local arak.

In its raw state, arak wasn't much to northern European tastes, and so a few drink companies took to blending it with grape brandy and various wines and cordials, in effect

Right: The real thing – Carlshamns, a cask-aged punsch from Sweden.

creating a kind of powerful punch in the process. Like a traditional punch, the mixture is also highly spiced.

The original punch was a British colonial invention, but by the 18th century, a vogue for it had spread not only to Scandinavia but into France as well. Rum was a favoured base ingredient, variously boosted with hot tea, lemon juice and sweet spices such as cinnamon. Punch was, in every way, the grand-daddy of the cocktail.

In an echo of the British habit, Swedish punch was also usually served hot, at least until the end of the 19th century.

How it is made
These days, punsch is exclusively a rum-based drink, to which other forms of alcohol, including wine, are added, together with a quantity of fragrant spices, such as cinnamon and cloves. It is sweetened and then aged for several months in cask, before being bottled at around 26% ABV.

Tastes good with
Punsch works reasonably well with little salty nibbles made with strong cheese. In its native Sweden, it is often taken in liqueur quantities with marinated fish, typically herring, when it should be vigorously chilled. In this context, it is effectively a rather gentler alternative to aquavit.

> ### HOW TO SERVE
> To relive the old days, warm the punsch gently (without letting it boil) in a small saucepan and serve it in big, heatproof wine glasses.

Pimm's

Forever associated with the English summer, Pimm's No. 1 Cup is a proprietary version of a fruit cup created by James Pimm in the 1820s. He devised his recipe to mark out his own establishment in the City of London from the run of other oyster bars, which traditionally served stout ale to wash the bivalves down.

Pimm did such a roaring trade with his fruit cup that he began to market it ready-mixed in 1859, at a stiffish three shillings a bottle. Popular throughout the British Empire during colonial times, it came to enjoy a sudden vogue in France and Italy after the Second World War.

There were once six different versions of Pimm's, each based on a different

Left: Pimm's is the quintessential flavour of an English summer.

spirit. The market has since whittled these down to just two: Pimm's Vodka Cup and the original, which is still sold as No. 1 Cup, and is based on London gin, with an unmixed strength of 25% ABV. Pimm's has suffered somewhat from being seen as too fiddly to prepare. Its present owner has tried to combat that by launching little cans of pre-mixed Pimm's.

Tastes good with

Pimm's works well with classic English picnic foods, such as cucumber sandwiches, hard-boiled quail's eggs, crackers with cream cheese, and

HOW TO SERVE

A double measure of Pimm's No. 1 should be poured over ice in a tall glass. (In Mr Pimm's oyster bar, it was knocked back by the pint.) It is then topped up with lemonade or soda, and garnished with slices of orange, lemon and lime, a wedge of apple and a dangling twist of pared cucumber rind. If you can find fresh borage, use some of its smaller leaves instead of the cucumber. Float a little bundle of mint leaves on top. If that sounds too much of a fandango, just throw in a slice of lemon and get on with it. It's just as nice.

crudités. In this context, it's as well to make a fairly dilute mixture, so as not to overwhelm the food.

Suze

If I had to nominate one other product to stand alongside champagne and fino sherry in a perfect trinity of aperitifs, it would unhesitatingly be Suze. It relies for its stimulating impact on gentian.

Gentian is a wild mountain plant found in the Alps and the mountains of the Jura. It has large yellow flowers, but is principally valued for its roots, which can grow up to a yard long and have an uncompromisingly bitter flavour. It was once the quinine of its day and, like quinine, is thought to be particularly good for ailments of the liver.

The Suze brand is owned by pastis manufacturers Pernod-Ricard, and it has a very delicate primrose colour. It is wine-based, and its

Right: It is well worth making a journey to France just to taste Suze.

flavour is so dry and bitter, even when mixed with a little water or served on ice, that it acts as an extraordinarily powerful appetite-rouser.

Other similar products may be labelled Gentiane in France and Switzerland, or Enzian in the German-speaking countries.

How it is made

An extract of gentian is steeped in a white wine base, imparting a little faint colour to the liquid. It is then clarified and bottled at 16% ABV.

Tastes good with

Suze is great served with any bitter nibbles,

HOW TO SERVE

Pour a measure of Suze into a tumbler with either the merest splash of very cold water or a single cube of ice, just to freshen it up.

and combines extremely well with the more pungent varieties of green olive. Strong marinades, such as those made with garlic and chillies, won't faze it.

Cuarenta y Tres

Cuarenta is a sweet liqueur made in the Cartagena of eastern Spain, and based on a recipe that supposedly dates from classical times, when the Phoenicians founded Carthage, in North Africa, and introduced viticulture. Its name is Spanish for "forty-three" (it has the alternative name in English-speaking markets of Licor 43), and is so named because that is the number of herbs and spices it contains. Its strength is 31% ABV.

Cuarenta is concocted from a brandy base, with infusions of the various aromatizers, but has a noticeably predominant

Right: Cuarenta y Tres is supposedly based on a 2000-year-old recipe.

flavour of vanilla, which rather torpedoes the Carthaginian theory since vanilla was only discovered in the 16th century by Spanish explorers in Mexico. Not much seen outside its region of production, it is nonetheless held in high regard locally.

Tastes good with

A small chilled measure of Cuarenta is surprisingly good with hot desserts of stewed fruit and cream. It also has fleeting hints of chocolate and honey in the flavour, making it an ideal accompaniment to a light, chocolatey dessert – or try it with *crema catalana*, the citrussy Spanish answer to crème brûlée.

HOW TO SERVE
Cuarenta y Tres should be served either on the rocks, or mixed with a small quantity of freshly squeezed orange juice.

Cynar

A liqueur for the truly intrepid, Cynar is a soupy, dark brown potion made in Italy, the flavouring of which is artichoke leaves (its name derives from the Latin word for artichoke, *cynarum*). It contains all of the savoury bitterness of the globe artichoke, which is boldly illustrated on its label. If that sounds like fun, go ahead and try it. I once swallowed a modest measure of it in a little backstreet bar in Venice, and of all my shimmering memories of the watery city, Cynar is not, I have to say, the loveliest.

Great claims are made for Cynar as a health tonic as it contains herbs as well as artichoke, itself known to be good for the liver. First formulated in 1949, the brand is owned by Campari. It has

a bottled strength of 20% ABV, putting it at the upper end of the aperitif range for strength.

Tastes good with

It is often claimed that there is no wine in the world that makes a good gastronomic match for artichoke, when it is served as an hors d'oeuvre, partly because this vegetable has the peculiar property of making everything else alongside it taste a little sweeter than it naturally is. Cynar – with its syrupy texture helping it along – could just be the answer. Otherwise, it is probably best to forget the matchmaking.

Left: Cynar, the world's only artichoke drink.

HOW TO SERVE
As an aperitif, mix Cynar with tonic or soda water, add a slice of orange or lemon, and be very broad-minded. Served very well chilled, it can be drunk on its own – slowly.

Kikor

The first of three products on this page made by the Italian liqueur-makers, Tuoni and Canepa of Livorno, the family company that also created Tuaca, Kikor is the one with most obvious commercial appeal. It is a more complex chocolate liqueur than basic crème de cacao, made by a lengthy maceration of cocoa beans in a neutral alcohol base.

The flavour is an irresistible combination of slightly bitter dark chocolate, sugar and deceptive hints of vanilla and coffee. It is thickly syrupy, but the bitterness of the cocoa used gives it exemplary balance. Its bottled strength is 30% ABV.

Tastes good with

The makers suggest pouring it over vanilla ice cream, and who am I to argue?

Left: Kikor is a sensuous liqueur flavoured with chocolate, vanilla and coffee.

HOW TO SERVE
Serve Kikor chilled with ice or mixed with cold full-cream (whole) milk.

Poncino Livornese

Poncino is a liqueur made for using in the classic Italian coffee preparation known as "ponch". This is basically a variant of the liqueur coffee procedure, in which sugar and lemon are added to a cup of hot, strong, boozy black coffee. It is an anis-based liqueur, infused with come-hither flavourings such as caramel, chocolate and coffee itself, and bottled at a fairly soul-stirring 47% ABV.

The aroma is a complex mixture of coffee, chocolate and a fleeting hint of citrus (either bitter orange or lemon), underpinned by anis. When tasted, the anis comes through strongly, and adds its liquoricey depth to the chocolate aftertaste. This is an altogether less sweet liqueur than Kikor, but an equally appealing one.

Right: Poncino Livornese is an anis-based Italian liqueur.

HOW TO SERVE
Add a measure of Poncino to a small coffee cup. Pour in an espresso, sweeten to taste, and finish by squeezing a piece of lemon rind over the top and dropping it in. When cool enough, drink in one gulp. Alternatively, serve small measures of the liqueur well-chilled in a liqueur glass. With its anis content in mind, it makes a rather special digestif served neat.

Monasterium

A liqueur made in tribute to the celebrated monastic preparations of southern Europe, Monasterium is derived from an infusion of various Mediterranean citrus fruits with essential oils of a number of flowers and herbs. It is based on an old recipe handed down from Franciscan monks, and is affectionately – if rather alarmingly – known in Italy as the "Green Monster", although its colour is a delicate yellowy-green. Its alcohol strength is the same as Poncino, at 47% ABV, indicating that it is meant to be taken seriously.

Monasterium may, in time, come to be seen as one of the world's great liqueurs. It has something approaching the ineffable complexity of Chartreuse, perhaps without some of the bitterness of that monastic classic. Strong citrus notes of lemon (and possibly lime) mingle with medicinal herbal tones, and fill the mouth. It is sweetish, but not too syrupy, and leaves a clean, surprisingly subtle aftertaste for such a powerful liqueur.

Left: Monasterium is an extremely fine herbal liqueur in the monastic style of Chartreuse.

HOW TO SERVE
Monasterium should be served in shot glasses, just as it is, or perhaps slightly chilled. It should certainly not be mixed.

WINE, CHAMPAGNE AND FORTIFIED WINES

Fermented drinks based on the wine grape, *Vitis vinifera*, are the most hugely varied of all drink categories.

Wine and champagne

At the heart of the enormous boom in wine consumption that has taken place in the English-speaking world over the last two decades or so is a fascinating, happy paradox. In the days when wine was exclusively the preserve of a narrow cultural elite, the ordinary drinker didn't get a look-in. Wine was considered a highly technical subject, in which anybody without the necessary ability could only fall flat on his or her face in embarrassment. It required an intimate knowledge of what came from where, and what it was supposed to taste like.

Those were times, however, when wine appreciation essentially meant a familiarity with the French classics, with perhaps a little sweet wine from Germany and a smattering of the traditional fortified wines: sherry, port and madeira. That was what the wine trade dealt in. These days, wine is bought daily in supermarkets to be consumed that evening; hardly anyone has a cellar

Below: Mature summer vines at the Robert Mondavi vineyard in the Napa Valley, northern California.

Above: Wine undergoing its fermentation in wooden vats.

Above: Champagne is the world's pre-eminent sparkling wine.

to store it in and many don't even possess a decanter. Wines from dozens of countries cram the retail shelves.

It seems, in other words, that the commercial jungle that wine has now become has not deterred people in the slightest from plunging adventurously into the thickets. Consumers are no longer intimidated by the thought of needing to know their Pouilly-Fumé from their Pouilly-Fuissé, their Bardolino

from their Brunello, just at the very moment when there is more to know than ever before.

The reason for this new mood of confidence is not hard to find. On virtually every wine label we come across is the name of the grape from which it is made. Consumers effectively recognize these as brand names, and have thus acquired a basic lexicon of wine that can serve them well.

In the wine heartlands of Europe, especially France, winemakers are scared to death of that trend. This is not because they think their wine isn't as good as the best from California or South Australia, but because they don't traditionally call their wines Cabernet Sauvignon or Chardonnay. They call them Château Ducru-Beaucaillou or Corton-Charlemagne, and they aren't about to change.

Wine consumption was also given a significant boost in the early 1990s by the pioneering work of Dr Serge Renaud, a nutritionist based at Lyon, who has spent many years investigating the reasons for the uncannily low incidence of coronary heart disease in the south of France. One of his findings

is that the fat-derived cholesterol that builds up in the arteries can be dispersed by the antioxidants in wine.

Champagne has its own story, but where it once had the field almost to itself, with other sparkling wines being seen as cheap and usually nasty imitations, it must now try its luck in the marketplace against products that have, in recent years, improved beyond recognition.

Fortified wines

There is one important difference between fortified wines and ordinary table wines. The former have all been strengthened with spirit: usually grape spirit. None of these types of wine could have existed before the discovery of distillation.

In most cases, the creation of the classic fortified wines was a chance discovery made while trying to find ways of preserving ordinary wines. It wasn't that some bright spark in Portugal once thought, "Let's add some brandy to our wines and see what they taste like." The addition of spirit was

Below: Flor yeast growing on the surface of fino sherry. The yeast forms spontaneously and protects the wine from air. The yeast cells are nourished by oxygen, with new ones continuously being formed.

Above: Krug Grande Cuvée bottles, stored in candlelit cellars in Reims, France.

intended to keep wines on the arduous sea voyages they had to undergo to their customers abroad.

In the days when the chemistry of fermentation was not so well understood, wine was often shipped in a micro-biologically unstable state. Its fermentation may have been interrupted by a sudden drop in the cellar temperature, as opposed to having run its natural course. When such wines arrived at their destinations, it was found that they had begun re-fermenting or, worse, that they would re-ferment after being bottled.

The yeasts that ferment in grape juice can only work as long as the amount of alcohol generated doesn't exceed a certain level, which is usually estimated to be in the range of 16 to 17% ABV. After that, they die off, and the wine becomes stable. If you add a healthy dose of brandy or other spirit to wine that has apparently finished fermenting, you raise the alcohol level to such a degree that the yeasts are killed off.

The normal strength of unfortified table wines is in the region of 11 to 13% ABV. But 15% is the *starting* point for fortified wines, and they can be fortified to a maximum of 22%, putting them not far off the strength of the average liqueur.

Each of the world's classic fortified wines has its own particular method of production. The majority are made from white grapes, the most notable exception being port, most of which is red. They tend to be sweet, but don't have to be; fino and manzanilla sherry are the driest of the dry. Most of them contain only wine and grape spirit, but in the case of vermouth and related products, a whole bunch of aromatizing ingredients (familiar to us from some of the herbal liqueurs) creates a style that is halfway between a fortified wine and a liqueur.

By the time the 19th century dawned, most of these wines were seen as premium products. Vintage port and madeira, in particular, were as highly acclaimed as claret and burgundy. Since that time a progressive decline has taken place, as international tastes in wine have tended towards the dry and light end of the spectrum, and away from the sort of sinew-stiffening brew to be sipped by the fireside on winter nights.

Despite that, there will always be a place for the traditional fortified wines. They are unique styles of wine.

White, red and rosé wines

The three colours that unfortified table wines come in all require different production processes.

White wines

Of the three colours of wine, white is the simplest of all to make, precisely because it has no colour. When the ripe grapes are harvested, they are brought to the winery, and immediately de-stemmed and crushed to extract the first (and best) juice from them. After that, they are likely to be treated to a slightly heavier pressing, and then the juice is separated off from all the solid matter, such as skins, pips, leaves, etc.

The juice must be stored at low temperatures, to minimize the risk of spoilage through oxidation. While standing, any remaining minute, solid particles settle to the bottom and thus clarify the juice; the process can be speeded up artificially by subjecting it to centrifugal force. The fermentation of white wine takes place at much lower temperatures than that of reds, typically around 12–18°C/54–64°F, which means that it tends to be a fairly slow process.

At some stage, the wine may be encouraged to undergo a secondary type of fermentation to the sort that turns grape juice into alcohol. This is called the malolactic fermentation, and is useful for converting hard-tasting malic acid, with which grape juice is naturally abundant, into softer, creamier lactic acid. Some white wines are better off with a noticeable bite to them, and for those, the winemaker will take positive steps to avoid a malolactic fermentation, usually by keeping the temperature low.

The final decision is whether to bottle the wine as it is, or give it a period of ageing in oak barrels, which adds spiciness and richness to the finished product. If so, the wine may well be left on its lees (fermentation

Above left: Maçon-Villages Chardonnay is a white wine from Burgundy.

Above middle: Orvieto Classico comes from Italy's Umbria region.

Above right: An Italian white wine from the Marches region.

Left: Different styles of wine need different glasses, but the middle one here is the classic shape.

sediments) to acquire extra character, and a periodic stirring up of the settled gunge with a wooden paddle helps to maximize that effect. Before bottling, the wine is generally subjected to a final filtration to ensure that it is absolutely bright and clear, but this has become a contentious issue in recent years, with some authorities feeling that it strips the wine of too much of its character.

Among the widely used international white grape varieties, whose names have become increasingly familiar, are: Chardonnay, Sauvignon Blanc, Sémillon, Riesling, Chenin Blanc, Gewürztraminer, Viognier and the various members of the Muscat family.

Below: Villa Montes Sauvignon Blanc from Chile is one of the band of southern hemisphere varietal wines that have taken Europe by storm.

Red wines

Making red wine is a more complicated process in that the grape juice has to be dyed. The skins of the grapes may be red (or deep purple, to be precise), but their juice is as colourless as that of white grapes. The colour has therefore to be put into the wine by leaching it out of the skins.

When the grapes have been de-stemmed and crushed, and perhaps pressed as well, the mass of smashed skins and pips is left sitting in the juice. A period of cold soaking before the fermentation begins is now common practice. It is thought to emphasize the wine's fruitiness, and to encourage the development of good, ripe fruit tannin which, together with acidity, will give the wine the structure to age well.

Red wine is fermented at higher temperatures than white: generally in the 25–30°C/77–86°F range, although some reds are allowed to go higher than this. The mass of skins, known as the pomace, is left in the fermenting juice. Of course, it's not doing any good merely floating on the surface, and so either the pomace is punched down manually a couple of times a day, or a device is used that pumps wine from the bottom of the vat over the floating cap of skins to give the fermenting juice the benefit of it. Malolactic fermentation is automatically carried out for the vast majority of red wines.

After the fermentation, the wine may be allowed a further few days of sitting in contact with the skins, before they are removed, and the wine transferred to its maturation vessel. This can be either stainless steel or oak, as in the case of white wine. Premium reds may be kept for a year or more in barrels in the winery cellar, during the course of which they may pick up more tannin (of a different kind, though, this time, from the wood) and undergo a very gentle process of oxygenation. Some reds are meant to be aged by the buyer; others, such as Spanish Reserva quality reds, have been aged for you by the winemaker, and are intended to be drunk on release.

Major international red grape varieties are: Cabernet Sauvignon, Merlot, Pinot Noir, Shiraz (or Syrah, as it is known in France) and Grenache. Grapes of importance in their homelands, but with international reputations, are the Gamay of Beaujolais, Spain's Tempranillo, Italy's Sangiovese and Nebbiolo, California's Zinfandel and South Africa's Pinotage.

Rosé wines

Rosé wine is basically a partially made red. It achieves its pale tint by virtue of the fact that the skins of the red grapes are only allowed a short maceration in the juice (usually less than 24 hours) before being removed. Some pink wine is made as an off-cut of a serious red, in that a little of the juice is siphoned off after the maceration has begun, with the rest going on to turn into fully fledged red.

In the case of pink champagne, a kind of cheat's approach has been sanctioned by the French wine authorities. The colour is attained by simply adding a slug of ready-made red wine to the finished white. If that sounds a little sloppy for a product as illustrious as champagne, rest assured that it is preferable to the colouring materials that were resorted to in the 19th century. The alternative method is to allow a short maceration period on the skins. Such a wine is said to have been *saignée*, or bled, but the technique is used for only about 2% of all pink champagne on the market. Although those who use it dispute the fact, the taste is essentially the same.

Below left: Chianti Classico comes from Tuscany in central Italy.

Below middle: Campo Viejo is a Rioja from northern Spain.

Below right: Chateau Saint-Maurice is from France's southern Rhône valley.

Champagne and sparkling wines

Although it was the winemakers of the Champagne region itself who perfected the various techniques indelibly associated with producing quality sparkling wines the world over, they would not have done so had the metropolitan English not developed a taste for deliberately spoiled wine. Effervescence in the wine was considered an exasperating liability in the cold, unforgiving northerly climate of Champagne.

The problem arose when the slow fermentation of the delicate and high-acid wines was interrupted by plummeting cellar temperatures as winter came on. When the time came

Below left: Moët & Chandon, from Epernay, is the world's most famous champagne.

Below right: Bollinger comes from the tiny Champagne village of Ay.

to bottle the wines the following spring, there was very often a certain amount of residual sugar left over from the uncompleted fermentation. As the weather warmed up again, the yeasts that had lain dormant in the wine over the winter now came back to life in the bottle and began feeding on the sugars once more. This time, however, the carbon dioxide gas that the fermentation process creates had no means of escape, so it dissolved into the wine until such time as the bottle came to be opened.

The British trade had, for sometime, been used to adding brandy and a little sugar to the wines it imported because it was the only way to save them from turning rank during the long sea voyages they had to endure. Champagne was the only wine, with the possible exception of burgundy, not to undergo this treatment as a matter of course, for the simple reason that, being the closest fine wine region to the British Isles, the journey was nowhere near as arduous as that made by other wines.

Since there was a marked British predilection, however, for sweetness and potency in wine, some merchants undoubtedly added a little sugar and a slug of spirit to the wines they brought in from Champagne as well. Given the fact that many of the wines were biologically unstable to begin with, this treatment, followed by early bottling, would have virtually assured anything from gentle *pétillance* to volcanic eruption when the bottle was broached.

Unbeknown to itself, the London demi-monde, having a rollicking good time drinking fashionable fizz in the cafés and playhouses, was assiduously

Left: Charles Heidsieck Brut Réserve is one of the richer and rounder styles of dry champagne.

developing the image that the champagne industry has traded on for most of the last three centuries. Fizzy wine is fun, and so champagne came to play a matchless role in partying and celebration.

If you visit the headquarters of the largest and most famous champagne producer of all, Moët & Chandon, in Epernay, you will encounter a rather stern-looking statue in the forecourt. It stands in commemoration of Dom Pérignon, a Benedictine monk who, in 1668, was appointed treasurer at the Abbey of Hautvillers near the town of Epernay, now the nerve centre of the region as a whole.

HOW TO SERVE

Champagne should be served in tall, narrow glasses known as flutes to minimize dispersal of its fizz, as the bubbles have a smaller surface area on which to break. Avoid the flat "saucer" glasses.

Among Dom Pérignon's formidable achievements were the perfecting of the technique of making a still white wine entirely from red grapes; the refinement of the art of blending wines from different vineyards in the region to obtain the best possible product from available resources; and advances in clarification treatments to ensure a brighter wine than was the turbid norm at the time.

Dom Pérignon also devoted much effort to researching ways of avoiding the dreaded re-fermentation that resulted in so many turbulent wines. His seminal place in the region's history is unquestionably merited, but not as the inventor of sparkling champagne.

As the process for making sparkling wines was rationalized, the inducement of the all-important second fermentation in the bottle was achieved by the addition of a little sugar solution to an already fully fermented wine. This then gave the surviving yeasts something more to chew over. The drawback to this was that the sediment of dead yeast cells then created remained trapped in the wine and gave it the cloudiness that Dom Pérignon had worked so hard to prevent. The house of Veuve Clicquot, founded in 1772, may take the credit for the solution to that particularly sticky problem.

Nicole-Barbe Clicquot-Ponsardin took over the running of the firm after her husband, the founder's son, left her widowed in her twenties. It was the development under her tutelage of the process of remuage that installed her unassailably in the region's hall of fame. By this method, the bottles are slowly tipped over a number of weeks, and the sediment gradually sinks

Right: Bluff Hill from New Zealand is typical of the sparklers now challenging French champagne.

towards the neck of the bottle until it all collects on the underside of the cap.

In time, the way to remove the accumulated deposit came to involve dipping the necks of the bottles in freezing brine so that the portion of wine containing the sediment is flash-frozen. When the metal cap is knocked away, the deposit flies out with it and the bottle is topped up and corked.

With the coming of prosperity after the Second World War, champagne began very gradually to trickle down the social scale and become less of a luxury. The industry lost its way somewhat in the 1980s when consumption in the UK reached unprecedented levels to coincide with relatively benign economic times. Some members of its controlling body felt that the wine was in danger of becoming too democratic and losing its aura of elite unaffordability. A more or less explicit attempt to ration consumption, using the sledgehammer of price inflation, was just beginning to work when the coming of severe recession did the job for them.

By the mid-1990s, champagne sales were once more on a gentle upward trajectory as prices moderated and a new quality charter came into effect to ensure that Champagne didn't just idly trade on its good name by selling wafer-thin, razor-sharp, watery wines as it had been tempted to do during the boom years. As a result, it is again possible to say that, when they play to the peak of their form, these are indeed the finest sparkling wines made anywhere.

Styles of champagne include: basic non-vintage (the flagship wine of each house); vintage-dated wine (the product of a single year's harvest); blanc de blancs (made only from Chardonnay grapes); blanc de noirs (made from either

Above left: Freixenet Cava comes from northern Spain, but is made by the same method as champagne.

Above right: Hardy's Nottage Hill Chardonnay Brut is a popular sparkling wine made in Australia.

or both the black grapes Pinot Noir and Pinot Meunier); and rosé. Brut is the classic ultra-dry style, Doux is distinctly sweet and Demi-Sec lies between the two.

Most champagne is released on to the market too young. In France, they rather like the rapier-like acidity of youthful champagne, but the British taste is for something softer and rounder. If you have the resources (a dark cupboard will do), it is always worth ageing it for some time. Six months will soften a non-vintage fizz considerably; a year is even better. Vintage-dated champagne should ideally not be breached at less than eight years old.

Port

Although it is one of the major fortified wines, port is the only example to be based on a red wine. True, there is such a thing as white port, but it accounts for only a fraction of the production. Port hails from only one delimited area, the Douro valley in northern Portugal. So popular has it traditionally been as a style of wine, that many non-European wine-making countries have been trying their hands at port lookalikes since the 19th century. The difference today is that, in the countries of the European Union at least, such products are no longer allowed to be called port.

The drink originated during one of the frequent periods of hostilities between the English and the French in the 17th century, as a consequence of which the English authorities declared a punitive tax levy on goods imported from France. This hit the wine trade hard. Wine shippers had to look to Portugal, England's oldest European ally, with whom there were preferential trade tariffs, to supply their customers. Journeying inland along the river Douro, the English merchants happened upon the fierce red wines of the region and found them pretty much to the domestic taste. As was common practice at the time, they fortified them with a little brandy for the sea voyage.

Thus was port born. Originally, it was of course a dry wine, since these were fully fermented wines that were being augmented with brandy. However, it took only the chance discovery of the effects of fortification on an extremely ripe, sweet wine to remodel port in the image with which we are familiar today. To preserve that sweetness, the wines would have their normal fermentation interrupted (or "muted") with brandy, so that some of the grape sugars would remain unconsumed by the yeasts.

Left: Cockburn's Vintage Port bears the year of its harvest on the label, and must be aged by the buyer.

Eventually, it was considered that using a simple, local grape spirit was cheaper than buying fine cognac for the fortification. Also, port was coming to be seen as a fine wine in its own right, and so it was desirable that the fortifying agent should be as neutral as possible, in order to allow the characteristics of the underlying wine to be shown off.

Port styles have since multiplied almost infinitely. At the top of the quality tree are the vintage ports, wines of a single year that must be bottled within two years of the harvest and are intended for long ageing. Late-bottled vintage (LBV) is also the product of a single year, but one that has been kept in cask in the shipper's premises for longer – around six years usually – in order to be more mature on bottling, and readier to drink on purchase. Vintage Character port is an everyday blended product and nothing special, while the fine old tawny ports are often aged for many years in barrel so that their initial full-blooded red fades to an autumnal brown.

Other countries producing good port-style fortified wines are Australia (where the favoured grape variety is the spicy Shiraz), South Africa and the United States. There is a very good

Right: Late Bottled Vintage Port matured in the cellars of the shipper.

Far right: Graham's Six Grapes is a sound blend of red wines from six different grape varieties.

Greek fortified red called Mavrodaphne that makes an agreeable alternative to the more basic offerings of the Douro.

How it is made
The fermentation of Douro wines is stopped part-way through by the addition of grape spirit, to produce a sweet, strong, liquorous wine. Various periods of cask-ageing are given to the various grades. The bottled strength is in the region of 18–20%, but can be as high as 22%.

Tastes good with
Port is excellent with nuts and with mature, strong hard cheeses, such as Cheddar, but less good with its traditional partner, Stilton, when the tannins in it always seem to me to clash. Some drink it with chocolate – I couldn't possibly comment.

Far left: Taylor's 20 Years Old is a fine example of a cask-aged port, in which the average age of the wine in the blend is 20 years.

Second from left: Cockburn's Fine Ruby is a good, simple, everyday port from one of the most widely known of the English shippers.

Third from left: Quinta do Crasto is an LBV from a small Portuguese producer. Such ports will always have a vintage year on the label, but are released a few years later than true vintage ports.

Left: Quady's Batch 88 Starboard is a Californian fortified wine made in punning homage to port. It is sweet and fruity, and can be drunk in much the same way, with mature cow's-milk cheeses.

HOW TO SERVE

Good port should be served in wine glass quantities, rather than in silly little liqueur glasses. It should be served unchilled, except in the case of white port. Older wines that have thrown a sediment may need to be decanted.

Although it may seem to have an assertive (even, in the case of the basic grades, aggressive) flavour, port is surprisingly useful in the cocktail repertoire. It is inevitably best mixed with other grape products, perhaps with a dash of

best cognac for a simple digestif cocktail, or maybe with unfortified red wine and brandy for something a little racier, when it's best to throw in a lump or two of ice as well. If you can stretch to it, a good LBV is probably best for mixing.

Sherry

Although fortified wines bearing the name of sherry have been produced around the world for well over a century, true sherry comes only from a demarcated region in the southern Spanish province of Andalucía. There are three main centres of production: Jerez de la Frontera, Puerto de Santa María and Sanlúcar de Barrameda. The last is the traditional home of a type of pale, delicate, notably tangy dry sherry called manzanilla.

The production process for sherry is one of the most complicated of any fortified wine. When the new white wine is made, it is fermented until fully dry, and then transferred into large butts. Some sherries, those that are destined

Below left: Tio Pepe's Muy Seco is the very driest style of sherry.

Below right: Harvey's Bristol Cream is a big-selling brown cream sherry.

HOW TO SERVE
Fino and manzanilla, and the sweetened pale sherries, should be served very well chilled, preferably from a freshly opened bottle. In Spain, they think nothing of drinking a bottle of dry sherry as we would a table wine. The other styles should be served at room temperature. Finos are brilliant aperitifs; old olorosos are best at the other end of the meal.

to end up as the pale dry styles known as fino or manzanilla, develop a film of yeast culture called *flor* on the surface of the wine. In some barrels, the layer of *flor* dies out because it has consumed all the remaining nutrients in the wine, whereupon it breaks up and sinks to the bottom of the butt. With the subsequent greater exposure to the air, the colour of the wine deepens through oxidation, and the style known as amontillado results.

Some wines develop no *flor* at all and go on to turn a deep, woody brown colour. These are oloroso sherries. The fortification of the wine varies according to the style. Fino may be fortified to only 15% ABV, whereas oloroso is generally bottled at around 20%. At this stage, all of the wines are naturally dry, and some – the true connoisseur's sherries – will be bottled in that condition after ageing in cask.

Many commercial sherries, however, are made sweet by the addition of a quantity of *mistela*, the juice of raisined

grapes to which grape spirit has been added. The best sweet sherries are sweetened with PX, which stands for Pedro Ximénez, the name of a grape variety whose berries are left to dry in the sun until loss of moisture has concentrated their sugars to an almost unbelievable degree. Some houses bottle some of their PX separately as a speciality product.

Other countries that produce sherry-style wines are Australia (which makes about the best outside Jerez), the United States, South Africa and Cyprus. Within Spain itself, there are two other regions near Jerez that produce similar fortified wines in the same range of styles, but they are not as distinguished as sherry. One is the distinctly cheaper Montilla-Morilés, the other the virtually forgotten Condado de Huelva.

Spain's other great, now sadly nearly extinct, fortified wine is Málaga, made around the Mediterranean port of that name. Its finest wines are deep brown, caramel-sweet creations of great power, once hugely popular in Britain, but now forsaken by the vagaries of fashion.

Tastes good with
Dry sherries are good with salted nuts such as almonds, piquant nibbles such as olives, salty fish like anchovies, and Serrano ham or its Mediterranean equivalents. The sweet old olorosos are wonderful with rich, dark fruitcake and hard Spanish sheep's-milk cheeses such as the tangily salty Manchego.

Right: Emva Cream is a Cypriot wine, no longer labelled as "sherry".

Madeira

Of all the classic fortified wines of southern Europe, madeira is the one with the most singular history. It comes from the island of the same name in the Atlantic Ocean, slightly nearer to the coast of North Africa than it is to that of Portugal, of which it is an autonomously governed region.

The evolution of this wine belongs to the days of the trading ships that plied the East India routes in the late 17th century. Madeira's geographical position made it a natural port of call for north European vessels on their way to Africa and the East Indies, and so they would load up with wine at the port of Funchal, the island

Right: Sercial is the palest and driest style of madeira.

Above: Verdelho is the second driest style; this five-year-old madeira is only very slightly sweet.

capital. It gradually came to be noticed that, whereas many more delicate table wines would be badly spoiled by the combination of violent shaking and the torrid heat in which they travelled the oceans, madeiras were eerily improved by the experience.

Eventually, it wasn't financially practical to keep treating the wine to a round-the-world cruise, and so the tortuous heat it endured at sea was recreated in the wineries or "lodges". Some madeira, known as *canteiro*, is heated simply by being left under the roof of the lodge to bake in the heat of the tropical sun. Some is stored in rooms where fat central-heating pipes radiate heat throughout the summer, and even the lowest grades are matured in vats that have hot-water pipes running through them.

Left: Rich Malmsey is the sweetest style of madeira.

There are four basic styles of madeira, named after their grape varieties. The palest and driest style is sercial. Then comes verdelho, a little sweeter and darker, then bual, and finally malmsey (the last is an English corruption of the Portuguese name Malvasia). The wines are also graded according to how long they have been aged. This is generally given as a minimum age on the label (five-year-old, ten-year-old and so on). Some madeira is vintage-dated, meaning it is the unblended produce of the stated year's harvest.

How it is made

A light, white base wine is made from any of the four main varieties, perhaps supplemented with some juice from the local red grape Tinta Negra Mole. For the sweeter styles, the fermentation may be interrupted by the addition of grape spirit, meaning that some natural sugar remains in them; the drier wines are fermented until more of the sugar has been consumed before being fortified. The wines are then subjected to heat during the cask-ageing, either by one of the heating systems known as an *estufa* (stove), or by being left in the hottest part of the lodge, in which case it is known as a *vinho canteiro*.

Tastes good with

The driest styles present the answer to that age-old problem of what to drink with soup. They are particularly good with clear, meaty consommé. As you proceed to the richer end of the scale, drink them with mince pies, Christmas cake and other dense fruitcake mixes or, of course, madeira cake.

HOW TO SERVE
Serve madeira in a good-sized sherry glass or small wine glass. The drier styles may benefit from a little light chilling, but the richer, darker, sweeter styles, with their overtones of treacle toffee and Christmas cake, should be served at room temperature.

Marsala

Sicily's very own fortified wine is named after the town of Marsala, in the province of Trapani at the western end of the island. Like many of the fortified wines of southern Europe, it has an English connection. It was effectively invented by a wine merchant, John Woodhouse, in 1773, in direct imitation of the sherry and madeira in which he was something of a specialist. He simply added a quantity of ordinary brandy to the traditional white wines of western Sicily, and found on shipping them that the result was a reasonably close approximation of the already established fortified wines.

Woodhouse founded a commercial operation on the island at the end of the 18th century, and won valuable orders from the British Royal Navy, among others. Marsala was carried on Nelson's ships during the hostilities with France, and the wine's reputation quickly spread. Although the early trade was dominated by English merchants, Italians themselves eventually got in on the act. The first significant house of Italian origin was Florio, founded in 1832.

The rules and regulations governing the production of marsala were only finally codified in 1969, and are considerably more flexible than those controlling the manufacture of the other famous fortified wines. Perhaps

Above left: Secco is the driest and lightest style of marsala.

Above right: Dolce is best suited for classic Italian desserts.

the least satisfactory aspect of them is the nature of the sweetening agent that may be added. It can be either a fortified grape juice, or just grape juice whose sweetness has been concentrated by cooking. This latter ingredient, known in Italian as *mosto cotto*, is not in itself alcoholic. The best marsalas have natural sweetness from ripe grapes, which is retained through interrupted fermentation.

Marsala is classified by age (Fine is one year old, Superiore two, Superiore Riserva four, Vergine five, Stravecchio ten), as well as by sweetness. Dry is labelled *secco*, medium-dry *semisecco* and the sweetest *dolce*. It also comes in three colours. The better grades are

Left: Terre Arse is a vintage-dated marsala from Florio.

both shades of tawny, either amber (*ambra*) or golden (*oro*), but there is a red version too (*rubino*).

How it is made

Light white wines from local grape varieties Grillo, Inzolia and Catarratto are turned into marsala by one of three methods. They can be fortified with grape spirit in the traditional way, or sweetened and strengthened with either alcohol-boosted juice from ultra-sweet, late-ripened grapes or with cooked grape juice concentrate. Concentrate is only permitted in ambra marsala. The wines are then cask-aged for varying periods.

Tastes good with

Marsala has come to be seen as even more of a kitchen ingredient than madeira. It is indispensable as the alcohol element in both zabaglione and tiramisu, and makes a sticky brown sauce to go with scallopini of veal.

HOW TO SERVE

Dry and medium-dry marsala, of which there is a regrettably small amount, should be served chilled in generously sized sherry glasses as an aperitif. The sweetest styles should be served at room temperature as digestifs or with certain types of old, dry cheese.

Muscat and Moscatel

Sweet fortified wines are made from Muscat all over the world. It is easy to imagine Muscat as a single grape variety, but it is in fact a family. Some of its offshoots are of the highest pedigree, notably a type the French call Muscat Blanc à Petits Grains. Others, such as Muscat of Alexandria and Muscat Ottonel, are of humbler extraction, and give correspondingly less exciting wines. Moscatel is the name the family assumes on the Iberian peninsula, in Portugal and Spain.

Australian liqueur Muscats

These are hugely rich, strong, fortified Muscats made in and around the town of Rutherglen, in north-west Victoria. They are produced by a method that seems to combine a little of all the ways of making fortified wine. The grapes are

Left: A Moscatel de Valencia sold in a bottle that is highly ornate for a very simple drink.

left to overripen and shrivel on the vine, so that they are halfway to becoming raisins. After pressing, they ferment part-way, but the fermentation is arrested by fortification with grape spirit, keeping massive quantities of natural sugar in the wine. The cask-ageing they then receive combines elements of the *solera* system used in Spanish brandy and sherry, with the action of searing sunshine, as in the *canteiro* madeiras.

Vin doux naturel Muscats

A group of Muscat wines made in southern France are made by virtually the same method as port. Their collective name, *vins doux naturels*, means "naturally sweet wines". The grapes are picked very ripe and the normal process of fermentation is stopped by the addition of a powerful grape spirit, so the natural grapey sweetness of Muscat is retained. There are six appellations for this type of wine, the most famous of which is Muscat de Beaumes de Venise from the southern Rhône.

Four of the others – Muscat de Frontignan, de Lunel, de Mireval and de St Jean de Minervois – are in the Languedoc, while the sixth, Muscat de Rivesaltes, is grown even further south, in Roussillon near the Spanish border. De Rivesaltes does not have to be made from the noblest Muscat, and the quality varies hugely. The best are honeyed and orangey; the worst cloyingly sweet like barley sugar.

Left: This 20-year-old Moscatel is made on western Portugal's Setúbal peninsula.

Left: This Muscat de Beaumes de Venise is made by Domaine de Coyeux, one of the best producers of Muscat.

Setúbal Moscatel

This is a traditional fortified wine based on the Muscat of Alexandria grape, together with a couple of its more obscure cousins. It is made on the Setúbal peninsula in western Portugal, and was recognized as a regionally demarcated wine in the early 20th century. The process is the same as for *vin doux naturel*, except that after fortification, the grape skins are allowed to macerate in the finished wine for several months. Some Setúbal Moscatel is released after five years or so, when its colour is already a vivid orange from the wood. Other wines are aged for a couple of decades, deepening to burnished mahogany.

Moscatel de Valencia

Around Valencia, on the eastern coast of Spain, they make what the French would call a *vin de liqueur*, that is, an unfermented grape juice fortified with grape spirit. Moscatel de Valencia is not made from the most distinguished Muscat variety. When very well chilled, it can be a pretty refreshing drink, particularly in the stunning heat of a Spanish summer.

Jerepigo

Jerepigo is the South African version of Moscatel de Valencia, except that it uses the aristocratic Muscat Blanc à Petits Grains variety, here known as Muscadel or Muskadel. Otherwise, the production is the same, with grape spirit being added to the very sweet, freshly pressed grape juice. Vintages of Jerepigo are occasionally released at around 15 years old, and are found to retain much of their initial freshness. Don't expect great complexity though: because these aren't fermented wines, they don't mature in the same way.

Vermouth

As far removed from the natural produce of the vine as it is possible for a fortified wine to get, vermouth is not only strengthened with spirit, but also heavily aromatized with herbs and botanical ingredients. The result is a distinctive type of drink intended for drinking as an aperitif, either mixed or straight. It is an everyday product made to a consistent and unchanging recipe by each manufacturer.

The presence in vermouth of such a cocktail of herbs and roots alerts us to the fact that this was originally a

Below left: Noilly Prat is a bone-dry vermouth produced in the south of France.

Below right: Martini Extra Dry is the top brand of vermouth internationally.

medicinal drink. A popular early additive was wormwood, villain of the piece when absinthe was outlawed, yet much prized as a tonic for the stomach, from classical antiquity to medieval times and the beginnings of distillation in Europe.

To find a drink identifiable as the precursor of modern vermouth, we have to travel back to the 16th century to find a merchant called d'Alessio selling a wormwood wine in Piedmont (north-west Italy). The inspiration had come from similar German products, produced on a domestic scale, and it is from the German word for wormwood, *Wermuth*, that the modern English word is derived. It was already popular in England by the middle years of the following century.

Two centres of vermouth production came to be established. One was in d'Alessio's part of Italy, close to the alpine hills where the botanical ingredients that went into the wine were sourced, and the other over the border in south-east France. As the big commercial companies were founded, two distinct styles of vermouth emerged: one pale and dry with pronounced bitterness; the other red and sweet and not quite so bitter. The former was the style associated with France, the latter with Italy. So ingrained did these definitions become that, even now, drinkers still use the terms "French" and "Italian" to mean dry and sweet respectively, when these may not necessarily always be the geographical origins.

In fact, sweet and dry vermouths are made in both of these countries, as well as elsewhere, including the United States. Brands vary according to the number and type of the herbal ingredients added, but the basic style remains the same from one batch to the next. Cloves, cinnamon, quinine, citrus rinds, ginger, and perhaps a touch of wormwood are typical elements in the potpourri of

HOW TO SERVE

A drop or two only of dry French vermouth is needed for the perfect dry Martini or Vodkatini. All these drinks should be served as aperitifs or at the cocktail hour. Vermouth is not as fragile once opened as pale dry sherry tends to be. It doesn't have to be drunk within a few days, and is able to withstand extremes of temperature far more hardily than the other light fortified wines.

aromatizers that goes to create the distinctive flavours of modern vermouths.

As with many of the traditional liqueurs, the medicinal image of vermouth was, by the onset of the 20th century, something of an albatross around its neck, rather than a marketing opportunity. It was once again the cocktail era that rode to its rescue, finding multifarious uses for both styles of vermouth. After all, if the traditional dry Martini was destined to be the only use to which dry vermouth could be put behind the bar, one drop at a time, then it was not going to sell in very large quantities. Because it is quite as perfumed, in its way, as gin, vermouth proved hugely versatile in a range of mixed drinks, and the demand for it today, which is thanks in part to the big proprietary brands, remains reasonably steady.

The bulk-producing Italian firm of Martini e Rossi, based at Turin, is still the vermouth name that springs most readily to mind for consumers today. Other Italian producers are Riccadonna, Cinzano and Gancia. In France, the Marseillan producer Noilly Prat makes one of the more highly regarded dry vermouths, although it also has a sweeter style. The region of Chambéry in eastern France has been awarded the *appellation contrôlée* for its vermouths, which include a strawberry-flavoured fruit version called Chambéryzette. As well as red and white styles of vermouth, there is a golden or amber variant, and a rosé.

Other similar branded products include Lillet of Bordeaux, owned by one of the high-ranking claret châteaux, which blends a proportion of fruit juice with the wine base along with the customary herbs; the French Dubonnet, a red or white sweet vermouth also full of highly appetizing quinine bitterness; and Punt e Mes, a similar but dark-coloured Italian product that combines sweetening and bittering elements in an intriguing balance. These are all, without exception, products that deserve a wider audience. They are versatile cocktail ingredients that also happen to be supremely appetizing on their own.

Left: Cinzano Bianco is a hugely popular brand of sweet white vermouth.

How it is made

A low-alcohol, and mostly white, wine is produced and may be allowed a short period of ageing. For the sweeter styles of vermouth, it then has a quantity of sugar syrup added to it before the fortification with spirit. This is usually grape spirit but may occasionally also be derived from vegetable sources such as sugar beet. The wine is then transferred into large barrels or tanks to which the dried aromatizing ingredients have already been added. From time to time, the mixture is stirred manually with wooden paddles. After the absorption of the flavourings, the vermouth will be bottled at around 17% ABV. Some producers insist that their vermouths will continue to age in the bottle for a couple of years if kept.

Tastes good with

Dry vermouths are particularly useful in the kitchen for adding to sauces to accompany fish. The herbal ingredients in the vermouth add an attractive savoury note to the dish. A seasoned reduction of Noilly Prat, lemon juice and single (light) cream is a fine way to treat good white fish such as sole or turbot. Try marinating chunks of monkfish in dry white vermouth.

Above left: A red version of vermouth, such as Dubonnet, mixes well with lemonade.

Above right: Carpano Punt e Mes is a deep red vermouth produced at Turin.

HOW TO SERVE

As one might expect, given the precedent of the classic Dry Martini, vermouth mixes superbly with gin in cocktails. It happily takes a dash of absinthe too, and gets along well with the herbal liqueurs such as Chartreuse, Glayva and Bénédictine.

BEER

An ancient drink with a chequered and varied history, beer has been used by preachers as a religious symbol, by doctors as a medicinal treatment and by workers as a means of relaxation after a hard day's toil. Throughout the ages, in different countries, beer has been both promoted as a health drink and reviled as the draught of the devil.

The brewing industry has changed fundamentally since the early medieval ale wives brewed from their kitchens, and it has been affected profoundly by advances in technology. Now the centre of one of the largest multinational industries, beer is shipped around the globe, with large companies often producing their brews thousands of miles from home, but there is thankfully still room for the small-scale producer in all this.

Tasting beer

Good beer should never be rushed. Take the trouble to pour the beer carefully into a clean glass, ensuring a reasonable head, and then savour the aroma. Some have a subtle scent; others can be almost overpowering.

When tasting, let the beer flow over your palate to pick up all the different taste sensations, savouring the flavours left behind after swallowing. A good beer should linger on the palate.

Generally, the best beer of most styles is hand-pumped, and the closer the pub or bar is to the brewery, the better the beer. It is at the heart of the community in many countries, whether it is served in a cosy English pub, a huge German beer cellar, a packed Czech bar or a roadside bar in Africa. Tasting local beer is often a good way to meet the locals, who will probably know where to find the best brews.

Styles of beer

It is only recently that beer has begun to be discussed with the same degree of attention that wine receives. Beer is at best a fine balance of malted grain and hops. There are different hop varieties, just as there are varieties of wine grapes, and there are many distinct styles of malt, as well as different cereal grains. In addition, there is an exotic store of extra spices for the more adventurous brewer.

There are basically two main beer categories: ale (or top-fermented beer) and lager (bottom-fermented). The range of different styles within these general terms is immense, from dark, hearty ales to tangy, spritzy Belgian beers. Here is a lightning tour of some of the most famous varieties.

Abbey beers Strong, fruity ales brewed in Belgium, sometimes under licence from religious communities. They copy the style of the surviving beers produced in monasteries, and usually name their brews after a church or saint.
Alt "Old" in German.

Left: Bitter beers usually have a floral, fruity flavour.

Indicates a bitter-tasting brew produced by top-fermentation. Copper-coloured and aromatic. Around 4.5% ABV.
Barley wine English name for a powerful, syrupy, strong ale usually sold in nip-size bottles. These well-matured brews can be golden or dark. Darker versions were once called "Stingo".
Berliner Weisse Light, sharply acidic German wheat beer made mainly in Berlin. Relatively low in alcohol. It has a cloudy, white (*weisse*) appearance.
Bière de Garde Top-fermenting "beer for keeping" from north-west France, which is medium to strong. Some are bottle-conditioned and sealed with champagne-style wired corks.
Bitter The distinctive dry and hoppy draught ale of England and Wales. Reddish amber in colour, although paler varieties are now popular. Alcohol content is usually 3–5%, but stronger versions exist, which are often called Best or Special.
Black beer (Schwarzbier) Strong-tasting, bitter-chocolate lager, a speciality of eastern Germany, but also made in Japan. In Yorkshire, black beers are strong, pitch-black, treacly malt extracts, usually bottled for mixing with lemonade as shandy.
Bock Strong, malty German beer of about 6.5% ABV. Traditionally dark, but now more likely to be golden bronze. Originated in Einbeck in Lower Saxony, but now brewed elsewhere. Doppelbocks are stronger versions, and Eisbocks stronger still.
Brown ale Sweetish, bottled mild ale, dark in colour and low in alcohol. North-east England classically produces stronger, drier versions. Sweet-and-sour ones are produced in East Flanders in Belgium.
Chilli beer Produced by a few American breweries, this is an odd, slow-burning speciality for drinking with Mexican food.
Cream ale Sweetish, smooth, golden ale from the USA. Originally produced by brewers trying to copy Pilsner.
Dortmunder Strong, malty full-bodied

Above: The term lambic indicates a Belgian wheat beer that is fermented by wild, airborne yeast.

lager from Dortmund, the biggest brewing city in Europe. 5.5% ABV.

Dry beer First produced in Japan by the Asahi Brewery in 1987, this is a super-dry Pils with a parching effect and little taste.

Dunkel Bavarian Dunkels are soft, malty, brown beers with 4.5% alcohol.

Framboise/Frambozen French and Flemish names for a Belgian fruit beer, made by adding raspberries to a lambic (lambic is a style of Belgian wheat beer that undergoes a spontaneous, as opposed to induced, fermentation). It has a sparkling "pink champagne" character with a light, fruity flavour. Other fruits have been tried with varying degrees of success.

Green beer Young beer that has not had time to mature. The term also denotes a beer made with organically grown malt and hops (*bioiogique* in France, *biologisch* in Germany).

Gueuze Blend of young and old lambics, triggering a secondary fermentation, which gives a sparkling beer with a fruity, sour, dry taste.

Hefe German for "yeast". Describes an unfiltered beer with sediment. Draught beers *mit Hefe* are usually cloudy.

Hell Means "pale". A mild, malty, golden lager, often from Munich.

Honey beer A few English breweries have revived an old tradition of producing a honey brew. Some innovative American and Belgian brewers have followed suit.

Ice beer A style in which the beer is frozen after fermentation, originally developed in Canada by Labatt. Sometimes the ice crystals are removed to increase the strength of the beer.

IPA India Pale Ale. A strong, heavily hopped beer, originally brewed in Britain to withstand long sea voyages to far-flung outposts of the British Empire. Now produced by specialist American brewers too.

Irish ale Soft, slightly sweet, reddish ale of which Smithwick's of Kilkenny is the best-known.

Kölsch Light, subtle, fruity-tasting, top-fermented beer, with 4–5% alcohol. Produced in Cologne.

Kriek Cherry-flavoured Belgian lambic beer with a delicate, bitter edge.

Kristall Usually indicates a crystal-clear, filtered wheat beer (*Weizenbier*).

Light ale Low-gravity bottled bitter in England. In Scotland, the term means the weakest brew.

Lite Denotes a thin, low-calorie beer in the USA. Also indicates low-alcohol beer in Australia.

Low alcohol Many breweries have added low-alcohol (up to 2.5%) or no-alcohol (less than 0.05%) beers to their range. Some of these "near beers" are produced by using yeasts that create little alcohol and sometimes fermentation is cut short. In others, the alcohol is removed from normal beer.

Malt liquor Strong US lager made with a high amount of sugar to produce a thin, potent brew (6–8% ABV).

Märzen Full-bodied and copper-coloured, 6% ABV lager originating in Vienna. Developed in Munich as a stronger Märzen (March) brew, and laid down in the spring to allow it to mature for the Oktoberfest.

Mild The dominant ale in England and Wales until the 1960s. Traditionally the worker's drink sold on draught. Relatively low-gravity, malty beer, lightly hopped. Can be dark or pale.

Old ale Strong, matured, rich dark ale, usually sold as a seasonal beer in England. Increasingly rare.

Oud Bruin Dutch for "Old Brown". Traditional, low-alcohol, sweetish, brown lager styles.

Pale ale English bottled beer, stronger than light ale, and usually based on the brewery's best bitter.

HOW TO SERVE

Lager should be served well chilled as it is primarily about refreshment rather than connoisseurial flavour appreciation. It should be poured fairly quickly into a tall, tilted glass, which should then be righted once it is three-quarters full, so that the last complement of beer forms a luxuriant, feather-light, frothy head. Drink the first of the beer through the head rather than waiting for it to subside.

Above: The Czech lager Pilsner has spawned many imitators.

Pilsner Strictly, a golden, hoppy, aromatic lager from Plzeň, Czech Republic. The original Pilsner Urquell is still brewed there. Czech Pilsner has a complex character, with a flowery hop aroma and a dry finish. German Pilsners, now the dominant imitator, are dry, hoppy, light golden lagers, of 5% alcohol.

Porter Traditional London-blended brown mild ale, more heavily hopped than usual to improve its keeping qualities. Matured for months to increase its alcohol. Once all but extinct, but now being revived.

Rauchbier The intense smokiness of these dark, bottom-fermented Franconia beers comes from drying the malt over beechwood fires. Speciality of Bamberg, Germany.

Red beer Reddish, sour beers of West Flanders, made with Vienna malt. Often dubbed the "Burgundies of Belgium".

Roggen Fairly rare German or Austrian rye beer.

Saison/Sezuen Refreshing, slightly sour Belgian summer beer mainly made in Wallonia. The orange, highly hopped,

top-fermenting ales are brewed in winter and laid down to condition in wine bottles until summer. Sold in corked bottles after ageing. Some contain spices such as ginger.

Scotch ale Scotland's ales tend to be maltier than England's.

Steam beer A cross between a bottom-fermented beer and an ale, brewed with lager yeasts at warm temperatures in shallow pans in the California Gold Rush. Now brewed only by the Anchor Steam Brewery of San Francisco.

Steinbier "Stone beer" is heated by red-hot rocks lowered into the brew to bring it to the boil. The sizzling stones become covered in burnt sugars, and are returned to the beer at maturation stage to spark a second fermentation.

Stout Dry, black brew using dark, roasted barley in the mash, heavily hopped. One of the classic styles of ale, as represented by Guinness. Draught stout is smoother and creamier than bottled because it uses nitrogen in the dispenser. Milk or sweet stout is weaker and smoother, made with lactose. Oatmeal stout, now mostly vanished, contained oats. Oyster stout is made to accompany oysters. Russian or Imperial stout, originally brewed in London in the 18th century, is a rich, intense, fruitcakey brew.

Trappist Refers strictly to beers from one of five Belgian Trappist monastery breweries or the single Dutch one. Strong, complex, spicy ales, top-fermented.

Weisse/Weizen White wheat beer popular in Bavaria. Made with 50–60% malted wheat. Pale, often cloudy, top-fermented brews popular in summer. Thirst-quenching as lager, but with true ale flavour. Hefeweizen is unfiltered and cloudy, Kristall filtered. Weizenbock is a stronger brew, Dunkelweizen a dark one.

Witbier/Bière blanche Belgian white wheat beers. Brewed using 50% wheat, typically aromatized with orange rind and coriander. Spicy, fruity flavour.

Below: Stout is a derivative of porter. There are many varieties available.

CIDER

The fruitier alternative to grain beer, cider – fermented apple juice – has a long and distinguished history on both sides of the English Channel. It was introduced into England by the Normans of northern France during the conquests after the Battle of Hastings in 1066. Production gradually acquired momentum through the Middle Ages, and came to be concentrated in the West Country. Devon, Somerset and Herefordshire are the premium apple-growing counties.

Cider remained very much a local taste in those areas until the time of the Civil War in the 1640s, when soldiers of the Royalist and Parliamentary armies criss-crossing England to do battle with each other carried its reputation further afield. Eventually, as a contemporary agricultural writer John Worlidge noted, it was "valued above the wines of France". Particular varieties of apple, and especially the Redstreak, were held to make the best ciders, and were correspondingly the most prized.

In the 18th century, when it was the custom to part-pay agricultural labourers in cider, the reputation of the drink started sliding. It was now seen as the corrupting brew of lolling farm-workers too smashed to pitch hay, and nobody considering themselves to be of quality wanted to be seen drinking it. Mass production in the 20th century didn't help matters, but

Left: Aspall Dry Cyder, with the antique spelling, is made in Suffolk, England.

among Britain's 400 cider producers, there is still a handful of small farms making unfiltered real cider, including the famous "scrumpy", a hazy, potent brew over twice as strong as commercial lager. The UK industry accounts for around 65% of European output.

French cider, from Normandy, is a distinctly different style of drink to British. It tends to be thinner in texture and lower in alcohol, even though it is often produced by the champagne method of allowing a secondary fermentation in the bottle. Look for the wired cork that seals it.

Cider can be dry, medium-dry or sweet, depending on the types of apples used and the degree of fermentation the juice is permitted. There are hundreds of different varieties of cider apple, classified into four broad taste groups: sweet, bitter-sweet, bitter and acid. When the fruit is picked, it is first subject to a light crushing, which reduces it to a rough pulp. That pulp, known in English as "cheese", is then wrapped in hessian blankets, and it is these that go into the press to extract the juice.

Even the lowest grades of commercial cider are at the stronger end of the alcohol range associated with beer, i.e. 5–6% ABV. Premium brands may reach double figures. Some, such as the famous English brand Merrydown, make a virtue of only using dessert apples rather than cider apples in their products. The best ciders are vintage-dated like wines, indicating that what's in the bottle is the exclusive produce of that particular year's harvest. Unlike wine, however, there is no significant gain in quality to be had from keeping them.

Cider is another of those products in which England has a rich, distinguished heritage, but which it has allowed to decline. It deserves to be accorded the same dignity and legal protection that the French afford their wines under the *appellation contrôlée* system.

Above left: Premium organic cider from a Herefordshire specialist.

Above right: Westons cider is aged in oak casks for greater complexity.

HOW TO SERVE
Cider should be served well-chilled in tall glasses, or else in the earthenware cups traditional in northern France.

NON-ALCOHOLIC MIXERS

Although many of the drinks talked about in this book are commonly drunk unmixed, such as single malt whiskies, aged brandies and rums, and the various wines and beers, the great majority of them would not be consumed at all were it not for non-alcoholic mixers. Some of these are so familiar as scarcely to need any explanation. Others may be used more rarely, but nonetheless constitute an important element in the mixed drink and cocktail repertoire

The following pages provide a brief guide to the range of non-alcoholic ingredients you will need to assemble if you are intending to test the full range of recipes in the third part of this book. You may have expected to buy fruit juices, sparkling drinks and syrups such as grenadine, but coffee, cocoa and block chocolate also play their parts. Good fresh mineral water is worth buying for mixing with fine Scotch, and you may decide to invest in a soda siphon.

Below: Fruit juices come in a huge variety of flavours these days, worth making the most of.

Right: Who would ever have thought that water would one day have its aficionados like wine? But it does.

Garnishing

As well as mixers, coffee and chocolate, there is the question of fruit garnishes. These are very much a matter of personal taste. The habit these days, and it is a wise one, is to keep garnishes nice and simple, and certain drinks don't need garnishing at all. Everybody remembers that first thrilling encounter in a cocktail bar with a drink that comes in a glass that looks like a flower vase, replete with slices of pineapple, wedges of citrus fruit and cherries on sticks, not to mention cocktail parasols and perhaps the odd fizzling sparkler. Apart from looking a trifle silly now, this over-the-top approach is not very sensible when making cocktails at home. If you've invited a few friends round, you'll spend the entire evening in the kitchen if you go to such extremes.

Slices and half-slices of citrus fruits are worth having to hand, as are twists of their peel pared off in spirals, and

you may want to invest in a jar of cocktail cherries (although even they aren't as popular now as they once were). That, apart from the odd Martini olive or slice of pineapple for the tropically inspired, rum-based recipes, is likely to be all you'll need. And perhaps coffee beans for the Sambucas.

Above: Coffee is the basis of many hot, alcohol-boosted after-dinner drinks, as well as being used iced in certain traditional cocktail recipes.

Water

The simplest of all mixers is the one that dilutes the strength of ardent spirits without altering the character of their basic flavour. Water is indispensable to whisky drinkers, who claim that it enhances rather than mutes the aromatic personalities of their favoured spirit. Water softens the olfactory impact of the alcohol, while allowing the complexities of grain, peat and wood to announce themselves. Pastis drinkers use plain water, too, since the cloudiness that gives the drinks their collective name can only be obtained by mixing. In all cases, good spring water or mineral water is preferable to heavily chlorinated tap water – especially so in the case of Highland and Lowland malts.

Below left: Badoit naturally sparkling mineral water comes from France.

Below right: Ty Nant is a Welsh mineral water that comes in a blue bottle.

Although the phenomenon would have been considered quite surreal a generation ago, something of a connoisseurship has arisen in the last few years with regard to bottled waters. Comparative tastings of spring waters and mineral waters from around the world are held, at which experts studiously roll one mouthful of water after another around their palates, looking for the telltale distinguishing characteristics in them, hoping to spot a slightly more obvious mineral content that would mark one sample out geographically from the next.

It is certainly the case that some waters have a distinctly higher presence of natural mineral salts than others. A celebrated example is the French mineral water Badoit, in such demand a few years ago that exports of it had to be rationed, and it is no longer available in retail outlets in the UK. It has a particularly salty, almost pungent flavour that is most definitely an acquired taste. Others occupy the other extreme of the spectrum, tasting as comfortingly neutral as one was always led to expect water to taste.

As a mixer for good spirits, completely neutral spring water should be used. In the case of single malt Scotch, the ideal water to choose is the one that the whisky itself was made with. Similarly, for a sparkling mixture, many people now prefer using a naturally effervescent, or even carbonated, water to the soda that was once traditional, and which is used extensively in the cocktail recipes that form the third part of this book. I still think soda has its place, but I can certainly see the attraction of sparkling spring water as an alternative. It definitely has a purer taste, by which I mean it has no taste at all.

Above left: Royal Deeside sparkling spring water is a Scottish product with an ultra-clean, pure taste.

Above right: Perrier from France is one of the most famous fizzy waters of them all, a superb palate-cleanser.

Should you doubt that different specimens of H_2O can taste different, try a comparative tasting of any bottled still spring water against what comes out of the kitchen tap. The presence of chlorine in the latter is quite a shock to the nose and tastebuds after the ethereal purity of the former.

Every now and then, some more or less alarming health hazard arises from tap water, which only goes to boost further the already explosively rising sales of bottled waters. Some authorities feel that if we carry on only drinking extremely pure water, we will dangerously lose much of our immunity to micro-organisms in the less pure variety.

Fruit juices

There are many different fruit juices, and blends of juices, on the market today, all of which can be pressed into service.

Orange juice
Of all the fruit juices, orange is probably the most important for mixing with single spirit shots, most notably with the white spirits that don't interfere with its colour. It is more versatile when used with more than one other ingredient in a cocktail, but when it does appear in a recipe, it will quite often be in conjunction with another fruit flavour, such as lemon or pineapple, or with a fizzy mixer. If you are buying commercial orange juice, the product to go for is the freshly squeezed or pressed article. The other stuff is made from concentrate, which is a dried fruit powder that has been reconstituted with tap water. All juices now are required to state on their packaging which kind they are.

Some squeezed orange juices make a virtue of having some fibrous fruit pulp left in them. From the cocktail point of view, these should be avoided, as pulp gets in the way of the correct composition of the drink. On the other hand, they do make for an extra-refreshing breakfast juice.

The best orange juice, as with all citrus juices, is the one you squeeze for yourself. It will have a noticeably thinner texture than packaged juice, but that is a welcome attribute to the cocktail maker. It makes for a less aggressive colour in the

Right: Orange juice labelled "squeezed" has not been reconstituted from powdered concentrate.

Above: Oranges are always best freshly squeezed at home, rather than coming from a carton.

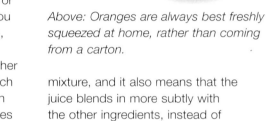

mixture, and it also means that the juice blends in more subtly with the other ingredients, instead of overwhelming them.

If you are prone to heartburn, or acid reflux, then you need to be careful with orange juice. It is exceptionally high in acidity. Lemon, lime, grapefruit and the smaller orange varieties such as clementines, satsumas, tangerines and mandarins are less acidic, but the regular orange is not your friend. A lemon may be sourer, but it has balancing alkalinity in it, whereas an orange contains just too much roaring, unadulterated acidity.

Lemon juice
Freshly squeezed lemon juice is undoubtedly the most versatile ingredient in the cocktail repertoire. The juice of lemons has the uncanny ability to accentuate the flavours of other fruits, almost in the manner of a seasoning (try tasting a fresh fruit purée with and without lemon juice to demonstrate this point), and so it complements the

fruit-flavoured liqueurs very well. Additionally, its sourness mitigates the syrupy sweetness of the traditional liqueurs.

Many of the classic cocktail recipes, such as Sours and Daiquiris, rely on lemon juice for their bite. Not only does it provide that all-important sour edge, but it disguises itself very obligingly. A cocktail with lemon juice in it very rarely tastes particularly lemony, unless a very generous measure has been used. It goes without saying that freshly pressed lemons are infinitely preferable to anything that comes in a bottle, or for that matter in a plastic container shaped like a lemon.

HOW TO SERVE
When drinking orange juice on its own, leave a little of the pulp to ensure a texturally interesting result. When mixing, it is better to strain the pulp out. Always drink fresh juice at once; don't keep it.

Right: Smooth-skinned lemons are best for juicing, as well as those with thin skins and relatively little pith.

Below: Limes have a sharper flavour than lemons. A little of their juice goes a long way.

Grapefruit juice

Grapefruit juice, with its bracing sourness, has more applications than you might anticipate in cocktail-making. Many of the modern recipes use it quite extensively. Pink grapefruit juice, with its slightly less acidic mien, is a particular boon, and should be used more often.

Other fruit juices

The more rarely encountered fruit juices, such as peach and apricot nectars, mango and passion fruit juice, diluted and sweetened cranberry drinks, and cherry and grape juices should all be used imaginatively in the cocktail repertoire. Tropical fruit flavours are especially good in rum-based cocktails.

In generous dilution and with plenty of ice, a lime and water (or soda) makes a fantastically thirst-quenching recourse on a hot day. It also serves its place with lager, adding a gentler note for palates that haven't quite got used to the bitter taste of the unmixed article.

Lime juice

Lime juice is even more sour, having a mere 0.5% natural sugar, and is used in drinks that should have a particularly biting tang. Unlike lemon, it advertises itself more assertively as a flavour, so that even half a measure in a welter of other ingredients makes its presence felt. Think of the limey tang in traditional Thai cooking, where it is one of the linchpins of the seasoning. To my mind, lime is a flavour that one can quickly have enough of, and if you are moving to a second cocktail after one that has had lime juice in it, it makes sense to choose a recipe without lime for the chaser.

As a cordial, lime is indelibly associated with one of the best-known British drink brands of all, Rose's.

Left: A bottle is the next best thing if fresh limes aren't available.

Pineapple juice

Pineapple makes a sweetly exotic element in some rum-based mixtures. Since the fruit itself is rather messy to prepare and so large, you will probably need to use packaged juice. Pineapple juice has breathtaking levels of natural sweetness, and it comes as something of a surprise to find 1920s cocktail recipes that use pineapple juice also adding a dash of sugar syrup. We rightly feel today that it doesn't need it.

Right: Pineapple juice is indispensable for many rum cocktails.

Above: A purée made of ripe apricots will work wonders with apricot brandy in a fruit Daiquiri, and bottled apricot nectar is a useful product too.

Tomato juice

The only juice that remains is tomato juice, which you may not find that useful. Until, that is, the morning comes when only a Bloody Mary will do, and then you'll be mighty glad you bought it. Only buy pure tomato juice, and not the varieties that have been pre-seasoned with Worcestershire sauce or salt, herbs or any sort of additive. Any seasoning you choose to add is up to you, the bartender.

Sparkling beverages

Fizzy drinks totally transform the character of a cocktail, whether they are neutral like soda, or assertively sharp like lemonade.

Soda water

To achieve the diluting effects of water without changing flavour, and to add a refreshing sparkle to a mixture, soda water is the required ingredient. At one time, no bar (or home, for that matter) was complete without a soda siphon. These were charged with tablets of sodium bicarbonate and dispensed a stream of bubbling water through a

Below left: Soda water in a bottle is the modern form of this staple cocktail ingredient.

Below right: A soda siphon was once an essential in all the best-equipped homes. They are efficient and fun to use.

pressurized nozzle. Nowadays, there is very little difference between bottled or canned soda and carbonated mineral water.

The siphon was an efficient means of keeping soda, as it allowed you to dispense it by one small squirt at a time. This was particularly useful for mixed drinks. Whisky and soda, Campari and soda, even a straightforward lime and soda, only needed a quick burst of the siphon. It came out fizzy and fresh, so that you didn't have to resort to the semi-flattened remains of an already opened bottle. The bicarbonate does give soda a slightly salty flavour, which was thought to add seasoning to a drink. Proprietary sparkling spring water really only introduces carbon dioxide and dilution.

If you are serious about testing out the full range of the cocktail repertoire, however, you will need to invest in some soda water. It is used widely, from old 19th-century recipes, through the Slings and Fizzes of the 1920s, and up to the more ostentatious creations of today.

Tonic water

Gin and tonic water go together like Fred Astaire and Ginger Rogers. A sweetened fizzy water flavoured with the bittering component, quinine, tonic is medicinally

Left: Tonic water isn't a very versatile cocktail ingredient, but many feel that gin would be nothing without it.

named for the anti-malarial properties it demonstrated in tropical climes. When first brought back to Europe from the Americas in the 17th century, quinine replaced the previously universal plant-derived liver tonic in European medicine, namely gentian. Tonic is useful not just with gin, but also with vodka and even calvados. Use it wherever the dryness of a drink can be made more appetizing with the addition of a little bitterness.

That said, tonic is probably the least useful of all the standard mixers when it comes to making cocktails, as its flavour is so assertive. Whatever bitterness it has also tends to be outweighed by the artificial sweeteners that are added to it, and to my tastebuds at least, these quickly cloy. One gin and tonic is usually enough. For that reason, you may find it as well to be fairly sparing when mixing with tonic. A half-and-half, or at a push two-thirds-to-one-third, mixture may be sufficient, as opposed to recklessly topping up a tall glass.

Lemonade

Far from being solely a children's drink, lemonade provides a useful way of administering citric sourness and fizz to a long drink. The best lemonades for bar use are not as sweet as the kids may like them. Some are actually still, in which case you may just as well use lemon juice and a pinch of sugar, or alternatively make your own still lemonade, following the recipe in this book.

Most of the recipes in which lemonade appears, though – and there are a surprising number of them – are

Above left: Lemonade adds sweetness, sharpness and fizz to a drink, but the home-made article is naturally still.

Above right: Coca-Cola is the first and most celebrated cola brand in the world, universally popular.

intended to be made with the fizzy variety. Go for one of those products that looks like the real thing, with an opaque, greyish-yellow appearance, rather than the crystal-clear products that just look like carbonated water.

Cola

All cola is derived from the invention of Coca-Cola in the United States in the late 19th century by one John Pemberton. The first version of a drink that was to become the most instantly recognizable multinational brand-name on the planet really was first mixed up in a tub in Mr Pemberton's back yard. There was very much a vogue for health-giving tonic beverages at the time, as indeed there is again today, and in some respects Coca-Cola can

be seen as the true forerunner of the isotonic sports drinks, vitaminized replacement drinks and energizing ginseng and guarana preparations of the modern era.

It was intended as a stimulating as well as a tonic drink, and included the ground nuts of the kola tree, along with crushed coca leaves. The latter are also the source of the drug cocaine, which was widely made illegal in the early years of the 20th century, and so the company removed them from the recipe. Rum and neutral vodka seem to be the main spirits with which cola mixes most happily, with coffee-flavoured Kahlúa and Tia Maria being its closest liqueur companions.

Cola is made by numerous rival companies today, and there is a kind of rudimentary connoisseurship among its drinkers, with some people, including children, genuinely able to tell one brand from another instantaneously. Not being able to get their preferred brand, and having to settle for another, causes as much distress to them as wine-drinkers face when confronted with the choice in the average pub or bar. Then there is a tiny minority of unusual people left in the world who can't stomach it in any form (the author, alas, included). Whether it's the sweetening, the aggressive carbonation, or just the flavour of the kola nut remains a mystery.

Right: Ginger ale is a traditional English summer concoction, working well as a mixer for basic Scotch, and with vodka and lime for a classic Moscow Mule.

Ginger ale

Also known as ginger beer, ginger ale also has its uses, with Scotch for example, and perhaps most famously with vodka and lime juice as a Moscow Mule. Vodka producer Smirnoff now makes a pre-mixed version of this drink, which appears to be a roughly reasonable approximation of the one you can make at home.

There is a long and distinguished folk history behind ginger ale in the English culinary tradition. It was brewed in country areas in centuries gone by not just as a refreshing summer tipple, but as a tonic remedy too. Ginger is good for aiding digestion, among a wide range of other medicinal applications, and as a spice it has always been held in great affection in the kitchen.

As with lemonade, there are both sparkling and still versions on the market. For cocktails, it's the sparkling you'll need, but go for one of the better brands. Fentiman's is a rightly celebrated example, full of the softly burning potency of this versatile spice. Some have a modicum of alcohol in them, which is not needed.

HOW TO SERVE
Ginger beer should be served on baking-hot summer days as an ice-cold drink in a tall glass. Some of the better brands will contain a little sediment, which is all to the good.

Syrups

Cocktail-making would not be quite what it is without the availability of a range of neutral or flavoured non-alcoholic syrups to add complexity and interest to a drink. Tastes in mixed drinks were often distinctly sweeter in the past than we might expect, and a dash, a teaspoon, even a half-measure of these products crops up quite regularly in older recipes.

Grenadine

The most famous of these syrups is grenadine, used to give a strong red colouring to otherwise clear mixtures, and to create the red-orange-yellow colour spectrum in the classic Tequila Sunrise. Grenadine is made principally from the juice of the pomegranate, the

Below: The principal flavour of grenadine is pomegranate.

peculiar Asiatic fruit that looks like a thick-skinned onion but, when cut, reveals a mass of jewel-like seeds within. It is thick, ruby-coloured and intensely sweet; some brands are made with a small alcohol quotient, but no more than about 3% ABV.

Grenadine, like all these products, should be used very sparingly, but it is an essential component of your starter kit, and you'll soon find that you won't get very far without it. Syrups are naturally loaded with sugar, so there is no need to worry about them going off. Even in the tiny measures in which it is used, you may be surprised how quickly you get through a bottle. Furthermore, grenadine is one of those ingredients for which there simply isn't any obvious alternative.

Orgeat

Orgeat is a much rarer syrup, although it was once used very widely in cocktails. It is flavoured with almonds and it adds that telltale taste of marzipan to a drink, even when used in very sparing quantities. Its name derives from the French word *orge*, meaning "barley", which was once one of its ingredients.

A few popular cockail recipes call for orgeat syrup. If you can't get hold of it, you can approximate the flavour of it by adding a similar quantity of amaretto, or other sweet almond liqueur. The only potential problem is that you will then be considerably increasing the quotient of alcohol in the drink, which in turn upsets the balance of flavours. The point of the syrups is that they added sweetness and flavour to a drink without strengthening the final mixture.

Left: Orgeat is an almond-flavoured syrup once widely used in cocktails.

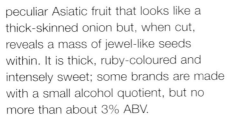

Above left: Kiwi-flavoured syrup would make a fine addition to one of the exotic, rum-based cocktail recipes.

Above right: A syrup flavoured with passion fruit should be used sparingly, but proves to be a surprisingly versatile cocktail ingredient.

Fruit syrups

Other syrups, flavoured with a whole greengrocer's shop of exotic ingredients, are now available. Pineapple, peach, apricot, strawberry, banana, even kiwi fruit are produced, and can add an appetizing dash of fruit flavour to a mixed drink, without the extra alcohol that the equivalent liqueurs bring.

These products may come in handy when making a drink that is based on a liquidization of fresh fruit. They help to concentrate the flavour. I haven't by and large given indications for them in the recipes in the third part of the book, as they should be left very much up the the individual user's discretion. If you do resort to fruit syrups, though – perhaps because a particular batch of fruit is not quite as full-flavoured as you might have hoped – use them only in very small quantities. They really are extremely sugary.

Sirop de gomme

Sugar syrup was used quite widely in cocktail recipes in the era before the huge range of sweet liqueurs that we know today was generally available.

Below left: Peach and passion fruit is an enticing combination that would work well added to a summer fruit cup.

Below right: Summer berries cordial is just asking to be added to some light red wine in a summer punch concoction.

Left: Gomme is simply a straight sugar and water syrup.

It is possible to buy a bottled neutral sugar syrup called gomme (from the French word for "gum"), but as it consists only of sugar and water, it is easy to make your own. The sugar solution should be boiled briefly, just until the texture of it has begun to turn syrupy, and then removed from the heat and left to cool. Large quantities can then be bottled, and used as needed.

As it is only used in small doses, however, the neutral sweetening element that sugar syrup contributes can be just as easily derived from adding 2.5ml/½ tsp caster (superfine) sugar to a drink. Use caster sugar for its finer grains, which dissolve more readily. (It is possible to turn ordinary granulated sugar into something a little finer than commercial caster by whizzing it briefly in a dry liquidizer.)

Tinned fruits

Although health-conscious shoppers go for fruits in natural juices now, the sort that are canned in syrup ("light" or "heavy") are still of course widely available. Drain off some of these syrups as a more economical replacement for bottled syrups. The canning liquors from tinned peaches, apricots and pineapple are all very handy.

HOW TO SERVE
Grenadine not only adds a vivid red colour to a cocktail, but it was also one of the main sweetening agents in an otherwise dry, spirity cocktail.

The almond flavour of orgeat syrup works well with fruit juices. Use amaretto as a near substitute.

It isn't always necessary to buy a bottled syrup. The juice from a tin of fruit in syrup will often do.

Coffee

Ever since its migration from Abyssinia (present-day Ethiopia) to Arabia many centuries ago, the coffee bean has played a multifaceted role in moulding history. That short hop across the Red Sea helped to alter social, political and economic life not only in Africa and the Middle East, but in mainland Europe, Britain and the Americas too. Coffee has made the fortunes and misfortunes of many, oiled the wheels of communication, inspired creative minds, stimulated the tired and, for countless imbibers the world over, become a daily necessity.

Coffee comes from the fruit of an evergreen shrub that flourishes in tropical and subtropical regions around the world. The trees produce delicate clusters of jasmine-scented blossoms, and fruit known as "cherries". Cocooned in each cherry, protected by pulp and parchment, are two coffee beans. Since around 4000 beans are needed to produce one pound of roasted coffee, few commodities require so much human effort.

Below: Colombian is one of the mildest and freshest varieties of coffee.

Below: Illy is an internationally renowned Italian brand.

Right: Coffee beans are best bought whole, and freshly ground for each brew.

Below: A medium-grind coffee gives a smoother drink.

As with the discovery of the plant and its journey to Arabia, the process of development from food to hot beverage is a matter of historical speculation.

The comments of early European explorers and botanists indicate that the Ethiopians chewed raw coffee beans, obviously appreciative of their stimulating effect. They also pounded ripe coffee cherries, mixed them with animal fat and moulded the resulting paste into pellets. This powerful cocktail of fat, caffeine and meat protein was a vital source of concentrated energy. The cherries were probably eaten as a ripe fruit, too, since the pulp is sweet and contains caffeine.

It seems possible that coffee was treated as a food in Arabia, too, and only later mixed with water to make a drink. The earliest version of the beverage was probably a liquid produced by steeping a few whole hulls in cold water. Later, the hulls were roasted over an open fire, and then boiled in water for about 30 minutes until a pale yellow liquid was produced.

By about AD 1000, the drink was still a relatively crude decoction made with green coffee beans and their hulls. It was probably not until around the 13th century that the beans were dried before use. They were laid out in the sun, and, once dry, could be stored for longer periods. After that, it was a small step to roasting them over a charcoal fire.

Coffee as a stimulant

Once in Europe, coffee became a vital part of the pharmacopoeia used by 17th-century doctors, chemists, herbalists and even midwives. Caffeine's qualities as a stimulant did not go unnoticed, even then. One

Below: Coffee in a can from Japan, a very modern product.

Dr Thornton was to assert: "A cup of Coffee strengthens and exhilarates our mental and bodily faculties; and nothing can be more refreshing either to the studious or the laborious."

Among coffee's opponents was an Italian medical writer, Sinibaldi. He stated: "[Coffee] has contributed most shockingly to the destruction of our constitutions... it produces debility, alters gastric juice, disorders digestion, and often produces convulsions, palsy of the limbs and vertigo."

The medical debate was to continue for many years, as doctors, pursuing new avenues of insight, argued the pros and cons of coffee, claiming it to be alternatively therapeutic and detrimental to the body and mind. This debate still continues today.

Coffee drinking today

Recent times have seen the development of speciality coffee shops, selling fine single-estate beans, treated as seriously as fine wine. Developing alongside them came a rash of modern coffee houses – the antithesis of the 1950s coffee bar – styled on minimalist lines and selling an extensive choice of coffee from around the world. Then there are the seemingly ubiquitous branches of American chains such as Starbucks, where coffee is sold in a variety of different presentations of Italian derivation, from long, hot, milky *latte* to small shots of black *ristretto*, the super-strength version of espresso.

The art of brewing coffee

From the moment coffee-drinking took hold, an enormous amount of ingenuity and effort went into perfecting the art of brewing. Not content with the simple act of pouring hot water over grounds and letting it sit, inventive minds in Europe and the United States managed to produce an astonishing variety of equipment: drips, filters, percolators and pressure machines, to name but a few.

One of the earliest devices was the cafetière, which made its debut in France around 1685. Its use became widespread throughout the reign of Louis XV. It was no more than a simple jug (carafe) with a heating plate warmed by a spirit lamp below. It was superseded in about 1800 by the first percolator, invented by Jean Baptiste de Belloy, the Archbishop of Paris. In Belloy's cafetière, the ground coffee was held in a perforated container at the top of the pot and hot water was poured over it. The water passed through the small holes in the container and into the pot below.

The cafetière still manages to produce a better cup of coffee than the elaborate coffee filter-machine that preceded it in British homes. Because the water only dribbles through it in a thin stream, a lot of the coffee in the filter paper doesn't get properly used, whereas in the cafetière, it is all sitting in the hot water. Not only that, but the filter machine doesn't boil the water properly, resulting in a

Above: Carte Noire Expresso is made exclusively from fine arabica beans.

Left: Lavazza is a good Italian arabica brand.

tepid brew. Going back for another cup from the jug after it has been sitting on the warm plate for an hour or so produces only a stewed, lukewarm drink. Note, however, that water should be allowed to come off the boil before adding to coffee beans; boiling water scalds them and spoils the taste.

Coffee mixes so very well with alcohol (and indeed makes the basis for some appetizing non-alcoholic mixtures) that we have included plenty of recipes for it. Dark-roast ground coffee is the best type for the great majority of these recipes.

HOW TO SERVE

A cup of normal espresso laced with an alcoholic spirit or liqueur is a favoured preparation in Italy, where a little sugar and even lemon zest may also be added.

Chocolate

One of the greatest discoveries in gastronomic history was the bean of the cocoa tree *Theobroma cacao*, the original source of chocolate. Smooth in texture, intense in taste, subtly perfumed and elegant to behold, chocolate is a rich source of sensory pleasure, adored by almost everyone.

It was Spanish colonists in the 17th century who, encountering chocolate use among the Aztecs in Mexico, first brought it back to Europe. It then followed the continental trade routes up to northern Europe, before making its way back across the Atlantic to the United States and Canada.

Initially known purely as a drink, as it had been among the Aztecs, chocolate soon became all the rage in the fashionable circles of most of the western European capitals. It made its debut as a hot beverage at almost exactly the same time as coffee and tea arrived, and speciality cafés and even gentlemen's clubs were established, specifically catering to a taste for one or the other of these beverages. The Cocoa Tree was the first London café establishment to specialize in hot chocolate.

Not only was chocolate valued for its stimulant properties (its essential alkaloid, theobromine, is a very efficient substance in this regard, and of course it also contains caffeine), it was also touted for a while as an aphrodisiac. Virtually all newly introduced foodstuffs following the discovery of the Americas, from the potato to the Jerusalem artichoke, were fanfared in this way at one time or another, but in chocolate's case, the image has never quite gone

Above: Chocolat Charbonnel is a premium French brand of instant drinking chocolate, with a particularly satisfying, rich flavour.

away. A box of chocolates is still seen as a romantic gift, and there is moreover a peculiar sensuousness to fine chocolate that no other confection can boast.

By the mid-18th century, chocolate had become more widely available and was often brought into Switzerland (eventually to become one of the great chocolate-producing nations of Europe) by travelling Italian merchants, known as *cioccolatieri*, who sold it at fairs and markets.

A colourful American chocolate producer was Domingo Ghirardelli, an Italian confectioner with useful South American connections. The Ghirardelli company was the first in America to make easily dissolvable powdered cocoa, which was another landmark stage in the continuing commercialization of chocolate.

Above: Ghirardelli makes easily dissolvable powdered cocoa.

Cocoa

This rich, strong, dark powder is made by extracting some of the cocoa butter during chocolate production. What remains is a block containing around 20% cocoa butter, but this varies with each manufacturer. The cocoa is then ground and mixed with sugar and starch. The addition of starch means that cocoa needs to be cooked briefly

Left: Quality blocks of white, milk and dark chocolate.

Above:
A layered bar
of plain, white
and milk chocolate.

to remove the raw, floury taste. This can be done by mixing it to a paste with a little boiling water, which is the usual technique when making a hot drink with it. If a richer mixture is required, it will probably be mixed with hot milk.

The very best cocoa is produced in Holland. It is alkalized, a process that removes the acidity and produces a cocoa with a mellow, well-rounded flavour. The technique was devised by the manufacturer, Van Houten, some 150 years ago and this is still the very best cocoa available. Although it is

more expensive than some other brands, it is definitely worth using for chocolate-flavoured cocktails.

It is always worth using true cocoa in the chocolate drink recipes provided in the third part of this book. The alternative, drinking chocolate, is a vastly inferior product, contains a much higher ratio of sugar to cocoa solids, and is really only suitable for children.

Garnishing with chocolate

As well as using cocoa as the basis for a chocolate drink, many of the cocktail recipes that use chocolate liqueurs are garnished with a sprinkling of grated chocolate. Always use a fine real chocolate for this purpose, and preferably one with a cocoa solids reading in the 60–70% range. Grate it roughly into coarse flakes so that its flavour is more readily appreciated. For more of a chocolate hit, pour a small quantity of good melted chocolate on to a baking tray, allow it to cool and then chisel it carefully away in long curls with the point of a knife.

Chocolate-coated coffee beans have become quite fashionable of late as an alternative to traditional petits fours. They too can be served on a chocolate cocktail, or perhaps as an exciting variation on the ordinary coffee beans served in a flaming Sambuca. They are naturally quite crunchy, but have the extra caffeine kick of the chocolate coating.

Left: Cadbury drinking chocolate is one of the most popular everyday brands for a sweet hot chocolate.

HOW TO SERVE

Whole block chocolate can be dissolved with hot milk and brown sugar to make a highly refined hot chocolate drink. It is particularly popular in Spain and Mexico.

Below: These bars of Lindt chocolate have a very high cocoa content.

Bartending techniques

In this part of the book, we shall find out what props and paraphernalia are needed to set up your own professional-looking bartending operation at home. After going through the bartender's equipment, and types of glasses and garnishes commonly used, we'll learn how to measure, mix and pour, and how to plan and carry off a successful cocktail party. We'll end with some useful advice on avoiding or mitigating the unwanted after-effects of such an occasion.

Bartending equipment

To make a successful cocktail bartender, you will need a few essential pieces of equipment. The most vital and flamboyant is the cocktail shaker, but what you have on hand in the kitchen can usually stand in for the rest. After a while, though, you may find the urge to invest in some of the following specialist pieces of equipment.

Measuring jug

Cocktail shakers usually come with standard measures for apportioning out the ingredients. These may be small cups, or something shaped like a double trumpet, one side of which is a whole measure, the other half. If you don't have one, then use a jug for measuring out the required quantities. The measurements can be in single (25ml/1fl oz) or double (50ml/2fl oz) bar measures. Do not switch from one type of measurement to another within the same recipe.

Below: Measuring jug and spoon measures.

Left: Cocktail shaker.

Below: Measure.

Measure

Be sure to buy a shaker that comes with a measure, known in American parlance as a "jigger". They usually come as a single-piece double cup, with one side a whole measure and the other a half. Once you have established the capacity of the two sides, you will save a great deal of bother apportioning out ingredients in a measuring jug. It also looks a lot more professional than using spoons.

Cocktail shaker

The shaker is used for drinks that need good mixing, but don't have to be crystal-clear. Once the ingredients have been thoroughly amalgamated in the presence of ice, the temperature clouds up the drink. Cocktail shakers are usually made of stainless steel, but can also be silver, hard plastic or tough glass. The Boston shaker is made of two cup-type containers that fit over each other, one normally made of glass, the other

of metal. This type is often preferred by professional bartenders. For beginners, the classic three-piece shaker is easier to handle, with its base to hold the ice and liquids, a top fitted with a built-in strainer and a tight-fitting cap. Make sure you hold on to that cap while you are shaking. As a rough rule, the drink is ready when the shaker has become almost too painfully cold to hold, which is generally not more than around 15–20 seconds.

Blender or liquidizer

Goblet blenders are the best shape for mixing cocktails that need to be aerated, as well as for creating frothy cocktails or ones made with finely crushed ice. Attempting to break up whole ice cubes in the blender may very well blunt the blades. Opt for an

Below: Blender.

ice bag or tea-towel, a rolling pin and plenty of brute force, or better still, use an ice crusher.

Ice bags

These plastic bags that can be filled with water and frozen are a kind of disposable ice tray. You simply press each piece of ice out of them, tearing through the plastic as you go. They also have the advantage of making a more rounded piece of ice, as opposed to the hard-angled cube that an ice tray produces.

Ice crusher

If the prospect of breaking up ice with a hammer and dish towel comes to seem almost as much of a penance as working on a chain gang, an ice-crushing machine is the answer. It comes in two parts. You fill the top with whole ice cubes, put the lid on and, while pressing down on the top, turn the gramophone-type handle on the

Below: Wooden hammer and towel.

side. Take the top half off to retrieve the crystals of ice "snow" from the lower part. Crushed ice is used to fill the glasses for drinks that are to be served frappé. It naturally melts very quickly, though, compared to cubes.

Wooden hammer

Use a wooden hammer for crushing ice. The end of a wooden rolling pin works just as well.

Ice bag or towel

A towel or bag is essential for holding ice cubes when crushing, whether you are creating roughly cracked lumps or a fine snow. It must be scrupulously clean and fresh for each repeated use.

Ice bucket and chiller bucket

An ice bucket with a close-fitting lid is useful if you are going to be making several cocktails in quick succession. They are not completely hermetic though, and ice will eventually melt in them, albeit a little more slowly

than if left at room temperature. It should not be confused with a chiller bucket for bottles of champagne and white wine, which is bigger and has handles on the sides, but doesn't have a lid. A chiller bucket is intended to be filled with iced water, as opposed to ice alone.

Left: Ice crusher.

Right: Chiller bucket.

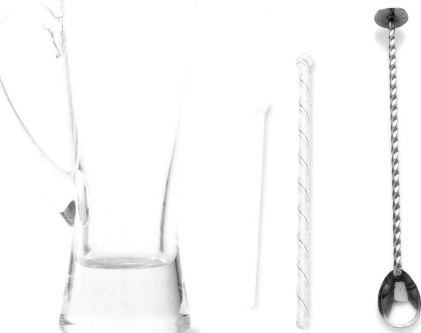

Above: Mixing pitcher and muddlers.

Above: Bar spoon.

Mixing pitcher or bar glass

It is useful to have a container in which to mix and stir drinks that are not shaken. The glass or pitcher should be large enough to hold two or three drinks. This vessel is intended for drinks that are meant to be clear, not cloudy.

Muddler

A long stick with a bulbous end, the muddler is used for crushing sugar or mint leaves, and so is particularly useful when creating juleps or smashes. A variety of sizes is available. It should be used like a pestle in a mixing jug; the smaller version is for use in an individual glass. At a pinch, a flattish spoon can be used instead of a muddler, but then you will find it more awkward to apply

Right: Strainer.

sideways rather than downward pressure when trying to press those mint leaves.

Bar spoon

These long-handled spoons can reach to the bottom of the tallest tumblers and are used in jugs, or for mixing the drink directly in the glass. Some varieties look like a large swizzle-stick, with a long handle and a disc at one end. They also look considerably more elegant than a dessert spoon.

Strainer

Used for pouring drinks from a shaker or mixing jug into a cocktail glass, the strainer's function is to remove the ice with which the drink has been prepared. Some drinks are served with the ice in (or "on the rocks") but most aren't, the reason being that you don't want the ice to unhelpfully dilute the drink. The best strainer, known professionally as a

Hawthorn strainer, is made from stainless steel and looks like a flat spoon with holes and a curl of wire on the underside. It is held over the top of the glass to keep the ice and any other solid ingredients back.

Corkscrew

The fold-up type of corkscrew is known as the Waiter's Friend, and incorporates a can opener and bottle-top flipper as well as the screw itself. It is the most useful version to have to hand as it suits all purposes. The spin-handled corkscrew with a blade for cutting foil is the best one for opening fine wines.

Right: Corkscrew.

Sharp knife and squeezer

Citrus fruit is essential in countless cocktails. A good quality, sharp knife is required for halving the fruit, and the squeezer for extracting its juice. Although fruit juice presses are quicker to use, they are more expensive and more boring to wash up afterwards.

Below: Sharp knife and squeezer.

Left: Nutmeg grater.

Right: Zester and canelle knife.

Nutmeg grater

A tiny grater with small holes, for grating nutmeg over egg-nogs, frothy and creamy drinks. If this sounds too fiddly, buy ready-ground nutmeg instead. It's almost as good.

Zester and canelle knife

These are used for presenting fruit attractively to garnish glasses. If you don't already have them, don't feel obliged to run out and buy them, since drinks can look equally attractive with simply sliced fruit. The zester has a row of tiny holes that remove the top layer of skin off a citrus fruit when dragged across it (although the finest gauge on your multi-purpose grater was also designed for just this job). A canelle knife (from the French word for a "channel" or "groove") is for making decorative stripes in the skins of a whole fruit. When sliced, they then have a groovy-looking serrated edge. It is, in effect, a narrow-gauged version of a traditional potato peeler, but is purely for decorative purposes.

Egg whisk

Use a whisk to beat a little frothy texture into egg white before you add it to the shaker. It helps the texture of the finished drink no end. An ordinary balloon whisk will do the trick, although for culinary uses, a rotary whisk with a handle (or the electric specimen) is best.

Straws, swizzle-sticks and cocktail sticks

These decorative items are used to add the finishing touches to a cocktail. It was once considered axiomatic to drink all cocktails through straws. They tend now to be the exception rather than the rule. The flavours of the drink are better appreciated if it is poured directly into the mouth, as opposed to being sucked up in a thin stream. A mythical belief that the alcohol took effect more quickly if taken through straws was responsible for their popularity in the 1980s.

A swizzle-stick is useful for stirring a drink, and may be substituted by such food items as a stick of celery in a Bloody Mary, or a length of whole cinnamon for a short creamy cocktail or a hot, spicy drink such as mulled wine or ale.

Cocktail sticks are purely decorative and are used for holding ingredients such as cherries or other items of fruit that would otherwise sink to the bottom of the glass.

And if you intend to eat the cherry or olive, it's handier if it's already speared, so that you don't have to commit the appalling faux pas of dipping a finger into the drink to catch it.

Above: Egg whisk.

Right: Cocktail sticks.

Left: Swizzle-sticks.

Glasses

To ensure that glasses are sparkling clean, they should always be washed and dried with a glass cloth. Although some recipes suggest chilled glasses, don't put best crystal in the freezer; leave it at the back of the refrigerator instead. An hour should be enough.

Cocktail glass or Martini glass

This elegant glass is a wide conical bowl on a tall stem: a design that keeps cocktails cool by keeping warm hands away from the drink. It is by far the most widely used glass, so a set is essential. The design belies the fact that the capacity of this glass is relatively small (about three standard measures). Uses: the classic Martini and its variations, and almost any short, sharp, strong cocktail, including creamy ones.

Collins glass

The tallest of the tumblers, narrow with perfectly straight sides, a Collins glass holds about 350ml/12fl oz, and is usually used for serving long drinks made with fresh juices or finished with a sparkling mixer such as soda. This glass can also stand in as the highball glass, which is traditionally slightly less tall. Uses: Tom Collins, and all drinks that are to be "topped up" with anything.

Old-fashioned glass, tumbler or rocks glass

Classic, short whisky tumblers are used for shorter drinks, served on the rocks, and generally for drinks that are stirred rather than shaken. They should hold about 250ml/8fl oz. Uses: Old-Fashioned, Manhattan, Sours, etc.

Liqueur glass

Tiny liqueur glasses were traditionally used to serve small measures of unmixed drinks, and hold no more than 80ml/3fl oz. They are a good alternative for making a pousse-café or layered cocktail. They are best not used for serving measures of fortified wines such as sherry, port and madeira, where they will look ridiculously mean.

Above: Tumbler.

Above: Liqueur glass.

Brandy balloon or snifter

The brandy glass is designed to trap the fragrance of the brandy in the bowl of the glass. Cupping the glass in the palm of the hand further helps to warm it gently and release its aromas. Not now considered the thing to use for best cognac, it nonetheless makes a good cocktail glass for certain short, strong drinks that have been stirred rather than shaken. The wide bowl makes them suitable for drinks with solids floating in them.

Below: Large cocktail glass.

Below: Collins glass.

Below: Cocktail glass.

Below: Brandy balloon.

Above: Champagne flute.   *Above: Champagne saucer.*   *Above: Red wine glass.*   *Above: White wine glass.*

Large cocktail goblet or poco

Available in various sizes and shapes, large cocktail goblets are good for serving larger frothy drinks, or drinks containing puréed fruit or coconut cream. Classically, they are the glasses for Piña Coladas. The wider rims leave plenty of room for flamboyant and colourful decorations.

Champagne flute

The champagne flute is the more acceptable glass to use for quality sparkling wines. It is more efficient at conserving the bubbles since there is less surface area for them to break on. It should be used for champagne cocktails too. Always choose one with good depth, as the shorter ones look too parsimonious.

Champagne saucer

The old-fashioned saucer glass may be frowned on now for champagne, but it is an attractive and elegant design and can be used for a number of cocktails, particularly those that have cracked ice floating in them. Because of the wider surface area, there is plenty of scope for fruity garnishes too.

Red wine glass

The most useful size of wine glass, the red wine glass holds about 500ml/ 16fl oz. It should only be filled about a third full to allow the wine to be swirled around, so that it releases its bouquet. It can be used for long wine cocktails too, and will do at a pinch as a stand-in for the large cocktail goblet.

White wine glass

A long-stemmed, medium-sized glass of about 250ml/8fl oz capacity, a white wine glass should be held by the stem so as not to warm the chilled wine or cocktail with the heat of the hand. Use it for short wine cocktails such as spritzers and wine-based punches.

Pousse-café

A thin and narrow glass standing on a short stem, a pousse-café is used for floating or layering liqueurs one on top of the other. If you haven't got one, use a liqueur glass or even an old-fashioned sherry schooner instead. This is not a type of drink you are likely to be making very often. Although they look impressive, the novely does rather wear off.

Shot glass

A tiny glass with a capacity of no more than 50ml/2fl oz, the shot glass is used for those very short, lethally strong cocktails known as shooters. If you're going to make a shooter, this is absolutely the only glass to use. No substitute will be accepted. The glass itself is usually extremely thick, as these drinks are intended to be thrown back in one, and then the glass slammed down fairly peremptorily on the bar counter. Go for it.

Below: Pousse-café.

Below: Shot glass.

Garnishes

It is far more elegant not to overdress cocktails, otherwise they all too quickly turn into a fruit salad with a drink attached. Less is best. The edible extras suggested on these pages add colour, flavour and visual interest to any glass.

Frosting

Frosting glasses with salt, sugar or cocoa is a simple but effective touch. It is extremely quick and easy, and means that the drink needs no other decoration.

Salt is absolutely indispensable for frosting the rim of a textbook Margarita, and is normally done with lime juice. For a sweet drink, sugar frosting makes for an appealingly festive look. It is appropriate for drinks such as Royal Silver, Golden Start and Brandy Crusta.

Left:
Many kinds of sugar can be added to drinks: soft brown, demerara, dark muscovado, sugar cubes, cane sugar and caster (superfine) sugar.

SALT
A traditional Margarita should always have salt around the rim of the glass. To do this, rub the rim of the glass with a wedge of fresh lime and then dip the glass in fine salt. This example has an additional twist of cucumber rind as a garnish – but try not to over-garnish your drinks. Less is more.

SUGAR AND SYRUP
This champagne saucer was dipped into a shallow bowl of grenadine, then dipped into caster (superfine) sugar to create a frosted rim. The grenadine makes the sugar go bright pink. The glass was then placed in the refrigerator so that it was well chilled before being filled.

SUGAR AND FRUIT JUICE
It is possible to frost a glass with any fruit that goes with the drink. For example, this drink consists of Galliano mixed with a variety of fruit juices and coconut cream. The rim of the glass has been dipped in pineapple juice, then covered in a fine coating of caster (superfine) sugar.

Alternatively, a dark brown frosting of cocoa powder can be applied to a glass for Brandy Alexander, Cara Sposa or any other creamy cocktail flavoured with chocolate, coffee or orange.

To frost a glass, tip the rim of the glass in water, egg white, citrus juice or one of the syrups, and then dip it again in the chosen frosting. The garnish will take on the colour of the liquid.

Citrus fruits

Edible garnishes should reflect the various contents of the cocktail. Citrus fruit is widely used because it is appetizing to look at, and can

be cut in advance and kept covered in the refrigerator for a day until needed. Whole slices cut halfway through can be balanced on the rim of a highball glass, while half-slices are best used for floating in a cocktail glass. Apple, pear and banana are also suitable, but they do discolour on exposure to the air; dip them in lemon juice first to preserve colour and flavour.

Lemon is probably the most important fruit of all for the bartender. It is handy in everything from a simple gin and tonic to almost any cocktail.

A lime is small enough for you to be able to use whole slices to garnish a sharp-tasting cocktail containing its juice, such as a Moscow Mule.

Orange is indispensable for garnishing not just orange-flavoured drinks, but old-time mixtures of vermouth and spirit, such as Negroni.

Kumquats are bitter little citrus fruits, which are eaten with the skin on. Use half of one on a stick to garnish a cocktail that has some bitter orange flavour in it.

Above: Oranges.

Left: Kumquats.

Left: Limes.

Left: Lemons.

USING CITRUS FRUITS
A twisted half-slice of lemon adds an elegant decoration to any cocktail containing lemon juice.

A simple twist of lime looks effective and adds to the taste of a tequila, banana and lime cocktail.

Grated orange rind goes well with drinks containing orange, such as this creamy chocolatey-orange Tuaca and orange curaçao cocktail.

Soft fruits

Fresh soft fruit such as strawberries, cherries, peaches, apricots, blackberries and redcurrants make fabulous splashes of colour and add a delicious flavour, although they still tend to be mainly available in the summer.

Quartered large strawberries or, better still, the whole, small, wild variety, such as the French *fraises des bois*, would look good on a Strawberry Kiss.

Whole fresh cherries, particularly the black varieties, can be used in place of standard cocktail cherries from a jar to adorn a drink containing cherry brandy or kirsch. Singapore Sling contains the former, Rose the latter. The maraschino cherry is a popular option too, even though it is seen as something of a cliché these days.

A thin slice of very ripe peach is appropriate for a drink containing peach schnapps or peach brandy, such as Sparkling Peach Melba. White peach is best.

If there's apricot brandy in the drink (for example, Festival), a thin slice of apricot will work well. Use only juicy-ripe fruits though. The French Bergeron is a good variety.

Blackberries are the only garnish to use for a Blackberry and Champagne Crush, so long as they're in season.

The endless supply of tropical fruits available all year long, such as mango, pineapple, star fruit, papaya, physalis and the various types of melon, offers numerous decorative ideas and combinations for garnishing. A twiglet of redcurrants, perhaps with a little sugar frosting, makes a rather Christmassy-looking garnish. Physalis is a favourite garnish for modern desserts. Bring it into the cocktail repertoire too for exotically flavoured drinks.

Below: Cherries.

Below: Strawberries.

Above: Peaches.

Left: Apricots.

Below: Blackberries.

USING SOFT FRUITS
A cherry and an apricot slice can be skewered with a cocktail stick to make a stylish, fruity garnish.

Above: Redcurrants.

Below: Physalis.

*Above:
Chocolate.*

Above: Nutmeg.

*Below: Cherry
tomatoes.*

*Above: Red
chillies.*

Above: Green and black olives.

*Right:
Mint.*

Above: Celery.

USING OTHER GARNISHES
A sprig of fresh mint adds
freshness to drinks such as this
Long Island Iced Tea, or anything
containing crème de menthe.

Grated dark chocolate adds flavour
to sweet cocktails such as this gin,
banana and cream mixture.

Whole cinnamon sticks can be
used as stirrers for hot drinks such
as coffee or hot chocolate.

Other garnishes

Not all garnishes and decorations need
be fruit, however. A block of chocolate
can be grated over a drink, or melted
and scraped into chocolate curls, to
decorate a cocktail such as Iced Mint
and Chocolate Cooler.

Ground (or whole) cinnamon makes
an appropriate garnish for hot mulled
wine or punch.

Nutmeg goes well with egg-nogs
and flips. Either grate whole nutmegs,
or add the powdered version to the
surface of cream cocktails containing
chocolate or coffee flavours. A Brandy
Alexander cries out for nutmeg.

To some, green olives are
indispensable in a Dry Martini; to others,
they are anathema. When Martinis do

call for a green olive, always opt for
those packaged in brine, not in oil.

Plain or chilli-pepper vodka can
stand up to pickled chillies, while the
Martini variant known as a Gibson
would not be a Gibson without a white
pearl onion.

Red chillies should certainly set
the palate alight in a drink already
containing pepper vodka.

Cherry tomatoes are an interesting
alternative for garnishing a Bloody Mary,
while celery is the Bloody Mary's very
own swizzle-stick.

As well as forming an integral
ingredient in some cocktails, a sprig
of fresh mint makes an appealing
garnish, perhaps to the creamy,
mint-flavoured Grasshopper.

Tricks and techniques of the trade

It is worth mastering the techniques for the preparation of good-looking drinks. The following pages give you precise directions for some of the essential procedures, such as crushing ice, as well as some not-so-essential skills, such as making decorative ice cubes. Mastering these tricks of the trade is what will distinguish the dedicated bartender from the amateur dabbler.

Crushing ice

Some cocktails require cracked or crushed ice for adding to glasses, or a finely crushed ice "snow" for blending. It isn't a good idea to break ice up in a blender or food processor as you may find it damages the blades. Instead:

1 Lay out a cloth, such as a clean glass cloth or dishtowel, on a work surface, and cover half of it with ice cubes. (If you wish, you can also use a cloth ice bag.)

2 Fold the cloth over and, using the end of a rolling pin, or better still a wooden mallet of the sort used for tenderizing meat, smash down on the ice firmly several times, until you achieve the required fineness.

3 Spoon the ice into glasses or a pitcher. Fine ice snow must be used immediately because it melts away like morning mist, but cracked or roughly crushed ice can be stored in the freezer in plastic bags. Stay up all night with a sledgehammer, and you should have enough to do a moderate-sized social gathering. Alternatively, just buy an ice crusher.

Making decorative ice cubes

Decorative ice cubes can instantly jolly up the simplest of cocktails. Flavour and colour the water with fruit juices or bitters, and freeze in three stages.

1 Half-fill each compartment of an ice cube tray with water and place in the freezer for 2–3 hours, or until the water has frozen.

2 Prepare the fruit, olives, mint leaves, lemon rind, raisins or borage flowers and dip each briefly in water. Place in the ice-cube trays, put in the freezer and freeze again.

3 Top up the ice-cube trays with water and return to the freezer to freeze completely. Use as required, but only in one drink at each session.

Frosting glasses

The appearance and taste of a cocktail are enhanced if the rims of the glasses are frosted. Use celery salt, grated coconut, grated chocolate, coloured sugars or cocoa for an eye-catching effect. Once it is frosted, place the glass in the refrigerator to chill until needed, if you have time.

1 Hold the glass upside down, so the juice does not run down the glass. Rub the rim of the glass with the cut surface of a lemon, lime, orange or even a slice of fresh pineapple.

2 Keeping the glass upside down, dip the rim into a shallow layer of sugar, coconut or salt. Redip the glass, if necessary, and turn it so that the rim is well-coated.

3 Stand the glass upright and let it sit until the sugar, coconut or salt has dried on the rim, then chill.

Bartending know-how
Instead of using fruit juice as the frosting liquid, you can rub a glass rim with egg white instead.

Shaking cocktails

Cocktails that contain sugar syrups or creams require more than just a stir; they are combined and chilled with a brief shake. Remember that it is possible to shake only one or two servings at once, so you may have to work quickly in batches. Always use fresh ice each time.

1 Add four or five ice cubes to the shaker and pour in all the ingredients.

2 Put the lid on the shaker. Hold the shaker firmly in one hand, keeping the lid in place with the other hand.

3 Shake vigorously for about 15 seconds to blend simple concoctions, and for 20–30 seconds for drinks with sugar syrups, cream or egg. By this time, the shaker should feel extremely cold.

4 Remove the small cap and pour into the prepared glass, using a strainer if the shaker is not already fitted with one.

Bartending know-how

Never shake anything sparkling, whether lemonade or best champagne. It will flatten it.

Making twists

As an alternative to slices of the fruit, many drinks are garnished with a twist of orange, lemon or lime rind. The most famous one is Horse's Neck, but twists are useful in many other recipes. They should be made before the drink itself is prepared, so that you don't keep a cold cocktail waiting. Here's how:

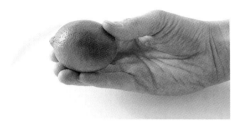

1 Choose a fruit with an unblemished skin and a regular shape.

2 Using a canelle knife or potato peeler, start at the tip of the fruit and start peeling round, as though you were peeling an apple.

3 Work slowly and carefully down the fruit, being sure to keep the pared-away rind in one continuous strip.

4 Trim it, if necessary, to a length that suits the glass.

Melon balling

A gadget exists for producing perfect little balls of melon that can be used to decorate a cocktail.

1 Cut the ripe melon in half, and scoop out the seeds with a dessert spoon.

2 Push the baller deeply into the flesh of the fruit, and then turn it through 360° to extract as near to a perfect sphere as you can.

3 Thread balls of different-coloured melon (e.g. Galia, Charentais and watermelon) on to a cocktail stick for full visual impact.

Bartending know-how

Choose ripe melon by its fully developed skin colour, which should be properly deep.

Muddling

A muddler – a long stick with a bulbous end – is the only thing to use for pressing the juice out of mint leaves for use in cocktails in which the mint is an ingredient, rather than just a garnish.

1 Put the mint leaves and caster (superfine) sugar or sugar syrup in the bottom of your glass.

2 Give the leaves an initial twist and turn to break them up and mix them into the sugar.

3 Press them forcefully, with repeated turns of the wrist, to extract their juices.

Bartending know-how
Muddling is a vigorous process that involves more force than any other technique, apart from ice-smashing.

Flaming sugar for absinthe

This technique of adding sugar to your absinthe is favoured by the Czechs. It is more dramatic than simply pouring water over it in the Parisian fashion, and is more efficient anyway.

1 Put a sugar cube on a perforated spoon and immerse it in a generous shot of absinthe until it is saturated.

2 Balancing the spoon across the top of the glass, use a match to set fire to the sugar cube.

3 As the sugar cooks, the flame will gradually die down, and when it does, gently lower the melting cube once more into the drink, and stir it in to dissolve it.

4 Add the same quantity of cold water as absinthe, and stir the drink once more. It's all a bit of a fuss, but worth it.

Making basic sugar syrup

A sugar syrup is sometimes preferable to dry sugar for sweetening cocktails, since it blends immediately with the other ingredients. This recipe makes about 750ml/1¼ pints.

350g/12oz sugar
60cl/1 pint water

1 Place the sugar in a heavy pan with the water, and heat gently over a low heat. Stir the mixture with a wooden spoon until all of the sugar has dissolved completely.

2 Brush the sides of the pan with a pastry brush dampened in water, to remove any sugar crystals that might cause the syrup to crystallize.

3 Bring to the boil for 3–5 minutes. Skim any scum away and when no more appears, remove the pan from the heat. Cool and pour into clean, dry, airtight bottles. Keep in the refrigerator for up to one month.

Bartending know-how
Homemade sugar syrup is a useful standby ingredient, and cheaper than buying sirop de gomme.

Making flavoured syrup

Syrup can be flavoured with anything: a split vanilla pod, mint leaves or citrus rind. Simply boil, and then bottle with the syrup. This recipe makes about 450ml/¾ pint syrup.

900g/2lb very ripe soft or stone fruit, washed
350g/12oz sugar

1 Put the washed fruit of your choice in a bowl and, using the bottom of a rolling pin, a wooden pestle or a potato masher, crush the fruit to release the juices.

2 Cover and allow to sit overnight to concentrate the flavour.

3 Strain the purée through a cloth bag or piece of muslin (cheesecloth). Gather the corners of the cloth together and twist them tight, to remove as much juice as possible.

4 Measure the amount of juice and add 225g/8oz sugar to every 300ml/½ pint fruit juice.

5 Place the pan on a low heat, and gently stir until all the sugar has dissolved. Continue as for basic sugar syrup. The syrup will keep in the refrigerator for up to one month.

Making flavoured spirits

Gin, vodka and white rum can be left to steep and absorb the flavours of a wide variety of soft fruits. This recipe makes about 1.2 litres/2 pints.

450g/1lb raspberries, strawberries, or pineapple
225g/8oz sugar
1 litre/1¾ pints gin, vodka or light rum

1 Put the fruit in a wide-necked jar, and add the sugar.

2 Add the spirit. Cover tightly. Leave in a cool, dark place for a month, shaking gently every week.

3 Strain through clean muslin (cheesecloth) or a cloth bag, and squeeze out the rest of the liquid from the steeped fruit. Return the flavoured liquor to a clean bottle and seal. Store in a cool, dark place. It will happily keep for a year.

Steeping spirits

The process of steeping any spirit with a flavouring agent, such as chillies, creates a whole new sensation. This recipe makes about 1 litre/1¾ pints.

25–50g/1–2oz small red chillies, or to taste, washed
1 litre/1¾ pints sherry or vodka

1 Using a cocktail stick, prick the chillies all over to release their flavours.

2 Pack the chillies tightly into a sterilized bottle.

3 Top up with sherry or vodka. Fit the cork tightly and leave in a dark place for at least ten days or up to two months.

Variations

Try the following interesting alternatives: gin with cumin seeds, star anise or juniper berries; brandy with 25g/1oz peeled and sliced fresh ginger, or 15g/½oz whole cloves; vodka with 50g/2oz washed raisins, or 15–30ml/1–2 tbsp cracked black peppercorns; rum with 2–3 pricked vanilla pods. The amount of flavouring used is of course a matter of personal taste.

Professional bartending

There is much more to becoming a successful bartender than being able to whip up a few cocktails at home. The job has something of the nature of a true vocation about it, with national and international professional associations for working bartenders, and a constant interchange of information taking place via trade journals and the internet. Educational courses, in both the theory and practice of what has come to be known quite seriously as "mixology", are organized, and the crowning events of each year are the cocktail competitions, at which aspiring grand masters produce their latest new creations for an international panel of judges.

While there is inevitably an air of commodious bonhomie about such occasions, that does not mean they are not taken extremely seriously. The fact that, when all is said and done, you are dealing in strong alcoholic drink is never forgotten, and there is a focus on

encouraging responsible drinking as well as dispensing enjoyment. Achieving a full understanding of the raw materials of your trade – learning the history of each drink, gaining familiarity with its range of flavours and its potential in the mixed drink repertoire – is absolutely essential. New products are coming on to the market at a faster rate than ever before. Some are likely to be here today and gone tomorrow; others are of more lasting importance. They must all become familiar to you.

The approach to cocktail creation must be taken as seriously and as studiously as learning to become a chef, and indeed there are obvious connections between the two professions. You don't just suddenly become a bartender overnight because you can make a Brandy Alexander that your friends like without spilling anything. The skills you will acquire will

Above: A good bartender needs to know his or her way around a bewildering array of products these days.

Below: Dealing with a press of thirsty customers can be a thoroughly daunting business.

include consistency (making sure the same drink turns out tasting the same way each time), dexterity (shaking up one cocktail after another for a bar full of thirsty customers is necessarily lightning-quick and exhausting work), and what is known in the educational courses as "flair training".

Putting it very roughly, flair training will enable you to withstand comparison to Tom Cruise in the famous, although universally derided, 1988 motion picture *Cocktail* (for which the tagline was "When he pours, he reigns"). Believe it or not, they really do teach aspiring young mixologists how to juggle with bottles, create pyrotechnical effects with flaming alcohol, and even set up little brain-teasers with matchsticks for those, perhaps sitting with their elders in a hotel bar, not quite old enough to drink.

Most countries have their own professional organizations. The American Bartenders' Guild, and its British equivalent the UKBG, are among the longest-established, and many now belong to an umbrella group called the International Bartenders Association.

Below: A professional barman at work is something of a showman too.

Above: The movie Cocktail *stars Tom Cruise as the flamboyant, bottle-throwing barman who tries to make it big in his own top-class bar.*

The IBA was founded with a meeting at the Grand Hotel in Torquay, south-west England, in 1951. Just seven European countries were represented at that inaugural gathering – Denmark, France, Italy, the Netherlands, Sweden, Switzerland and the UK – but the group now claims members from all around the world. It held its first cocktail competition at its 1955 conference, the prize being carried off by an Italian bartender, Giuseppe Neri. In 1975, the IBA took the revolutionary step of admitting female members, and at the beginning of the new century, 50 years after its foundation, it now boasts over 50 international affiliates.

If you should feel yourself drawn to this very singular vocation, the first step is to acquire the skills and techniques we have been looking at in this book. Hosting even a small cocktail party, and keeping things flowing without either major spillages or (even worse) running out of ice, is almost as challenging as organizing army manoeuvres. Only when you have reached an elevated

level of aptitude in that department should you go on to the really fun side of the business, namely, inventing your own cocktail recipes.

Useful professional publications to help get you started are the UKBG's *International Guide to Drinks*, or, in the United States, *The Original Guide to American Cocktails and Drinks (The Bartender's Companion)*. The UKBG also publishes a magazine, *Spirit*, which is packed with news from the frontline, features and reports of tastings; *Class*, "the magazine of bar culture", is a vibrant and entertaining consumer journal that keeps tracks of what's going on in fashionable bars around the world. Good websites that are worth a look include *www.cocktailtimes.com* and *www.webtender.com*. Both are full of recipes, as well as containing plenty of invaluable reference information.

Planning a party

The key to planning and carrying out your first successful cocktail party is to start small. Inviting the entire neighbourhood to a riotous bash might sound rather tempting, but you will only come unstuck by overreaching your own resources. A small group of old friends – say, half a dozen – is a good starting point.

Browse through the third part of this book, try out for yourself a few of the recipes that appeal to you, and whittle them down to two or three that you think will prove popular with guests whose tastes are familiar to you. A pleasing balance of sour and sweet, or sour, sweet and fizzy, drinks will make for a satisfying evening. Choosing one cocktail that can be made in the liquidizer, one that is made in the shaker and one that is mixed in a pitcher would make logistical sense, so that you are not frantically rinsing out the shaker as guests move from one cocktail to another.

State your start and end times in advance when you invite people. That way, you can ensure that you are not still dealing with thirsty stragglers at one o'clock in the morning.

Provide food, but make it clear that this is a cocktail evening, not a dinner

Below: Champagne chilling in a bucket of iced water needs about 15 minutes.

Above: Nibbles will help absorb some of the alcohol consumed.

party. You are going to be quite busy enough with drink preparation, without having to cook. However, the more guests are encouraged to eat, the slower the intoxication effect will set in. Little salty and cheesy nibbles, tortilla chips with dips, and nuts are always popular. If you really want to splash out, you could make or buy some canapés ahead of time as well.

Decide on which glasses you are going to use for which cocktail, and make sure there is one of each for each guest. Go through your checklist of vital equipment several times, to be certain you haven't forgotten anything: shaker (with measures), liquidizer, pitcher, glasses, fruit for garnishing (remember that citrus fruit slices and twists can be prepared in advance before anyone arrives), a knife for last-minute slicing, bags of ice, and any special opening implements for flipping off bottle-tops or pulling corks. Serving each drink on a little folded paper napkin is the kind of touch that really impresses.

Quantities will depend on how many people you invite, but it is worth doing some initial calculations. A standard measure in these recipes is 25ml/1fl oz,

of which there are 28 in a standard bottle of spirits and 20 in a 50cl bottle of liqueur. Divide each bottle not by single measures, but by the number of measures in each recipe, which may be higher or lower than one. For some drinks, you may find a half-bottle will be quite enough to be going on with.

If there is one golden rule, it has to be that you can never have too much ice. Cocktail-making uses an enormous amount, as each batch is used for the few seconds it takes you to shake the cocktail, and is then thrown away. But ice is only water after all, so be extravagant, and if you aren't sure you have enough ice trays or bags to cope, then buy one of those industrial-sized bags of ice from the supermarket. Better still, buy two or three, which shouldn't set you back too much. They aren't very cost-effective, I admit, but at some late stage in the evening, you'll be mighty glad it's there, if only to clamp firmly on your head as you see the last happy guests away.

So good luck, and have fun!

Alcohol and health

It has now been established that one to three glasses of wine a day is good for you. It is a bulwark in the body's defence against coronary heart disease because its antioxidants help to break down bad cholesterol in the arteries. To some extent, ethanol (alcohol) itself in any of its forms can assist in this, as has been found by scientists in Denmark, but there are obviously limits. Alcohol is virtually worthless in terms of nutritional value and, if drunk in excess, is positively harmful.

Heavy drinking damages the liver, possibly irreparably, and puts strain on its normal day-to-day functioning. It also depletes nutrients, such as vitamins A and C, the B vitamins, magnesium, zinc and the essential fatty acids, and leads to severe dehydration.

Modern methods of producing alcoholic drinks often mean that your average glass of wine, beer or spirit will contain chemical pesticides, colourants

Below: Nuts and fruits are efficient sources of protein and vitamins to replace essential nutrients.

and other noxious additives, which you might be a lot more circumspect about if you found them in food products.

Each drinker famously has his or her own limit. What may be no more than a convivial evening's imbibing to one would have the next person sliding under the table. As a very general rule, an adult woman's capacity is thought to be about two-thirds that of a man's, so women shouldn't feel under any pressure to keep pace.

It would be disingenuous to pretend that you won't at some stage wake up feeling so unutterably lousy that you'll swear to forgo all strong liquors forever more. Welcome to the wonderful world of the alcohol hangover, caused by dehydration and too much toxin in the bloodstream. Everybody has his or her own best cure, whether it be milk, fried foods, black coffee, the rather dubious hair-of-the-dog approach (i.e. another small drink) or my own indispensable standby: aspirin.

Far smarter than a hangover cure, though, is knowing how to avoid such a ghastly outcome in the first place. Ways

Above: Fruit juices will help to make life fun during periods of abstinence.

of doing this include: lining the stomach with lactic fat (300ml/½ pint whole milk) before you embark on the evening's drinking; taking 500mg of aspirin beforehand; downing a glass of water between drinks to rehydrate; and (most important of all) slowly drinking a pint of water before falling into bed.

Treat yourself to a break from it all periodically. Non-alcoholic juices made from fruits and vegetables stimulate the body, speed up metabolism, encourage the elimination of toxins via the lymphatic system, and strengthen the body's overall immunity. They play a vital role in detoxing – everyone's favourite pastime in January – and should be drunk fresh. When making juices at home, choose ripe fruits and vegetables. Fresh juices can be very strong, so dilute with filtered or mineral water to taste. They should always be drunk as soon as they are made.

Health-food stores and pharmacies sell a natural remedy called milk thistle in capsule form, which has been clinically proven to assist in liver cell regeneration. Take it in doses of up to 200mg per day, especially during periods of abstinence. It really will make you feel better.

Making drinks

Now we can get down to business. The recipes in
this part of the book are a mixture of old formulas
that go back to the America of the 19th century;
cocktails from the great jazz era of the 1920s;
drinks that came to prominence in the cocktail
revival of the 1980s; and new ones being drunk in
trendsetting bars today. They are grouped into
their basic drink categories in the same order that
we encountered them in the first part of the book.
For all recipes, 1 measure should be taken as the
standard cocktail measure, that is 25ml or 1fl oz.
A "dash" is the amount that escapes from the
bottle by tilting it and righting it again over the
shaker in about half a second. Where orange,
lemon and lime juices are specified, they should
ideally be from the freshly squeezed fruit.

Gin

Of the six basic spirits that are used in cocktail-making, gin is the most versatile. That may seem strange in view of its assertively perfumed character, but it is precisely the herb and spice aromatics in its composition that enable it to blend well with a range of liqueurs and fruit juices, and even other spirits. In addition to that, it has in common with plain vodka, white rum and silver tequila the useful attribute of colourlessness, so that it makes a neutral background for some flamboyant-looking creations. Use a good brand of London gin in these recipes, except where one of the other types, such as Plymouth or Dutch genever, is specifically called for.

As with each section in this part of the book, we shall begin with the old classic recipes, which tend to do no more than slightly modify the flavour of the essential ingredient, before progressing on through the ages to today's more complex and challenging mixtures.

Gin Fizz

The combination of sourness and fizziness in this 19th-century recipe is what makes it so refreshing.

2 measures/3 tbsp gin
juice of half a large lemon
5ml/1 tsp caster (superfine) sugar
soda water

Shake the gin, lemon juice and sugar with ice until the sugar is properly dissolved. Pour out into a frosted, tall, narrow glass half-filled with ice, and top up with soda. Add two straws. There should ideally be a little less soda than the other combined ingredients, but it is very much a matter of personal taste.

Tom Collins

This is similar to a Gin Fizz, except that it isn't shaken and tends to be made with a little less soda. Originally known as John Collins, after the head waiter at a London hotel in the early 19th century, it changed its name when it began to made with the Old Tom brand of gin.

2 measures/3 tbsp gin
juice of half a large lemon
5ml/1 tsp sugar
soda water

Pour the gin and lemon juice into a frosted, tall glass half-filled with ice. Add the sugar and stir to dissolve. Add roughly a measure and a half of soda, a slice of lemon and a couple of straws.

Gin Swizzle

The Swizzle dates from the early 19th century, and was originally a drink made frothy purely by energetic stirring. The implement used for this, the swizzle-stick, took its name from the drink.

2 measures/3 tbsp gin
¼ measure/1 tsp sugar syrup
juice of a lime
2 dashes Angostura bitters

Beat all the ingredients together (as if you were preparing eggs for an omelette) in a large jug, with ice. When the drink is good and foaming, strain it into a tall glass. Alternatively, make the drink in the tall glass, but remember to stir it up vigorously with a swizzle-stick. Some recipes add soda water to achieve the swizzle effect, but originally it was all done by elbow grease. The froth will subside fairly quickly anyway.

Bartending know-how

The invention of gin is apocryphally credited to one Franciscus de la Boë, a medical professor at the University of Leiden in the Netherlands, sometime in the mid-17th century. Even if he is the true progenitor of gin, however, he was almost certainly not the first to add juniper berries for medicinal reasons to a pure distilled spirit. The 12th-century monastery at Salerno, where European distillation was born, is the most likely origin of the basic recipe.

Gin Sling

Precursor of the Fizz, the Sling started life in the mid-18th century as a mixture of gin, lemon juice and sugar, but used plain water instead of sparkling. In later times, it also came to have a bittering element added to the sour, as here.

2 measures/3 tbsp gin
juice of half a lemon
5ml/1 tsp sugar
dash of Angostura bitters
still mineral water

Mix the gin, lemon juice, sugar and Angostura in a tumbler with plenty of ice until the sugar is fully dissolved. Top up the glass with cold water straight from the refrigerator. Add a twist of lemon rind and straws.

Gin Cocktail

A very simple preparation of fruity, bittered gin, this makes a highly sophisticated aperitif.

2 measures/3 tbsp gin
5 dashes orange bitters

Shake the ingredients well with ice and strain into a cocktail glass. This is one of those drinks that needs no garnish, but is perfect just as it is.

Gin Sour

The Sour dates from the 1850s, and can be made with any of the basic spirits. Fresh lemon juice is naturally the key to it, with the edge taken off it by means of a pinch of sugar. However, it should never taste at all sweet, otherwise it wouldn't be worthy of its name.

2 measures/3 tbsp gin
juice of half a large lemon
5ml/1 tsp caster (superfine) sugar

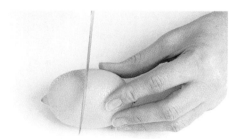

Shake all the ingredients together with ice and strain into a rocks glass or small tumbler. Some bartenders add the briefest squirt of soda just before serving for extra pep, but it is better served wholly still.

Dry Martini

No cocktail recipe is more energetically argued over than the classic dry Martini. It is basically a generous measure of virtually neat, stone-cold gin with a dash of dry white vermouth in it. But how much is a dash? Purists insist on no more than a single drop, or the residue left after briefly flushing the glass out with a splash of vermouth and then pouring it away. (They puzzlingly refer to such a Martini as "very dry", as if adding more vermouth would sweeten it. In fact, the terminology

harks back to the original recipe, when the vermouth used was the sweet red variety.) Some go for as much as half a measure of vermouth, which is guaranteed to send the purist into paroxysms of horror. If in doubt, it makes more sense to incline towards the purist philosophy: the vermouth should be added as if it were the last bottle in existence. Inevitably, individual preference remains the crucial factor.

The drink should properly be mixed gently in a large pitcher, with ice, and then strained into the traditional cocktail glass (the real name of which is a Martini glass), which should be straight out of the freezer. A twist of lemon rind should be squeezed delicately over the surface, so that the essential oil floats in globules on top of the drink, but don't put the lemon twist in the glass. The addition of a green olive to the glass is traditional, but definitely disliked by some for its salty pungency.

Gibson

Well loved in Japan, this version of the Martini is named after one Charles Gibson, an American illustrator who found a cocktail onion in the drink more to his taste than the traditional olive. You can afford to be a little more generous with the vermouth.

½ measure/2 tsp dry white vermouth
2½ measures/3½ tbsp gin
2 cocktail onions

Pour the vermouth and gin into a large glass or pitcher with plenty of ice, and stir for at least 30 seconds to chill well. Strain into a Martini glass. Skewer the onions on to the end of a cocktail stick and add to the glass, so that they sit temptingly at the bottom. Better still, pour out the drink over the onions to release their flavours.

Orange Blossom

The original gin and orange, much drunk during the Prohibition era in the United States, where the fruit juice masked the ghastly flavour of bathtub gin. Note that the spirit isn't drowned with too much juice. Some recipes add a pinch of sugar, but it doesn't need it.

1½ measures/6 tsp gin
1½ measures/6 tsp freshly squeezed
  orange juice

Shake the ingredients with ice, and strain into a cocktail glass.

Clover Club

A traditional recipe from the 1920s cocktail era, named after a celebrated nightclub in Chicago.

2 measures/3 tbsp gin
juice of half a large lemon
1 measure/1½ tbsp grenadine
1 egg white

Shake all the ingredients with ice for at least 30 seconds to make sure the egg white is thoroughly incorporated. Strain into a rocks glass, and garnish with a half-slice of lemon.

Gimlet

Like the Sour, the Gimlet is a small, sharply flavoured drink, but it is made with lime rather than lemon. As fresh lime juice is exceptionally sour, lime cordial is used, which is classically Rose's, as this was once the only brand available. The gin should ideally be Plymouth. The 1930 recipe in the *Savoy Cocktail Book* uses half-and-half proportions, but these days it is better adjusted to the quantities below so as not to be too syrupy. Some bartenders add a touch of soda.

2 measures/3 tbsp Plymouth gin
¾ measure/3 tsp Rose's lime cordial

Shake both ingredients well with ice and strain into a cocktail glass.

Bitter Gimlet

This is an old-fashioned aperitif, which could easily be turned into a longer drink by finishing it with chilled tonic or soda water.

1 lime, cut into wedges
1 measure/1½ tbsp gin
2 dashes Angostura bitters

Put the lime into a pitcher and, using a muddler, press the juice out of it. Add the cracked ice, gin and bitters and stir well until chilled. Strain the cocktail into a short tumbler over ice cubes. Add a triangle of lime rind to the drink.

Horse's Neck

The name derives from the shape of the lemon rind that hangs in the glass. There are various versions of this mix, the earliest using bourbon or brandy, but gin eventually became the most popular.

1 lemon
2 measures/3 tbsp gin
dry ginger ale

Cut the entire rind from a lemon, spiral-fashion, as in the recipe for Gin Crusta. Dangle it from the rim of a tall glass so that it hangs down inside. Add plenty of cracked ice and the gin, and then top up with ginger ale. You can also add a dash of Angostura bitters if the mood takes you, but it is by no means essential.

My Fair Lady

This frothy, fruity cocktail was invented at London's Savoy Hotel in the 1950s to coincide with a production of the much-loved Lerner and Loewe musical based on George Bernard Shaw's play *Pygmalion*.

1 measure/1½ tbsp gin
½ measure/2 tsp orange juice
½ measure/2 tsp lemon juice
¼ measure/1 tsp crème de fraise
1 egg white

Shake all the ingredients thoroughly with ice, and strain into a cocktail glass.

Gin and Lemon Fizz

If gin and tonic is your tipple, try this chilled alternative. The fruit and flower ice cubes make a lively decoration for any iced drink. This recipe serves two.

mixture of small edible berries or currants
pieces of thinly pared lemon or orange rind
tiny edible flowers
4 scoops of lemon sorbet
30ml/2 tbsp gin
120ml/4fl oz chilled tonic water

To make the decorated ice cubes, place each fruit, piece of rind or flower in a section of an ice-cube tray. Carefully fill with water and freeze for several hours until the cubes are solid. Divide the sorbet into two cocktail glasses or use small tumblers, with a capacity of about 150ml/¼ pint. Spoon over the gin and add a couple of the ornamental ice cubes to each glass. Top up with tonic water and serve immediately.

Bartending know-how
When making the ice cubes, choose small herb flowers such as borage or mint, or edible flowers such as rose geraniums, primulas or rose buds.

Gin Cobbler

The Cobbler is a very early drink, American in origin, that was served in the summer. It is basically sweetened spirit lavishly decorated with fruit. Brandy, whisky and dry sherry make popular alternatives to the gin version described here.

5ml/1 tsp caster (superfine) sugar
2 measures/3 tbsp gin
soda water
fruit, to garnish

Dissolve the sugar in a little water in a large goblet. Half-fill the glass with cracked ice and add the gin. Stir well and then double the quantity of liquid with soda water. The drink should then be adorned with slices of orange, lemon, pineapple, or whatever comes to hand, and drunk through straws.

White Lady

This is one of the classic cocktail recipes of the 1920s, and is still going strong today. The high strength of the alcohol ingredients and the sharpness of the lemon quite belie its innocuous reputation as a "lady's drink".

1 measure/1½ tbsp gin
1 measure/1½ tbsp Cointreau
1 measure/1½ tbsp lemon juice

Shake the ingredients with ice and strain into a frosted cocktail glass. Some recipes also add 5ml/1 tsp egg white. The *Savoy Cocktail Book* makes no mention of it. It simply gives the drink a frothier texture, if that's what you like. Garnish with a lime twist.

Perfect Lady

A blended cocktail with a nice sharp edge, given a frothy texture with a little egg white.

1 measure/1½ tbsp gin
½ measure/2 tsp peach brandy
½ measure/2 tsp lemon juice
1 measure/1½ tbsp egg white

Put all the ingredients into a liquidizer with a good handful of crushed ice, blend for a few seconds, and then pour into a champagne bowl. Garnish with a slice of juicy fresh peach.

Bartending know-how
When using eggs, always be sure that they are very fresh. The whites will whip better in this condition.

Tod's Cooler

The name of this cocktail refers to Tod Sloan, an American jockey of the era before the First World War, who invented this drink at one of his favourite haunts, the bar of the Palace Hotel in Brussels. Known to English racegoers as Toddy, his more famous nickname, coined in the States, was Yankee Doodle Dandy.

2 measures/3 tbsp gin
⅔ measure/1 tbsp crème de cassis
⅔ measure/1 tbsp lemon juice
soda water

Half-fill a tall glass with cracked ice, add the first three ingredients and then top up with soda. Garnish with a spiral twist of lemon rind.

Gin Smash

Try this cocktail with any fresh mint you can find: peppermint and spearmint would each contribute their own flavour to this simple and very refreshing summery drink.

15ml/1 tbsp sugar
4 sprigs fresh mint
2 measures/3 tbsp gin

Dissolve the sugar in a little water in the cocktail shaker. Add the mint and, using a muddler, bruise and press the juices out of the leaves. Then add plenty of crushed ice, and finally the gin. Shake for about 20 seconds. Strain into a small wine glass filled with crushed ice. If desired, add fresh mint sprigs and drinking straws.

Leap Year

The particular year in question was 1928, when Harry Craddock, a barman at the Savoy Hotel in London, created this drink for a party held there on February 29.

2 measures/3 tbsp gin
½ measure/2 tsp Grand Marnier
½ measure/2 tsp sweet red vermouth
dash lemon juice, plus lemon rind

Shake well and strain into a cocktail glass. Squeeze a bit of lemon rind over the surface of the drink so that a little of its oil sprays out.

Gin Rickey

The Rickey was invented in the last decade of the 19th century in the United States. It is almost the same as a Gimlet, only without the sweetening element of the cordial, which makes it a much more acerbic proposition. It can be made with any spirit, although gin is the original version.

juice and rind of half a lime
2 measures/3 tbsp gin
soda water

Half-fill a tall glass with ice. Squeeze the lime directly into the glass and then drop in the empty rind. Add the gin and stir vigorously, before topping with soda.

Gin Crusta

Prepare the glass in advance and keep it chilled in the refrigerator ready for instant use. The depth of pink colour will depend on the strength of the maraschino cherry juice you use.

1 lemon
25g/2 tbsp golden granulated sugar
3 dashes sugar syrup
2 dashes maraschino cherry juice
2 dashes Angostura bitters
1 measure/1½ tbsp gin

Cut both ends off the lemon and, using a canelle knife, peel it thinly in one long, continuous piece. Halve the lemon and rub the rim of a glass with the cut surface. Dip it into the sugar to create a decorative rim. Arrange the lemon rind in a scroll on the inside of a high-sided glass. Add the sugar syrup, cherry juice, Angostura, gin and juice of a quarter of the lemon to a cocktail shaker, half-filled with ice. Shake well and strain into the prepared glass.

Monkey Gland

From the classic cocktail era of the early 1920s, this drink was created at Ciro's Club in London, a legendary jazz nightspot just off the Charing Cross Road. Head bartender Harry McElhone later moved to Paris to run Harry's New York Bar, where he ascended to true international renown.

2 measures/3 tbsp gin
1 measure/1½ tbsp orange juice
½ measure/2 tsp grenadine
½ measure/2 tsp absinthe

Shake the ingredients with plenty of ice, and strain into a large wine glass. Garnish with a slice of orange.

Amsterdam

This deliciously orangey cocktail is unusual in having the ice left in it. It was invented in the city whose name it bears. Squeeze a fresh mandarin if you have one, or else use unsweetened juice from a can of mandarin segments.

1½ measures/6 tsp gin
½ measure/2 tsp Cointreau
¾ measure/3 tsp mandarin juice
1–2 mandarin segments

Shake the gin, Cointreau and mandarin juice with cracked ice and pour, without straining, into a rocks glass. Add a mandarin segment or two.

Lady Killer

A lusciously fruity, tropical-flavoured cocktail from a bar called the Wantagh Arms in New York State. It would make a good summer's afternoon cocktail.

1 measure/1½ tbsp gin
¾ measure/3 tsp apricot brandy
¾ measure/3 tsp Cointreau
2 measures/3 tbsp passion fruit juice
2 measures/3 tbsp pineapple juice

Shake all the ingredients together with ice, and strain into a highball glass half-filled with cracked ice. Garnish with a wedge of pineapple.

Pink Pussycat

An object-lesson in how easily gin takes to a range of tangy fruit flavours in a mixed drink, Pink Pussycat also has – as its name suggests – a most beguiling colour.

2 measures/3 tbsp gin
3 measures/4½ tbsp pineapple juice
2 measures/3 tbsp grapefruit juice
½ measure/2 tsp grenadine

Shake all the ingredients well with ice, and strain into a tall glass. Garnish with a segment of grapefruit.

Wilga Hill Boomerang

This sundowner is mixed in a large pitcher half-filled with ice cubes, and is served extremely cold.

1 measure/1½ tbsp gin
¼ measure/1 tsp dry vermouth
¼ measure/1 tsp sweet red vermouth
1 measure/1½ tbsp apple juice
dash Angostura bitters
2 dashes maraschino cherry juice

Pour the gin, dry and sweet vermouths and apple juice into a pitcher half-filled with cracked ice, and stir until the outside of the glass has frosted. Add the Angostura bitters and cherry juice to the bottom of a cocktail glass and add crushed ice, and then strain in the mixed cocktail. Prepare a strip of orange rind and a maraschino cherry to decorate the glass.

Arctic Summer

This is a very appealing, sunset-coloured cocktail. Don't stint on the ice.

1½ measures/6 tsp gin
¾ measure/3 tsp apricot brandy
¼ measure/1 tsp grenadine
4 measures/6 tbsp sparkling bitter lemon

Fill a highball glass with cracked ice, and add the ingredients one by one in the order above. Do not stir. Garnish with a slice of lemon and a cocktail cherry.

Vunderful

A long, lazy Sunday afternoon tipple, conjured up in the heat of southern Africa. Leave the fruits in the gin for as long as possible. This recipe contains 20 servings.

400g/14oz can lychees
2 peaches, sliced
¾ bottle gin

For each serving you will need:
1 measure/1½ tbsp Pimm's
2–3 dashes Angostura bitters
5 measures/120ml/4fl oz chilled tonic water or lemonade

Strain the lychees from the syrup and place them in a wide-necked jar with the peach slices and the gin. Let them sit overnight or for anything up to a month. For each serving, mix in a large pitcher a measure of the lychee gin with the Pimm's and the bitters to taste. Strain into tall tumblers filled with ice cubes. Add chilled tonic water or lemonade to top up. Put a couple of the drained gin-soaked lychees and peach slices into each glass, stirring and crushing the fruit into the drink with a muddler. Add a half-slice of lime to the rim of each glass.

Luigi

A 1920s classic, Luigi was created at the Criterion restaurant on London's Piccadilly Circus by one Luigi Naintré.

1½ measures/6 tsp gin
1½ measures/6 tsp dry vermouth
¼ measure/1 tsp grenadine
dash Cointreau
juice of half a tangerine or mandarin orange

Shake well with ice and strain into a glass. Add a segment of tangerine.

Bartending know-how
Mandarins and tangerines taste much the same, but the latter are full of pips.

Mistress

This is a long, delicately creamy cocktail. The Campari topping just gives it a tantalizing edge of bitterness.

1½ measures/6 tsp gin
1 measure/1½ tbsp white crème de cacao
2 measures/3 tbsp pineapple juice
1 measure/1½ tbsp passion fruit juice
1 measure/1½ tbsp whipping cream
¼ measure/1 tsp Campari

Shake all the ingredients except the last with ice, and then strain into a highball glass, half-filled with ice cubes. Drizzle the Campari on top.

Mayfair

Also dating from the 1920s, Mayfair was invented at the Embassy Club in that district of London. The recipe calls for syrup of cloves, which you may have difficulty tracking down, but its flavour is quite inimitable if you can. It has a sweetly floral quality.

1½ measures/6 tsp gin
¾ measure/3 tsp apricot brandy
¾ measure/3 tsp orange juice
¼ measure/1 tsp clove syrup

Shake all the ingredients well with ice, and strain into a cocktail glass.

Pink Lady

Yet another of the "Ladies", this one is more venerable than most. It dates from before the First World War, and was named after a now forgotten, hit stage play. The pink colour is achieved by means of a relatively large quantity of the pomegranite syrup, grenadine.

caster (superfine) sugar, for frosting
1½ measures/6 tsp Plymouth gin
½ measure/2 tsp grenadine, plus extra for frosting
½ measure/2 tsp double (heavy) cream
¼ measure/1 tsp lemon juice
1 measure/1½ tbsp egg white

Dip the rim of a champagne saucer or bowl-shaped cocktail glass into grenadine and then into caster sugar to create a bright pink, frosted rim. Shake the cocktail ingredients with ice and strain into the prepared glass. Garnish with a cherry.

Blue Star

The unearthly colour produced by mixing blue and orange in this drink is further enhanced by serving it frappé, over crushed ice.

1 measure/1½ tbsp gin
¾ measure/3 tsp Noilly Prat or other dry vermouth
⅓ measure/1½ tsp blue curaçao
1 measure/1½ tbsp orange juice

Shake all the ingredients well with ice, and strain into a cocktail glass full of finely crushed ice. Garnish with a half-slice of orange.

Jockey Club

This 1920s mixture of gin with dashes of this, that and the other came to Europe all the way from a nightclub in the Cuban capital, Havana.

2 measures/3 tbsp gin
⅓ measure/1½ tsp crème de noyau (or amaretto)
dash orange bitters (or orange curaçao)
dash Angostura bitters
⅓ measure/1½ tsp lemon juice

Shake all the ingredients well with ice and strain into a cocktail glass. Garnish with a half-slice of lemon.

RAC

This was created on the eve of the First World War by the barman of the Royal Automobile Club in London's Pall Mall.

1½ measures/6 tsp gin
¾ measure/3 tsp dry vermouth

¾ measure/3 tsp sweet red vermouth
¼ measure/1 tsp orange bitters

Shake well with ice, and strain into a glass. Squeeze a twist of orange rind over the top to release its oil.

Little Red Riding Hood

Vivid summery fruit flavours make a cocktail that tastes as innocent as Grandma, but has a bite more reminiscent of the Wolf!

1 measure/1½ tbsp gin
¾ measure/3 tsp crème de mûre

¾ measure/3 tsp crème de fraise
1½ measures/6 tsp orange juice

Shake the ingredients with ice and strain into a large cocktail glass filled with crushed ice. Garnish with a strawberry, a blackberry and a cherry.

Carla

This fruity concoction owes its character to Dutch genever, which should be used in preference to ordinary London gin.

1½ measures/6 tsp jonge genever
2 measures/3 tbsp orange juice
1 measure/1½ tbsp passion fruit juice
2 measures/3 tbsp lemonade

Shake the first three ingredients together with a couple of handfuls of crushed ice, and pour, unstrained, into a highball glass. Add the lemonade. You could garnish with a slice of orange.

Bartending know-how
In the Netherlands, genever is nearly always drunk neat, accompanied by a chaser of the local beer.

Bridesmaid

This drink sounds as though it would be perfect for a summer wedding, as long as the bridesmaids have fulfilled their duties by the time it's served.

2 measures/3 tbsp gin
1 measure/1½ tbsp lemon juice
¾ measure/3 tsp sugar syrup
dash Angostura bitters
4 measures/6 tbsp sparkling ginger ale

Add the first four ingredients to a tall glass filled with cracked ice, stir well and add the ginger ale. Garnish with a twist of lemon.

Bennett

Dating from the 1920s, this short drink is sometimes seen spelt with only one "t", and with a small quantity of sugar syrup added to it, but this is the original formula, which on the whole I prefer for its sharper edge.

1½ measures/6 tsp gin
½ measure/2 tsp lime juice
2 dashes Angostura bitters

Shake well with ice and strain into a cocktail glass.

César Ritz

Created at the Paris Ritz Hotel, this was named after the legendary chef of the 19th century.

2 measures/3 tbsp gin
⅔ measure/1 tbsp dry vermouth
⅓ measure/1½ tsp cherry brandy
½ measure/2 tsp kirsch

Stir the ingredients gently in a pitcher with ice cubes, until a frost of condensation mists the outside. Strain into a cocktail glass. Add a cocktail cherry that has been liberally dunked in kirsch.

Space

... the final frontier? Not quite, but this is a very moreish modern cocktail recipe made with hazelnut liqueur. A good aperitif.

1½ measures/6 tsp gin
1 measure/1½ tbsp Frangelico (or crème de noisette)
½ measure/2 tsp lemon juice

Shake all the ingredients well with ice, and strain into a rocks glass. Add a couple of pieces of cracked ice.

Bartending know-how
The monk after whom Frangelico is named, and who is credited with its recipe, lived as a hermit in north-west Italy in the 17th century.

Honolulu

This fruity little shooter should be served in a shot glass.

1 measure/1½ tbsp gin
¼ measure/1 tsp pineapple juice
¼ measure/1 tsp orange juice
¼ measure/1 tsp lemon juice
¼ measure/1 tsp pineapple syrup (from a can)
1 drop Angostura bitters

Shake all but the last ingredient with ice and strain into a shot glass. Add a single drop of Angostura to the drink, and knock back in one.

Caruso

Towards the end of his life, the celebrated Italian opera singer Enrico Caruso stayed at the Hotel Sevilla in Cuba, where an obliging barman created this cocktail in his honour.

1 measure/1½ tbsp gin
1 measure/1½ tbsp dry vermouth
1 measure/1½ tbsp green crème de menthe

Shake well with ice and strain into a cocktail glass. Some versions these days use a little less crème de menthe than a whole measure, as the flavour is so strong, but this is the original recipe.

Barbarella

This is a colourful drink named after the title character in the classic sci-fi movie, played by Jane Fonda.

1 measure/1½ tbsp Plymouth gin
1 measure/1½ tbsp dry vermouth
½ measure/2 tsp Galliano
¼ measure/1 tsp blue curaçao
2 measures/3 tbsp sparkling bitter lemon

Shake the first four ingredients well with ice, and strain into a rocks glass that has been half-filled with cracked ice. Add the bitter lemon, and garnish with a slice of lemon.

Damn the Weather

This cocktail has been around since the 1920s, and presumably commemorates a particularly persistent gloomy spell.

1 measure/1½ tbsp gin
½ measure/2 tsp sweet red vermouth
½ measure/2 tsp orange juice
¼ measure/1 tsp orange curaçao

Shake well with ice, and strain into a chilled whisky tumbler. Add a twist of orange wrapped around a cocktail stick.

Park Avenue

This sharp and fruity cocktail takes its name from one of the smartest thoroughfares in New York City.

1½ measures/6 tsp gin
½ measure/2 tsp cherry brandy
½ measure/2 tsp lime juice
¼ measure/1 tsp maraschino

Shake all the ingredients well with ice, and strain into a cocktail glass. Garnish with a cocktail cherry and add a thin slice of lime.

Derby

This classic, old, American short drink is just a barely modified gin. Instead of garnishing the glass with a mint leaf, you could add a couple of mint sprigs to the alcohol in the shaker, and then strain them out.

2 measures/3 tbsp gin
¼ measure/1 tsp peach bitters

Shake with ice and then strain into a liqueur glass. Garnish with a leaf of garden mint.

Red Cloud

Although red clouds at night were once said to be a sailor's delight, you don't have to be ocean-bound to enjoy one of these.

1½ measures/6 tsp gin
¾ measure/3 tsp apricot brandy
½ measure/2 tsp lemon juice
¼ measure/1 tsp grenadine
dash Angostura bitters

Shake all the ingredients well with ice, and strain into a champagne saucer or cocktail glass. Garnish with a half-slice of lemon and a cherry.

Bartending know-how
The oversized label around each Angostura bitters bottle was an administrative error that just stuck!

Maiden's Blush

There were two quite distinct recipes for Maiden's Blush, even in the 1920s. The first mixed gin with orange curaçao, lemon juice and grenadine. This one was a slightly more lethal proposition, and the blush effect in the colour is more apparent, if you need any excuse to up the ante.

2 measures/3 tbsp gin
1 measure/1½ tbsp absinthe
¼ measure/1 tsp grenadine

Shake all the ingredients well with ice, and strain into an ice-cold cocktail glass.

Bartending know-how
Cocktails containing absinthe should be served sparingly. Too many aren't necessarily very nice.

Bee's Knees

The name should give a clue as to the essential ingredient in this rather restorative mixture. The honey and lemon together give the drink a particularly comforting note.

1½ measures/6 tsp gin
¼ measure/1 tsp honey
¼ measure/1 tsp lemon juice

Shake the ingredients very well with ice to integrate the honey, and strain into a cocktail glass.

Cloister

A strong lemony/herbal flavour pervades the Cloister. It is a short drink that delivers a strong kick-start to the tastebuds.

1½ measures/6 tsp gin
½ measure/2 tsp yellow Chartreuse

Grapefruit Cocktail

If you have a grapefruit on the go after making a Cloister, it makes sense to move on to this classic preparation next. Waste not, want not.

1½ measures/6 tsp gin
1 measure/1½ tbsp grapefruit juice
¼ measure/1 tsp maraschino

Shake all the ingredients well with ice, and strain into a champagne saucer or cocktail glass. Garnish with a sliver of grapefruit and a cherry.

½ measure/2 tsp grapefruit juice
¼ measure/1 tsp lemon juice
¼ measure/1 tsp sugar syrup

Shake all the ingredients well with ice, and strain into a cocktail glass. Garnish with a twist of grapefruit rind.

Tangier

A four-city cocktail tour on this page starts in Morocco with this sweetly orangey number. The choice of city for the name distantly reflects the tangerines that go into Mandarine Napoléon.

1 measure/1½ tbsp gin
1 measure/1½ tbsp Cointreau
1 measure/1½ tbsp Mandarine Napoléon

Shake all the ingredients well with ice, and strain into a cocktail glass. Decorate the glass with a spiral twist of orange rind, wrapped around a cocktail stick.

Berliner

A dry, and very grown-up sort of drink, Berliner is full of herbal flavours from the vermouth and kümmel and has a finishing tang of lemon.

1½ measures/6 tsp gin
½ measure/2 tsp dry vermouth
½ measure/2 tsp kümmel
½ measure/2 tsp lemon juice

Shake all the ingredients well with ice, and strain into a chilled cocktail glass. Squeeze a bit of lemon rind over the top, and garnish with a half-slice of lemon.

Parisian

Another 1920s recipe that nicely balances the sweetness of blackcurrant liqueur with the acerbic dryness of good dry French vermouth.

1 measure/1½ tbsp gin
1 measure/1½ tbsp Noilly Prat
1 measure/1½ tbsp crème de cassis

Shake all the ingredients well with ice, and strain into a cocktail glass. Add three or four blackcurrants to the glass to add touches of sharpness to the drink. They can be eaten at the end.

Dundee

What else but Scottish ingredients (two of them, in fact) could give a drink a name like this? This is a dry, sour cocktail with quite a kick.

1 measure/1½ tbsp gin
¾ measure/3 tsp Scotch
½ measure/2 tsp Drambuie
½ measure/2 tsp lemon juice

Shake all the ingredients well with ice, and strain into a whisky tumbler. Squeeze a twist of lemon rind over the drink, and then drop it into the glass.

Juan-les-Pins

Once the preferred destination of the Mediterranean jet-set, the Riviera resort is fittingly honoured by this appetizing mixture of gin, an aperitif and a liqueur.

1 measure/1½ tbsp gin
¾ measure/3 tsp white Dubonnet
½ measure/2 tsp apricot brandy
dash lemon juice

Shake all the ingredients well with ice, and strain into a cocktail glass. Garnish with a slice of apricot and a cherry speared by a cocktail stick.

Bloodhound

The drink takes its name from the rather gory colour and texture produced by including whole strawberries in the blend.

1½ measures/6 tsp gin
½ measure/2 tsp dry vermouth
½ measure/2 tsp sweet red vermouth
¼ measure/1 tsp crème de fraise
6 strawberries

Put all the ingredients into a liquidizer with ice, and blend for about 20 seconds. Strain into a cocktail glass, and garnish with a final whole strawberry dipped in crème de fraise.

Princeton

This cocktail was created in the early 20th century to honour one of America's Ivy League universities. It was originally made with a sweet gin called Old Tom, but the drier version tastes better.

1½ measures/6 tsp gin
¾ measure/3 tsp ruby port
¼ measure/1 tsp orange bitters

Stir the ingredients together with plenty of ice in a large pitcher, and then strain into a rocks glass or cocktail glass. Squeeze a piece of lemon rind over the surface to release a spray of oil, and then drop it into the drink.

Whiteout

A highly indulgent preparation with which to conclude the gin collection, this is a sweet, chocolate cream cocktail that tastes far more innocuous than it actually is.

1½ measures/6 tsp gin
1 measure/1½ tbsp white crème de cacao
1 measure/1½ tbsp double (heavy) cream

Shake all the ingredients very well with ice to amalgamate the cream fully, and then strain into a chilled cocktail glass. Grate a small piece of white chocolate over the surface.

Bartending know-how
It is estimated that, at the time the Gin Act was introduced in 1736, average consumption in London had hit something like two-thirds of a bottle per head *per day*.

Vodka

Vodka may not seem the most obviously useful ingredient in the cocktail cupboard, in the sense that it is typically just a neutral, colourless spirit that at most can only add a further shot of alcohol to a mixed drink. However, many of the modern cocktails are based on the principle of blending a range of different, often exotic fruit flavours over an alcohol base that doesn't interfere with the taste of them. If there are surprisingly few vodka cocktails from the classic era, that is because vodka wasn't then generally commercially available. Some of the recipes here use one of today's ultra-fashionable flavoured vodkas.

Screwdriver

The Screwdriver is the original vodka and orange, so named – as the story has it – after an American oil-rig worker developed the habit of stirring his drink with a screwdriver. Presumably, swizzle-sticks are in rather short supply on oil-rigs. As a member of the classic cocktail repertoire, it probably only dates from the 1950s, which is when vodka made its first, tentative appearance on Western markets. The rest is history.

2 measures/3 tbsp vodka
4 measures/6 tbsp orange juice

Add the ingredients, spirit first, to a rocks glass or whisky tumbler loaded with ice cubes, and throw in a slice of orange. Made with freshly squeezed rather than commercial juice, the drink tastes more grown-up and appears to pack more of a punch, as the juice is naturally thinner than concentrate orange juice from a carton.

Moscow Mule

One of the classic American vodka-based cocktails, the Moscow Mule was invented at a Los Angeles restaurant in 1947 as part of the first US sales drive for the Smirnoff brand. It should contain enough vodka to give the drink a real kick, as befits a mule.

2 measures/3 tbsp vodka
¼ measure/1 tsp lime juice
3 measures/4½ tbsp sparkling ginger ale

Pour the vodka and lime juice into a highball glass half-filled with ice. Mix together well with a bar spoon. Top up the mixture with ginger ale, and add a few halved slices of lime to the cocktail.

Black Russian

The true Black Russian is simply equal measures of vodka and Tia Maria, or Kahlúa, mixed with ice cubes in a tumbler. However, the fashion in recent years has been to serve it as a long drink in a big glass, topped up with cola.

Proportions of the classic Black Russian vary according to taste. Two parts vodka to one part Tia Maria on ice, with no mixer, makes a very adult drink. Certain aficionados insist on Kahlúa rather than Tia Maria with the vodka. Either way, it is as well not to adulterate the drink with cola.

White Russian

The White Russian is a creamy version of the Black, which needs shaking rather than stirring, so as to incorporate the cream.

1 measure/1½ tbsp vodka
1 measure/1½ tbsp Kahlúa or Tia Maria
1 measure/1½ tbsp whipping cream

Shake all the ingredients well with ice, and strain into a cocktail glass.

Blenheim

A further twist on the basic Black Russian idea, Blenheim uses orange juice instead of cola, if you want a non-alcoholic mixer in there. The resulting colour is not the loveliest, but the flavour is better than it sounds.

1½ measures/6 tsp vodka
¾ measure/3 tsp Tia Maria
¾ measure/3 tsp orange juice

Shake all the ingredients well with ice, and strain into a cocktail glass.

Golden Russian

This is a quite distinct drink from the preceding two Russians, in which the vodka acts to take a little of the sweetness off the liqueur, while the lime sharpens it all up still further. It's a very ingenious (and powerful) mixture, and one that should not be taken lightly.

1½ measures/6 tsp vodka
1 measure/1½ tbsp Galliano
¼ measure/1 tsp lime juice

Pour all the ingredients into a rocks glass over plenty of cracked ice, and stir. Add a slice of lime.

Bullshot

The Bullshot is a sort of Bloody Mary, only with beef consommé replacing the tomato juice. It too is thought to have amazing restorative powers as a reviving breakfast drink after the previous night's indulgence. It can be handy if you really can't bear to eat anything, but drink some water first.

2 measures/3 tbsp vodka
4 measures/6 tbsp cold beef consommé
 (classically Campbell's)
½ measure/2 tsp lemon juice
¼ measure/1 tsp Worcestershire sauce
2 dashes Tabasco
pinch celery salt
pinch cayenne pepper

Mix all the ingredients with ice in a pitcher, and then strain into a highball glass half-filled with ice.

Bloody Mary

Everybody has his or her own recipe for the next best hangover cure after aspirin. Some strange people even put tomato ketchup into it. Others round out the alcohol with a splash of dry sherry. Here is my own formula.

Put a slice of lemon and 2–3 ice cubes in a tall glass, add 5ml/1 tsp Worcestershire sauce, 5ml/1 tsp freshly squeezed lemon juice, a pinch of celery salt, about six drops of Tabasco and six twists of the black pepper mill. Stir to coat the ice. Fill the glass to about 4cm/1½in from the top with tomato juice and pour in a generous measure of vodka. Stir well.

Dickson's Bloody Mary

This recipe has plenty of spicy character, with horseradish, sherry and Tabasco. Made with chilli or pepper vodka, it is a much hotter proposition than the standard recipe.

Gipsy

The ingredients in this recipe make for an exotically scented, and slightly bittersweet mixture. It would make a highly unusual digestif for the end of a grand dinner.

2 measures/3 tbsp vodka
1 measure/1½ tbsp Bénédictine
dash Angostura bitters

Add the ingredients to a whisky tumbler or Old-Fashioned glass half-full of cracked ice, and stir gently.

2 measures/3 tbsp chilli-flavoured
 vodka
1 measure/1½ tbsp fino sherry
7 measures/150ml/¼ pint tomato juice
1 measure/1½ tbsp lemon juice
2–3 dashes Tabasco
10–15ml/2–3 tsp Worcestershire sauce
2.5ml/½ tsp creamed horseradish
5ml/1 tsp celery salt
salt and ground black pepper
celery stalk, stuffed green olives and a
 cherry tomato, to decorate

Fill a pitcher with cracked ice and add the vodka, sherry and tomato juice. Stir well. Add the lemon juice, Tabasco, Worcestershire sauce and horseradish. Stir again. Add the celery salt, salt and pepper, and stir until the pitcher has frosted and the contents are chilled. Strain into a tall tumbler, half-filled with ice cubes. Add a stick of celery.

Mint Collins

The original Tom Collins recipe has been adapted since the 1950s to be made with vodka rather than gin. This refreshing, summery variation also adds the cool flavour of mint for extra class.

2 measures/3 tbsp vodka
⅓ measure/1½ tsp green crème de menthe
1 measure/1½ tbsp lemon juice
dash sugar syrup
5 measures/120ml/4fl oz soda water

Half-fill a highball glass with cracked ice, and then add the first four ingredients. Give the drink a good stir and then top up with the soda. Float a sprig of fresh mint on the top.

Chilli Vodkatini

Not quite a Vodkatini, but almost. This recipe produces a hot, savoury drink that is stirred in the manner of the original Dry Martini, and served with a couple of chilli peppers in it.

1 measure/1½ tbsp chilli or pepper vodka
¼ measure/1 tsp dry French vermouth
2 small pickled or vodka-soaked chillies and
    1 pitted green olive, to garnish

Vodkatini

This variation on a Dry Martini was popularized by James Bond. Famously, it should be "shaken, not stirred", which gives the drink a cloudiness not achieved in the classic recipe.

The mixture is basically that of a classic Dry Martini, but with vodka replacing the gin. Since vodka lacks the aromatic character of gin, it is generally served with a twist of lemon rind immersed in the drink, as well as being squeezed over it.

Add the chilli or pepper vodka to a bar glass of ice and mix for about 30 seconds, until the outside of the glass is frosted over. Add the vermouth to a chilled cocktail glass, swirl it around to wet the inside of the glass, and then pour it away. Cut one of the pickled chillies in half and discard the seeds. Thread it through the pitted green olive, and then thread the stuffed olive on to a cocktail stick with the other chilli. Strain the cocktail into the prepared glass. Add the olive and chilli decoration to the drink before serving.

Bartending know-how
There are two kinds of pepper vodka. Some is flavoured with red chillies, but most is spiced with crushed black peppercorns.

Après-Ski

Certainly not to be tried before skiing anyway. The intriguing mixture of aniseed, mint and lemon in this drink is quite a challenge. Somehow the mint emphasizes the flavour of the Pernod. One should be enough, not least because the drink has an exceedingly long aftertaste.

1 measure/1½ tbsp vodka
1 measure/1½ tbsp Pernod
½ measure/2 tsp green crème de menthe
5 measures/120ml/4fl oz sparkling lemonade

Shake the first three ingredients with ice, and then strain into a highball glass with a couple of ice cubes in it. Add the lemonade. Garnish the drink with a sprig of mint and a slice of lemon.

Harvey Wallbanger

This is the next step up from a Screwdriver, with a dash of Galliano added. It is a 1970s recipe that supposedly derives its name from having left a gentleman called Harvey, who had downed several of them, in the walking-into-walls state. There is no need to go quite that far, but it's easy to see why the formula became such a popular one in nightclubs.

2 measures/3 tbsp vodka
¾ measure/3 tsp Galliano
5 measures/120ml/4fl oz orange juice

Add the vodka and orange juice to a highball glass half-filled with cracked ice. Pour the Galliano carefully over the top so that it floats above the other ingredients. Garnish with a half-slice of orange, decorated with a canelle knife.

Kiss and Tell

A thoroughly exotic mixture of flavours goes into this modern cocktail, and the resulting throbbingly vibrant colour is something to be seen.

Bartending know-how
The blue Bols curaçao is so popular that it is probably now the flagship product of their liqueur range.

1 measure/1½ tbsp vodka
½ measure/2 tsp Galliano
¼ measure/1 tsp dry vermouth
¼ measure/1 tsp blue curaçao
2 measures/3 tbsp orange juice
1 measure/1½ tbsp passion fruit juice

Shake all the ingredients with roughly crushed ice and pour everything out into a tall glass. Garnish with a half-slice of orange and a cherry.

Liberator

Here is another of those cocktails full of blended, tropical fruit flavours, to which a vodka base lends itself so well.

1½ measures/6 tsp vodka
½ measure/2 tsp Midori or other melon liqueur
2 measures/3 tbsp mango juice
½ measure/2 tsp lime juice

Shake all the ingredients well with ice, and strain into a cocktail glass. Garnish with a neatly cut sliver of mango and a slice of lime.

Barbara

This is a variation on the White Russian, but with a chocolatey flavour replacing the original coffee.

1 measure/1½ tbsp vodka
1 measure/1½ tbsp white crème de cacao
½ measure/2 tsp double (heavy) cream

Shake all the ingredients well with ice, and strain into a cocktail glass. The surface of the drink can be sprinkled with grated chocolate.

Piranha

This is one of those deceptive cocktails that tastes relatively harmless, but in fact packs quite a bite, much like the predatory flesh-eating fish after which it is named.

1½ measures/6 tsp vodka
1 measure/1½ tbsp of brown crème de cacao
1 measure/1½ tbsp ice-cold cola

Pour the alcohol into a rocks glass containing plenty of cracked ice and stir vigorously, before adding the cola.

Bartending know-how
Brands of cola have proliferated like wildfire ever since the success of the original Coca-Cola. There are low-sugar and caffeine-free versions, and there is now a French brand aimed at the Muslim market.

Camshaft

I am not at all certain how this drink came to be named after part of a car engine. Perhaps the fruit juices in it act as sliding parts to facilitate the passage of the alcohol.

1 measure/1½ tbsp vodka
½ measure/2 tsp Campari
1 measure/1½ tbsp passion fruit juice
1 measure/1½ tbsp orange juice
1 measure/1½ tbsp sparkling lemonade

Pour the ingredients in this order into a rocks glass half-full of cracked ice. Stir briefly and gently, being careful not to neutralize the fizz in the lemonade. Garnish with a half-slice of orange and a half-slice of lemon.

Katinka

This fruity mixture achieves a nice balance of sweet and sour flavours, and is revved up with the added horsepower of the vodka. A good Russian brand such as Stolichnaya would be the optimum choice for the drink.

1½ measures/6 tsp vodka
1 measure/1½ tbsp apricot brandy
½ measure/2 tsp lime juice

Shake all the ingredients well with ice, and strain into a cocktail glass heaped with slivered ice. Add a slice of lime.

SOS

Lemon vodka is called for in this drink. Russian types are termed limonnaya and flavoured with natural lemon essence, or there is a mixed citrus version made by the Swedish Absolut company called Citron.

1 measure/1½ tbsp lemon vodka
1 measure/1½ tbsp peach schnapps
2 measures/3 tbsp unsweetened mandarin juice (from a can, if necessary)
¼ measure/1 tsp grenadine

Shake all the ingredients well with ice, and strain into a large cocktail glass. Garnish with a slice of lemon and a mandarin segment on a cocktail stick, and add a short straw.

Cooch Behar

This drink was supposedly created in an idle moment by the Maharajah of that eponymous part of India. It is basically a stripped-down, hot Bloody Mary.

2 measures/3 tbsp chilli or pepper vodka
4 measures/6 tbsp tomato juice

Add the ingredients to a rocks glass or whisky tumbler packed with ice cubes.

Czarina

A recipe from the age when vodka was still enough of a commercial novelty for a drink containing it to be given a name with glamorous Russian connotations.

1 measure/1½ tbsp vodka
½ measure/2 tsp apricot brandy
½ measure/2 tsp dry vermouth
dash Angostura bitters

Stir all the ingredients well with ice in a pitcher, and then strain into a chilled cocktail glass.

Graffiti

Grape juice isn't used that often in the cocktail repertoire, which is a pity, as its natural sweetness works well, particularly with the clear spirits.

1½ measures/6 tsp vodka
2 measures/3 tbsp white grape juice

2 measures/3 tbsp sparkling cherryade

Pour the vodka and grape juice into a large wine goblet half-filled with cracked ice. Stir to combine, and then add the cherryade. Garnish with a green seedless grape and a cocktail cherry.

Balalaika

My note on the Czarina applies equally here. The formula is basically a variation on the White Lady recipe, with vodka replacing the gin. As such, it has a slightly milder spirit flavour, but the sharp citrus flavours are still appetizingly apparent.

1½ measures/6 tsp vodka
¾ measure/3 tsp Cointreau
¾ measure/3 tsp lemon juice

Shake the ingredients well with plenty of ice, and strain into a cocktail glass. Add an orange-and-cherry garnish.

Kew Punch

This is a very drinkable concoction of vodka, sweet vermouth, curaçao, gin and cherry brandy served over fresh summer fruits.

1 measure/1½ tbsp vodka
1 measure/1½ tbsp sweet red vermouth
1 measure/1½ tbsp orange curaçao
⅔ measure/1 tbsp gin
⅔ measure/1 tbsp cherry brandy
assorted soft summer fruits, sliced
1–2 dashes Angostura bitters

2 measures/3 tbsp American dry ginger ale
2 measures/3 tbsp sparkling lemonade

Measure the vodka, vermouth, curaçao, gin and cherry brandy into a pitcher of ice and stir well to chill. Strain into a highball glass full of ice cubes and the sliced summer fruits (peach, apricot, strawberries, raspberries, etc). Add the bitters, and then pour in the chilled ginger ale and lemonade. Garnish with twists of lemon rind and leaves of lemon balm or mint.

Salty Dog

The name refers to the salt frosting that the glass is given. Otherwise, this is a bracingly sour and simple mixture of vodka and grapefruit juice that makes a good aperitif.

2 measures/3 tbsp vodka
5 measures/120ml/4fl oz grapefruit juice

Salt the rim of a highball glass by dipping it first in grapefruit juice and then in fine-ground sea salt. Half-fill it with cracked ice. Shake the liquid ingredients together with ice, and then strain into the prepared chilled glass. Add a decorative twist of grapefruit rind.

Black Cossack

You may think its presence will hardly be noticed, but the extra kick given to the beer by the slug of vodka in a Black Cossack is an appreciable one.

1 measure/1½ tbsp vodka
300ml/½ pint Guinness

Add well-chilled Guinness to a highball or half-pint glass into which a measure of ice-cold vodka has already been poured. Wait for the head on the beer to settle before drinking.

Ménage-à-Trois

Many modern cocktails have ice cream added to them. It gives a richer flavour and creamier texture, and makes for an altogether luxurious mixture. This is a particularly naughty example.

1 measure/1½ tbsp vodka
4 strawberries
1 measure/1½ tbsp coconut cream
30ml/2 tbsp rich chocolate ice cream

Add all the ingredients to a liquidizer with cracked ice and blend for 20 seconds or so, until the strawberries are quite pulverized. Strain into a chilled rocks glass. Garnish with another whole strawberry.

Slow Comfortable Screw

The 1970s idea of a joke in the drink's name may be a touch embarrassing now, but the mixture is a good one, and the drink was something of a modern classic a generation ago.

1 measure/1½ tbsp vodka
¾ measure/3 tsp Southern Comfort
¾ measure/3 tsp sloe gin
5 measures/120ml/4fl oz orange juice

Add the first three ingredients to a highball glass half-packed with ice. Stir to combine, and then top up with the orange juice. Garnish with a cocktail cherry on a stick for the essential seventies touch, and add two long straws. A plastic novelty will add that final note of sheer class, as will throwing back three of them and then slow-dancing with somebody ghastly.

Cosmopolitan

This drink has a similar bracing flavour to a Sea Breeze, but the sweet liqueur shows through the bitter juices.

1½ measures/6 tsp vodka
1 measure/1½ tbsp Cointreau
1 measure/1½ tbsp cranberry juice
½ measure/2 tsp lime juice

Shake all the ingredients well with ice, and strain into a large cocktail glass. Dangle a twist of orange in the drink.

Bailey's Comet

The spirit turns the popular creamy liqueur into a rather stiffer proposition.

1 measure/1½ tbsp vodka
1 measure/1½ tbsp Bailey's

Combine the ingredients with cracked ice in a rocks glass. The quantity can safely be doubled to save time, as you're bound to want another.

Sea Breeze

One of today's most requested cocktails, Sea Breeze was one of the first popular cocktails to use cranberry juice. Ocean Spray is one of the most famous brands, but the supermarkets nearly all have a proprietary version.

2 measures/3 tbsp vodka
2 measures/3 tbsp grapefruit juice
3 measures/4½ tbsp cranberry juice

Shake all the ingredients well with plenty of ice, and pour everything into a chilled highball glass. Add a wedge of lime and a few cranberries.

Bartending know-how
Cranberry juice is a sugar-and-water product. It is possible to buy apple juice with cranberry if you want neither sugar nor water.

Pompanski

This drink specifically calls for one of the premium Polish vodkas. Its soft texture and rounded feel in the mouth are a world away from neutral commercial vodka.

1 measure/1½ tbsp Wodka Wyborowa
½ measure/2 tsp dry vermouth
¼ measure/1 tsp Cointreau
1 measure/1½ tbsp grapefruit juice

Shake all the ingredients together with three or four ice cubes and then pour everything, unstrained, into a rocks glass. Add a twist of grapefruit rind.

Hammer Horror

Use the best vanilla ice cream you can find for this, and preferably one that is made with whole egg and real vanilla, for extra richness.

1 measure/1½ tbsp vodka
1 measure/1½ tbsp Kahlúa
60ml/4 tbsp vanilla ice cream

Add all the ingredients to a liquidizer with cracked ice, blend for a few seconds and then strain into a cocktail glass. Sprinkle the surface of the drink with grated dark chocolate.

French Horn

The drink is so called because it calls for a particular variety of French liqueur called Chambord, made from black raspberries. If you can't find it, substitute ordinary crème de framboise. Its sweetness is thrown into relief with the neutrality of the vodka and the sharpness of the lemon juice.

1 measure/1½ tbsp vodka
¾ measure/3 tsp Chambord (or crème de framboise)
½ measure/2 tsp lemon juice

Stir the ingredients in a pitcher with plenty of ice. Strain into a cocktail glass and garnish with a whole raspberry.

Hot Cherry

Solve the Russo-Polish dispute as to which of them originally invented vodka by combining both nationalities (in even-handed measure of course) in this exciting cocktail. The tonic water adds a pleasantly bitter note to the rich cherry fruitiness of the mixture.

1 measure/1½ tbsp Stolichnaya vodka
1 measure/1½ tbsp Wisniowka (Polish cherry vodka)
2 measures/3 tbsp tonic water

Shake the vodkas with plenty of cracked ice, strain into a rocks glass containing two ice cubes and add the tonic. Garnish with a cherry.

Kir Lethale

The raisins for this cocktail should be soaked overnight in vodka to give the drink that extra kick. This is a party recipe to serve six.

6 vodka-soaked raisins
30ml/2 tbsp vodka
3 measures/4½ tbsp crème de cassis
1 bottle brut champagne or dry sparkling wine, chilled

Place a vodka-soaked raisin at the bottom of each glass. Add ¼ measure/1 tsp plain vodka or the vodka from the steeped raisins, if using, to each glass. Add ½ measure/2 tsp crème de cassis to each and finish the drinks with the champagne or sparkling wine.

Pushkin's Punch

This powerful cocktail is named after the great Russian writer. Use a good sparkling wine from Australia or California.

1 measure/1½ tbsp vodka
1 measure/1½ tbsp Grand Marnier
dash lime juice
dash orange bitters (or orange curaçao)
dry sparkling wine

Shake the first four ingredients with ice, and strain into a chilled, large wine goblet. Top up with sparkling wine.

Soft Fruit and Ginger Cup

This colourful medley of soft fruits is steeped in vodka and served with an icy blend of sorbet and ginger ale. You will definitely need to use spoons. The recipe serves four, and can be used as a summer dinner-party dessert.

115g/4oz strawberries, hulled
115g/4oz raspberries, hulled
50g/2oz blueberries
15ml/1 tbsp caster (superfine) sugar
4 measures/6 tbsp vodka
600ml/1 pint still ginger ale
4 large scoops orange sorbet
1 measure/1½ tbsp grenadine

Cut the strawberries in half and put them in a bowl with the raspberries, blueberries and sugar. Pour over the vodka and toss lightly. Cover and chill for at least 30 minutes. Put the ginger ale and sorbet in a blender or food processor and process until smooth. Pour into four bowl-shaped glasses and

add a couple of ice cubes to each glass of sorbet mixture. Spoon ¼ measure/1 tsp grenadine over the ice cubes in each glass, then spoon the vodka-steeped fruits on top of the sorbet mixture and ice cubes. Garnish each glass with a physalis and serve.

Vodka and Kumquat Lemonade

This is a mild-sounding name for what is a strong concoction of kumquat and peppercorn-flavoured vodka and white curaçao. The recipe comfortably serves two, in long glasses.

90g/3oz kumquats
5 measures/120ml/4fl oz vodka
3 black peppercorns
⅔ measure/1 tbsp white curaçao
⅔ measure/1 tbsp lemon juice
7 measures/150ml/¼ pint sparkling mineral or soda water
fresh mint leaves

Thickly slice the kumquats and add to the vodka in an airtight jar with the cracked black peppercorns. Set aside for at least a couple of hours or overnight if possible. Fill a pitcher with cracked ice and then add the curaçao, the lemon juice and the kumquat-flavoured vodka with the sliced kumquats (but not the peppercorns). Using a long swizzle-stick, stir together well. Add the mineral or soda water and a few fresh mint leaves and gently stir everything together. Pour the drink into chilled glasses of ice. Add slices of kumquats to the glasses and garnish with extra mint sprigs.

Woo Woo

A creation of the 1980s, Woo Woo was one of the first cocktail recipes to use peach schnapps. Archer's Peach County was the brand preferred, and the recipe is still a popular one on today's cocktail lists.

1 measure/1½ tbsp vodka
1½ measures/6 tsp peach schnapps
4 measures/6 tbsp cranberry juice

Shake all the ingredients well with ice, and strain into a highball glass half-filled with cracked ice.

Bartending know-how
Peach schnapps is not really a true schnapps, but a sort of schnapps-based liqueur. Archer's now make lime and cranberry versions to supplement the original peach.

Nevsky Prospekt

The Russian reference here is to a boulevard in Moscow. You can add ¼ measure/1 tsp sugar syrup if you feel it needs a touch of extra sweetness, but I prefer it quite sour.

1½ measures/6 tsp Stolichnaya vodka
½ measure/2 tsp light rum
½ measure/2 tsp orange curaçao
¼ measure/1 tsp lime juice

Shake all the ingredients well with ice, and strain into a cocktail glass. Garnish with a half-slice of lime.

Green Dragon

You will find one glass of this dry, savoury and extremely strong cocktail is more than enough. Sip it slowly, or be brave and take it at a couple of gulps. Then lie down.

Blackhawk

A lustrous purple is more the colour here than black, and the combination of fruit flavours is quite enchanting. This is a very moreish short drink with an appealing balance of sweet and sour.

1½ measures/6 tsp vodka
½ measure/2 tsp crème de mûre
½ measure/2 tsp lime juice

Shake all the ingredients well with ice, and strain into a cocktail glass. Add a whole, perfectly ripe blackberry and a half-slice of lime.

2 measures/3 tbsp Stolichnaya vodka
1 measure/1½ tbsp green Chartreuse

Shake the ingredients well with ice, and strain into a cocktail glass.

Blue Shark

Blue curaçao mixes so well with clear spirits that it would seem a shame not to include a vodka-based recipe, and here is a popular American one.

1 measure/1½ tbsp vodka
1 measure/1½ tbsp tequila
½ measure/2 tsp blue curaçao

Shake all the ingredients well with ice, and strain into a small rocks glass. Squeeze a little orange rind over the drink to release the oil, but don't add the rind itself.

Bartending know-how
The kümmel you will buy for making a Boyar will most probably be the pre-eminent Wolfschmidt brand. It has been sold in the UK since the late Victorian era, having originally made its name in the Baltic state of Latvia.

Genoa

This is something like a strong Screwdriver with the bittering element of Campari adding savoury appeal.

1½ measures/6 tsp vodka
2 measures/3 tbsp orange juice
¾ measure/3 tsp Campari

Shake all the ingredients well with ice, and strain into a rocks glass containing a couple of cubes of ice. Add a twist of orange rind.

Boyar

This very dry and herb-tinged mixture would make a good appetite-whetter at a party where nibbles are going to be served. The tiny quantity of kümmel shines through, and leaves a very appetizing aftertaste in its wake.

Borodino

Let's get serious. This is a strong cocktail, with the ingredients in the 37.5% to 40% alcohol range, but the result is a virginal-looking white drink.

1 measure/1½ tbsp vodka
1 measure/1½ tbsp gin
1 measure/1½ tbsp Cointreau

Shake all the ingredients well with ice, and strain into a cocktail glass. Add a small piece of orange rind.

2 measures/3 tbsp vodka
½ measure/2 tsp dry vermouth
¼ measure/1 tsp kümmel

Shake with ice, and strain into a cocktail glass. The drink doesn't need a garnish.

Sex on the Beach

A variation on Woo Woo, this version has more fruit juice. The name has, not surprisingly, kept it popular in seaside resorts, as the next best resort after sex.

1 measure/1½ tbsp vodka
1 measure/1½ tbsp peach schnapps
3 measures/4½ tbsp cranberry juice
3 measures/4½ tbsp pineapple juice

Half-fill a highball glass with cracked ice, add all the ingredients in the above order, and stir vigorously. Garnish with pieces of pineapple and orange.

Soviet Cocktail

This is an American drink intended as a sort of grudging acknowledgement of its old adversary, the USSR.

1½ measures/6 tsp vodka
½ measure/2 tsp dry vermouuth
½ measure/2 tsp medium-dry (amontillado) sherry

Shake all the ingredients well with ice, and strain into a cocktail glass. Squeeze a twist of lemon rind over the top and drop it into the drink.

Prussian Salute

This is one of those hardcore cocktails that's all alcohol with no mixers. The sweet fruit notes in it help to soften its impact a little – but not much.

1½ measures/6 tsp vodka
½ measure/2 tsp crème de mûre
½ measure/2 tsp slivovitz
½ measure/2 tsp Cointreau

Shake all the ingredients well with ice, and strain into a cocktail glass. Garnish with a slice of lemon.

Kempinsky Fizz

A luxuriously fruity, fizzy mixture with a delicate pinkish colour, this would kick off a dinner party in fine style.

1½ measures/6 tsp vodka
½ measure/2 tsp crème de cassis
¼ measure/1 tsp lemon juice
4 measures/6 tbsp sparkling ginger ale

Half-fill a chilled tall glass with ice, add the first three ingredients, stir briskly and then top up with ginger ale.

Bartending know-how
The original home of syrupy crème de cassis is Burgundy in eastern France, where much is made in Dijon. As a classic fruit liqueur, it dates back to the mid-19th century, and its principal export market today – somewhat surprisingly – is Japan, where they mix it with soda.

Rum

Before the advent of vodka cocktails, rum was the spirit with which all the exotic flavours were mixed. Coming from the tropical climates of the Caribbean and South America, it was felt to lend itself to all kinds of racy preparations, so unlike the comparative staidness of gin, whisky and brandy. There are basically three grades in the cocktail repertoire: white, light (or golden) and dark. The top-strength naval rums, known as "overproof", are sometimes added in droplets to a mixture: not just to fortify it, but to concentrate the flavour of what is still an under-appreciated spirit.

Tom and Jerry

A cold weather drink invented in the 1850s by the legendary Jerry Thomas of St Louis, Missouri, Tom and Jerry is one of the oldest cocktails in this book. It is said that Mr Thomas would serve these at the first snows of winter. This recipe serves four to six people.

For the batter:
3 eggs
45ml/3 tbsp caster (superfine) sugar
pinch bicarbonate of soda (baking soda)
1 measure/1½ tbsp dark rum
1.5ml/¼ tsp ground cinnamon
pinch ground cloves
pinch allspice

Separate the eggs and beat the whites into stiff peaks, adding 15ml/1 tbsp of the sugar with the bicarbonate. Mix the yolks separately with the rum, the rest of the sugar and the spices. Then fold in the whites with a metal spoon.

For each drink:
1 measure/1½ tbsp dark rum
1 measure/1½ tbsp brandy
4 measures/6 tbsp boiling milk

Using heatproof glasses, put in 15ml/1 tbsp of the batter and 1 measure/1½ tbsp each of rum and brandy, then top up with boiled milk. Dust with nutmeg.

Bacardi Cocktail

The original recipe, this must (legally, in the USA) be made with the world's biggest-selling white rum brand. It's short and sour and altogether perfect.

1½ measures/6 tsp Bacardi white rum
juice of half a lime
¼ measure/1 tsp grenadine

Shake all the ingredients well with ice, and strain into a cocktail glass. Add a slice of lime. (Add a measure of gin to turn it into a Bacardi Special, a variation created in the 1920s.)

Caribbean Breeze

This bang-up-to-date mixture of exotic fruit flavours will have party guests coming back for more.

1½ measures/6 tsp dark rum
½ measure/2 tsp crème de banane
3 measures/4½ tbsp pineapple juice
2 measures/3 tbsp cranberry juice
¼ measure/1 tsp lime cordial

Shake all the ingredients well with ice, and strain into a large wine goblet, generously filled with crushed ice. Garnish with a slice of pineapple and a wedge of lime.

Cuba Libre

This is a brand-specific cocktail if ever there was one. Created in Cuba – where Bacardi was then produced – in the late 19th century, the novelty value of Cuba Libre lay in its use of Coca-Cola, a newfangled tonic beverage, then less than ten years on the market.

juice and rind of half a lime
2 measures/3 tbsp Bacardi white rum
5 measures/120ml/4 fl oz Coca-Cola

Squeeze the juice directly into a highball glass half-filled with cracked ice, and then put the empty rind in too. Add the rum, stir, and finally top up with ice-cold Coca-Cola.

Ti Punch

This is a great favourite in the originally French Caribbean islands.

1 lime
2 measures/3 tbsp French Caribbean white rum
¼ measure/1 tsp sugar syrup

Cut the lime into wedges and put them in a wide-based rocks glass. Pound and crush them with a blunt instrument to release the juices, but leave all the residue in the glass. Add the syrup and the rum, and plenty of cracked ice.

Saoco

I have drunk this cocktail on Barbados served in half a hollowed-out coconut shell, but it does nearly as well served in a plain glass tumbler. Coconut milk is the watery liquid that is released from the centre of a coconut when the end is pierced, and not to be confused with canned coconut cream.

2 measures/3 tbsp white rum
4 measures/6 tbsp coconut milk

Shake both the ingredients well with ice, and then strain into a rocks glass that has been half-filled with finely crushed ice. Drink through two short straws.

Waikiki Beach

This creamy, nutty, exotic cocktail has the power to call up memories of Caribbean beach holidays gone by.

1½ measures/6 tsp white rum
½ measure/2 tsp amaretto
½ measure/2 tsp canned coconut cream
2 measures/3 tbsp pineapple juice
1 measure/1½ tbsp passion fruit juice
1 measure/1½ tbsp double (heavy) cream

Shake all the ingredients well with ice, and strain into a bowl-shaped cocktail glass half-filled with cracked ice. Garnish with a cube of pineapple and a cocktail cherry.

Mary Pickford

A 1920s recipe in tribute to one of the greats among the first generation of silent movie stars.

1½ measures/6 tsp white rum
1½ measures/6 tsp pineapple juice
¼ measure/1 tsp grenadine
dash maraschino

Shake all the ingredients well with ice, and strain into a cocktail glass filled with crushed ice. Garnish with a cocktail cherry.

Daiquiri

The Daiquiri is one of the most adapted and abused cocktails in the repertoire. Created in the 1890s, it is named after a town in Cuba and was originally nothing more than a white rum sour. Despite its extreme simplicity, this really is one of the all-time perfect cocktail recipes, standing proud above the fashionable fruit versions mentioned below.

2 measures/3 tbsp white rum
juice of half a lime or a quarter of a lemon
5ml/1 tsp caster (superfine) sugar

Shake all the ingredients well with ice to dissolve the sugar, and strain into a well-chilled cocktail glass. Serve ungarnished.

Fruit Daiquiri

The original Daiquiri recipe of white rum shaken with lemon or lime juice and a pinch of sugar can be adapted by adding a measure of any of the fruit liqueurs to it, with about 50g/2oz of the equivalent puréed fruit as well. The sugar can then be left out. A strawberry version, made with crème de fraise and pulped fruit, is especially enticing, and banana is a crowd-pleaser too.

Presidente

Another 1920s Cuban recipe, this is named in honour of one of the island's old military rulers.

2 measures/3 tbsp white rum
1 measure/1½ tbsp orange curaçao
½ measure/2 tsp dry vermouth
¼ measure/1 tsp grenadine

Stir the ingredients with ice in a pitcher to chill them well, and then strain into a frozen rocks glass. Add a slice of lemon, decorated around the edges with a canelle knife.

Planter's Punch

This long, refreshing, old colonial drink originates from the sugar plantations that are dotted throughout the West Indian islands.

1 measure/1½ tbsp fresh lime juice
1 measure/1½ tbsp orange juice
2 measures/3 tbsp dark rum
½ measure/2 tsp grenadine
dash Angostura bitters
soda water or lemonade, chilled

Columbus

A simple and appealing mixture of sweet and sour, Columbus must absolutely be made with light rum, but if that's the only colour you haven't got, use a half-and-half mixture of dark and white.

1½ measures/6 tsp light rum
¾ measure/3 tsp apricot brandy
1 measure/1½ tbsp lime juice

Shake all the ingredients well with ice, and strain into a cocktail glass. Garnish with a slice of lime.

Squeeze the lime and orange juices and add them to a pitcher of ice. Add the dark rum and the grenadine, and mix them together well for about 20 seconds. Add a dash of Angostura bitters to the bottom of a wide tumbler filled with cracked ice cubes. Strain the rum and grenadine mixture into the chilled tumbler. Finish with plenty of chilled soda water or lemonade, according to taste.

Garnish with two skewered peach slices and a physalis, complete with its leaves attached.

Mai Tai

This is a very refreshing, long but strong party drink that slides down easily – just before you do!

1 measure/1½ tbsp light rum
1 measure/1½ tbsp dark rum
1 measure/1½ tbsp apricot brandy
3 measures/4½ tbsp orange juice
3 measures/4½ tbsp pineapple juice
1 measure/1½ tbsp grenadine

Shake the first five ingredients well with ice, and strain into a highball glass half-filled with cracked ice. Slowly pour the grenadine into the glass, letting it sink to the bottom of the drink to make a glowing red layer. The cocktail could be lavishly garnished with tropical fruits.

Monkey Wrench

Deliciously refreshing, despite its indelicate name, this makes a fine drink for a summer afternoon in the garden.

1½ measures/6 tsp white rum
3 measures/4½ tbsp grapefruit juice
3 measures/4½ tbsp sparkling lemonade

Half-fill a highball glass with roughly cracked ice, and add the rum and grapefruit juice. Stir briskly, before topping up with the sparkling lemonade. Decorate with intertwined twists of grapefruit and lemon rind in a suitably artistic arrangement.

Blue Hawaiian

This drink can be decorated as flamboyantly as Carmen Miranda's headdress with a mixture of fruits and leaves. It is an eye-catching, colourful cocktail that you'll find very drinkable.

1 measure/1½ tbsp blue curaçao
1 measure/1½ tbsp coconut cream
2 measures/3 tbsp light rum
2 measures/3 tbsp pineapple juice
leaves and wedge of pineapple, slice of
    prickly pear or orange, a wedge of lime and
    a maraschino cherry, to garnish

Escape Route

Punt e Mes, made by the Carpano company of Turin, is one of the classic vermouth brands, and is a must for this elegant cocktail.

1 measure/1½ tbsp light rum
1 measure/1½ tbsp Punt e Mes
½ measure/2 tsp crème de fraise
4 measures/6 tbsp sparkling lemonade

Half-fill a highball glass with cracked ice, and add the first three ingredients. Stir vigorously before topping up with the lemonade. Garnish with a slice of lemon and a couple of mint leaves.

Put the curaçao, coconut cream and light rum in a blender with a few cubes of ice. Process very briefly until the colour is even. Add the pineapple juice to the blender and process the mixture once more until frothy. Spoon crushed ice into a large cocktail glass or goblet until three-quarters full. Strain the cocktail from the blender over the crushed ice.

Garnish with a wedge of pineapple, a slice of prickly pear or orange, a wedge of lime and a maraschino cherry.

Zombie

This legendary 1930s recipe was created at Don the Beachcomber restaurant in Hollywood, reportedly as a hangover cure! It has everything but the kitchen sink in it, and yet is a harmonious (and dynamic) mixture.

1 measure/1½ tbsp light rum
½ measure/2 tsp dark rum
½ measure/2 tsp white rum
1 measure/1½ tbsp orange curaçao
¼ measure/1 tsp Pernod
1 measure/1½ tbsp lemon juice
1 measure/1½ tbsp orange juice
1 measure/1½ tbsp pineapple juice
½ measure/2 tsp papaya juice
¼ measure/1 tsp grenadine
½ measure/2 tsp orgeat (almond syrup)
¼ measure/1 tsp overproof rum

Blend all but the last ingredient with ice, and strain into an ice-packed highball glass. Sprinkle with overproof rum. Garnish with a slice of pineapple, a slice of lime and a mint sprig.

Piña Colada

This has to be one of the most popular cocktails worldwide, with a name meaning "strained pineapple". For that extra Caribbean touch, the drink may be served in a hollowed-out pineapple shell, which also means that you can liquidize the flesh for the juice in the recipe, but a bowl-shaped cocktail glass is the next best thing.

2 measures/3 tbsp white rum
2 measures/3 tbsp pineapple juice
1½ measures/6 tsp coconut cream
5ml/1 tsp caster (superfine) sugar (if freshly blended fruit is used)

Shake all the ingredients well with ice, and strain into a cocktail goblet. Garnish with a slice of pineapple and a cherry. (If you can't get hold of coconut cream, the equivalent quantity of any coconut liqueur such as Malibu may be used to good effect.)

Passion Punch

Although it is not really a punch at all, the combination of passion fruit and grape juices in this recipe is a winning one. The acidity of the one is mitigated by the sweetness of the other, with the pineapple syrup adding a viscous texture to the drink.

Hustler

This is a sharply tangy drink. I prefer it without sugar to emphasize its bite, but around 5ml/1 tsp will not go amiss, if you find it just too sour without.

1 measure/1½ tbsp light rum
1 measure/1½ tbsp white rum
1 measure/1½ tbsp passion fruit juice
juice of a lime
5ml/1 tsp caster (superfine) sugar (optional)

Shake all the ingredients well with ice (especially well to dissolve the sugar if you are using it), and strain into a large wine goblet. Add the empty shell of the lime to the drink.

1½ measures/6 tsp light rum
1 measure/1½ tbsp red grape juice
1 measure/1½ tbsp passion fruit juice
¼ measure/1 tsp pineapple syrup (from a can)

Shake all the ingredients well with ice, and strain into a rocks glass.

Sun City

A similar type of blend to the Mai Tai, and almost as lethal, this is a drink with plenty of personality.

1 measure/1½ tbsp white rum
½ measure/2 tsp dark rum
½ measure/2 tsp Galliano
½ measure/2 tsp apricot brandy
2 measures/3 tbsp pineapple juice
¼ measure/1 tsp lime juice
3 measures/4½ tbsp sparkling lemonade

Shake all but the last ingredient with ice, and then strain into a highball glass. Top up with the lemonade. Garnish with slices of lemon and lime.

Captain's Cocktail

This is named after Captain Morgan rum. Cocktail author Robert Cross suggests that the port be added to half of the drink's surface, so that it can be imbibed from the port side, as it were.

1 measure/1½ tbsp white rum
½ measure/2 tsp Captain Morgan spiced rum
1 measure/1½ tbsp lime juice
2.5ml/½ tsp caster (superfine) sugar
½ measure/2 tsp good ruby port

Shake the first four ingredients well with ice, and strain into a small tumbler. Sprinkle the port on top, and garnish with a slice of lime.

Costa del Sol

This is a light, sweet, fizzy drink with a gentle flavour, one of the less tastebud-startling rum cocktails.

2 measures/3 tbsp white rum
1 measure/1½ tbsp sweet red vermouth
1 measure/1½ tbsp sugar syrup
½ measure/2 tsp lemon juice
3 measures/4½ tbsp soda water

Half-fill a highball glass with cracked ice, and then add the first four ingredients. Stir, before adding the soda. Garnish with lemon pierced by a cocktail stick.

Beach Peach

The flavour of this cocktail is largely derived from pure, thick peach nectar, and the drink has a nice balance of sweet and sharp flavours. It tastes alluring when sipped on the beach.

1½ measures/6 tsp white rum
¾ measure/3 tsp peach brandy
1 measure/1½ tbsp peach nectar
½ measure/2 tsp lime juice
¼ measure/1 tsp sugar syrup

Shake all the ingredients well with ice, and strain into a rocks glass half-filled with cracked ice. Garnish with a slice of ripe peach and a cherry.

Frozen Coconut

You may well have tasted something like this ice cream drink at a Thai restaurant with a cocktail list.

1½ measures/6 tsp white rum
1 measure/1½ tbsp Malibu or other coconut liqueur
45ml/3 tbsp coconut ice cream

Frost the rim of a large goblet by dipping it in coconut liqueur and then into grated or desiccated coconut. Half-fill it with finely crushed ice. Process all the ingredients thoroughly in a blender with plenty of ice, and strain into the prepared glass. Drink through a short straw, quickly.

Mulata

A Cuban creation of the 1940s, Mulata offers a beguiling combination of chocolate and lime flavours. It's a short but delicious drink that may well have you wanting a second one.

1¾ measures/2½ tbsp of light rum
¼ measure/1 tsp brown crème de cacao
juice of half a lime

Shake all the ingredients well with ice, and strain into a cocktail glass. Garnish with a half-slice of lime.

Jamaica Sunday

A spoonful of honey adds sweetness and an exotic note to this cocktail, the name of which indicates that it should specifically be made with a good Jamaican brand of rum. The darker and stronger the brand, the better.

2 measures/3 tbsp dark rum
¼ measure/1 tsp acacia honey

½ measure/2 tsp lime juice
2 measures/3 tbsp sparkling lemonade

In a separate glass, stir the honey into the dark rum until it is dissolved. Half-fill a rocks glass with cracked ice, and then add the honey-rum mixture and the lime juice, and stir again. Add the lemonade. Garnish with lime slices.

Goldilocks

The name is a rough approximation of the final colour of this appealing fruit-juice cocktail.

1 measure/1½ tbsp dark rum
1 measure/1½ tbsp Malibu
3 measures/4½ tbsp pineapple juice
2 measures/3 tbsp orange juice

Shake with ice, and strain into a tall glass half-filled with cracked ice. Garnish with slices of pineapple and orange.

Angel's Treat

The addition of cocoa powder to the mixture makes this an unusual but successful recipe. It should be sieved to remove any lumps, and combines very well with the almond-paste flavour of amaretto.

1½ measures/6 tsp dark rum
1 measure/1½ tbsp Disaronno Amaretto
1½ measures/6 tsp double (heavy) cream
2.5ml/½ tsp cocoa powder

Shake all the ingredients very vigorously with ice to dissolve the cocoa, and strain into a bowl-shaped cocktail glass. Sprinkle the surface with grated dark chocolate.

Arrowhead

The peachy flavour of Southern Comfort works well with fruity banana and lemon notes in this lightly fizzy rum cocktail.

1 measure/1½ tbsp dark rum
½ measure/2 tsp Southern Comfort
½ measure/2 tsp crème de banane
¼ measure/1 tsp lime juice
3 measures/4½ tbsp sparkling lemonade

Fill a rocks glass with ice nearly to the brim, and then add the ingredients in the order above. Give the drink a gentle stir without dispersing the fizz, and garnish with a half-slice of lemon.

Hurricane

There are almost as many different recipes for a drink called Hurricane as there are cocktail books, but this particular one, with its exuberantly fruity character, is my favourite.

1½ measures/6 tsp dark rum
1 measure/1½ tbsp white rum
1 measure/1½ tbsp lime juice
2 measures/3 tbsp passion fruit juice
1 measure/1½ tbsp pineapple juice
1 measure/1½ tbsp orange juice
½ measure/2 tsp blackcurrant syrup (from a can of fruit)

Chop Nut

An ingenious blend of coconut, chocolate and hazelnut flavours, all sharpened up with orange, this is a most satisfying drink.

1 measure/1½ tbsp white rum
¾ measure/3 tsp Malibu
½ measure/2 tsp white crème de cacao
¼ measure/1 tsp Frangelico
1½ measures/6 tsp mandarin juice

Shake all the ingredients well with ice, and strain into a bowl-shaped cocktail glass. For a slightly frothier texture, add 5ml/1 tsp egg white as well. Garnish with a twist of mandarin rind.

Shake all the ingredients well with ice, and strain into a highball glass. Decorate with slices of pineapple and orange and a cherry.

Emerald Star

Despite the presence of the green melon liqueur, the colour of this drink isn't exactly emerald. It's a pretty name nonetheless.

1 measure/1½ tbsp white rum
⅔ measure/1 tbsp Midori
⅓ measure/1½ tsp apricot brandy
⅓ measure/1½ tsp lime juice
1 measure/1½ tbsp passion fruit juice

Shake all the ingredients well with ice, and strain into a cocktail glass. Garnish with a slice of star fruit.

Bartending know-how
When the Japanese melon liqueur, Midori, was launched in New York in 1978, the party was held at the fabled Studio 54 nightclub. John Travolta, who had just made *Grease*, was among the guests.

Eye of the Tiger

This is another drink that has a dark rum float on top. It adds a suitably tigerish bite to what otherwise tastes like a rather innocent fruity mixture.

1 measure/1½ tbsp light rum
1 measure/1½ tbsp Malibu
1 measure/1½ tbsp cranberry juice
1 measure/1½ tbsp lemon juice
1 measure/1½ tbsp orange juice
1 measure/1½ tbsp sugar syrup
½ measure/2 tsp dark rum, preferably overproof

Shake all but the last ingredient well with ice, and strain into a highball glass half-filled with cracked ice. Sprinkle the dark rum on to the surface of the drink, and garnish with a slice of orange.

Petite Fleur

This tangy, refreshing cocktail makes a good aperitif. I'm not sure what flower is meant to be invoked by its name. Perhaps you can decide as you drink it.

1 measure/1½ tbsp white rum
1 measure/1½ tbsp Cointreau
1 measure/1½ tbsp grapefruit juice

Shake all the ingredients well with ice, and strain into a cocktail glass. Add a twist of grapefruit rind.

Rompope

Legend has it that this rich egg-nog was first made in the kitchens of a convent in Puebla, Mexico. It is traditional to seal bottles of Rompope with rolled corn husks, or corn cobs that have been stripped of their corn. The recipe makes 1.5 litres/2½ pints, and will keep for up to one week in the refrigerator.

1 litre/1¾ pints milk
350g/12oz sugar
2.5ml/½ tsp bicarbonate of soda (baking soda)
1 cinnamon stick
12 large egg yolks
300ml/½ pint dark rum

Pour the milk into a pan and stir in the sugar and bicarbonate of soda. Add the cinnamon stick. Place the pan over a medium heat and bring the mixture to the boil, stirring constantly. Immediately pour the mixture into a bowl and cool to room temperature. Remove the cinnamon stick, squeezing it gently to release any liquid.

Put the egg yolks in a heatproof bowl over a pan of simmering water and whisk until the mixture is very thick

and pale. Add the whisked yolks to the milk mixture a little at a time, beating after each addition.

Return the mixture to a clean pan, place over a low heat and cook until the mixture thickens and the back of the spoon is visible when a finger is drawn along it. Stir in the rum, pour into sterilized bottles and seal tightly with stoppers or clear film (plastic wrap). Chill until required, and serve very cold.

Yum Yum

The name of this drink is an indication of most people's reactions to this exotically fruity recipe with a fleeting hint of coconut.

1½ measures/6 tsp white rum
½ measure/2 tsp Malibu
1 measure/1½ tbsp mango juice
1 measure/1½ tbsp peach juice
½ measure/2 tsp lime juice

Shake all the ingredients well with ice, and strain into a highball glass half-filled with roughly cracked ice. Garnish with a slice of lime.

Bartending know-how
Malibu is from Jamaica, but its white rum base comes from Barbados.

Poker

Here is a simple cocktail from the 1920s. The preference now is for the proportions given below, although it was originally half-and-half. It may also be made with light rum instead of white, if you prefer.

1½ measures/6 tsp white rum
¾ measure/3 tsp sweet red vermouth

Shake the ingredients well with ice, and strain into a cocktail glass. Squeeze a twist of orange rind over the surface of the drink to release a spray of oil and then drop it in.

Bartending know-how
Recipes based on white rum are far more interesting if made with one of the small producers' island rums, rather than one of the big multi-national proprietary products.

Morning Joy

One wouldn't necessarily recommend making a habit of these, but the idea is of a more robust approach than usual to the glass of breakfast juice. How much joy it spreads over the morning may well depend on how joyful the night before was.

1½ measures/6 tsp light rum
6 measures/135ml/4½fl oz grapefruit juice
¼ measure/1 tsp sloe gin

Half-fill a highball glass with cracked ice, and then add the ingredients in this order, sprinkling the sloe gin on top as a float.

X.Y.Z.

The significance of its mysterious algebraic name escapes me, but this is a 1920s recipe that has survived the test of time. It's a strong one too.

2 measures/3 tbsp dark rum
1 measure/1½ tbsp Cointreau
1 measure/1½ tbsp lemon juice

Shake all the ingredients well with ice, and strain into a large cocktail glass. Add a half-slice of lemon.

Trade Winds

The correct rum brand to use for this cocktail is Mount Gay, made on Barbados. It is properly served frappé.

2 measures/3 tbsp light rum
½ measure/2 tsp slivovitz
½ measure/2 tsp lime juice
½ measure/2 tsp orgeat (almond syrup)

Shake the ingredients well with ice, and strain into a cocktail glass filled with crushed ice. Add a half-slice of lime.

Kingston

This is named after the Jamaican capital, so it would be inappropriate to use rum from any other location.

1½ measures/6 tsp dark Jamaica rum
¾ measure/3 tsp gin

Continental

An old-fashioned mixture of rum and peppermint cordial was once a popular drink. This cocktail presents a more adventurous spin on that formula. The colour is an attractive shade of tawny, and the mint flavour is agreeably set off by the piercing note of lime.

1½ measures/6 tsp light rum
½ measure/2 tsp green crème de menthe
½ measure/2 tsp lime juice

juice of half a lime
¼ measure/1 tsp grenadine

Shake all the ingredients well with ice, and strain into a cocktail glass. Garnish with a half-slice of lime.

Shake all the ingredients well with ice, and strain into a cocktail glass. If available, add a sprig of mint to the drink.

Bolero

Here is one of those cocktails that's all alcohol and no mixers. Stirring the drink gently, as opposed to shaking it, emphasizes its strength, in the sense that the mixture doesn't become quite as chilled as it would in the shaker.

1½ measures/6 tsp light rum
¾ measure/3 tsp calvados
¼ measure/1 tsp sweet red vermouth

Mix the ingredients gently in a pitcher with a couple of ice cubes, and then strain into a pre-chilled rocks glass. Squeeze a twist of lemon over the drink, and then drop it in.

Pilot Boat

With its mixture of dark rum and banana, this is the most tropical-tasting cocktail imaginable. The relatively high proportion of citrus helps to sharpen it up most agreeably.

1½ measures/6 tsp dark rum, preferably Jamaica
1 measure/1½ tbsp crème de banane
2 measures/3 tbsp lemon juice

Shake all the ingredients well with ice, and strain into a bowl-shaped cocktail glass. Garnish with a slice of lemon.

Canteloupe Cup

Another recipe containing puréed fruit. If a Canteloupe melon isn't available, use any other sweet, green-fleshed variety. Note that the flavour of honeydew melon isn't strong enough for this drink.

1½ measures/6 tsp light rum
90g/3½oz ripe Canteloupe melon, diced
½ measure/2 tsp lime juice
½ measure/2 tsp orange juice
dash sugar syrup

Process all the ingredients with smashed ice in the blender, and then strain into a goblet. Garnish with a thin slice of melon.

Strawberry and Banana Preparado

Similar to a smoothie, this is a thick, creamy fruit drink. You could leave out the alcohol if you prefer, but it would miss the point somewhat. The recipe serves four.

200g/7oz strawberries (plus a few extra to garnish)
2 bananas
115g/4oz block creamed coconut
120ml/4fl oz water
175ml/6fl oz white rum
60ml/4 tbsp grenadine

Pino Frio

Another in this mini-section of blended fruit cocktail recipes, this is a pineapple one with plenty of fruity zest to it.

1½ measures/6 tsp light rum
2 measures/3 tbsp pineapple juice
½ measure/2 tsp lemon juice
two slices of pineapple, about 2cm/1in thick, cut into chunks

Put all the ingredients into a blender with plenty of cracked ice, and whizz up until perfectly smooth. Pour the mixture into a chilled, tall glass, and garnish with a couple of extra chunks of fresh pineapple.

Hull the strawberries and chop them into halves, or quarters if they are large fruits. Peel the bananas and chop them into rough chunks. Put the fruit in a food processor or blender, crumble in the coconut and add the water. Process until smooth, scraping down the sides of the goblet as necessary. Add the rum, grenadine, and about ten ice cubes, crushing the ice first unless you have a heavy-duty processor. Blend until smooth and thick. Serve at once, garnishing the drink with the extra strawberries.

Bartending know-how
Creamed coconut not only makes for a luxuriously textured drink; it also has a wonderful concentrated coconutty flavour.

Havana Bandana

Use Cuban rum for this cocktail if you can get it. A drink full of liquidized banana makes for a very sumptuous and filling blend. Use one that has the mottled dark brown patches of a very ripe fruit.

2 measures/3 tbsp light rum
½ measure/2 tsp lime juice
1 ripe banana, sliced
¼ measure/1 tsp crème de banane

Add the first three ingredients to a blender with plenty of cracked ice, and process until the banana is fully incorporated into the liquids. Pour out into a chilled goblet, and spoon the banana liqueur on to the surface. Sprinkle some grated nutmeg over the top too, if desired.

Hot Tea Toddy

Rum isn't just a good partner for coffee. It also goes unexpectedly well with tea. Use a good Indian leaf, such as Assam or Darjeeling in this recipe, and strain it.

1½ measures/6 tsp light rum
2.5ml/½ tsp clear honey
2.5ml/½ tsp ground cinnamon
slice of lemon
1 teacup hot black tea
piece of crystallized (candied) ginger

Add all but the last ingredient to a pan and gently warm until just about to boil. Pour out into a mug and add the ginger.

Bartending know-how

Hot tea cocktails are pretty few and far between. Use a fairly straightforward blend such as English Breakfast tea or perhaps Assam or Darjeeling. China teas will be too assertively flavoured to sit easily in the mix.

Jamaican Black Coffee

There are any number of combinations of alcohol with hot brewed coffee, some more successful than others. This delicious version of black coffee is in fact only slightly alcoholic but gains extra allure from the inclusion of citrus fruits. The recipe serves eight.

1 lemon and 2 oranges, finely sliced
1.5 litres/2½ pints black coffee (filter/cafetière brewed using 55g/2oz coffee per 1 litre/ 1¾ pints water)

Hot Buttered Rum

Another hot preparation for winter drinking, this will cheer the heart if you've just come in from the cold.

2 measures/3 tbsp dark rum
5ml/1 tsp light muscovado (raw) or demarara (brown) sugar
2.5ml/½ tsp ground cinnamon
15g/½oz unsalted butter

Mix the rum and sugar in a tall glass. Add the cinnamon and butter, and then fill with hot water. Remember to stand a spoon in the glass to conduct the heat if the water has just boiled. Stir well to dissolve the butter and sugar.

2 measures/3 tbsp light rum
85g/3oz caster (superfine) sugar

Place the lemon and orange slices in a pan. Add the coffee and heat. When the mixture is about to boil, pour in the rum and sugar, stirring well until the sugar dissolves, then immediately remove from the heat. While the coffee is still very hot, pour or ladle into heatproof glasses, and garnish with a fresh lemon slice.

San Juan

A coconutty, fruity and strong cocktail seems the only fitting way to conclude our repertoire of rum recipes.

1½ measures/6 tsp light rum
1 measure/1½ tbsp grapefruit juice
1 measure/1½ tbsp lime juice
½ measure/2 tsp coconut cream
¼ measure/1 tsp overproof dark rum

Blend all except the last ingredient with cracked ice in the liquidizer, and then pour into a bowl-shaped cocktail glass. Sprinkle the surface of the drink with the overproof rum, and add a half-slice of lime.

Whisky

It is perhaps whisky that is the trickiest base ingredient to use in cocktails. Its flavour doesn't take quite as obligingly as the other spirits do to being mixed with liqueurs and fruit juices, although it is by no means bereft of its classic recipes. The rich, sweetly woody flavours of American whiskeys such as bourbon and rye, and the fruitiness of Canadian whisky, are better in this respect than Scotch. It is the iodiney pungency of much single malt Scotch that gets in the way. Perhaps these products really are best enjoyed on their own, or else with nothing more elaborate than fresh spring water.

Whisky Sour

Mix the juice of half a lemon with 5ml/ 1 tsp caster (superfine) sugar in a small tumbler with two or three cubes of ice. When the sugar is dissolved, add a generous measure of whisky and stir again – American whiskeys are best for this preparation. Some people add a brief squirt of soda. If you find this formula a little too sour, add a little more sugar, but this is the way I like it.

Perfect Manhattan

When making Manhattans it's a matter of preference whether you use sweet vermouth, dry vermouth or a mixture of the two. Both of the former require a dash of Angostura bitters. The last, given here, is such a harmoniously balanced mixture that it doesn't need it.

2 measures/3 tbsp rye whiskey
¼ measure/1 tsp dry vermouth
¼ measure/1 tsp sweet red vermouth

Pour the whiskey and vermouths into a bar glass half-full of ice. Stir well for 30 seconds to mix and chill. Strain on the rocks or straight up into a chilled cocktail glass. Pare away a small strip of lemon rind. Tie it into a knot to help release the oils from the rind, and drop it into the cocktail. Add a maraschino cherry with its stalk left intact. As any Manhattan drinker wil tell you, the cherry is essential.

Rob Roy

A further modification of the Perfect Manhattan recipe, Rob Roy is made with Scotch, and inclines very much to the sweeter end of the spectrum. It has traditionally been drunk on St Andrew's Day, November 30, but may with confidence be drunk all year round now.

1 measure/1½ tbsp Scotch
1 measure/1½ tbsp sweet red vermouth

Shake the ingredients well with ice, and strain into a cocktail glass. Some recipes add a dash of Angostura bitters to the mix as well, but I leave that to your discretion.

Mint Julep

One of the oldest cocktails of them all, this originated in the southern states of the USA, probably in the 18th century. It's the drink of tradition at the Kentucky Derby, the first Saturday in May, and is an incomparably refreshing mixture that has deservedly become a classic.

15ml/1 tbsp caster (superfine) sugar
8–10 fresh mint leaves
⅔ measure/1 tbsp hot water
2 measures/3 tbsp bourbon

Place the sugar in a mortar or bar glass. Tear the mint leaves into small pieces and add them to the sugar. Bruise them with a pestle or use a muddler to release their flavour and colour. Add the hot water and grind well together. Spoon into a highball glass and half-fill with crushed ice. Add the bourbon.

Stir until the outside of the glass has frosted. Allow to stand for a couple of minutes until the ice melts slightly and dilutes the drink.

Whisky Mac

The classic cold remedy is half-and-half good Scotch and green ginger wine (preferably Crabbie's). These days, it is generally served over ice in a rocks glass, but traditionally it was taken straight up. Whether it actually gets rid of a cold must be open to doubt, but it certainly makes you feel better.

Canada Cocktail

An engagingly sweet and fruity cocktail that obviously has to be made with whisky from Canada. Canadian Club is a fine brand, and is generally available.

1½ measures/6 tsp Canadian whisky
¼ measure/1 tsp Cointreau
2 dashes Angostura bitters
5ml/1 tsp caster (superfine) sugar

Shake all the ingredients well with ice, and strain into a cocktail glass. Garnish with a twist of orange rind.

Bobby Burns

Similar to Rob Roy, but with the herbal tang of Bénédictine coming through it, this is a drink named after Scotland's national poet. It is best served on Burns Night, January 25.

1½ measures/6 tsp Scotch
¾ measure/3 tsp sweet red vermouth
¼ measure/1 tsp Bénédictine

Stir all the ingredients well with ice, and strain into a chilled cocktail glass. Squeeze a spray of oil from a piece of lemon rind over the surface, but in this case don't add the rind to the drink. In the 1920s, the cocktail was shaken, but it seems to work better stirred, which gives a less cloudy result.

Old-Fashioned

The Old-Fashioned is only a modified bourbon or rye whiskey, but quickly established itself as one of the all-time classic preparations. It is usually heavily garnished, and served in a particular kind of squat tumbler that is named after the drink.

¼ measure/1 tsp sugar syrup
2 dashes Angostura bitters
2 measures/3 tbsp bourbon or rye whiskey

Mix the sugar and Angostura in an Old-Fashioned glass until the sugar is dissolved. Add plenty of cracked ice and then the whiskey. Throw in a twist of lemon rind, a slice of orange cut laterally from the fruit and a cocktail cherry, and serve with a stirring implement in it. This is the most old-fashioned formula for an Old-Fashioned.

New York

This is another simple preparation for whisky that was made in the 1920s with Canadian whisky, despite its name. Scotch can also successfully be used, however, as can, seemingly, anything but American whiskey.

2 measures/3 tbsp Canadian whisky or Scotch
5ml/1 tsp caster (superfine) sugar
juice of half a lime
dash grenadine

Stir all the ingredients vigorously with ice in a pitcher, and then strain into a chilled cocktail glass. Squeeze a twist of lemon over the drink, but don't drop it in.

Bartending know-how
Bourbon and rye whiskeys have quite distinctive flavours. In each case, the chosen grain must constitute at least 51% of the mash (corn being used in bourbon). Rye results in a thicker, heavier-tasting whiskey with a rather more rustic appeal than classic bourbon.

Rusty Nail

A short, sharp drink, this is another classic half-and-half recipe, and one that still manages to do perfect justice to both ingredients.

1½ measures/6 tsp Scotch
1½ measures/6 tsp Drambuie

Pour both ingredients over crushed ice in a rocks glass or whisky tumbler, and stir gently. No garnish is necessary. Some prefer to leave the ice cubes whole so as not to dilute the drink too much. It should be drunk quickly.

Bartending know-how
A Rusty Nail is really *the* Drambuie cocktail. Attempts to make this fine Scottish liqueur blend with anything other than Scotch always seem to come to grief. It genuinely seems to be too good to mix.

Sea Dog

This is a long Scotch whisky drink with a citrus twist. For a sweeter drink, add a second sugar cube.

1–2 sugar cubes
2 dashes Angostura bitters
2 orange wedges
2 lemon wedges
⅔ measure/1 tbsp Scotch
1 measure/1½ tbsp Bénédictine
2 measures/3 tbsp soda water

Put the sugar cube at the bottom of a highball glass, add the bitters and allow to soak into the sugar cube. Add the orange and lemon wedges and, using a muddler, press the juices from the fruit. Fill the glass with cracked ice. Add the whisky and Bénédictine, and mix together well with a swizzle-stick. Add the chilled soda water. Serve with the muddler, so that more juice can be pressed from the fruit by the drinker. Garnish with a maraschino cherry.

Gall Bracer

Short and smart, this drink is served on the rocks in a tumbler, or in a long-stemmed glass with a maraschino cherry. It all depends on the drinker and the occasion.

2 dashes Angostura bitters
2 dashes grenadine
2 measures/3 tbsp bourbon or rye whiskey

Millionaire

Several cocktails have been recorded over the years under this name. The *Savoy Cocktail Book* lists two alternatives, one based on rum, the other on gin. This one is from roughly the same era, though.

1½ measures/6 tsp bourbon
¾ measure/3 tsp Cointreau
dash grenadine
½ egg white

Shake all the ingredients well with ice, and strain into a cocktail glass. Garnish with a half-slice of lemon.

Half-fill a bar glass with ice cubes. Add the Angostura bitters, grenadine and whiskey, and stir well to chill. Place some ice in a small tumbler and pour the cocktail over it. Squeeze lemon rind over the top and then discard. Garnish with a cherry, if desired. For a longer drink, finish with soda or sparkling mineral water.

Buckaroo

Not many cocktails work well with cola, but this is an honourable exception. The pronounced bittering note contributed by the Angostura is essential and should not be omitted.

1½ measures/6 tsp bourbon
2.5ml/½ tsp Angostura bitters
5 measures/120ml/4fl oz Coca-Cola

Add the first two ingredients to a highball glass containing plenty of cracked ice. Stir briskly and then top up with cola. Serve with a swizzle-stick for further stirring.

Loch Lomond

This is another very simple treatment for Scotch for those who are not quite up to taking it neat.

1½ measures/6 tsp Scotch
¼ measure/1 tsp sugar syrup
2 dashes Angostura bitters

Shake all the ingredients well with ice, and strain into a cocktail glass. Squeeze a piece of lemon over the surface and discard.

Bartending know-how
When Scotch is given as few additives as it is in the Loch Lomond cocktail, you can afford to be as choosy as any whisky connoisseur about which type you use. Even fine single malt will not suffer unduly in this simple preparation.

Duck Soup

A fruity preparation in which bourbon is given the treatment more normally accorded to rum. It works well, though, showing what a versatile drink American whiskey is.

2 measures/3 tbsp bourbon
½ measure/2 tsp apricot brandy
¾ measure/3 tsp lemon juice
¾ measure/3 tsp pineapple juice
5ml/1 tsp caster (superfine) sugar

Modern Cocktail

The meaning of "modern" here is not as in 21st century, but as in 1920s. There were two cocktails with this name even then. One had whisky and sloe gin in it, but this seems to have been the original. It has a strong and unusual flavour that is an acquired taste, but one that you may well find yourself acquiring.

2 measures/3 tbsp Scotch
⅓ measure/1½ tsp dark rum
¼ measure/1 tsp absinthe
¼ measure/1 tsp orange bitters (or curaçao)
⅓ measure/1½ tsp lemon juice

Shake all the ingredients well with ice, and strain into a cocktail glass. Garnish with a twist of lemon.

Shake all the ingredients well with ice, and strain into a rocks glass that is half-filled with cracked ice. Garnish with a slice of lemon and a cherry.

Bartending know-how
Bourbon can technically be made anywhere in the United States, as its name isn't a geographical designation. Its traditional home state, however, is Kentucky, which is the only one allowed to put its name on the label. Tennessee whiskey may not be called Tennessee bourbon because when the labelling laws were drawn up in the 19th century, Kentucky had more senators than its southern neighbour.

Brainstorm

Here is a recipe that specifically calls for Irish whiskey. Its smooth, triple-distilled flavour works exceptionally well with the other ingredients. Jameson's would be a particularly good brand to use.

2 measures/3 tbsp Irish whiskey
2 dashes dry vermouth
2 dashes Bénédictine

Half-fill an Old-Fashioned glass with cracked ice, and then add the ingredients in this order. Stir gently, add a twist of orange rind, and serve with a swizzle-stick for stirring.

Churchill

The British wartime leader is well-served by having this sophisticated and powerful cocktail named after him, even though Scotch wasn't his favourite tipple.

1½ measures/6 tsp Scotch
½ measure/2 tsp sweet red vermouth

½ measure/2 tsp Cointreau
½ measure/2 tsp lime juice

Shake all the ingredients well with ice, and strain into a chilled cocktail glass. Garnish with a half-slice of orange and a slice of lime.

Jack Frost

The Jack in the name refers to the ever-popular Tennessee whiskey brand, Jack Daniel's, and so that is the type that must be used. This is an exotic and highly appealing cocktail.

1 measure/1½ tbsp Jack Daniel's
¾ measure/3 tsp dry vermouth
⅓ measure/1½ tsp crème de banane

1 measure/1½ tbsp passion fruit juice
⅓ measure/1½ tsp pineapple juice

Shake all the ingredients well with ice, and strain into a large cocktail glass that has been half-filled with crushed ice. The drink could be garnished with a slice of lemon on a stick with a chunk of juicy, ripe pineapple.

Kentucky Kernel

The geographical reference of this drink indicates that it's a bourbon cocktail, and the second half of the name refers to the apricot kernels from which its other alcoholic ingredient is made. The grapefruit juice brings it all into focus.

1½ measures/6 tsp bourbon
½ measure/2 tsp apricot brandy
1 measure/1½ tbsp grapefruit juice
¼ measure/1 tsp grenadine

Shake all the ingredients well with ice, and pour the drink – ice and all – into a rocks glass.

Plank Walker

Another recipe that puns on a famous name, this one being the celebrated Scotch brand, Johnnie Walker. It's a hardcore, all-alcohol mixture.

1½ measures/6 tsp Johnnie Walker Red Label Scotch
½ measure/2 tsp sweet red vermouth
½ measure/2 tsp yellow Chartreuse

Shake all the ingredients well with ice, and strain into a rocks glass half-filled with roughly cracked ice. Add a wedge of lemon.

Pleasant Dreams

This fruity treatment for bourbon would make a very comforting nightcap – so long as you confine yourself to just the one, that is.

1½ measures/6 tsp bourbon
¾ measure/3 tsp crème de mûre
¼ measure/1 tsp peach schnapps

Shake all the ingredients well with ice, and pour without straining into a chilled rocks glass.

Artists' Special

This drink is so-named because it was invented at the Artists' Club in the rue Pigalle, Paris, in the 1920s. The red ingredient was originally redcurrant syrup, but grenadine can be used to perfectly good effect instead. The mixture of Scotch and sweet sherry at its heart is a very appealing one.

1 measure/1½ tbsp Scotch
1 measure/1½ tbsp sweet brown sherry
½ measure/2 tsp lemon juice
½ measure/2 tsp grenadine

Shake all the ingredients well with ice, and strain into a cocktail glass. Add a half-slice of lemon.

Algonquin

This is named after the elegant New York hotel where Dorothy Parker once ruled the roost. The types of whisky to be used are once again quite specific.

2 measures/3 tbsp rye or Canadian whisky
1 measure/1½ tbsp dry vermouth
1 measure/1½ tbsp pineapple juice

Shake all the ingredients well with ice, and strain into a rocks glass half-filled with cracked ice. Garnish with lemon.

Pamplemousse

The name is the French word for "grapefruit", and so it's not hard to work out what the principal flavour of this charming cocktail should be.

1½ measures/6 tsp Canadian whisky
½ measure/2 tsp Southern Comfort
2 measures/3 tbsp grapefruit juice
¼ measure/1 tsp pineapple syrup

Shake all the ingredients well with ice, and then strain into a rocks glass half-filled with cracked ice. Add a short twist of grapefruit rind and a cocktail cherry.

Bartending know-how

Both Canadian whisky and Southern Comfort have a pronounced fruity flavour, the latter derived at least partly from the use of peaches. They work particularly well in fruity mixtures such as this one.

Rocky Mountain

Here is another of those cocktails that calls for three specific brands, and wouldn't be quite the same with substitutes. Its light, delicately herbal tinge is very attractive.

1½ measures/6 tsp Canadian Club
½ measure/2 tsp Glayva
¼ measure/1 tsp Punt e Mes

Shake all the ingredients well with ice, and pour without straining into a chilled rocks glass.

Bartending know-how
The Italian aperitif Punt e Mes, created in Turin in 1870, contains around four dozen herbs and spices on a white wine base. In Italy, it is traditionally accompanied by a piece of strong, dark chocolate.

Blizzard

The trick with this drink is to shake it for longer than normal with masses of ice until the mixture is extremely frosty-looking. That incidentally goes some way to disguise the high proportion of bourbon in it.

3 measures/4½ tbsp bourbon
1 measure/1½ tbsp cranberry juice

Grenoble

This is a superbly fruity cocktail with quite a kick, and one that demonstrates what a good mixer Kentucky whiskey is.

1½ measures/6 tsp bourbon
½ measure/2 tsp crème de framboise
½ measure/2 tsp Cointreau
1 measure/1½ tbsp orange juice
¼ measure/1 tsp orgeat syrup

Shake all the ingredients well with ice, and strain into a cocktail glass. Garnish with a half-slice of orange and a raspberry on a cocktail stick.

⅔ measure/1 tbsp lemon juice
30ml/2 tbsp sugar syrup

Shake all the ingredients extremely well with plenty of large ice cubes, and pour the mixture unstrained into a chilled highball glass. Garnish with a slice of lemon, and perhaps a couple of cranberries.

Tivoli

There is an Italian connection in this powerful little cocktail to reflect its name, but it comes by way of Scandinavia and Kentucky.

1½ measures/6 tsp bourbon
½ measure/2 tsp sweet red vermouth
½ measure/2 tsp aquavit
dash Campari

Shake all the ingredients well with ice, and strain into a chilled cocktail glass. Garnish the drink with a half-slice of lemon.

Paddy

Another traditional one, this was originally made with the Irish whiskey brand of the same name. In the 1920s, it had equal quantities of whiskey and vermouth and slightly less Angostura, which would obviously make for a sweeter result. This is today's drier and more sophisticated formula.

1½ measures/6 tsp Irish whiskey
¾ measure/3 tsp sweet red vermouth
3 dashes Angostura bitters

Shake all the ingredients well with ice, and strain into a chilled cocktail glass. Garnish with a half-slice of lemon.

Tipperary

You'll certainly know you've had one of these! Tipperary is an old 1920s mixture that's all alcohol, and packs the considerable punch of Chartreuse. If you're feeling brave, the Chartreuse was originally a whole measure too.

1 measure/1½ tbsp Irish whiskey
1 measure/1½ tbsp sweet red vermouth
½ measure/2 tsp green Chartreuse

Add the ingredients to a pitcher with plenty of cracked ice, and stir until cold enough to frost the sides of the glass. Strain into a pre-chilled cocktail glass.

Highland Morning

Although the name seems to be encouraging you to drink one of these for breakfast, a little later in the day might be wiser.

1 measure/1½ tbsp Scotch
¾ measure/3 tsp Cointreau
3 measures/4½ tbsp grapefruit juice

Shake all the ingredients well with ice, and pour (unstrained if you really are having it in the morning) into a chilled rocks glass. The drink could be garnished with a twist of grapefruit rind and perhaps a half-slice of orange to reflect the presence of Cointreau in the mix.

Loch Ness

A pair of Scottish and a pair of Irish cocktails rounds off with this tough cookie, which dates from the 1920s.

1½ measures/6 tsp Scotch
1 measure/1½ tbsp Pernod
¼ measure/1 tsp sweet red vermouth

Shake all the ingredients well with ice, and pour without straining into a chilled rocks glass or Old-Fashioned glass. Do not garnish.

Coffee Egg-Nog

This is a rather special coffee drink, particularly suitable for daytime summer-holiday festivities. The recipe serves six to eight.

8 eggs, separated
225g/8oz sugar
250ml/8fl oz cold strong coffee (espresso strength or filter/cafetière brewed at 75g/3oz coffee per 1 litre/1¾ pints water)
220ml/7½fl oz Scotch or bourbon
220ml/7½fl oz double (heavy) cream
120ml/4fl oz whipped cream
ground nutmeg, to decorate

Thoroughly beat the egg yolks, then add the sugar, mixing well. Heat gently in a pan over a low heat, stirring with a wooden spoon. Allow to cool a few minutes, stir in the coffee and whisky, and then slowly add the cream, stirring well. Beat the egg whites until stiff and stir into the egg-nog, mixing well. Pour into small round cups, top each with a small dollop of whipped cream and sprinkle nutmeg on top.

Jamaica Shake

Combining the best of both worlds, this cream cocktail brings together the complementary richnesses of American whiskey and Jamaica rum. It's a milkshake for adults.

1½ measures/6 tsp bourbon
1 measure/1½ tbsp dark Jamaica rum
1 measure/1½ tbsp double (heavy) cream

Shake all the ingredients well with ice to amalgamate the cream, and strain into a cocktail glass. Sift grated chocolate over the top.

Irish Chocolate Velvet

This is a luxurious creamy hot chocolate drink, with just a touch of alcohol to fortify it. It would be the perfect antidote to a winter morning spent working outdoors. The recipe serves four.

250ml/8fl oz double (heavy) cream
400ml/14fl oz milk
115g/4oz milk chocolate, chopped into small pieces
30ml/2 tbsp cocoa powder
60ml/4 tbsp Irish whiskey
whipped cream, for topping

Ring of Kerry

Since Irish whiskey lends itself so well to these creamy treatments, here is another one, in which it appears with its much-loved compatriot, Bailey's Irish Cream.

1½ measures/6 tsp Irish whiskey
1 measure/1½ tbsp Bailey's Irish Cream
½ measure/2 tsp Kahlúa

Shake all the ingredients well with ice, and strain into a chilled cocktail glass. Sprinkle 5ml/1 tsp grated chocolate over the top.

Whip half the cream in a bowl until it is thick enough to hold its shape. Place the milk and chocolate in a pan and heat gently, stirring, until the chocolate has melted. Whisk in the cocoa, then bring to the boil. Remove from the heat and stir in the remaining cream and the Irish whiskey. Pour quickly into four warmed heatproof mugs or glasses and top each serving with a generous spoonful of the whipped cream, finishing with a garnish of milk chocolate curls.

Tequila

Being even more of a recent commercial phenomenon than vodka, tequila has acquired correspondingly fewer recipes so far in the cocktail repertoire. That is gradually changing on modern bar menus as the salty, savoury, slightly feral aroma and flavour of the drink are appreciated. It mixes well with most fruit juices, and although combinations with liqueurs are still only at a fairly tentative stage, they are developing. There is therefore an experimental quality to some of the recipes that follow. Don't forget that, as well as basic, so-called "silver" tequila, there is also the richer and more complex oro, or "gold", style that has been aged in wooden casks.

Tequila Sunrise

This classic Mexican recipe of the 1930s takes its name from the way the grenadine – that bright red pomegranate cordial – first sinks in the glass of orange juice and then rises to the surface. Add it too slowly and it will simply blend into the drink, turning it a fetching (but totally incorrect) scarlet colour.

2 measures/3 tbsp gold tequila
4 measures/6 tbsp freshly squeezed orange
    juice
½ measure/2 tsp grenadine

Half-fill a highball glass with crushed ice. Pour in the tequila, then the orange juice, which must be freshly squeezed. Quickly add the grenadine, pouring it down the back of a spoon held inside the glass so that it sinks to the bottom of the drink. You could garnish the drink with a slice of orange and a cherry.

Tequila Sunset

This variation on the popular party drink can be mixed and chilled in a pitcher, ready to pour into glasses, and finished at the last minute with the addition of crème de cassis and honey.

1 measure/1½ tbsp gold tequila
5 measures/120ml/4fl oz lemon juice
1 measure/1½ tbsp orange juice
15–30ml/1–2 tbsp clear honey
⅔ measure/1 tbsp crème de cassis

Pour the tequila, and lemon and orange juices into a well-chilled cocktail glass. Using a swizzle-stick, mix the ingredients together well. Trickle the honey into the centre of the drink. It will sink and create a layer at the bottom of the glass. Add the crème de cassis, but do not stir. It will create a glowing layer above the honey at the bottom of the glass.

Margarita

With the Tequila Sunrise, Margarita (created in Tijuana in the late 1940s) is probably the best-known tequila cocktail of them all, and these days is a sight more popular. Its saltiness and sourness make it a great aperitif, and it is pleasingly strong too. Some recipes use lemon juice instead of lime, but lime juice sharpens its bite.

1½ measures/6 tsp silver tequila
½ measure/2 tsp Cointreau
juice of a lime

Rub the rim of a cocktail glass with a wedge of fresh lime, and then dip it in fine salt. Shake the tequila, Cointreau and lime juice with plenty of ice, and strain into the prepared glass. Garnish with a twist of cucumber rind or a half-slice of lime.

Iced Margarita

This smooth sorbet drink has all the punch of Mexico's renowned cocktail. This recipe makes two drinks.

2½ measures/3½ tbsp silver tequila
1¼ measures/5½ tsp Cointreau
1¼ measures/5½ tsp lime juice
6–8 small scoops lime sorbet
150ml/¼ pint chilled lemonade

Frost the rims of the glasses with cut lime and caster (superfine) sugar. Add lime and lemon slices to each. Mix the tequila, Cointreau and lime juice in a jug. Scoop the sorbet into the glasses. Pour an equal quantity of the drink into each glass. Top with lemonade and garnish with lemon balm.

Mango and Peach Margarita

Adding puréed fruit to the classic tequila mixture alters the consistency. This recipe serves four.

2 mangoes, peeled and sliced
3 peaches, peeled and sliced
5 measures/120ml/4fl oz silver tequila
2½ measures/3½ tbsp Cointreau
2½ measures/3½ tbsp lime juice

Blend the mango and peach slices in a liquidizer until a smooth paste is obtained. Add the tequila, Cointreau and lime juice, blend for a few seconds more, then add the ice. Blend again until the drink has the consistency of a milkshake. Pour into pre-chilled cocktail glasses, and garnish with slices of mango with the skin left on. Create other fruit variations on the basic Margarita, using this recipe.

Cactus Juice

In this modern recipe, the roundness of flavour of gold tequila is enhanced by marrying it with a little of the herb-flavoured Scotch liqueur, Drambuie.

2 measures/3 tbsp gold tequila
¼ measure/1 tsp Drambuie

1 measure/1½ tbsp lemon juice
5ml/1 tsp caster (superfine) sugar

Shake all the ingredients well with ice until the sugar is dissolved, and pour without straining into a rocks glass. Add a slice of lemon.

Pineapple Tequila

Flavours such as almond and quince have been added to silver tequila for some time. Many bars have developed unique flavours by combining ingredients such as chillies with tequila, and leaving them to infuse. The method below will make a smooth, fruity drink to serve six.

1 large pineapple
50g/2oz soft dark brown sugar
1 litre/1¾ pints silver tequila
1 vanilla pod

Rinse a large (about 2 litre/3½ pint) wide-necked bottle or demijohn and sterilize by placing it in an oven and then turning on the oven and setting it at 110°C/225°F/Gas ¼. After 20 minutes remove the bottle from the oven with oven gloves and allow it to cool down.

Cut the top off the pineapple and then cut away the skin. Cut the flesh in half lengthways, then remove the hard centre core and discard it. Chop the rest of the pineapple into chunks, ensuring that they are small enough to fit in the bottle neck.

When the bottle is completely cold, put the pineapple into the bottle. Mix the sugar and tequila together in a pitcher until the sugar dissolves and then pour into the bottle. Split the vanilla pod and add it to the rest of the ingredients.

Gently agitate the bottle a few times each day to stir the contents. Allow the tequila to stand for at least a week before drinking with ice. (When all the tequila has been drunk, use the pineapple in desserts such as ice cream, or warm with butter and cinnamon and serve with cream.)

Home infusions of tequila like this are very popular in its native Mexico.

TNT

With a bit of twisting, the initials of the name just about indicate the ingredients of the drink: tequila, Napoléon and Tia (Maria). Rather more accurately, they mirror the effect of the drink, which is all alcohol with no mixers. The flavour is very satisfying, though.

1 measure/1½ tbsp gold tequila
½ measure Mandarine Napoléon
1 measure/1½ tbsp Tia Maria

Stir all the ingredients gently with ice in a pitcher until very cold, and then strain into a rocks glass half-filled with cracked ice. Suspend a twist of orange rind in the drink.

Tequila and Orange

Have done with the lemon-squeezing and salt-licking fuss associated with traditional tequila-drinking, and try tequila on the rocks with fresh orange juice and a half-slice of orange. It makes an enlivening change for those grown weary of vodka-and-orange. Silver tequila will do for this mix.

Mexican Chocolate

A chillier, and more inspiring, version of boozy hot chocolate, this makes a refreshingly original drink for a hot summer afternoon. It beats chocolate ice cream, anyway.

1½ measures/6 tsp gold tequila
1 measure/1½ tbsp Kahlúa
4 measures/6 tbsp prepared cocoa or drinking chocolate, made with full-cream (whole) milk

Shake all the ingredients well with ice, and strain into a large goblet. Drink through straws.

Tequila Slammer

The Slammer reflects something of the bravado with which tequila is traditionally drunk in Mexico. It is a drink in which one takes over the bartender's performance ethic for oneself, and it has not surprisingly become internationally practised among a certain age group.

1 measure/1½ tbsp silver or gold tequila
1 measure/1½ tbsp sparkling mixer (usually either lemonade or ginger ale, but can be sparkling wine)

Pour the two measures into a shot glass, cover with the palm of your hand (or a beer mat, if you don't fancy getting messy) and slam the glass down a couple of times on the bar counter. The drink will then fizz wildly up, and you have something less than a second to get it to your mouth, and down it in one.

Bloody Maria

A close cousin of the original vodka-based Bloody Mary, this simple cocktail consists of tequila and tomato juice mixed together with spicy seasonings. The quantities here make two drinks, just in case that hangover is particularly persistent, or you have a fellow sufferer.

Bar Bandit

A long, fruity drink with a subtle, but nonetheless recognizable punch behind it. The inclusion of both types of vermouth proves once again the versatility of this style of fortified wine.

1 measure/1½ tbsp gold tequila
½ measure/2 tsp dry vermouth
½ measure/2 tsp sweet red vermouth
½ measure/2 tsp crème de framboise
¼ measure/1 tsp lime juice
4 measures/6 tbsp sparkling cherryade

Pack a highball glass with cracked ice, and add all but the last ingredient in the order above. Stir briskly with a swizzle-stick, and then top up with cherryade. Garnish with a slice of lime and a couple of cocktail cherries.

250ml/8fl oz tomato juice, chilled
2 measures/3 tbsp silver tequila
5ml/1 tsp Worcestershire sauce
few drops Tabasco
juice of half a lemon
pinch celery salt
salt and freshly ground black pepper

Pour the chilled tomato juice into a large pitcher and stir in the tequila. Add the Worcestershire sauce and stir the mixture well. Add a few drops of Tabasco and the lemon juice. Taste and season with celery salt, salt and pepper. Serve over ice cubes in highball glasses, with celery sticks standing in the drink for stirring it. The tequila naturally makes its presence felt in this mixture more obviously than vodka does.

Boomer

This is one of those recently popular drinks known as shooters, which are small, assertively flavoured preparations for downing at one gulp. It should be served either in a shot glass or small liqueur glass, when its short, sharp shock can be best appreciated.

⅔ measure/1 tbsp gold tequila
½ measure/2 tsp apricot brandy
½ measure/2 tsp orange juice
¼ measure/1 tsp lemon juice
¼ measure/1 tsp sugar syrup

Shake all the ingredients well with ice, and strain into a tiny glass.

Firebird

This is a fairly sweet, fizzy concoction that's shorter than most other sparkling cocktails.

1½ measures/6 tsp silver tequila
½ measure/2 tsp crème de banane
½ measure/2 tsp lime juice

2 measures/3 tbsp sparkling lemonade

Fill a rocks glass nearly to the brim with cracked ice. Add the first three ingredients, give them a quick stir and then add the lemonade. Garnish with a slice of lemon.

Sangrita

Sipping sangrita and tequila alternately is a taste sensation not to be missed, the warm flavours of the first balancing the strength of the second. The drinks are often served with *antojitos* (nibbles) as an appetizer. This recipe serves eight.

450g/1lb ripe tomatoes, or one 400g/14oz can chopped tomatoes
1 small onion, finely chopped
2 small fresh green chillies, seeded and chopped
120ml/4fl oz freshly squeezed orange juice
juice of 3 limes
2.5ml/½ tsp caster (superfine) sugar
pinch of salt
1 small shot glass gold or aged tequila per person

Cut a large cross in the base of each tomato. Place the tomatoes in a heatproof bowl and pour over boiling water to cover. Leave for 3 minutes. Lift the tomatoes out on a slotted spoon, and plunge them into a second bowl of cold water. Remove the skins, then cut the tomatoes in half and scoop out the seeds with a spoon. Chop the tomato flesh and put in a food processor. Add the onion, chillies, orange juice, lime juice, sugar and salt. Process until all the mixture is very smooth, then pour into a pitcher and chill for at least an hour before serving. Offer each drinker a separate shot glass of neat tequila as well. The drinks are sipped alternately.

Last Chance

A drop of honey makes a good companion for mellow, cask-aged tequila in this drink. It would make a rather comforting nightcap.

1¾ measures/2½ tbsp gold tequila
½ measure/1 tsp apricot brandy
1 measure/1½ tbsp lime juice
10ml/2 tsp clear honey

Shake all the ingredients very well with ice, ensuring that the honey is fully dissolved, and strain into a rocks glass. Garnish with a slice of lime.

Cherry Coco

Here is a sumptuously creamy, exotically flavoured cocktail that would look very elegant served in a champagne flute. It's both creamy and sour – a nice combination.

1½ measures/6 tsp silver tequila
¾ measure/3 tsp coconut cream
1 measure/1½ tbsp lemon juice
¼ measure/1 tsp maraschino

Shake all the ingredients well with ice, and strain into a tall, narrow glass. Drop a cocktail cherry into the drink.

Zorro

John J. Poister, author of *The New American Bartender's Guide*, has created this winning tequila recipe that uses the Balkan plum spirit, slivovitz.

1½ measures/6 tsp silver tequila
1 measure/1½ tbsp slivovitz
1 measure/1½ tbsp lime juice
¼ measure/1 tsp sugar syrup

Shake all the ingredients well with ice, and strain into a chilled cocktail glass. You could garnish with a slice of lime.

Bartending know-how
The best brands of slivovitz hail from Bosnia, Croatia and Serbia, and are made with a local plum variety called pozega, sourced from trees with a minimum age of 20 years.

Piñata

An odd name this, as you might think it contained pineapple, but no – banana and lime are the fruit flavours. It is, nonetheless, quite delicious enough to be going on with.

1½ measures/6 tsp gold tequila
1 measure/1½ tbsp crème de banane
1 measure/1½ tbsp lime juice

Shake all the ingredients well with ice, and strain into a cocktail glass. Dangle a twist of lime rind in the drink.

Rosita

A drink that bears some distant kinship to the Negroni, and is prepared in roughly the same way.

1½ measures/6 tsp silver tequila
1 measure/1½ tbsp Campari
½ measure/2 tsp dry vermouth
½ measure/2 tsp sweet red vermouth

Add the ingredients in this order to an Old-Fashioned glass or small rocks glass, half-filled with cracked ice. Stir. Squeeze a small twist of orange rind over the drink and then drop it in.

Mockingbird

A good balance of sweet and sour is achieved in this minty, but sharp-edged cocktail. It's one of those tastes of which one can say that a little goes a long way.

1½ measures/6 tsp silver tequila
¾ measure/3 tsp white crème de menthe
juice of half a lime

Shake all the ingredients well with ice, and strain into a chilled cocktail glass. Garnish with a half-slice of lime and a sprig of mint.

Brandy

In his strange, single-gendered world, Dr Johnson was quite clear about the status of brandy: "Claret is the liquor for boys; port for men; but he who aspires to be a hero must drink brandy." Indeed, fine cognac has for a long time been associated with a certain swaggering demeanour. Not for nothing is one of the top grades of cognac called Napoleon brandy. As well as cognac, there is armagnac from the south-west of France, and brandies from Spain, Germany, Mexico and the USA. They are good mixers in cocktails, and although, understandably, you wouldn't want to use your best Fine Champagne cognac in a mixed drink, it pays not to go for the cheapest grades either. They largely taste horrible, and will ruin the resulting cocktail.

Brandy Cocktail

Over time, this drink became modified to include Cointreau instead of curaçao, a little sugar syrup and a dash of Angostura. However, the earliest versions of it are nothing more than cognac with a soupçon of bitterness.

1½ measures/6 tsp cognac
2 dashes orange curaçao

Stir the ingredients gently with ice in a bar glass, and then strain into a brandy balloon. Do not garnish.

Brandy Fix

A Fix is a mixture of spirit with lemon juice, sweetening and in this case another alcohol flavour, with the shell of the lemon and a pile of ice left in the drink for good measure.

5ml/1 tsp sugar
juice and rind of half a lemon

1½ measures/6 tsp cognac
¾ measure/3 tsp cherry brandy

Dissolve the sugar in a little water in the bottom of a small tumbler, and then fill it with crushed ice. Add the lemon juice and alcohol and stir the drink well. Drop in the squeezed lemon rind.

Bonnie Prince Charlie

As its name indicates, this drink contains Drambuie, the liqueur that was given to Prince Charlie by the MacDonald family on his flight to Skye. The mixture is a strong one, but one that seems to do justice to the liqueur.

1 measure/1½ tbsp cognac
½ measure/2 tsp Drambuie
1 measure/1½ tbsp lemon juice

Shake all the ingredients well with ice, and strain into a cocktail glass. Garnish with a twist of lemon.

Brandy Blazer

A warming after-dinner tipple, this is ideally served with fresh vanilla ice cream or caramelized oranges.

½ orange
1 lemon
2 measures/3 tbsp cognac
1 sugar cube
½ measure/2 tsp Kahlúa

Pare the rind from the orange and lemon, removing and discarding as much of the white pith as possible. Put the cognac, sugar cube, lemon and orange rind in a small pan. Heat gently, then remove from the heat, light a match and pass the flame close to the surface of the liquid. The alcohol will burn with a low, blue flame for about a minute. Blow out the flame. Add the Kahlúa to the pan, and strain into a heat-resistant glass. Garnish with a cocktail stick threaded with orange rind, and serve warm.

B&B

The traditional mix of this world-famous cocktail is half-and-half Bénédictine and good brandy (cognac for preference), stirred not shaken, and not usually iced. In fact, for true authenticity, you don't even need a stirrer. The two drinks are simply poured into a balloon glass, the brandy first, and the drink swirled in the hand before being passed to its recipient. No garnish is needed.

Brandy Smash

The excitingly named Smash is essentially a miniaturized julep (or Mint Julep). It may be made with any spirit, but is particularly successful with brandy.

5ml/1 tsp caster (superfine) sugar
4 mint leaves
2 measures/3 tbsp cognac
1 measure/1½ tbsp soda water

Dissolve the sugar in a little water in a tumbler. Add the mint leaves and press them into the sugar solution to express some of the juices. Put in a couple of ice cubes, and then add the brandy and stir vigorously. Add the soda. Squeeze a piece of lemon rind over the top of the drink, and decorate with a half-slice of orange.

Brandy Crusta

The sweet, frosted rim is all-important in this most appealing drink. It mitigates some of the sourness in the drink itself.

1½ measures/6 tsp cognac
½ measure/2 tsp Cointreau
¼ measure/1 tsp maraschino
dash Angostura bitters
¼ measure/1 tsp lemon juice

Frost the rim of a wide tumbler by dipping it first in lemon juice and then in caster (superfine) sugar. Hang a twist of lemon rind in it, and then fill it with cracked ice. Stir all the ingredients well with ice in a pitcher until the mixture is well-chilled, and then strain into the prepared glass. Garnish further with a half-slice of orange.

Brandy Alexander

One of the greatest cocktails of them all, Alexander can be served at the end of a grand dinner with coffee as a creamy digestif, or as the first drink of the evening at a cocktail party, since the cream in it helps to line the stomach. It was possibly originally made with gin rather than brandy, and the cream was sweetened, but the formula below is undoubtedly the best of all possible worlds.

1 measure/1½ tbsp cognac
1 measure/1½ tbsp brown crème de cacao
1 measure/1½ tbsp double (heavy) cream

Shake the ingredients thoroughly with ice, and strain into a cocktail glass. Scatter ground nutmeg, or grate a little whole nutmeg, on top. Alternatively, sprinkle with grated dark chocolate.

Corpse Reviver 1

Not the most delicately named cocktail, this is a 1970s recipe intended of course as a morning-after remedy. I'm not sure I'd make quite that claim for it myself, but in its bitterly minty way, it tastes convincingly medicinal, which is what matters.

1 measure/1½ tbsp cognac
1 measure/1½ tbsp Fernet Branca
1 measure/1½ tbsp white crème de menthe

Shake all the ingredients well with ice, and strain into a cocktail glass. Do not garnish. If you really are taking it at 10 o'clock in the morning, you're not likely to care about twists of this and slices of that anyway.

Corpse Reviver 2

This was the 1920s idea of a morning-after remedy, and is probably the first recipe that can lay claim to this name. It looks much more like a night-before drink to me – and a good one at that.

1½ measures/6 tsp cognac
¾ measure/3 tsp calvados
¾ measure/3 tsp sweet red vermouth

Shake all the ingredients well with ice, and strain into a cocktail glass. Again, no garnish is required.

Morning Glory Fizz

A good early-morning drink, this should be consumed as soon as it is made, before it loses its bubbles.

⅔ measure/1 tbsp cognac
¼ measure/1 tsp orange curaçao
¼ measure/1 tsp lemon juice
dash anisette
2 dashes Angostura bitters
4 measures/6 tbsp soda water

Shake all but the last ingredient well with ice, and strain into a chilled highball glass. Finish with the soda water. Garnish the drink with a twist of lemon rind.

Bartending know-how
Always choose lemons that feel heavy for their size: they're the ones with the most juice.

Frozen Strawberry Daiquiri

This is a spinoff version of the rum original. When the fresh fruit isn't in season, use drained, canned strawberries instead, but wash off the sugar syrup.

4 strawberries
½ measure/2 tsp lime juice
1 measure/1½ tbsp cognac
1 measure/1½ tbsp light rum
dash grenadine

Vanderbilt

This cocktail was created in 1912 in honour of Cornelius Vanderbilt, member of one of America's great plutocratic families. The flavour is certainly rich enough to do justice to the name.

1½ measures/6 tsp cognac
½ measure/2 tsp cherry brandy
2 dashes Angostura bitters
¼ measure/1 tsp sugar syrup

Shake all the ingredients well with ice, and strain into a cocktail glass. Garnish with a twist of lemon, and a couple of cherries on a cocktail stick.

Put the strawberries, lime juice and brandy in a liquidizer and process to a purée. Add the light rum, grenadine and half a glass of finely crushed ice and process once more to a smooth slush. Pour the resulting mixture into a well-chilled cocktail glass. Garnish with a strawberry and a small sprig of fresh mint.

Connoisseur's Treat

Certainly a treat for somebody, this is a very strong, all-alcohol mix, not to be taken lightly. The flavour is a heady combination of herbs, vanilla and orange.

1½ measures/6 tsp cognac
½ measure/2 tsp Grand Marnier
½ measure/2 tsp Galliano

Stir the ingredients in a pitcher with ice until thoroughly chilled, and strain into a rocks glass. Garnish with a twist of orange rind.

Bombay

A very strong and challenging mixture, this is the kind of drink that comes in handy in situations where Dutch courage is called for. Or should that be Indian courage?

1½ measures/6 tsp cognac
¾ measures/3 tsp dry vermouth
¾ measure/3 tsp sweet red vermouth
¼ measure/1 tsp Cointreau
¼ measure/1 tsp absinthe

Shake all the ingredients well with ice, and strain into a cocktail glass or champagne saucer filled with crushed ice. Do not garnish.

East India

This short and elegant drink can be served as an aperitif, as it has a pleasantly bitter note to it.

⅔ measure/1 tbsp cognac
2 dashes white curaçao
2 dashes pineapple juice
2 dashes Angostura bitters

Stir all the ingredients well with ice in a pitcher until chilled, and strain into a small tumbler or Old-Fashioned glass, half-filled with broken ice. Garnish with a twist of lime and a cherry.

Apple Sour

For those who don't fancy swallowing raw egg, this drink can be made without the egg white. Applejack or apple schnapps also work well in place of the calvados.

1 measure/1½ tbsp cognac
1 measure/1½ tbsp calvados
⅔ measure/1 tbsp lemon juice

5ml/1 tsp sugar
dash Angostura bitters
1 egg white

Shake all the ingredients well with ice, and strain into a tumbler half-filled with cracked ice. Garnish the drink with slices of red and green apple dipped in lemon juice.

Brandy Punch

This old-fashioned punch recipe might have graced the table of an elegant Victorian party. It's a chilled punch as well, which tends to be a bit more popular these days than the hot version. The recipe should serve around 12 guests.

1 × 700ml/1 pint bottle of cognac
150ml/¼ pint orange curaçao
1 measure/1½ tbsp grenadine
juice of 5 lemons
juice of 2 oranges
250ml/8fl oz mineral water
orange and lemon slices
400ml/14fl oz sparkling ginger ale

Bartending know-how
Always ice the individual glasses rather than the punch bowl itself.

Mix all but the last ingredient in a punch bowl and add the ginger ale just before serving. Ladle into highball glasses packed with ice.

Lemon Lady

This is a delightful concoction that will have guests coming back for more. It could be served between courses as a more invigorating alternative to a straight sorbet.

1 measure/1½ tbsp cognac
½ measure/2 tsp Cointreau
3 measures/4½ tbsp light, partially melted lemon sorbet

Shake well with ice to combine the sorbet, and strain into a chilled cocktail glass. Garnish with a slice of lemon.

Never on Sunday

This recipe uses Metaxa, the softly caramelly Greek brandy, together with its compatriot, aniseedy ouzo, for a thoroughly Mediterranean experience.

1 measure/1½ tbsp Metaxa
½ measure/2 tsp ouzo
dash lemon juice

dash Angostura bitters
2 measures/3 tbsp dry sparkling wine
2 measures/3 tbsp sparkling ginger ale

Stir the first four ingredients in a pitcher with ice, strain into a tall glass and top up with the sparkling wine and ginger ale. Garnish with a slice of lemon.

Grenadier

This drink is a brandy variation on the Whisky Mac, and equally good at cheering up those suffering with a winter chill.

1 measure/1½ tbsp cognac
1 measure/1½ tbsp green ginger wine
5ml/1 tsp caster (superfine) sugar

Shake all the ingredients well with ice, and strain into a small tumbler. Drink quickly so that the warmth of the alcohol pervades the system in a comforting way.

Cranberry Kiss

In this delicious, full-flavoured cocktail, the tang of cranberry and pink grapefruit juices is balanced by the toffeeish sweetness of marsala.

redcurrants, to garnish
1 egg white, lightly beaten, and 15ml/1 tbsp caster (superfine) sugar, to garnish
1 measure/1½ tbsp cognac
2 measures/3 tbsp cranberry juice
2 measures/3 tbsp pink grapefruit juice
2 measures/3 tbsp marsala dolce

For the garnish, lightly brush the redcurrants with the egg white. Shake sugar over them to cover with a frosting. Set aside to dry. Shake the brandy, and cranberry and grapefruit juices with ice and strain into a well-chilled glass. Tilt the glass slightly before slowly pouring in the marsala down the side. Garnish with the frosted redcurrants.

Hard Case

For a small drink with a sharply fruity flavour, this is something of a misnomer. It's a (relatively) harmless customer.

1½ measures/6 tsp cognac
½ measure/2 tsp crème de cassis
¼ measure/1 tsp lemon juice

Shake all the ingredients well with ice, and strain into a cocktail glass. Garnish with a half-slice of lemon.

Champarelle

Dating from the late 19th century, this is one of the oldest recipes for the layered drink known as a pousse-café. It helps if the ingredients and the glass itself are pre-chilled, as they are not mixed in any way, and you can't put ice in the drink.

½ measure/2 tsp orange curaçao
½ measure/2 tsp yellow Chartreuse

Brandy Fino

The name tells you more or less what's in this, though the splash of Glayva may sneak craftily up on you.

1½ measures/6 tsp cognac
½ measure/2 tsp pale dry (fino) sherry
¼ measure/1 tsp Glayva

Stir all the ingredients well in a pitcher with ice until the mixture is properly chilled, and strain into a balloon glass. Do not garnish.

½ measure/2 tsp anisette
½ measure/2 tsp cognac

Carefully pour each of the ingredients in this order over the back of a large spoon into a liqueur glass or sherry schooner, ensuring that they remain in separate layers. Use a clean spoon for each ingredient.

Blackjack

Perhaps invented to steady nerves at the gaming table, this mix is more likely to impair concentration. It is a stimulating one nonetheless.

1 measure/1½ tbsp cognac
½ measure/2 tsp kirsch
½ measure/2 tsp Kahlúa
2 measures/3 tbsp cold black coffee

Shake all the ingredients well with ice, and pour without straining into a rocks glass. Do not garnish.

Bartending know-how
Kirsch made in Germany tends to be drier and higher in alcohol than the versions made in the Alsace region of France. The best French grade is labelled "pur". Avoid anything labelled "Kirsch de Cuisine".

Arago

This delightful creamy creation is quite as irresistible as the Pompeii, below.

1½ measures/6 tsp cognac
1 measure/1½ tbsp crème de banane
1 measure/1½ tbsp double (heavy) cream

Shake all the ingredients well with ice, and strain into a cocktail glass. Sprinkle the surface of the drink with grated dark chocolate.

Pompeii

Here is a different spin on the Alexander formula, but with the chocolate component given a sweeter, nutty edge.

1 measure/1½ tbsp cognac
¾ measure/3 tsp white crème de cacao
½ measure/2 tsp amaretto
1 measure/1½ tbsp double (heavy) cream

Shake all the ingredients well with ice, and strain into a cocktail glass. Sprinkle the drink's surface with flaked almonds.

Last Goodbye

The flavours of cherry brandy and Cointreau are seen as being particularly compatible with cognac, and this is another appealing mixture.

1 measure/1½ tbsp cognac
¾ measure/3 tsp cherry brandy
¼ measure/1 tsp Cointreau
½ measure/2 tsp lime juice
¼ measure/1 tsp grenadine

Shake all the ingredients well with ice, and strain into a balloon glass. You could garnish with a lime slice and a cherry.

Incredible

Chartreuse doesn't often mix well with other spirits, but this is definitely worth a go, Incredible as it may seem.

1 measure/1½ tbsp cognac
½ measure/2 tsp green Chartreuse
½ measure/2 tsp cherry brandy

Stir all the ingredients gently with ice in a pitcher until well-chilled, and then strain into a rocks glass. Garnish with a cocktail cherry.

Missile Stopper

On a military hardware theme, this fruity little number should stop anyone in their tracks.

1 measure/1½ tbsp cognac
½ measure/2 tsp crème de fraise
1 measure/1½ tbsp grapefruit juice
1 measure/1½ tbsp pineapple juice
¼ measure/1 tsp grenadine

Shake all the ingredients well with ice, and strain into a chilled balloon glass. Garnish with a sliver of pineapple and a strawberry.

Port Side

The purply-red colour of this very sophisticated short drink looks very fetching sinking through a snowdrift of crushed ice.

1½ measures/6 tsp cognac
½ measure/2 tsp ruby port
½ measure/2 tsp crème de mûre

Stir all the ingredients with ice in a pitcher, and strain into a rocks glass half-filled with crushed ice. Garnish with a blackberry, if you happen to have one to hand.

Torpedo

I have come across various different mixtures going under this title. This seems to me to be the one most worthy of the name. It's very dry, spirity and strong, and its name reflects something of the force with which it will go through you.

1½ measures/6 tsp cognac
¾ measure/3 tsp calvados
dash gin

Shake all the ingredients well with ice, and strain into a pre-chilled cocktail glass. Garnish with a twist of lemon.

Coterie

Strong and sour, this is just the way a grown-up cocktail should be. Robert Cross's recipe suggests Chartreuse as an alternative to the hard-to-find, but similar, Basque liqueur, Izarra.

1 measure/1½ tbsp cognac
½ measure/2 tsp yellow Chartreuse
½ measure/2 tsp gin
¼ measure/1 tsp lemon juice
¼ measure/1 tsp sugar syrup

Stir all the ingredients well with ice in a pitcher, and strain the drink into a chilled small tumbler. Garnish with a half-slice of lemon.

Fighter

This combative mixture is rendered seemingly tamer by the sparkling top-up. Do not be deceived.

1 measure/1½ tbsp cognac
½ measure/2 tsp vodka
½ measure/2 tsp Mandarine Napoléon
4 measures/6 tbsp sparkling bitter lemon

Add the first three ingredients to a highball glass half-filled with cracked ice. Stir vigorously. Top up with the bitter lemon. Garnish with a slice of mandarin orange, clementine, satsuma or similar.

Pisco Sour

The origin of pisco, the colourless brandy of South America, is energetically disputed between Peru and Chile. This is the classic way of taking it locally.

juice of half a lime
5ml/1 tsp caster (superfine) sugar
2 measures/3 tbsp pisco

Half-fill a small tumbler with smashed ice. Squeeze the lime juice directly into the glass and drop in the wrung-out shell. Add the sugar and stir well to dissolve it. Now add the pisco, and give the drink a final stir. A dash of Angostura bitters can be added too, if desired, but it isn't essential.

Bayou

The peachiness of this cocktail evokes the southern United States, as does its name. It's rich and fruity, with a refreshing sour finish.

1½ measures/6 tsp cognac
½ measure/2 tsp peach brandy
1 measure/1½ tbsp peach juice
⅓ measure/1½ tsp lime juice

Shake all the ingredients well with ice, and strain into a rocks glass. Garnish with a slice of ultra-ripe white peach.

Apricot Bellini

This is a version of the famous aperitif served at Harry's Bar in Venice. Instead of the usual sparkling wine and peach juice, apricot nectar and apricot brandy make this a tempting, and stronger, variation. This recipe serves six to eight.

3 ripe apricots
½ measure/2 tsp lemon juice
½ measure/2 tsp sugar syrup
1 measure/1½ tbsp cognac
1 measure/1½ tbsp apricot brandy
1 bottle brut champagne or dry sparkling wine, chilled

Plunge the apricots into boiling water for 2 minutes to loosen the skins, then peel and pit them. Discard the pits and skin. Process the apricot flesh with the lemon juice until you have a smooth purée. Sweeten to taste with sugar syrup, then strain. Add the brandy and liqueur to the apricot nectar and stir together. Divide the apricot nectar among chilled champagne flutes. Finish the drinks with chilled champagne or sparkling wine.

Dizzy Dame

Well, she will be after drinking two or three of these. Another of those creamy cocktails full of rich, indulgent flavours (and calories).

1 measure/1½ tbsp cognac
¾ measure/3 tsp Tia Maria
½ measure/2 tsp cherry brandy
¾ measure/3 tsp double (heavy)
   cream

Shake all the ingredients well with ice, and strain into a cocktail glass. Garnish with a cherry.

Captain Kidd

Brandy and dark rum make a heady, but very successful mix in a powerful cocktail, and this one is further enhanced by the addition of strong chocolate flavour. There are no non-alcoholic ingredients, you'll notice, so watch out.

Mikado

This is a 1920s Savoy Hotel recipe of great charm. The Gilbert and Sullivan work of the same name was premiered at the Savoy Theatre in 1885.

1½ measures/6 tsp cognac
2 dashes orange curaçao
2 dashes crème de noyau
2 dashes orgeat syrup (or amaretto)
2 dashes Angostura bitters

Shake all the ingredients well with ice, and strain into a cocktail glass. Garnish with a half-slice of orange and a cherry.

1½ measures/6 tsp cognac
1 measure/1½ tbsp dark rum
1 measure/1½ tbsp brown crème de cacao

Shake well with ice, and strain into a chilled champagne saucer. Garnish with a physalis or a half-slice of orange.

Savoy Hotel

It's a short step from London's Savoy Theatre to the American Bar in the hotel itself, where this delightful cocktail (like many another) was created. It's a pousse-café or layered drink that requires a steady hand.

1 measure/1½ tbsp brown crème de cacao
1 measure/1½ tbsp Bénédictine
1 measure/1½ tbsp cognac

Carefully pour each of the ingredients, in this order, over the back of a spoon into a liqueur glass or sherry schooner to create a multi-layered drink. Serve immediately, while the effect is intact.

Harvard

This mixture was invented at the distinguished Ivy League university in the 1920s. It originally had equal quantities of brandy and vermouth and no lemon juice, but this is a less sweet and altogether more balanced mixture.

1½ measures/6 tsp cognac
½ measure/2 tsp sweet red vermouth
¼ measure/1 tsp lemon juice
¼ measure/1 tsp grenadine
2 dashes Angostura bitters

Shake all the ingredients well with ice, and strain into a cocktail glass. Garnish with a twist of lemon.

Brandy Melba

As might be expected, this is a very fruity cocktail that could almost pass as a sort of dessert. It uses the combination of peach and raspberry in the classic Peach Melba dessert.

1½ measures/6 tsp cognac
½ measure/2 tsp peach schnapps
¼ measure/1 tsp crème de framboise
½ measure/2 tsp lemon juice
¼ measure/1 tsp orange bitters (or curaçao)

Shake well with ice, and strain into a chilled cocktail glass. Garnish with a slice of ripe peach and a raspberry.

Lake Como

The geographical reference recalls the origins of the excellent Italian liqueur used in this recipe. You'll never want another Black Russian after tasting this.

1½ measures/6 tsp cognac
¾ measure/3 tsp Tuaca

Mix the ingredients well with ice in a large glass, and strain into an Old-Fashioned or small rocks glass. Squeeze a twist of lemon rind over the drink and then drop it into the glass. This is one for drinking quickly and confidently.

Fjord

Good Scandinavian aquavit is needed for this recipe. The name suggests Norwegian, but Swedish or Danish would do quite as well.

1 measure/1½ tbsp cognac
½ measure/2 tsp aquavit
1 measure/1½ tbsp orange juice

½ measure/2 tsp lime juice
¼ measure/1 tsp grenadine

Shake all the ingredients well with ice, and strain into a chliled rocks glass half-filled with cracked ice. Garnish the drink with half-slices of orange and lime.

Booster

This egg-white drink has a powerful kick. You may find it helps to whisk the egg white for a few seconds before adding it to the shaker, just to ensure the right kind of foamy texture in the finished drink.

2 measures/3 tbsp cognac
1 measure/1½ tbsp orange curaçao
½ egg white

Shake all the ingredients very thoroughly with ice, and strain into a cocktail glass. Sprinkle the surface with ground nutmeg.

Via Veneto

Named after the street in Rome that was once a scene of bohemian glamour, this cocktail contains the Italian elderberry-flavoured liqueur Sambuca Romana.

1½ measures/6 tsp cognac
½ measure/2 tsp Sambuca
½ measure/2 tsp lemon juice
¼ measure/1 tsp sugar syrup
½ egg white

Shake all the ingredients well with ice, and strain into a chilled rocks glass. Garnish with a slice of lemon.

Memphis Belle

One of the earliest cocktail recipes to use Southern Comfort, this may look an unlikely idea, in that it blends a whiskey-based liqueur with brandy, but in its dry, sharply sour way, it works.

1½ measures/6 tsp cognac
¾ measure/3 tsp Southern Comfort
½ measure/2 tsp lemon juice
¼ measure/1 tsp orange bitters (or curaçao)

Shake all the ingredients well with ice, and strain into a pre-chilled cocktail glass. Garnish with a twist of lemon.

Kiss the Boys Goodbye

As the name suggests, this is a cocktail with which American troops going off to serve in the Second World War were toasted. It seemed to do the trick.

1 measure/1½ tbsp cognac
1 measure/1½ tbsp sloe gin
¼ measure/1 tsp lemon juice
½ egg white

Shake all the ingredients well with ice, and strain into a rocks glass half-filled with cracked ice. Garnish with a wedge of lemon.

Coffee Cognac Cooler

This drink is unabashedly decadent, and not for those counting calories. The recipe serves two, so you can both feel guilty together.

250ml/8fl oz cold strong dark-roast coffee
80ml/3fl oz cognac
50ml/2fl oz coffee liqueur
50ml/2fl oz double (heavy) cream
10ml/2 tsp sugar
2 scoops coffee ice cream

Shake or blend all the ingredients except the ice cream, together with plenty of crushed ice. Pour into tall glasses and gently add a scoop of ice cream to each. Garnish with chocolate shavings, and serve with a long-handled spoon.

Coffee and Chocolate Flip

Use only the freshest egg in this recipe, as it isn't cooked. You could replace the Kahlúa with Tia Maria for a slightly sweeter version. The result is a smoothly frothy, intensely rich drink with a strong, beguiling coffee flavour. The chocolate element is confined to the garnish.

1 egg
5ml/1 tsp sugar
1 measure/1½ tbsp cognac
1 measure/1½ tbsp Kahlúa
5ml/1 tsp dark-roast instant coffee granules
3 measures/4½ tbsp double (heavy) cream

Separate the egg and lightly beat the white until frothy. In a separate bowl, beat the egg yolk with the sugar. In a small pan, combine the brandy, Kahlúa,

coffee and cream and warm over a very low heat. Allow the mixture to cool, then whisk it into the egg yolk. Add the egg white to the egg and cream, and pour the mixture briefly back and forth between two glasses until it is smooth. Pour into a tall glass over coarsely crushed ice and sprinkle the top with cocoa powder.

Café Royale

This is a highly sophisticated, and rather ostentatious digestif. The recipe serves four.

4 sugar cubes
300ml/½ pint hot, strong, black filter or cafetière coffee
4 measures/6 tbsp cognac

Rinse out four coffee cups with boiled water and pour away. Add a sugar lump to each cup and then fill with coffee to a little way below the rim. Float a measure of cognac on the surface, and then set it alight. Guests should allow the drink to flame for a few seconds, and then extinguish it by stirring with a spoon.

Alhambra Royale

We conclude our brandy repertoire with a hot chocolate mixture that tastes even more luxurious than the preceding coffee recipes.

hot chocolate, made up to just short of the cup's brim
1 small piece orange rind
1½ measures/6 tsp cognac
15ml/1 tbsp whipped cream

Drop the orange rind into the hot chocolate. Heat the cognac in a metal ladle over a gas flame or over boiling water, and set it alight. Pour it, flaming, into the chocolate. Stir it in, and spoon a blob of whipped cream on to the surface of the drink. Sprinkle with cocoa powder.

Bartending know-how

When using hot chocolate in a cocktail, it is always preferable to use proper cocoa with a good, high proportion of real cacao solids in it. The alternative – drinking chocolate – is mostly sugar and has a much less concentrated flavour.

Other spirits

In this section, we deal with those less well-known spirits that fall outside the main six. These will include the bitter aperitifs, such as Campari, as well as the concentrated bitters like Angostura; the apple brandies, such as France's calvados and America's applejack; and the traditional European fruit distillates, such as kirsch (made from cherries) and slivovitz (plums). Despite their minority status, these products have played an integral part in the cocktail repertoire, and will no doubt continue to do so.

Americano

A recipe going back to the early years of the 20th century, Americano was the one of the first to make a feature of the bitter red Italian *aperitivo*, Campari.

2 measures/3 tbsp sweet red vermouth
1 measure/1½ tbsp Campari
1 measure/1½ tbsp soda water

Add the first two ingredients to a rocks glass or Old-Fashioned glass with two or three cubes of ice in it. Stir, and add the soda. Squeeze a twist of orange rind over the drink and then drop it in.

Negroni

The Negroni is an Americano with gin, making an altogether drier drink. It is named after one Count Negroni who invented this formula at a bar in Florence just after the First World War. The addition of gin elevates the drink into a different class altogether. This is a brilliant aperitif.

2 measures/3 tbsp gin
1 measure/1½ tbsp sweet red vermouth
¾ measure/3 tsp Campari
1 measure/1½ tbsp soda water

Mix the first three ingredients in a tumbler with ice and then add the soda. Finish with orange, as for Americano.

Pink Gin

The famous tipple of British naval officers (the lower ranks drank rum), this is simply a neat, bittered gin. Classically, it should be made with Plymouth gin, for its milder aromatic quality and its naval associations.

Sprinkle about six drops of Angostura bitters into a goblet-shaped glass, roll it around to coat the inner surfaces, then dash it out. Add ice-cold gin, which will then take on the faintest pink tint.

Normandy Cooler

This refreshing summer drink is perfect for afternoons in the garden. It can be made with applejack instead of calvados and renamed a Harvard Cooler, in which it is as well to leave out the grenadine.

2 measures/3 tbsp calvados
1 measure/1½ tbsp lemon juice
¼ measure/1 tsp grenadine
½ measure/2 tsp sugar syrup
4 measures/6 tbsp soda water

Fill a highball glass with cracked ice and dangle a twist of lemon in it. Add the first four ingredients, give the drink a good stir, and then top up with the soda water.

Calvados Cream

The cheaper grades of calvados can be a little fiery. If that's what you have to hand, this should sort it out. It's a creamy, but sharply flavoured cocktail.

2 measures/3 tbsp calvados
½ measure/2 tsp lemon juice

1 measure/1½ tbsp double (heavy) cream
¼ measure/1 tsp pineapple syrup (from a can)

Shake the first three ingredients thoroughly with ice, and strain into a bowl-shaped cocktail glass. Sprinkle the pineapple syrup over the surface.

Depth Charge

This is one of several 1920s cocktails that owe their names to the World War then still fresh in everyone's memory.

1 measure/1½ tbsp calvados
1 measure/1½ tbsp cognac

½ measure/2 tsp lemon juice
¼ measure/1 tsp grenadine

Shake all the ingredients well with ice, and strain into a cocktail glass. Garnish with a twist of lemon.

Calvarniac

The name of this drink is a combination of its three alcoholic ingredients. It is an impeccably French mixture, and a very fine one.

1 measure/1½ tbsp calvados
⅔ measure/1 tbsp Grand Marnier
⅓ measure/1½ tsp cognac
1 measure/1½ tbsp sparkling lemonade

Half-fill a rocks glass with cracked ice, and add the first three ingredients. Stir briskly, and then add the lemonade. Garnish with a slice of lemon.

French Toddy

This is a variation of a very old French recipe, said to have been a favourite of the novelist Gustave Flaubert, to which coffee and sugar have been added. This recipe serves two.

120ml/4fl oz calvados
50ml/2fl oz apricot brandy
20–30ml/4–6 tsp sugar, to taste
300ml/½ pint very strong coffee (filter/
    cafetière brewed at about 45g/8 tbsp
    coffee per 500ml/17fl oz water)

Applecart

This is another American recipe, but one that can just as easily be made with calvados as with applejack – or with home-grown Somerset cider brandy, for that matter.

1 measure/1½ tbsp applejack
¾ measure/3 tsp Cointreau
½ measure/2 tsp lemon juice

Shake all the ingredients well with ice, and strain into a chilled cocktail glass. Garnish the drink with a half-slice of lemon.

25ml/1½ tbsp double (heavy) cream

Very gently warm the calvados and apricot brandy together over a low heat, and transfer to large balloon glasses. Dissolve the sugar in the coffee and add to the liquor. Stir vigorously. While the contents are still rotating from the stirring, pour the cream over the surface in a circular motion. Do not stir further, just sip and savour.

Apple Blossom

The slightly sweeter finish of applejack is better suited than calvados in this American cocktail. Use ordinary sugar syrup if you can't get hold of maple, although it won't be quite the same.

1½ measures/6 tsp applejack
1 measure/1½ tbsp apple juice
½ measure/2 tsp lemon juice
¼ measure/1 tsp maple syrup

Shake all the ingredients well with ice, and strain into a cocktail glass or champagne saucer. Garnish with a wafer-thin slice of red apple with the skin left on, and a half-slice of lemon.

Bartending know-how
Applejack was the second-choice product of early American settlers. It was only when the hops they tried to make beer with failed that they turned to apples instead.

Rose

Although it looks delicately pink and sweet, the cocktail that this 1920s recipe actually produces is very dry, and would make a good aperitif.

1 measure/1½ tbsp kirsch
1½ measures/6 tsp dry vermouth
dash grenadine

Shake all the ingredients well with ice, and strain into a cocktail glass. You could garnish the drink with a cherry.

Bartending know-how
Kirsch and cherry brandy are not interchangeable, since the former is drier than the latter, and colourless. Cherry brandy is also lower in alcohol.

Vruiça Rakia

This is how slivovitz, the Balkan plum spirit, is often drunk in its regions of origin. It is a cold-weather preparation intended to insulate the outdoor worker. This recipe serves two.

4 measures/6 tbsp slivovitz
10ml/2 tsp soft brown sugar

Pit Stop

If Rose is too dry for you, this fizzy, fruity kirsch cocktail is definitely a more sweet-natured proposition.

1 measure/1½ tbsp kirsch
1 measure/1½ tbsp cherry brandy
¼ measure/1 tsp amaretto
2 measures/3 tbsp sparkling lemonade

Half-fill a rocks glass with cracked ice. Add the first three ingredients, stir and add the lemonade. Garnish with a twist of lemon and a couple of cherries on a cocktail stick.

4 measures/6 tbsp water

Put all the ingredients in a small pan and bring nearly to the boil, stirring to dissolve the sugar. Pour into mugs or heatproof glasses, and garnish with blueberries skewered on to a swizzle-stick. Drink while hot.

Slivovitz Fizz

A refreshing, cold, sparkling cocktail to complement the hot slivovitz above, this makes a original alternative to more mainstream long drinks.

2 measures/3 tbsp slivovitz
½ measure/2 tsp lime juice
¼ measure/1 tsp sugar syrup
4 measures/6 tbsp soda water

Shake the first three ingredients well with ice, and strain into a highball glass, half-filled with cracked ice. Top up with soda. Garnish with a slice of black plum.

Liqueurs

The world of cocktails would be virtually nothing without liqueurs. They are what give character and personality to many recipes. Sometimes they can be relied on to add sweetness as well as flavour to a drink, so that no other sugaring agent is needed, and sometimes – as in the case of the old herbal liqueurs like Chartreuse, Bénédictine and Strega – they add their peculiar aromatic quality to basic spirits. New liqueurs are being produced and included all the time (Malibu and Midori became firm cocktail flavourites in the 1980s), and, among the recipes that follow, you will find at least one or two appearances of nearly all the liqueurs discussed earlier.

Sidecar

Cointreau can successfully be mixed with virtually any spirit (except perhaps whisky) and a quantity of lemon juice, and shaken with ice. Start with gin and you have a White Lady, vodka for a Balalaika and even tequila for a lemon Margarita. The brandy version is a Paris classic called Sidecar, after the preferred means of travel of a French army officer.

1½ measures/6 tsp cognac
¾ measure/3 tsp Cointreau
¾ measure/3 tsp lemon juice

Shake well with ice and strain into a rocks glass with a little cracked ice. Garnish with a half-slice of lemon.

Rum Sidecar

Just to complete the Sidecar repertoire, here's a version of the basic mix that uses light or golden rum. It produces a very slightly sweeter final result.

1½ measures/6 tsp light rum
¾ measure/3 tsp Cointreau
¾ measure/3 tsp lemon juice

Shake all the ingredients well with ice, and strain into a cocktail glass. Garnish with a half-slice of lemon.

Between the Sheets

A 1920s recipe that suddenly became very fashionable again in the 1980s, this is a powerful, sharply flavoured cocktail. Some recipes use light rum instead of white, but the resulting colour is inevitably slightly muddier.

1 measure/1½ tbsp Cointreau
1 measure/1½ tbsp cognac
1 measure/1½ tbsp white rum
½ measure/2 tsp lemon juice

Shake all the ingredients well with ice, and strain into a bowl-shaped cocktail glass. Garnish with a twist of lemon.

Bartending know-how
The principal flavouring element in crème de menthe – green or white – is peppermint. Its flavour is more subtly aromatic and refreshing than that of spearmint.

Stinger

The adaptable Stinger is simply a two-thirds-one-third mixture of any spirit with white crème de menthe, shaken with ice and served over smashed ice in a cocktail glass. The prototype version, dating from around the time of the First World War, is with cognac, as in the following recipe.

2 measures/3 tbsp cognac
1 measure/1½ tbsp white crème de menthe

Shake both the ingredients well with ice, and strain into a cocktail glass. You could garnish it with a tuft of mint, although it is fine without.

Grasshopper

This is a minted, creamy cocktail in an attractive shade of green. If you use dark crème de cacao, the cocktail will not be as vibrant a colour, but you'll find that it tastes just as good.

1 measure/1½ tbsp green crème de menthe
1 measure/1½ tbsp white crème de cacao
1 measure/1½ tbsp double (heavy) cream

Charlie Chaplin

The first, and in many ways the greatest, cocktail era was also the age of silent films, and it is no surprise to hear that, just as Mary Pickford was honoured with a cocktail named after her, so was the greatest silent comic of them all.

1½ measures/6 tsp sloe gin
½ measure/2 tsp apricot brandy
½ measure/2 tsp lime juice

Shake all the ingredients well with ice, and strain into a chilled cocktail glass. Garnish with a slice of lime, and perhaps a sliver of apricot.

Shake all the ingredients very well with ice, and strain into a cocktail glass. Sprinkle the surface with grated chocolate. Alternatively, decorate with chocolate curls, made by pouring melted chocolate on to a cold baking tray, allowing to harden and then scraping gently off with the point of a knife.

Snowball

This is the kind of cocktail generally considered safe to give to minors, since it resembles nothing so much as a particularly rich milkshake. It is almost the only thing worth doing with advocaat. If you require a bit more of a kick, add ½ measure/2 tsp sweet brown cream sherry as well.

2 measures/3 tbsp advocaat
5 measures/120ml/4fl oz ice-cold sparkling
    lemonade

Add to a highball glass half-filled with cracked ice, and stir gently. You could garnish with a cherry on a stick.

Bartending know-how
Snowball needs plenty of lemonade to avoid its texture being too cloying.

Hollywood Nuts

Almond and hazelnut are among the flavours in this cocktail. The original recipe has egg white in it too, but I don't tend to feel it needs it.

1 measure/1½ tbsp white rum
½ measure/2 tsp amaretto
½ measure/2 tsp brown crème de cacao
½ measure/2 tsp Frangelico
1 measure/1½ tbsp sparkling lemonade

Shake all but the last ingredient with ice, and strain into a rocks glass half-filled with cracked ice. Add the lemonade and stir. Garnish with a slice of lemon.

B52

This cocktail depends on the difference in specific weight or densities of each of the liqueurs to remain separated.

1 measure/1½ tbsp Kahlúa
1 measure/1½ tbsp Bailey's Irish Cream
1 measure/1½ tbsp Grand Marnier

Round the World

This cocktail certainly contains a cosmopolitan mix of ingredients. I can think of no other obvious explanation for its name.

1½ measure/6 tsp green crème de menthe
1 measure/1½ tbsp gin
2½ measures/3½ tbsp pineapple juice

Shake all the ingredients well with ice, and strain into a chilled wine goblet. Garnish with a chunk of pineapple on a cocktail stick.

Pour the ingredients in this order over the back of a cold teaspoon into a shot glass or liqueur glass, remembering to change the spoon between shots. If you can't get the hang of the layering, just shake it all up with ice and strain it into a cocktail glass.

Hooded Claw

Syrupy-sweet prune juice with amaretto and Cointreau makes a delicious digestif when poured over a snow of finely crushed ice. If you can't get it, you could try using the liquor from a can of prunes, although it may well be composed of other fruit juices. This recipe serves four people.

5 measures/120ml/4fl oz prune juice
2 measures/3 tbsp amaretto
1 measure/1½ tbsp Cointreau

Shake all the ingredients well with ice, and strain into four small liqueur glasses loosely filled with crushed ice.

Shamrock

Best described as something of an acquired taste, your view of this drink will depend crucially on how well you get on with the combination of green Chartreuse and mint. The Irish theme accounts for all the greenery. And it is, of course, an incredibly strong alcoholic drink.

1 measure/1½ tbsp Irish whiskey
1 measure/1½ tbsp dry vermouth
¼ measure/1 tsp green Chartreuse
¼ measure/1 tsp green crème de menthe

Stir all the ingredients well with ice in a pitcher, and strain into a cocktail glass. Garnish with a green olive.

Airstrike

This is a burning drink, similar to the Italian flaming Sambuca tradition.

2 measures/3 tbsp Galliano
1 measure/1½ tbsp cognac
1 star anise

Heat the Galliano and brandy in a small pan until just warm. Pour into a heat-resistant glass and add the star anise. Using a long match, pass the flame over the surface of the drink to ignite it, being careful not to burn yourself. Let it burn for a couple of minutes, until the star anise has begun to sizzle a little and released its aroma into the drink. Leave to cool slightly before drinking.

Bullfrog

This is a very simple mix for apricot brandy, in which the generous quantity of lemon juice takes all the sweetness off the liqueur.

1½ measures/6 tsp apricot brandy
juice of a lemon

Shake both the ingredients well with ice and strain into a cocktail glass. Garnish with a slice of lemon.

Long Island Iced Tea

Las Hadas

This contemporary classic spin on the traditional Sambuca presentation is for those who aren't quite up to tackling a drink that's been set on fire.

1 measure/1½ tbsp Sambuca
1 measure/1½ tbsp Kahlúa

Stir both ingredients well with ice in a mixing glass, and strain into a pre-chilled wine goblet. Float a few coffee beans on the surface of the drink.

Alaska

This drink is intended to evoke the frozen wastes, so make sure it's shaken until the cocktail shaker is almost too cold to hold.

1½ measures/6 tsp gin
½ measure/2 tsp yellow Chartreuse

Shake both the ingredients very well with plenty of ice, and strain into a cocktail glass. No garnish is necessary.

This is a long, powerful drink with a rumbustiously intoxicating effect, its potency well disguised by the cola. For a simpler version, use equal quantities of rum, Cointreau, tequila and lemon juice, and top up with cola. The recipe does not contain tea. It's a facetious way of referring to the fact that it looks innocuously like a glass of non-alcoholic iced tea.

½ measure/2 tsp white rum
½ measure/2 tsp vodka

½ measure/2 tsp gin
½ measure/2 tsp silver tequila
½ measure/2 tsp Cointreau
juice of half a lemon
½ measure/2 tsp sugar syrup
4 measures/6 tbsp cola

Stir all but the last ingredient well with ice for about 30 seconds in a pitcher to chill. Strain into a highball glass filled with ice cubes and a twist of lemon. Add chilled cola, and finish with a sprig of fresh mint.

Old William

This is a gorgeously fruity mixture that brings out the best in the delightful liqueur Poire William. The citrus juices take the edge off its sweetness.

2 measures/3 tbsp Poire William
½ measure/2 tsp maraschino

½ measure/2 tsp orange juice
½ measure/2 tsp lemon juice

Add the ingredients in this order to a rocks glass half-filled with broken ice. Stir briskly, and garnish with half-slices of orange and lemon.

Bijou

This recipe dates from the 1920s. The mix of Chartreuse and vermouth does indeed create a rather jewel-like colour. It must be Plymouth gin, by the way.

1 measure/1½ tbsp Plymouth gin
1 measure/1½ tbsp green Chartreuse
1 measure/1½ tbsp sweet red vermouth
dash orange bitters (or curaçao)

Stir all the ingredients well with ice in a pitcher, and then strain into a cocktail glass. Squeeze a twist of lemon over the drink, drop it in and add a cherry.

Frosty Amour

This drink would make a good tipple for a Valentine's Day evening in. Any frostiness will soon be dispelled after downing one.

1 measure/1½ tbsp vodka
1 measure/1½ tbsp apricot brandy
1 measure/1½ tbsp Southern Comfort
¼ measure/1 tsp Parfait Amour
¼ measure/1 tsp crème de banane
4 measures/6 tbsp 7-Up

Frost the rim of a highball glass with lemon juice and caster (superfine) sugar. Half-fill it with ice. Shake all but the last ingredient with ice, and strain into the prepared glass. Top with 7-Up. Garnish with a cherry and a slice of orange.

Fuzzy Navel

The evocative name of this drink plays on the ideas of the fuzzy-skinned peach and the navel orange. If it tastes a little too tame, add a measure of vodka to it and call it a Hairy Navel, a grown-up version of the same body part.

2 measures/3 tbsp peach schnapps
4 measures/6 tbsp orange juice

Add the ingredients to a highball glass half-filled with cracked ice, and stir well. Garnish with a slice of orange.

Singapore Sling

One of the all-time greats, Singapore Sling was created in 1915 at the world-famous Raffles Hotel in Singapore. Some recipes omit the soda for a slightly stronger drink. Some add a dash of grenadine just to deepen the pink colour, but it should nonetheless be no more than a fairly delicate blush.

2 measures/3 tbsp gin
⅔ measure/1 tbsp cherry brandy
⅔ measure/1 tbsp Cointreau
juice of 1 lemon
5ml/1 tsp caster (superfine) sugar
3 measures/4½ tbsp soda water

Shake all but the last ingredient well with ice, and strain into a highball glass. Add the soda, and decorate with a twist of lemon and a black cherry pierced with two cocktail sticks.

Zam

This is a very resourceful cocktail that uses no fewer than three liqueurs, without the need for a plain spirit base. This enhances the herbal flavours well, and the overall effect is nicely balanced between sweet and dry.

1 measure/1½ tbsp Glayva
½ measure/2 tsp Bénédictine
½ measure/2 tsp Sambuca
1½ measures/6 tsp orange juice
¼ measure/1 tsp sugar syrup
¼ measure/1 tsp lemon juice

Shake all the ingredients well with ice, and strain into a chilled champagne saucer or wine goblet loaded with crushed ice. Garnish with a strawberry.

Blanche

Another three-way liqueur blend, this one is fairly sweet, although the curaçao adds a balancing bitter note. To live up to its name, the curaçao really ought to be the white variety, but nobody will know if you use orange.

1 measure/1½ tbsp Cointreau
1 measure/1½ tbsp white curaçao
1 measure/1½ tbsp anisette

Shake all the ingredients well with ice, and strain into a cocktail glass. Emphasize the drink's purity of colour by refraining from any garnish.

Godfather

Like the Godmother, this drink uses amaretto, but substitutes Scotch for the vodka. This makes for a more complex flavour, and the drink would make a good aperitif.

Godmother

Another very simple mixture, this is a formula to throw the sweetness of almond liqueur into relief for the more savoury-toothed. It should properly be made with the most famous brand of amaretto, Disaronno Originale, but won't come to any harm if you use another.

1½ measures/6 tsp amaretto
1½ measures/6 tsp vodka

Mix both ingredients well in a tumbler full of cracked ice. The drink does not need any garnish.

1½ measures/6 tsp amaretto
1½ measures/6 tsp Scotch

Mix both ingredients well in a tumbler full of cracked ice. Do not garnish.

Bunny Hug

This one is not for the novice cocktail drinker as it consists only of strong alcohol, and the flavour is very dry.

1 measure/1½ tbsp gin
1 measure/1½ tbsp Scotch
1 measure/1½ tbsp Pernod

Bartending know-how
Pernod and other forms of pastis will give an instant natural cloudiness to any mixture.

Shake all the ingredients well with ice, and strain into a pre-chilled cocktail glass. The drink can be garnished with a twist of lemon.

Festival

Strictly for the sweet and creamy brigade, this is the sort of drink that might well kick off a hen night, assuming the girls need any further egging on.

1 measure/1½ tbsp apricot brandy
¾ measure/3 tsp white crème de cacao
¼ measure/1 tsp grenadine
½ measure/2 tsp double (heavy) cream

Shake all the ingredients well with ice, and strain into a chilled cocktail glass. Garnish with a cherry or two speared on a cocktail stick.

Lost Bikini

The name seems to evoke memories of Ursula Andress emerging from the waves in the first James Bond movie, or is that just wishful thinking?

¾ measure/3 tsp Galliano
¾ measure/3 tsp amaretto
½ measure/2 tsp white rum
½ measure/2 tsp lime juice
2 measures/3 tbsp unsweetened mandarin juice (from a can)

Shake all the ingredients well with ice, and strain into a champagne saucer or cocktail glass. Garnish with a half-slice of orange and a cherry.

Kir

This world-famous gastronomic aperitif was created in Burgundy, and was originally named after a mayor of Dijon. It consists of a glass of light, dry, acidic white wine with a shot of crème de cassis stirred into it (¼–½ measure/ 1–2 tsp, depending on taste). The classic wine to use is a Bourgogne Aligoté of the most recent vintage, but any fairly neutral-tasting white wine will do, so long as it is sharp with acidity.

Add the cassis to a glass of non-vintage brut champagne and the drink becomes a Kir Royale.

Stratosphere

A few drops of crème de violette are added to a glass of champagne until a mauve colour is obtained. The scentedness is then enhanced by adding a whole clove to the glass.

Oracabessa

A recipe that will use your garnishing skills to the full. The more fruit it has piled on to it, the better, but the banana slices are essential.

1 measure/1½ tbsp dark rum
1 measure/1½ tbsp crème de banane
juice of half a lemon
thin banana slices
4 measures/6 tbsp sparkling lemonade

Shake the first three ingredients well with ice, and strain into a large cocktail goblet. Float some banana on the surface of the drink, and top it up with the lemonade. Garnish lavishly with fruits.

An American violet liqueur, Crème Yvette, was at one time the only correct product to use in this very ladylike aperitif. Parfait Amour might also do.

Blackout

The name of this cocktail does not mean it necessarily induces the said state, but is more of a description of the resulting colour of the drink. It is a very harmonious and appealing cocktail mixture.

1¾ measures/2½ tbsp gin
¾ measure/3 tsp crème de mûre
juice of half a lime

Shake all the ingredients well with ice, and strain into a cocktail glass. Garnish with a slice of lime and a couple of ripe blackberries threaded carefully on to a cocktail stick.

Silver Jubilee

This was created for Queen Elizabeth's Silver Jubilee in 1977. There is a tendency now to up the gin quotient to as much as double this quantity, but I find that these proportions work perfectly well.

1 measure/1½ tbsp gin
1 measure/1½ tbsp crème de banane
1 measure/1½ tbsp double (heavy) cream

Shake all the ingredients thoroughly with ice to amalgamate the cream, and strain into a chilled cocktail glass. Grate a little dark chocolate over the surface, if desired.

Bartending know-how
Cream cocktails should generally be made with double cream, as the single version tends to be too runny.

Oasis

Blue cocktails suddenly became all the rage during the cocktail boom of the 1980s. This is a particularly satisfying mixture that's not too sweet.

2 measures/3 tbsp gin
½ measure/2 tsp blue curaçao
4 measures/6 tbsp tonic water

Pour the gin into a highball glass half-filled with cracked ice. Add the curaçao, top up with the tonic and stir gently. Garnish with a slice of lemon and a sprig of mint.

English Rose

If you can find crème de roses, snap it up and use it in this very fetching cocktail that would make a fine Mother's Day toast. (Before you crack open the pink champagne, that is.)

1½ measures/6 tsp gin
¾ measure/3 tsp crème de roses
½ measure/2 tsp lemon juice
2.5ml/½ tsp caster (superfine) sugar
½ egg white

Shake all the ingredients thoroughly with ice, and strain into a wine glass. Alternatively, you can make this in the blender for that extra frothiness.

Olympic

Created for the 1924 Olympic Games in Paris, this is a gold medal-winning recipe.

1 measure/1½ tbsp cognac
1 measure/1½ tbsp orange curaçao

1 measure/1½ tbsp orange juice

Shake all the ingredients well with ice, and strain into a cocktail glass. Garnish with a twist of orange rind.

Whip

This lethally violent 1920s cocktail contains a lot of strong alcohol and no mixers. Caution is advised. One should be more than enough.

1 measure/1½ tbsp cognac
½ measure/2 tsp dry vermouth

½ measure/2 tsp sweet red vermouth
¼ measure/1 tsp orange curaçao
dash absinthe

Shake all the ingredients well with plenty of ice, and strain into a cocktail glass. You could garnish with a lemon twist.

Golden Tang

This recipe can be prepared short or long, depending on how the fancy takes you. If you serve it short, as here, use a wine glass. If you serve it long, increase the amount of orange juice to 4 measures/6 tbsp and serve it in a highball glass. The resulting drink is obviously more innocuous, but is an equally appealing aperitif long drink.

2 measures/3 tbsp vodka
1 measure/1½ tbsp Strega
½ measure/2 tsp crème de banane
½ measure/2 tsp orange juice

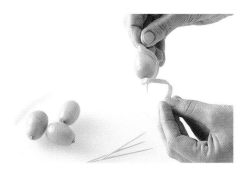

Shake all the ingredients well with ice, and strain into a large wine glass. Garnish with a twist of kumquat.

Golden Slipper

A group of "Golden" recipes continues with this American novelty drink from before the Second World War. I confess I haven't tried it; I suspect it may look rather prettier than it tastes.

1 measure/1½ tbsp yellow Charteuse
1 egg yolk
1 measure/1½ tbsp Goldwasser

Pour the yellow Chartreuse into a copita or sherry glass. Drop the egg yolk whole on to the surface, and then carefully pour the Goldwasser on top.

Golden Start

An ingenious mix of Galliano, fruit juices and coconut. It also works if the curaçao is replaced with white crème de cacao.

2 measures/3 tbsp Galliano
1 measure/1½ tbsp orange juice
1 measure/1½ tbsp pineapple juice
1 measure/1½ tbsp white or orange curaçao
1 measure/1½ tbsp coconut cream

Golden Dream

This fancifully named cocktail was created by the Galliano company itself in the 1960s. It's a sweetly delicious, creamy concoction.

1 measure/1½ tbsp Galliano
1 measure/1½ tbsp Cointreau
1 measure/1½ tbsp orange juice
1 measure/1½ tbsp whipping cream

Shake all the ingredients well with ice, and strain into a bowl-shaped cocktail glass. Decorate the surface with grated orange rind.

Process the Galliano, fruit juices and curaçao in a blender. Add the cream of coconut with 15ml/1 tbsp finely crushed ice, and process until smooth and frothy. Frost the rim of the cocktail glass by dipping it into pineapple juice and caster (superfine) sugar. Pour the cocktail into the prepared glass while still frothy.

Gloom Chaser

There was once a gin cocktail called Gloom Raiser, on account of the depressant qualities that spirit was mythically supposed to have. This, presumably, was intended as the antidote to it. I think we can safely say it works. Certainly, a couple of them will probably manage to dispel (temporarily) whatever it was that was bothering you.

1 measure/1½ tbsp Grand Marnier
1 measure/1½ tbsp orange curaçao
½ measure/2 tsp lemon juice
¼ measure/1 tsp grenadine

Shake all the ingredients well with ice, and strain into a chilled cocktail glass. Garnish the drink with a single slice of orange.

Paradise

A winning 1920s formula that should certainly waft you somewhere in the direction of paradise, however fleetingly.

1½ measures/6 tsp gin
¾ measure/3 tsp apricot brandy
¾ measure/3 tsp orange juice
dash lemon juice

Shake all the ingredients well with ice, and strain into a flared wine glass. Garnish with a slices of orange, lemon and lime.

Alexander the Great

Another variation on the chocolate/coffee/cream combination, and distantly related to the classic Alexander, this drink is reputed to have been invented by the late Hollywood singing star Nelson Eddy. Indeed, in some quarters, he may well be more respectfully remembered for this recipe than for his films.

1½ measure/6 tsp vodka
½ measure/2 tsp Kahlúa
½ measure/2 tsp brown crème de cacao
½ measure/2 tsp double (heavy) cream

Tovarich

There are not many cocktail recipes with caraway-flavoured kümmel in them, but this one works very well, in its tartly bracing way.

1½ measures/6 tsp vodka
1 measure/1½ tbsp kümmel
juice of half a lime

Shake all the ingredients well with ice, and strain into a cocktail glass. Garnish the drink with a couple of rings of thinly sliced lime.

Shake all the ingredients well with plenty of ice, and strain into a cocktail glass. Add a couple of chocolate-coated coffee beans to the drink.

Bartending know-how
The liqueur components in Alexander the Great are Kahlúa and the brown version of chocolate liqueur. If your guests are sweeter-natured than this, substitute Tia Maria and white crème de cacao.

Batida Banana

A recipe created specifically for the Brazilian coconut liqueur, Batida de Coco, this is dangerously moreish, and is effectively little more than a grown-up milkshake, but none the worse for that. The fact that it uses milk rather than cream means that the sweetness of its flavours is not as cloying as it might be.

1 measure/1½ tbsp Batida de Coco
1 measure/1½ tbsp crème de banane
5 measures/120ml/4fl oz full-cream (whole) milk

Mix the liqueurs with several ice cubes in a highball glass. Top with milk. Garnish with sliced banana and orange.

Pick-Me-Up

This is but one of the many recipes for pick-me-ups. As with all of them, it is intended to be drunk PDQ or, as Harry Craddock – Cocktail King of London's Savoy Hotel in the 1920s – used to put it, "while it's laughing at you".

1 measure/1½ tbsp dry vermouth
1 measure/1½ tbsp cherry brandy
2 dashes gin

Add the ingredients to a tumbler packed with cracked ice. Stir once, then drink.

Wally

This drink can be prepared with any apple spirit: calvados, applejack or English cider brandy. I have no idea who the gentleman was after whom it is named.

1 measure/1½ tbsp calvados
1 measure/1½ tbsp peach brandy
1 measure/1½ tbsp lime juice

Shake all the ingredients well with ice, and strain into a cocktail glass. Garnish with a thin slice of peach and a slice of lime on a cocktail stick.

Angel Face

To be dedicated to the one you love, perhaps, although after a couple of these, almost anyone will start to look good. It's another all-alcohol mix, and a pretty dry and bracing one at that, although the liqueur contributes a touch of almondy sweetness to the finish.

1 measure/1½ tbsp gin
1 measure/1½ tbsp apricot brandy
1 measure/1½ tbsp calvados

Shake all the ingredients well with ice, and strain into a cocktail glass. Garnish with a half-slice of lemon.

Tropical Cocktail

Not, as you might expect, a rum cocktail, this was the 1920s idea of tropical. In other words, it has a hint of chocolate in it. Use the brown version of crème de cacao for a less sweet result, but the attractively pale colour of the original will obviously be lost.

1 measure/1½ tbsp dry vermouth
1 measure/1½ tbsp maraschino
1 measure/1½ tbsp white crème de cacao
dash Angostura bitters
dash orange bitters (or curaçao)

Shake all the ingredients well with plenty of ice, and strain into a wine glass. Garnish with a slice of orange and a cherry.

Pink Almond

The colour of this isn't actually pink, more a sort of off-puce, but the flavour is indubitably of almond, so at least half the name is right.

1 measure/1½ tbsp Scotch
½ measure/2 tsp crème de noyau
½ measure/2 tsp kirsch
½ measure/2 tsp lemon juice
½ measure/2 tsp orgeat syrup

Shake all the ingredients well with ice, and strain into a wine goblet. Garnish with a twist of lemon and two or three slivers of flaked almond.

Green Caribbean

One of the 1980s creations that accompanied the launch of the delectable Japanese melon liqueur Midori, the name of which simply means "green". It's a supremely refreshing long drink with an appreciable kick.

Titanic

A modern recipe that should, not surprisingly, be served on a great heap of ice.

1½ measures/6 tsp vodka
1½ measures/6 tsp Mandarine Napoléon
3 measures/4½ tbsp soda water

Mix the vodka and Mandarine Napoléon with ice in a wide tumbler, and top up with soda water. Garnish with a twist of mandarin or tangerine rind.

1½ measures/6 tsp white rum
1½ measures/6 tsp Midori
4 measures/6 tbsp soda water

Shake the first two ingredients with ice, and strain into a highball glass. Add the soda and a slice of lemon.

Mad Monk

This is a cocktail I invented myself on first tasting the excellent hazelnut and herb liqueur, Frangelico, in its monk-shaped bottle.

1 measure/1½ tbsp gin
1 measure/1½ tbsp Frangelico
juice of half a lemon

Shake all the ingredients well with ice, and strain into a wine glass. You could garnish with a half-slice of lemon.

Bartending know-how
Yellow Chartreuse, formulated in 1840, is a more recent product than its green sibling. The colour of both is achieved by the natural colouring of their ingredients.

Walnut Whirl

This one sounds and, for that matter, tastes as though it ought to be lurking somewhere in the bottom layer of a box of fine chocolates.

1 measure/1½ tbsp cognac
1 measure/1½ tbsp crème de noix (walnut liqueur)
1 measure/1½ tbsp double (heavy) cream

Shake all the ingredients well with ice, and strain into a cocktail glass. Garnish with a sprinkling of grated dark chocolate and a walnut half.

Yellow Parrot

This is a powerful 1920s cocktail. It is essential to serve it over crushed ice, to mitigate a little of its firepower.

1 measure/1½ tbsp absinthe
1 measure/1½ tbsp yellow Chartreuse
1 measure/1½ tbsp apricot brandy

Shake all the ingredients well with ice, and strain into a cocktail glass filled almost to the brim with crushed ice. Do not garnish.

Eagle's Dream

The vanilla tones in purple Parfait Amour come through admirably in this foamy, gently flavoured 1920s cocktail. It should be served to your loved one on Valentine's Day, naturally.

1½ measures/6 tsp gin
1 measure/1½ tbsp Parfait Amour
juice of half a lemon
2.5ml/½ tsp caster (superfine) sugar
1 egg white

Whizz up all the ingredients with plenty of crushed ice in a blender, and strain into a large wine goblet. Garnish with a slice of lemon, or dangle a spiral twist of lemon or lime off the side of the glass, just to show you care.

Red Witch

In northern Europe and the United States, pastis is more often mixed with fruit juices than with water. Its colourlessness makes it a useful base; sharper flavours such as grapefruit are the most successful. A fashion for drinking it with blackcurrant cordial was quite the thing in Britain in the 1970s. It perhaps reminded the drinker of a certain type of childhood boiled sweet with a chewy centre that combined the flavours of liquorice and blackcurrant. Pernod and black in a tall glass topped up with sweet cider, known in the bars of the north of England as Red Witch, was a popular way of achieving oblivion in my own happily misspent youth.

Grand Slam

This is another recipe using punsch, which mixes very suavely with both shades of vermouth. Here is an aperitif cocktail, if ever there was one.

2 measures/3 tbsp punsch
1 measure/1½ tbsp dry vermouth
1 measure/1½ tbsp sweet red vermouth

Stir all the ingredients well with ice in a pitcher, and then strain over crushed ice in a wine glass. You could garnish the drink with a half-slice of orange.

Diki-Diki

I have no idea what the name of this cocktail refers to, but it was a very popular one in the Savoy American Bar in the 1920s. It is one of many from the period to use Swedish punsch.

2 measures/3 tbsp calvados
½ measure/2 tsp punsch
½ measure/2 tsp grapefruit juice

Shake all the ingredients well with ice, and strain into a cocktail glass. Add a small piece of pink grapefruit rind to the drink.

Rite of Spring

Green cocktails that don't somehow taste of mint are pretty few and far between. The relatively rare green version of curaçao is worth buying if you come across it, and here is a recipe of my own, tailor-made for it, if I say so myself.

2 measures/3 tbsp vodka
1 measure/1½ tbsp green curaçao
4 measures/6 tbsp sparkling lemonade

Mix the vodka and curaçao with ice in a pitcher until well-chilled. Pour without straining into a highball glass, and top up with the lemonade. Dangle a long twist of lemon rind in the drink.

Ojen Cocktail

This recipe was created specifically for the Spanish version of pastis, ojen. For that authentic touch, the twist should really be of the bitter Seville orange variety.

2 measures/3 tbsp dry ojen
5ml/1 tsp caster (superfine) sugar
½ measure/2 tsp still mineral water
dash orange bitters (or curaçao)

Shake all the ingredients well with ice, and strain into a small tumbler. Garnish with a twist of orange rind.

Absinthe Cocktail

This original 19th-century recipe could just be the most perfect cocktail in the world, for its simplicity and unforgettable power. Now that absinthe is widely commercially available again, it cries out to be tried. As a wise man once said, "Absinthe makes the heart grow fonder."

2 measures/3 tbsp absinthe
2 measures/3 tbsp still mineral water
dash sugar syrup
dash Angostura bitters

Shake all the ingredients well with ice, and strain into a cocktail glass. No garnish is needed. Sip slowly.

Matinée

In this nourishing, creamy, eggy mixture, the relatively small amount of Sambuca shines forth. Whip up the egg white a little before adding it to the shaker.

1 measure/1½ tbsp gin
½ measure/2 tsp Sambuca
½ measure/2 tsp double (heavy) cream
½ egg white
dash lime juice

Shake all the ingredients well with plenty of ice, and strain into a chilled cocktail glass. Sprinkle with finely grated nutmeg.

Bartending know-how
When three coffee beans are taken in a flaming Sambuca, they represent health, wealth and happiness.

Block and Fall

Cocktails that include pastis tend to be the most dramatic in the repertoire. Many of these contain no non-alcoholic ingredients. That is because a relatively small amount of pastis will have plenty to say for itself in even the most ferocious of mixes, concoctions that would drown the presence of many of the more delicate liqueurs.

1 measure/1½ tbsp cognac
1 measure/1½ tbsp Cointreau
½ measure/2 tsp Pernod
½ measure/2 tsp calvados

Stir all the ingredients together with ice in a pitcher, and then strain into a tumbler half-filled with cracked ice. Add a twist of lemon.

Drought

If you should bring back a bottle of delightful Suze from a trip to France, here is a good alternative to serving it neat. This is an unimaginably dry mixture, and a particular energizer to the appetite. It makes a fabulous lunchtime aperitif – or evening one, for that matter.

1 measure/1½ tbsp gin
1 measure/1½ tbsp Suze
dash orange juice

Shake all the ingredients well with ice, and strain into a small wine glass containing a single cube of ice. Add a little piece of orange rind.

Sundowner

This recipe uses the bitter, orange-flavoured South African liqueur, Van der Hum, in a variation on the formula for Sunburn (see below). Instead of using cognac, though, you could substitute a good South African brandy if you come across it. Many of them are surprisingly fine in quality.

1½ measures/6 tsp cognac
1 measure/1½ tbsp Van der Hum
½ measure/2 tsp orange juice
½ measure/2 tsp lemon juice

Shake all the ingredients well with ice, and strain into a cocktail glass. Garnish with a physalis fruit.

Southern Peach

The peach notes in America's classic whiskey liqueur are accentuated by its being mixed with peach brandy in this cream cocktail.

1 measure/1½ tbsp Southern Comfort
1 measure/1½ tbsp peach brandy
1 measure/1½ tbsp double (heavy) cream
dash Angostura bitters

Shake all the ingredients well with plenty of ice, and strain into a tumbler. Garnish with a wedge of ripe peach.

Sunburn

A dark and brooding combination of brandy and coffee liqueur is brightened up with fresh citrus juices. The effect is an unusual one, but you will find that you have grown to love it by the time you finish the drink.

1 measure/1½ tbsp cognac
1 measure/1½ tbsp Tia Maria
½ measure/2 tsp orange juice
½ measure/2 tsp lemon juice

Shake all the ingredients well with ice, and strain into a cocktail glass. Garnish with half-slices of orange and lemon.

Amsterdammer

Here is one of those bet-you-can't-drink-more-than-one-of-these recipes. I have never seen this on any cocktail list in Amsterdam. It seems more likely to be an American recipe.

1½ measures/6 tsp advocaat
1½ measures/6 tsp cherry brandy

Shake the ingredients very thoroughly with ice, and strain into a champagne saucer. Garnish with a cocktail cherry.

Milano

The assertive flavour of Galliano comes through strongly in this short, sour cocktail, which has a long aftertaste.

1 measure/1½ tbsp gin
1 measure/1½ tbsp Galliano

Duchess

This is a 1920s recipe in which the pungency of absinthe is tamed – if that's the right word – by a mixture of red and white vermouths.

1 measure/1½ tbsp absinthe
1 measure/1½ tbsp dry vermouth
1 measure/1½ tbsp sweet red vermouth

Shake all the ingredients well with ice, and strain into a cocktail glass. Add a small piece of lemon rind.

juice of half a lemon

Shake all the ingredients well with ice, and strain into a cocktail glass. Garnish with a cherry and slices of lemon and lime on a cocktail stick.

Saracen

This impeccably Scottish cocktail recalls the story of the Saracen's head, with which Glayva is associated. Good malt whisky is often matured in old sherry casks, so there is a Highland connection even in the use of dry sherry in the recipe.

1 measure/1½ tbsp Scotch
½ measure/2 tsp Glayva
½ measure/2 tsp pale dry (fino) sherry
dash orange bitters (or curaçao)
1 measure/1½ tbsp soda water

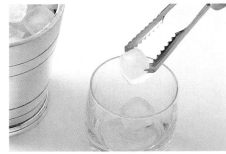

Shake all but the last ingredient well with ice, and pour without straining into a tumbler. Add the soda, and garnish with a piece of orange rind.

Bartending know-how
The tall fluted bottle in which Galliano is packaged is based on the classical design of Roman columns.

Strega Daiquiri

This is more or less a standard Daiquiri, in which the liqueur forms an additional element, rather than replacing the rum.

1 measure/1½ tbsp Strega
1 measure/1½ tbsp white rum
½ measure/2 tsp lemon juice
½ measure/2 tsp orange juice
2.5ml/½ tsp orgeat syrup (or sugar syrup)

Shake all the ingredients well with ice, and strain into a chilled cocktail glass. Garnish with a slice of lemon and a maraschino cherry.

Midori Sour

Tuaca Cocktail

The combined flavours of vanilla, orange and lime in this heavenly mixture will test your moderate-drinking resolution to its limit. Once breached, you can then go on to enjoy another couple with a clear conscience.

1 measure/1½ tbsp vodka
1 measure/1½ tbsp Tuaca
½ measure/2 tsp lime juice

Shake well with ice, and strain into a cocktail glass. Garnish with orange rind.

The standard Sour treatment works quite well with Midori, and certainly makes for a more exotic alternative to yet another Whisky Sour, but it's better shaken than stirred. You may well find it doesn't really need the sugar syrup.

2 measures/3 tbsp Midori
1 measure/1½ tbsp lemon juice
¼ measure/1 tsp sugar syrup

Shake well with ice, and strain into a tumbler. Garnish with a melon ball.

Café Kahlúa

This long, strong, creamy cocktail is pure self-indulgence. The addition of an optional cinnamon stick makes an imaginative alternative decoration to a plastic stirrer, and has the extra benefit of flavouring the drink as you swizzle it.

3 measures/4½ tbsp Kahlúa
1½ measures/6 tsp light rum
2 measures/3 tbsp whipping cream

Shake thoroughly with ice to incorporate the cream, and strain into a chilled tumbler. Add a stick of cinnamon.

Chrysanthemum

A 1920s recipe that, according to the *Savoy Cocktail Book*, was once popular in the bar of the Europa, one of the great passenger liners of the period.

1 measure/1½ tbsp Bénédictine
2 measures/3 tbsp dry vermouth
¼ measure/1 tsp absinthe

Shake all the ingredients well with ice, and strain into a cocktail glass. Squeeze a twist of orange rind over the surface of the drink and then drop it in.

Bartending know-how
Among the many herbal and aromatic ingredients that go to make up the flavour of Bénédictine are: saffron, myrrh, aloes, hyssop, pine, cloves, nutmeg and tea.

Cara Sposa

Liqueurs and cream without the addition of a spirit base add up to a sweet, rich cocktail, and if that's your tipple, this luxurious creation is a well-nigh unbeatable one. Serve it at the end of dinner after a correspondingly light dessert.

1 measure/1½ tbsp Tia Maria
1 measure/1½ tbsp Cointreau
½ measure/2 tsp double (heavy) cream

Shake all the ingredients well with ice, and strain into a champagne saucer. Garnish with a twist of orange.

Viking

It has to be a thoroughly Scandinavian cocktail with that name, and so it is. The marriage of Swedish punsch and aquavit is, logically enough, a happy one.

1½ measures/6 tsp punsch
1 measure/1½ tbsp aquavit
1 measure/1½ tbsp lime juice

Shake all the ingredients well with ice, and strain into an Old-Fashioned glass or small tumbler. Garnish with lime.

Summertime

For the very sweet of tooth, this is a perfect way of livening up a dish of vanilla ice cream on a long, hot afternoon.

½ measure/2 tsp white crème de menthe
½ measure/2 tsp green crème de menthe
2 scoops vanilla ice cream

Process all the ingredients briefly in the blender, and then pour into a sundae glass. Sprinkle with grated dark chocolate.

Melon Patch

Another recipe for Midori, or indeed for any other melon liqueur you may have to hand.

1 measure/1½ tbsp Midori
½ measure/2 tsp Cointreau
½ measure/2 tsp vodka
4 measures/6 tbsp soda water

Shake the first three ingredients well with ice, and strain into a highball glass half-filled with cracked ice. Top up with soda, and garnish with a slice of orange.

Peugeot

This very French cocktail is intended, unexpectedly, as a tribute to the car manufacturer. Owners of their cars may justifiably drink it with pride, though not of course immediately before driving anywhere, as it's quite strong.

Kowloon

Coffee and orange make a successful partnership again in this recipe named after the Chinese district that faces Hong Kong Island.

1 measure/1½ tbsp Grand Marnier
1 measure/1½ tbsp Kahlúa
3 measures/4½ tbsp orange juice

Stir all the ingredients well with ice in a pitcher, and strain into a wine goblet half-filled with cracked ice. Add a slice of orange.

1½ measures/6 tsp Cointreau
¾ measure/3 tsp calvados
2 measures/3 tbsp orange juice

Shake well with ice and strain into a cocktail glass. Garnish with orange.

La Bomba

This explosive mixture has more than a touch of the Zombie about it.

1 measure/1½ tbsp light rum
½ measure/2 tsp orange curaçao
½ measure/2 tsp anisette
½ measure/2 tsp apricot brandy
½ measure/2 tsp lemon juice

Shake all the ingredients well with ice, and strain into a chilled cocktail glass. The drink could be garnished with a couple of chunks of pineapple and a cherry on a cocktail stick.

Bartending know-how
The variety of orange whose peel is used to flavour Grand Marnier is called *Citrus bigaradia*. It produces a bitter, orangey flavour that marries well with fine brandy.

Grand Hotel

This is a charming 1920s cocktail, the name of which may well refer to London's Savoy, one of the grandest of them all.

1½ measures/6 tsp Grand Marnier
1½ measures/6 tsp gin
½ measure/2 tsp dry vermouth
dash lemon juice

Shake all the ingredients well with ice, and strain into a large cocktail glass. Squeeze a twist of lemon over the surface and drop it into the glass.

Blue Lady

We have a Lemon Lady, a Scarlet Lady, a Pink Lady and a White Lady elsewhere, and here is their Blue sister. It's a sweet, creamy one that combines the flavours of orange and chocolate, but in a most peculiar hue.

Love

This sweet old 1920s cocktail is obviously made for sharing, so the recipe below serves two.

4 measures/6 tbsp sloe gin
1 measure/1½ tbsp lemon juice
1 egg white
¼ measure/1 tsp grenadine

Shake all the ingredients well with ice and then strain into two cocktail glasses. Garnish each with a pair of cherries joined at the stalk.

1½ measures/6 tsp blue curaçao
½ measure/2 tsp white crème de cacao
½ measure/2 tsp double (heavy) cream

Shake thoroughly with ice, and strain into a cocktail glass. Do not garnish.

Il Paradiso

Not to be confused with Paradise, this is a creamy, sumptuous, chocolate-orangey cocktail with a nice balance of sweet and bitter flavours.

1 measure/1½ tbsp Tuaca
1 measure/1½ tbsp orange curaçao
1 measure/1½ tbsp double (heavy) cream

Shake all the ingredients thoroughly with ice, and strain into a cocktail glass. Alternatively, whizz it up in the blender for an extra-frothy texture. Garnish with grated orange rind.

Bartending know-how
The credit for the formulation of the recipe on which the orangey Italian liqueur Tuaca is based is said to go to the Florentine politican Lorenzo de Medici in the 16th century – along with his many other achievements.

After-Dinner Coffee

This makes a superb Mexican-style way to end a meal. Kahlúa, the coffee liqueur used in this drink, is also delicious served in a liqueur glass topped with a thin layer of cream. This recipe serves four.

50g/2oz dark-roast ground coffee
475ml/16fl oz boiling water
120ml/4fl oz tequila
120ml/4fl oz Kahlúa
5ml/1 tsp natural vanilla essence (extract)
30ml/2 tbsp soft dark brown sugar
150ml/¼ pint double (heavy) cream

Put the ground coffee in a heatproof pitcher or cafetière, pour on the boiling water and leave until the coffee grounds settle at the bottom. Strain the coffee into a clean heatproof pitcher. Add the tequila, Kahlúa and vanilla essence to the coffee, and stir well to mix. Add the sugar and continue to stir until it has dissolved completely. Pour the mixture into small coffee cups or tall heat-resistant glasses. Hold a spoon just above the surface of each coffee. Pour the cream very slowly down the back of the spoon so that it forms a pool on top. Serve at once.

Highland Milk Punch

This is just the sort of thing to keep the cold at bay on cold nights in the frozen north, or anywhere else for that matter.

2 measures/3 tbsp Scotch
1 measure/1½ tbsp Drambuie
1 egg, beaten
250ml/8fl oz full-cream (whole) milk

Ski Lift

Here's another comforting hot drink for a rainy day. This gives ordinary drinking chocolate a real lift, and may well provide some compensation if the snow isn't good enough for skiing on.

1 measure/1½ tbsp peach schnapps
½ measure/2 tsp Malibu
hot chocolate

Make a pan of hot chocolate or cocoa in the normal way, but add the liqueurs to your mug before pouring it. Stir briskly, and top with a blob of whipped cream dusted with ground cinnamon.

Put all the ingredients into a small pan and heat gently, stirring all the time to incorporate the egg and prevent the milk from burning on the bottom of the pan. Just before the mixture boils, pour it into a mug and sprinkle the surface of the drink with powdered cinnamon.

Coffee Orloff

A John J. Poister recipe from the *New American Bartender's Guide*, this would make a very sexy after-dinner drink with a good, strong kick. Be sure to use the cream version of Grand Marnier.

¾ measure/3 tsp vodka
¾ measure/3 tsp Tia Maria
hot black coffee
¾ measure/3 tsp Crème de Grand Marnier

Add the vodka and Tia Maria to a large cup, and then top up with coffee. Pour the Crème de Grand Marnier over the back of a spoon so that it floats on top.

Café à l'Orange

This is one of numerous drink possibilities in which the flavours of orange and coffee are combined. The recipe serves four.

120ml/4fl oz whipping cream
30ml/2 tbsp icing (confectioners') sugar
5ml/1 tsp grated orange rind
600ml/1 pint hot black coffee
150ml/¼ pint any orange-flavoured liqueur, such as Grand Marnier, Cointreau, triple sec, etc
4 orange wedges, to garnish

In a clean bowl, whip the cream until stiff. Fold in the icing sugar and zest. Chill for 30 minutes, or until the cream mixture is firm enough to hold a wedge of orange on top. Divide the black coffee equally among tall glass mugs and stir about 30ml/2 tbsp liqueur into each. Top with chilled whipped cream and balance an orange wedge on top. Serve immediately.

Lisbon Flip Coffee

Here the coffee is not so much a main ingredient. It provides instead a subtle undertone to an interesting and profoundly satisfying cocktail. The recipe serves two.

4 measures/6 tbsp red port
2 measures/3 tbsp orange curaçao
1 measure/1½ tbsp very strong coffee
10ml/2 tsp icing (confectioners') sugar
2 eggs
20ml/4 tsp condensed milk
60ml/4 tbsp crushed ice
grated chocolate and orange rind shavings, to garnish

Place all the ingredients in a cocktail shaker, including the crushed ice. Shake vigorously and serve immediately in cocktail glasses. Top with the finely grated chocolate and orange rind.

African Coffee

In parts of Africa, coffee is often drunk with condensed milk. This recipe is an adaptation of an African brew with a luxurious liqueur finish.

250ml/8fl oz cold strong coffee (four generous espressos or cafetière coffee brewed using 70g/12 tbsp coffee per 1 litre/1¾ pints water)
40ml/8 tsp condensed milk
20ml/4 tsp brown crème de cacao

Shake well with ice, and strain into a tall glass half-filled with cracked ice.

Grasshopper Coffee

The name of this drink recalls the creamy crème de menthe cocktail we came across earlier, and the coffee will need to be good and strong to stand up to the flavours of the liqueurs. This recipe makes two servings.

dark and white chocolate mints
2 measures/3 tbsp green crème de menthe
2 measures/3 tbsp coffee liqueur, such as Tia Maria or Kahlúa
350ml/12fl oz hot strong black coffee
50ml/2fl oz whipping cream

Cut the dark and white chocolate mints diagonally in half. Divide the two liqueurs equally into two tall, strong latte glasses. Combine well. Fill each glass with the hot coffee and top them with whipped cream. Decorate with the chocolate mint triangles, dividing the white and dark chocolate evenly.

Easy Café Brûlot

This is a traditional coffee drink from New Orleans, where all the ingredients except the coffee are "flamed" in a bowl at the table. The flame is extinguished by pouring the coffee into the bowl. Except for the dramatic visual effects, this recipe achieves the same flavour with less fuss. It serves three to four.

3 measures/4½ tbsp brandy or rum
2 measures/3 tbsp Cointreau or other orange-flavoured liqueur
30ml/2 tbsp caster (superfine) sugar
6–8 cloves
2 sticks cinnamon
a strip of lemon and/or orange rind
700ml/24fl oz strong hot dark-roast coffee

Heat the brandy or rum, Cointreau, sugar, cloves, cinnamon sticks and lemon or orange rind in a large pan. Stir to dissolve the sugar. Pour the black coffee, brewed at about 65g/2½oz per 1 litre/1¾ pints water by the cafetière method, into the mixture. Stir and serve in coffee cups. Garnish with a cinnamon stick and orange rind.

Coffee Colada

This coffee cocktail is a riot of bold Caribbean flavours. A pitcher can be made up a couple of hours in advance, then allowed to freeze partially, before topping with plenty of whipped cream. This recipe serves four.

450ml/¾ pint cold, very strong coffee (filter/cafetière brewed using 80g/14 tbsp coffee per 1 litre/1¾ pints water)
2 measures/3 tbsp tequila (or white rum)
2 measures/3 tbsp Malibu
4 measures/6 tbsp coconut cream
2.5ml/½ tsp vanilla essence (extract)
350ml/12fl oz crushed ice
60ml/4 tbsp whipped cream and toasted coconut shavings, to garnish

Combine all the ingredients in a blender and process on a high speed. Serve in tall wine glasses. Garnish with whipped cream, topped with toasted coconut shavings.

White Hot Chocolate

This new spin on hot chocolate matches white chocolate with orange liqueur. The recipe serves four.

1.75 litres/3 pints milk
175g/6oz white chocolate, broken into small pieces
½ measure/2 tsp coffee powder
4 measures/6 tbsp Cointreau or other orange-flavoured liqueur
whipped cream and ground cinnamon, to serve

Heat the milk in a large heavy pan until almost boiling. Remove from the heat. Add the white chocolate, coffee powder and liqueur. Stir until all the chocolate has melted. Pour into four mugs. Top each with a spoonful of whipped cream and a sprinkling of ground cinnamon. Serve immediately.

Peanut Coffee

Fans of peanut butter will love this iced drink with a coffee flavour. It's rich and filling, like a sumptuous dessert.

1½ measures/6 tsp Kahlúa
3 measures/4½ tbsp full-cream (whole) milk
30ml/2 tbsp vanilla ice cream
10ml/2 tsp smooth peanut butter
3 measures/4½ tbsp 7-Up

Put all but the last ingredient into the blender with crushed ice, and combine. Pour into a cocktail glass, and add the 7-Up. Stir once more.

Wine and champagne

Table wines are used surprisingly seldom in cocktails. That may at first seem odd, but the reason is that their flavours are so hugely various that it is difficult to give recipes that are guaranteed to come out tasting the same each time. For the following recipes, where a dry white wine is specified, go for something like a light, unoaked Chardonnay from Chile, South Africa or the south of France, and where red is used, choose something like a Côtes du Rhône or other southern French blend. When it comes to sparkling wine recipes, it isn't really worth using champagne where lots of other flavours are involved. A less expensive sparkler from another region (Australia, New Zealand, South Africa or Spain) will do quite as well.

Spritzer

The most famous white wine cocktail is this simple fizzy creation. Everyone who drinks spritzers seems to have his or her own preferred proportions, but this recipe should be reliable. The point is that the drink is lower in alcohol than a standard glass of wine.

3 measures/4½ tbsp dry white wine
4 measures/6 tbsp soda water

Half-fill a highball glass with cracked ice, and add the wine and soda. Garnish with mixed berries if you like, but the drink doesn't really need them.

Operator

Another low-alcohol preparation, Operator is to my mind a rather more satisfying drink than basic Spritzer, although along the same lines. At least it tastes of something.

2 measures/3 tbsp dry white wine
2 measures/3 tbsp sparkling ginger ale
¼ measure/1 tsp lime juice

Half-fill a rocks glass with cracked ice, and then add all the ingredients. Stir, and garnish with a slice of lime.

Crimean

You might think this would have vodka in it with a name like that, but it's actually quite innocent of the stuff. It needs straining through something like a tea-strainer in order to remove the lemon rind as well as the used ice.

2 measures/3 tbsp dry white wine
⅔ measure/1 tbsp Cointreau
grated rind of one lemon
1 measure/1½ tbsp soda water

Stir the first three ingredients well with ice in a pitcher, and strain into a rocks glass. Add the soda and garnish with a half-slice of lemon.

Fantaisie

This appealing cocktail is best made with an off-dry or medium-dry white wine, rather than the very driest. An aromatic, floral-scented Gewurztraminer from Alsace would suit the recipe down to the ground.

4 measures/6 tbsp off-dry white wine
¾ measure/3 tsp apricot brandy

Pour the wine into a well-chilled goblet. Add the liqueur and stir well. No garnish is necessary.

Sonoma Cup

The Sonoma Valley in California produces some of the world's very best Chardonnays. However, a simpler white wine will do just as well.

3 measures/4½ tbsp dry white wine
½ measure/2 tsp Cointreau

3 measures/4½ tbsp orange juice
4 measures/6 tbsp soda water

Shake all but the last ingredient well with ice, and strain into a highball glass. Add the soda, stir gently and garnish with a half-slice of orange.

Waltzing Matilda

A longer, stronger drink than most white wine cocktails, the name of this cocktail suggests that an Australian Chardonnay would be the best wine to use. If so, go for an unoaked one, as anything else will probably be too overwhelming for the mixture. Even the simplest wines should have a ripe, buttery flavour.

4 measures/6 tbsp dry white wine
1 measure/1½ tbsp gin
1½ measures/6 tsp passion fruit juice
¼ measure/1 tsp orange curaçao
3 measures/4½ tbsp sparkling ginger ale

Shake all but the last ingredient well with ice, and strain into a highball glass. Add the ginger ale and a lemon slice.

Sangria

Testament to the Spanish influence on Mexican cooking, this popular thirst-quencher is traditionally served in large pitchers, with ice and citrus fruit slices floating on top. This recipe serves six.

750ml/1¼ pints red wine
juice of 2 limes
4 measures/6 tbsp orange juice
4 measures/6 tbsp brandy
50g/2oz caster (superfine) sugar
1 lime, sliced, to garnish

Combine the wine, lime juice, orange juice and brandy in a large glass pitcher. Stir in the sugar until it has dissolved completely. Serve in tall glasses with ice. Garnish each glass with a slice of lime.

English Christmas Punch

This old Victorian recipe for a red wine punch uses tea. It may not taste like any punch you've previously been used to, but it makes a properly festive tipple. It would once have contained about twice this quantity of sugar, so add more if you think the resulting mixture isn't sweet enough. The recipe makes about 24 servings.

2 bottles red wine
3 teacups strong tea
juice of an orange
juice of a lemon
225g/8 oz caster (superfine) sugar
a 700ml/1 pint bottle dark rum
orange and lemon slices, to garnish

Heat the wine, tea and fruit juices in a pan, without allowing them to boil. Simmer for about 5 minutes, and then add the sugar, stirring until it has all dissolved. Transfer to a punchbowl. Using the same pan, heat about a quarter of the rum until it starts seething and set it alight. Pour the flaming rum into the punchbowl, and then add the rest of the rum. Stir well, and throw in some orange and lemon slices.

Bordeaux Cocktail

A good way of disguising any harshness in a young red wine, this recipe is classically made with a young claret from Bordeaux. Wine-tasters claim to find the taste of blackcurrant in the Cabernet Sauvignon grape that most claret contains, but you can make sure of that by adding the blackcurrant liqueur, cassis.

2 measures/3 tbsp red Bordeaux
1 measure/1½ tbsp cognac
¾ measure/3 tsp crème de cassis

Stir all the ingredients well with ice in a pitcher, and strain into a large wine glass. Do not garnish.

Mulled Red Wine

This is an excellent warm drink to serve on a cold winter's evening (at Christmas, traditionally), as it will really get the party started. The word "mulled" is derived from an old English dialect word of the late 14th or early 15th century, meaning "mixed" or "muddled", which is how you may feel after over-indulging in it. Then again it might only mull you into a false sense of security. This recipe serves six.

1 bottle red wine
75g/3oz soft light brown sugar
2 cinnamon sticks
1 lemon, sliced
4 whole cloves
150ml/¼ pint brandy or port

Put all the ingredients, except the brandy or port, into a large pan. Bring the wine to the boil to dissolve the sugar. Remove immediately, cover the pan and leave it to stand for 5 minutes, allowing the flavours to infuse. Strain to remove the spices and lemon slices. Add the brandy and serve warm, with a fresh slice of lemon in each glass.

Royal Silver

A sparkling wine cocktail should always look grand, and this one benefits from the frosted red rim given to the glass.

½ measure/2 tsp Poire William
½ measure/2 tsp Cointreau
1½ measures/6 tsp pink grapefruit juice
champagne or sparkling wine

Frost the rim of a large wine goblet by dipping it into grenadine and then caster (superfine) sugar. Shake the first three ingredients well with ice, and strain into the prepared glass. Top up with champagne or sparkling wine, and garnish with a chunk of ripe pear and a half-slice of orange on a cocktail stick.

Champagne Cocktail

The original champagne cocktail is an American recipe dating from the 19th century, although nobody appears to know precisely when it was first invented. It certainly makes a change from serving champagne straight, but I would only use a relatively inexpensive, non-vintage wine. As a rule, the very best stuff should never be mixed.

1 sugar cube
2 dashes Angostura bitters
¼ measure/1 tsp cognac
champagne

Drop the sugar cube into a champagne flute, and add the Angostura, rolling the sugar lump to soak it. Pour in the brandy, and then top the glass up with freshly opened champagne.

Marilyn Monroe

The drink named in honour of one of the great screen sirens of all time should really be made not just with champagne, but with the premium brand Dom Pérignon. It is fearfully expensive, though. Moet & Chandon Brut Impérial, made by the same house, might suffice instead.

4 measures/6 tbsp well-chilled champagne
1 measure/1½ tbsp applejack or calvados
¼ measure/1 tsp grenadine

Add all the ingredients to a champagne saucer, and give the drink the gentlest of stirs. Garnish with a couple of cocktail cherries.

Night and Day

This is an elegant recipe full of complementary flavours. The mixture should not be stirred, so that the layers of different drinks come at the drinker one by one.

3 measures/4½ tbsp champagne or sparkling wine
¾ measure/3 tsp cognac
½ measure/2 tsp Grand Marnier
¼ measure/1 tsp Campari

Add the ingredients in this order to a large wine goblet filled with crushed ice.

Sparkling Peach Melba

This refreshing fruit fizz is an excellent choice for summer celebrations. As with most soft fruit recipes, its success depends on using the ripest, tastiest peaches and raspberries available. This recipe serves four.

3 ripe peaches
90ml/6 tbsp orange juice
75g/3oz raspberries
10ml/2 tsp icing (confectioners') sugar
about 500ml/17fl oz raspberry sorbet
about 400ml/14fl oz medium sparkling
  wine, chilled

Put the peaches in a heatproof bowl and cover with boiling water. Leave for a minute, then drain and peel off the skins. Cut the fruit in half and remove the stones. Chop the peach halves roughly, and purée them with the orange juice in a blender until smooth. Transfer to a bowl.

Put the raspberries in the blender with the icing sugar, and process until smooth. Press the raspberry purée through a sieve into a separate bowl. Chill both purées for at least an hour.

Spoon the chilled peach purée into four tall glasses. Add scoops of sorbet to fill the glasses. Spoon the raspberry purée around the sorbet. Top up each glass with sparkling wine. Garnish with mint sprigs.

Buck's Fizz

Hugely popular in the 1980s, Buck's Fizz is a simple mixture of two-thirds champagne to one-third orange juice; it is not half and half, as is often suggested. It is a 1920s recipe invented at a club called Buck's in London. Some recipes add ¼ measure/1 tsp grenadine to it, to deepen the colour, but it isn't necessary. It is best served in flute glasses, but you can use a large wine goblet instead if you want to appear more generous.

Mustique

This rum drink was invented on the Caribbean island of Mustique.

1 measure/1½ tbsp light rum
1 measure/1½ tbsp orange juice
½ measure/2 tsp lemon juice
¼ measure/1 tsp grenadine
champagne or sparkling wine

Shake all but the last ingredient with ice, and strain into a large wine glass. Top with fizz, and garnish with a half-slice of lemon.

Blackberry and Champagne Crush

This sparkling blend makes a good brunch alternative to Buck's Fizz. For a party, divide the blackberry purée among six glasses and top up with champagne. This recipe, though, is just for two.

175g/6oz blackberries
15ml/1 tbsp icing (confectioners') sugar
30ml/2 tbsp cognac
250ml/8fl oz champagne or sparkling wine,
  chilled

Purée the blackberries in a food processor. Push the purée through a sieve, and then add the sugar. Pour the brandy into two glasses. Return the blackberry purée to the food processor, add the sparkling wine and blend for no more than two or three seconds. Pour into the glasses and serve immediately.

Bocuse Special

This recipe was created by the French master-chef Paul Bocuse at his restaurant in the south of France.

½ measure/2 tsp crème de cassis
½ measure/2 tsp crème de framboise
champagne

Mix the liqueurs together with ice in a small pitcher until well-chilled. Strain into a flute glass, and top up with champagne. Drop a raspberry into the glass if you have one to hand.

Southern Champagne

This is how they like a champagne cocktail in the southern states of America.

1 measure/1½ tbsp Southern Comfort
dash Angostura bitters
ice-cold champagne or sparkling wine

Add the liqueur and bitters to a champagne flute. Mix briefly and top up with champagne or sparkling wine. Squeeze a small twist of orange rind over the drink, and then drop it into the glass.

B2 C2

The story goes that American troops advancing through Germany in 1945 stumbled on a wine merchant's premises, and cobbled together their own cocktail from whatever came to hand. The name refers of course to the initials of the four ingredients.

1 measure/1½ tbsp brandy (cognac)
1 measure/1½ tbsp Bénédictine
1 measure/1½ tbsp Cointreau
4 measures/6 tbsp well-chilled champagne

Add the ingredients in this order to a large wine goblet. No garnish is necessary.

Pizzetti

This charming cocktail was created at a hotel in the Cortina region of Italy, and its name literally means "little pizzas". You work it out.

1 measure/1½ tbsp cognac
2 measures/3 tbsp orange juice
2 measures/3 tbsp grapefruit juice
champagne or sparkling wine

Shake the first three ingredients well with ice, and strain into a chilled wine goblet. Top up with champagne or sparkling wine, and stir gently. Garnish with a cherry.

Fortified wines

The most resourceful fortified wine of all for cocktail-making is vermouth. Whether in its dry white or sweet red version, its aromatic, herbal flavours equip it handsomely for mixing with any of the spirits and a fair few of the liqueurs. We shouldn't forget the other fortified wines, though: those that haven't had herbs infused in them, but are basically ordinary table wines boosted with the addition of grape spirit. Sherry and port are used quite widely, and I have even managed to track down a couple of recipes that use madeira and marsala.

Gin and It

The name of this drink is a shortened form of gin and Italian, so-called in the days when Italian vermouths were inaccurately thought to be always of the sweet red variety. (By the same token, gin and dry vermouth was known as Gin and French.) Proportions vary according to individual taste, and many recipes show the gin and vermouth in equal quantities. This is my preference.

2 measures/3 tbsp gin
1 measure/1½ tbsp sweet red vermouth

Add both ingredients to a rocks glass with a couple of ice cubes in it. Stir, and add a twist of lemon rind.

Bronx

An utterly satisfying mixture of gin and both vermouths, Bronx is basically a sort of gin Manhattan with a little orange juice. It is, naturally, a New York cocktail that dates back to the early years of the 20th century. Like all such mixtures, it makes a very effective aperitif.

1½ measures/6 tsp gin
¾ measure/3 tsp dry vermouth
¾ measure/3 tsp sweet red vermouth
juice of a quarter of an orange

Shake all the ingredients well with ice, and strain into a cocktail glass. Garnish with a half-slice of orange.

Bentley

Dubonnet has one of the most captivating flavours of all vermouth brands, derived in part from its long maturation in cask. Unless otherwise stated, these recipes call for the red version. Bentley is a fine aperitif mixture dating from the 1920s.

1½ measures/6 tsp calvados
1½ measures/6 tsp Dubonnet

Shake well with ice, and strain into a glass. Garnish with an orange twist.

Boston

This is another egg recipe containing a little sugar too, although the underlying mixture is quite dry.

1½ measures/6 tsp dry (sercial) madeira
1½ measures/6 tsp bourbon

Coronation

The Coronation for which this cocktail was created was that of George V in 1910. It's a strong, forthright mixture, much like King George himself.

1 measure/1½ tbsp sweet red vermouth
1 measure/1½ tbsp dry vermouth
1 measure/1½ tbsp calvados
¼ measure/1 tsp apricot brandy

Shake all the ingredients well with ice, and strain into a cocktail glass. Garnish with a half-slice of orange.

2.5ml/½ tsp caster (superfine) sugar
1 egg yolk

Shake all the ingredients with ice and strain into a small wine glass. Sprinkle with grated nutmeg.

Golf

This is an old 1920s recipe for a very short drink that is a distant relation of the Martini. It was indeed originally known as the Golf Martini, but is clearly for those who like a little more vermouth with their gin.

1 measure/1½ tbsp gin
½ measure/2 tsp dry vermouth
2 dashes Angostura bitters

Stir all the ingredients well with ice in a small pitcher, and strain into a tumbler. Garnish with a green olive.

Bartending know-how

Vermouth comes in a variety of styles. The red is made with red wine; the dry white gains an amber tinge from ageing in oak casks; bianco is sweetened-up dry white; the pink version is based on rosé wine.

Lily

Lillet is an aromatized, bittersweet, French fortified wine that comes in both red and white versions. It's hard to find now. It obviously bestowed its name (more or less) on this cocktail, but if you can't find it, use ordinary dry white vermouth instead.

1 measure/1½ tbsp gin
1 measure/1½ tbsp white Lillet or dry vermouth
1 measure/1½ tbsp crème de noyau
dash lemon juice

Shake all the ingredients well with ice, and strain into a wine glass. Garnish with a half-slice of lemon.

Midsummer Night

The orangey, quinine flavour of Italian Punt e Mes goes well with gin and a modest amount of blackcurrant liqueur in this modern recipe.

1 measure/1½ tbsp gin

1 measure/1½ tbsp Punt e Mes
½ measure/2 tsp crème de cassis

Shake all the ingredients well with ice, and strain into a cocktail glass. You could garnish with a twist of lemon.

Devil's Cocktail

For some reason, this old cocktail has come to be given the Spanish name, Diablo, in modern bar books, but the mixture remains essentially the same. It was probably originally made with red port, but white produces a more harmonious result.

1½ measures/6 tsp dry vermouth
1½ measures/6 tsp white port
2 dashes lemon juice

Shake all the ingredients well with ice, and strain into a cocktail glass. Garnish with a twist of lemon.

Breakfast

Save a tiny quantity of egg white before you scramble your breakfast eggs, and this cocktail might well make a good accompaniment to them. Then again, it would make a much better nightcap.

2 measures/3 tbsp red port
1 measure/1½ tbsp brown crème de cacao
¼ measure/1 tsp light rum
½ measure/2 tsp lemon juice
5ml/1 tsp egg white

Shake all the ingredients well with ice, and strain into a wine glass. Dust the surface with ground nutmeg.

Perfect Cocktail

Another gin and vermouths recipe from the 1920s, this is a little like Bronx, but without the orange juice. Then again, substitute Pernod for the gin and you have a Duchess.

1 measure/1½ tbsp gin
1 measure/1½ tbsp dry vermouth
1 measure/1½ tbsp sweet red vermouth

Shake all the ingredients well with ice, and strain into a cocktail glass. Garnish with a twist of lemon rind.

Bartending know-how
Use an LBV port if you can, in preference to plain ruby.

Bamboo

An exceedingly dry aperitif cocktail, with a slight bittering element, this makes a change from the usual neat dry sherry. One or two recipes add sweet red vermouth to it too, but that really is missing the point. If you have it, you could use orange bitters instead of the Angostura version.

Sloppy Joe

Strong and exotic, this is an American recipe of the postwar years. Some suggest adding 2.5ml/½ tsp grenadine to the mixture, but it doesn't really make much difference.

1 measure/1½ tbsp red port
1 measure/1½ tbsp cognac
2 measures/3 tbsp pineapple juice
2 dashes Cointreau

Shake all the ingredients well with ice, and strain into a wine goblet. Garnish with a half-slice of orange.

2 measures/3 tbsp pale dry (fino) sherry
2 measures/3 tbsp dry vermouth
2 dashes Angostura bitters

Stir all the ingredients well with ice, and strain into a large, chilled cocktail glass. You could garnish the drink with a twist of lemon.

First Avenue

A fine, slightly effervescent cocktail that uses one of the sweeter styles of sherry. Use decent oloroso, though, rather than cream sherry.

1½ measures/6 tsp sweet (oloroso) sherry
½ measure/2 tsp Cointreau
¾ measure/3 tsp soda water
¼ measure/1 tsp Campari

Half-fill a rocks glass with cracked ice. Add the first two ingredients and stir well. Add the soda, and then float the Campari on top. Do not garnish.

Prairie Oyster

I'm cheating a little by including this most challenging of hangover cures here, largely because it was once common in America to substitute sweet madeira for the brandy in a Prairie Oyster. If you're a stickler for tradition, use cognac, but you might find this a touch less aggressive if you are resorting to the drink medicinally.

1 measure/1½ tbsp sweet (malmsey)
   madeira, or cognac
¼ measure/1 tsp white wine vinegar
¼ measure/1 tsp Worcestershire sauce
pinch cayenne pepper
dash Tabasco
1 egg yolk

Add the first five ingredients to a small tumbler. Mix well without ice, and then spoon the yolk very gently on top. The preparation should then be swallowed in one gulp, without breaking the yolk.

Casanova

Marsala, from the island of Sicily, comes in various styles, but everyone seems agreed that the sweet version, dolce, is the best. That's what's used in this strong cream cocktail.

1 measure/1½ tbsp bourbon
½ measure/2 tsp marsala dolce
½ measure/2 tsp Kahlúa
1 measure/1½ tbsp double (heavy) cream

Shake all the ingredients well with plenty of ice to amalgamate the cream, and strain into a cocktail glass. Sprinkle the top with ground nutmeg.

Downhill

The name of this drink reflects pretty much where you'll be going if you try to take more than one. It's a knee-trembling, all-alcohol cocktail for the truly intrepid.

1 measure/1½ tbsp sweet (oloroso) sherry
½ measure/2 tsp gin
½ measure/2 tsp dry vermouth
½ measure/2 tsp orange curaçao
¼ measure/1 tsp cognac

Stir the ingredients with ice in a pitcher to chill them, and strain into a rocks glass half-filled with cracked ice. Add an orange twist and a cherry.

Third Rail

There isn't much call for the peppermint cordial that was once used in this American cocktail. If you can't get hold of it, use the white version of crème de menthe instead. It ups the alcohol ante of the drink, but only just.

3 measures/4½ tbsp dry vermouth
¼ measure/1 tsp orange curacao
¼ measure/1 tsp peppermint cordial

Stir all the ingredients well with ice in a pitcher, and strain into a chilled cocktail glass. Squeeze a piece of lemon rind over the drink, and then drop it into the glass.

Marsala Cocktail

This is my own preferred way of showing marsala to its best advantage if you don't want to drink it straight. The teaspoon of spirit and dash of acidity mingle very subtly with its toffee sweetness.

2 measures/3 tbsp marsala dolce
¼ measure/1 tsp cognac
dash lemon juice

Stir well with ice in a pitcher, and strain into a wine glass. Add a cube of ice.

Port Cocktail

Here is another very simple preparation that goes back a long way. Like the Sherry Cocktail, it uses a hint of orange.

2 measures/3 tbsp good red port (LBV)
dash cognac

Stir the ingredients well with ice in a small pitcher until quite cold, and strain into a wine glass. Squeeze a piece of orange rind over the drink so that plenty of its oil is released, but don't put it in.

Sherry Cocktail

This was very popular in the 1920s as a sophisticated aperitif, and deserves to be so now too.

2 measures/3 tbsp pale dry (fino or manzanilla) sherry
¼ measure/1 tsp dry vermouth
¼ measure/1 tsp orange bitters (or curaçao)

Stir all the ingredients with plenty of ice in a pitcher, and strain into a large wine glass. Do not garnish.

Dubonnet Cocktail

A quartet of recipes named after four of the basic fortified wine types concludes with this one using the French proprietary classic. Be sure to use the red version.

1½ measures/6 tsp gin
1½ measures/6 tsp Dubonnet

Shake both ingredients well with ice, and strain into a small wine goblet. Squeeze a twist of lemon rind over the drink and drop it in.

Adonis

If you don't care for the sweetness of sweet sherry, go for this 1920s recipe. A dry style is given the herbal sweetness of red vermouth instead.

2 measures/3 tbsp pale dry (fino) sherry
1 measure/1½ tbsp sweet red vermouth
2 dashes orange bitters (or curaçao)

Stir all the ingredients well with ice in a pitcher, and strain into a wine glass. Garnish with a twist of orange rind.

Sherry Flip

The recipe for a Flip would seem to go back to the 17th century, in that a mixture of alcohol, sugar and egg was being made then. In the pre-cocktail-shaker era, they were mixed by being repeatedly poured, or "flipped", between two glasses. A version using sweet sherry has proved the most enduringly popular of them all. The nutmeg is de rigueur.

Straight Law

This century-old recipe is as straight as they come. Both the ingredients are very dry and very strong in flavour. It's a real appetite awakener.

2 measures/3 tbsp pale dry (fino) sherry
1 measure/1½ tbsp gin

Stir both ingredients well with ice, and strain into a cocktail glass. Squeeze a piece of lemon rind over the surface and drop it into the drink.

2 measures/3 tbsp brown cream sherry
2.5ml/½ tsp caster (superfine) sugar
1 egg, beaten

Shake all the ingredients well with ice, and strain into a small wine glass. Sprinkle grated nutmeg on the surface. Alternatively, you can whizz it up in the blender if quite convenient.

Merry Widow

This is another 1920s recipe, this time at the bone-dry end of the spectrum, notwithstanding that splash of Bénédictine. It's a strong one too, all alcohol, which explains the merriness of the widow.

1 measure/1½ tbsp gin
1 measure/1½ tbsp dry vermouth
2 dashes absinthe
2 dashes Bénédictine
2 dashes Angostura bitters

Stir all the ingredients well with ice in a pitcher, and then strain into a large wine glass. Squeeze a twist of lemon rind over the drink, and then drop it in.

Havana Cobbler

This is an old-fashioned drink that is delightfully refreshing served in sultry, Caribbean-type weather, or in an English summer, at a push.

¼ measure/1 tsp sugar syrup
½ measure/2 tsp green ginger wine
1 measure/1½ tbsp light rum (preferably Cuban)
1 measure/1½ tbsp red port

Shake the first three ingredients well with ice, and strain into a chilled short tumbler. Tilt the glass, and slowly pour the port down the side to form a floating layer on top of the cocktail.

Bartending know-how
Stone's Special Reserve is the most gingery ginger wine of them all.

Parkeroo

This is a dry and rather startling mixture, which is worth trying at least once, just so you can say you have. I can't say it's one of my own favourites, but who's asking?

2 measures/3 tbsp pale dry (fino) sherry
1 measure/1½ tbsp tequila

Mix both ingredients in a pitcher with ice. Strain into a champagne flute filled with shaved ice, and add a twist of lemon rind.

Inigo Jones

Here is the only cocktail in this book to use rosé wine. Choose one from a southern-hemisphere country such as South Africa or Argentina. These wines tend to be much fruitier than the European ones, and you will of course have to finish the bottle straight after you've made this cocktail.

1 measure/1½ tbsp marsala dolce
1 measure/1½ tbsp dry rosé wine
1 measure/1½ tbsp cognac
dash orange juice
dash lemon juice

In a pitcher, stir together all the ingredients with plenty of ice. Strain into a tumbler half-filled with crushed ice. Garnish with a slice of orange.

Port in a Storm

I have always loved this poetically named cocktail, in which the port does indeed get buffeted by a storm of other ingredients.

2 measures/3 tbsp red wine
1½ measures/6 tsp red port
½ measure/2 tsp cognac

Stir all the ingredients with plenty of ice in a pitcher, and pour without straining into a large wine glass. You could garnish with a half-slice of orange.

Nightmare Abbey

Despite sounding like an adaptation of a Gothic novel starring Vincent Price, this mixture is perfectly sweet-natured.

1½ measures/6 tsp red Dubonnet
1 measure/1½ tbsp gin
1 measure/1½ tbsp orange juice
¾ measure/3 tsp cherry brandy

Shake all the ingredients well with ice, and strain into a bowl-shaped cocktail glass. Garnish with a twist of orange rind and a black cherry.

Soul Kiss

This fine American cocktail productively brings together three good fortified wines with orange to bind them.

1 measure/1½ tbsp red Dubonnet
1 measure/1½ tbsp sweet red vermouth
1 measure/1½ tbsp dry vermouth
1 measure/1½ tbsp orange juice

Shake all the ingredients well with ice, and strain into a large wine goblet. Garnish with a half-slice of orange.

Caffè Vermouth

Vermouth is not an obvious choice to partner coffee, but the resulting flavour is good: original and sophisticated. This recipe serves two.

4 measures/6 tbsp sweet red vermouth
60ml/4 tbsp very strong cold coffee (espresso strength or filter/cafetière brewed at 75g/3oz coffee per 1 litre/1¾ pints water)
250ml/8fl oz milk
10ml/2 tsp caster (superfine) sugar

Funchal Flip

This cocktail is named after Funchal, the capital of the island of Madeira, where some of the best fortified wines in the world are made.

1 measure/1½ tbsp sweet madeira
¾ measure/3 tsp cognac

Shake all the ingredients well with ice, and strain into cocktail glasses or tumblers. Garnish with a few roasted coffee beans.

Bartending know-how
Madeira is the hardiest of the fortified wines. An opened bottle will keep for years without declining.

½ measure/2 tsp Cointreau
¼ measure/1 tsp grenadine
1 egg yolk, beaten

Shake all the ingredients well with ice, and strain into a cocktail glass. Garnish with a half-slice of orange and a cherry.

Tinton

A traditional 1920s formula named after some long-forgotten worthy, this cocktail gives a sweet kick to apple brandy for those who find it too dry as it comes. It could be taken as an after-dinner digestif.

2 measures/3 tbsp calvados
1 measure/1½ tbsp red port

Shake both ingredients well with ice, and strain into a cocktail glass. There is no need for any garnish.

Dubonnet Fizz

This American recipe makes for a sweetly aromatic cocktail. High rollers might fill it up with champagne, but soda will do quite nicely, thank you.

4 measures/6 tbsp red Dubonnet
½ measure/2 tsp cherry brandy
2 measures/3 tbsp orange juice

Wine Collins

The wine named here is the fortified variety. Port, sweet madeira or marsala dolce can all be used as the base for this fizzy drink, but be generous.

4 measures/6 tbsp red port, malmsey
    madeira or marsala dolce
½ measure/2 tsp lime juice
sparkling lemonade

Add the first two ingredients to a highball glass half-filled with cracked ice, and stir well. Top up with lemonade, and garnish with a slice of lemon and a cherry.

1 measure/1½ tbsp lemon juice
soda water or champagne

Shake all but the last ingredient well with ice, and strain into a highball glass. Top up with soda water or champagne. You could garnish the drink with half-slices of orange and lemon.

Reform

Invented at the Reform Club at London in the 1920s, this cocktail is – as eagle-eyed drinkers will note – essentially a dry version of Adonis.

2 measures/3 tbsp pale dry (fino) sherry
1 measure/1½ tbsp dry vermouth
dash orange bitters (or curaçao)

Stir all the ingredients well with ice in a pitcher, and strain into a cocktail glass. Garnish with a cherry.

Bartending know-how
Pale dry sherry should always be treated with kid gloves. It needs drinking within a few days of the bottle being broached, and should always be served well-chilled. More than any other drink in this book, it is served in sub-standard condition in many bars and restaurants.

Beer and cider

Beer and cider are the least used of all alcoholic drinks in cocktails. They do come in handy for punches and mulled ale recipes, but as ingredients in short mixed drinks, they have only a limited number of applications. Probably the simplest beer "cocktail" of them all is shandy, which is roughly equal measures of beer and lemonade, and is always worth making for yourself, as opposed to resorting to one of the bottled proprietary brands. Good cider is one of the glories of the English brewing industry, as was once the now-forgotten perry, a refreshing sparkling drink made from pears.

Lamb's Wool

A kind of 17th-century punch, this was traditionally drunk on All Saints' Day, November 1. This recipe serves four.

1 litre/1¾ pints English bitter ale
4 baked apples
2.5ml/½ tsp ground nutmeg
2.5ml/½ tsp ground ginger
60g/2oz sugar

Heat the ale gently in a large pan without boiling it. When the apples have finished baking in the oven, peel them, remove the cores and mash the soft flesh with a potato masher. Stir the apple into the beer with the spices and sugar, and serve in warm glasses or mugs. It's a real treat that will warm you up on a dark autumn day.

Black Velvet

This simple but mightily effective drink was invented at Brooks' Club in London in 1861, following the death of Queen Victoria's husband, Prince Albert. It was considered an appropriate sign of mourning to dress the champagne up in black livery. As a popular mixture ever since, it has an appeal all its own.

Half-fill a tall, narrow beer glass with Guinness. Wait for the head to settle, and then without tilting the glass, gently top it up with good brut champagne.

Devon Gin

This is a short individual drink that will prove peculiarly potent on a cold winter's day. Tread warily.

3 measures/4½ tbsp strong sweet cider
¾ measure/3 tsp gin
¼ measure/1 tsp Cointreau

Half-fill a rocks glass with cracked ice, and add the first two ingredients, Stir gently, and then pour the Cointreau carefully on to the surface to form a float. Drink quickly.

Wassail Bowl

The wassail bowl was a wide-mouthed bowl from which hot punches were drunk. Cheer your Christmas carol-singers by offering them a bowl (or mug) each of this warming, festive drink. The recipe serves six.

2 litres/3½ pints strong bitter or brown ale
150ml/¼ pint brown cream sherry
90g/3oz caster (superfine) sugar
5ml/1 tsp ground nutmeg
5ml/1 tsp ground ginger
6 baked apples

Heat the beer, sherry, sugar and spices in a pan until gently simmering, stirring to dissolve the sugar. After about 5 minutes, decant the mixture into mugs or drinking bowls, each containing a whole mashed apple. Serve with spoons for stirring it up as it is drunk.

Cider Cup

A cup makes an excellent long and refreshing drink for an aperitif or party starter. It should be prepared shortly before serving so that the ice doesn't have time to melt. This recipe serves six.

rind of 1 lemon
slices of orange
5 measures/120ml/4fl oz pale dry (fino) sherry
3 measures/4½ tbsp cognac
3 measures/4½ tbsp white curaçao

2 measures/3 tbsp amaretto
600ml/1 pint good-quality strong dry cider

Partially fill a pitcher with cracked ice and stir in the lemon rind and the orange slices. Add the sherry, brandy, curaçao and amaretto, and stir well to mix. Pour in the cider and stir gently. Serve the cocktail in chilled tall glasses, including some of the citrus fruit in each one, and add a twist of cucumber rind.

Somerset Punch

This is a very appealing cider punch for serving at a garden party. The recipe makes around 14–16 servings.

1 litre/1¾ pints strong dry cider
150ml/¼ pint dry white wine
2 measures/3 tbsp cider brandy
150ml/¼ pint orange juice
2 measures/3 tbsp lemon juice
150ml/¼ pint pressed apple juice (not from concentrate)
300ml/½ pint sparkling ginger ale

Mix all the ingredients with ice in a punchbowl, and decant into wine glasses for serving. Garnish with thin slices of unpeeled apple.

Bartending know-how

The best ciders are those that come in a bottle with a champagne-style cork. They may be cloudy, but the quality is incomparable.

Non-alcoholic drinks

Not every cocktail session has to involve intoxication. There will be times, such as when dealing with a party of drivers, or in the course of a detox diet, or even in the middle of a raging hot day, when an alcoholic drink is not what's wanted. The non-alcoholic section of many cocktail books often has an air of "These are the also-rans" about it. That is not so here. There are enough recipes in the following pages to keep even the most determined mixologist going for a fair old time and, even more than their alcohol-based cousins, these drinks can be freely adapted as you see fit. Let your imagination off the leash.

Horse's Fall

This is a long drink to serve on a summer's day. The addition of strongly flavoured tea is a matter of taste.

1 lemon
dash Angostura bitters
2 measures/3 tbsp raspberry, Orange Pekoe or Assam tea, chilled (optional)
1 measure/1½ tbsp unsweetened apple juice
5 measures/120ml/4fl oz dry ginger ale or lemonade

Cut the rind from the lemon in one continuous strip and use it to line and decorate a long cocktail glass. Chill the glass until needed. Add a dash of Angostura to the bottom of the glass. Measure the tea, if using, into the cocktail shaker and add the apple juice. Shake for about 20 seconds. Strain into the prepared chilled glass. Finish with ginger ale or lemonade straight from the refrigerator, to taste.

Sunburst

Bursting with freshness and vitamins, this drink is a good early morning pick-me-up. This recipe makes two.

1 green apple, cored and chopped
3 carrots, peeled and chopped
1 mango, peeled and pitted
7 measures/150ml/¼ pint orange juice, chilled
6 strawberries, hulled

Place the apple, carrots and mango in a blender or food processor and process to a pulp. Add the orange juice and strawberries and process again. Strain well through a sieve, pressing out all the juice with the back of a wooden spoon. Discard any pulp left in the sieve. Pour into tumblers filled with ice cubes and serve immediately, garnished with a slice of orange on the side of the glass.

Virgin Prairie Oyster

This superior pick-me-up is a variation on the Bloody Mary. The tomato base can be drunk without the raw egg yolk if it does not appeal to you. Use only fresh free-range eggs.

175ml/6fl oz tomato juice
½ measure/2 tsp Worcestershire sauce
¼–½ measure/1–2 tsp balsamic vinegar
1 egg yolk
cayenne pepper, to taste

Measure the tomato juice into a large bar glass and stir over plenty of ice until well chilled. Strain into a tall tumbler half-filled with ice cubes. Add the Worcestershire sauce and balsamic vinegar to taste and mix with a swizzle-stick. Float the egg yolk on top and lightly dust with cayenne pepper.

Scarlet Lady

On the first sip, with its fruity and fresh tones, this drink could fool a fair few into thinking it was an alcoholic wine-based cocktail.

125g/4oz cubed melon, preferably Galia or Canteloupe
5 small red seedless grapes
3 measures/4½ tbsp unsweetened red grape juice

Fruit and Ginger Ale

This is an old English mulled drink, served chilled over ice. Of course it can be made with ready-squeezed apple and orange juices, but roasting the fruit with cloves gives a much better flavour. This recipe makes four to six servings.

1 cooking apple
1 orange, scrubbed
1 lemon, scrubbed
20 whole cloves
7.5cm/3in piece fresh ginger, peeled
30g/1oz light brown sugar
375ml/13fl oz bitter lemon

Put the melon and grapes in a blender and process until they form a smooth purée. Add the red grape juice and continue to process for another minute. Strain the juice into a bar glass of ice and stir until chilled. Pour into a chilled cocktail glass. Dip some red, seedless grapes in the lightly beaten white of an egg, and then into 15ml/1 tbsp sugar. Thread on to a cocktail stick to garnish.

Preheat the oven to 200°C/400°F/Gas 6. Score the apple around the middle and stud the orange and lemon with the cloves. Bake the fruits in the oven for about 25 minutes, until soft and completely cooked through. Quarter the orange and lemon, and mash the apple, discarding the peel and the core.

Finely grate the ginger. Place the fruit and ginger in a bowl with the light brown sugar. Add 300ml/½ pint boiling water. Using a spoon, squeeze the fruit to release more flavour. Cover and let sit for an hour until cool. Strain into a pitcher of cracked ice and use a spoon to press out all the juices from the fruit. Add the bitter lemon. Garnish with orange wedges and whole cloves.

Volunteer

This drink is ideal for a lazy summer afternoon. It's also a fine cocktail to serve the designated driver at a party. It was devised and drunk during a very rough Channel crossing in an undersized boat, a tribute to human resourcefulness!

2 measures/3 tbsp lime cordial
2–3 dashes Angostura bitters
7 measures/150ml/¼ pint chilled tonic water
decorative ice cubes, to serve

Pour the lime cordial into the bottom of the glass, and shake in the Angostura to taste. Add a few decorative ice cubes to the glass, if liked. Finish with tonic water and garnish with frozen lime slices.

Variation
Use fresh lime or grapefruit juice and a splash of sugar syrup instead of the lime cordial, and finish with ginger ale.

Blushing Piña Colada

This is good with or without the rum that is part of the original recipe. Don't be tempted to put whole ice cubes into the blender; the result won't be as smooth and you may ruin the blades. Make sure you crush it well first. The recipe serves two.

1 banana, peeled and sliced
1 thick slice pineapple, peeled
3 measures/4½ tbsp pineapple juice
1 scoop strawberry ice cream or sorbet
1 measure/1½ tbsp unsweetened coconut milk
30ml/2 tbsp grenadine

Roughly chop the banana. Cut two small wedges from the pineapple and set aside. Cut up the remainder of the pineapple and add it to the blender with the banana. Add the pineapple juice and process until smooth.

Add the ice cream or sorbet with the coconut milk and a little finely crushed ice, and process until smooth. Pour into two large cocktail glasses. Pour the grenadine syrup slowly on top of the drink; it will filter down, creating a dappled effect. Garnish each glass with a wedge of pineapple and a cherry.

Steel Works

This thirst-quenching drink can be served at any time of the day.

2 measures/3 tbsp passion fruit juice
dash Angostura bitters
3 measures/4½ tbsp soda water, chilled
3 measures/4½ tbsp lemonade, chilled
1 passion fruit

Pour the passion fruit juice into a tumbler. Add the Angostura, with some ice cubes. Finish the drink with the chilled soda water and lemonade and stir briefly. Cut the passion fruit in half; scoop out the seeds and flesh and add to the drink. Stir gently before serving.

Variation
For a Rock Shandy, pour equal parts of lemonade and soda over bitters or use your favourite variety of the naturally flavoured and unsweetened fruit drinks.

Bandrek

This is a rich and creamy version of a spicy Indonesian drink. Serve it either warm or chilled. If you like, add a very fresh egg to the syrup and mix in the blender, and you'll have something like an egg-nog.

3 whole cloves
3 juniper berries, bruised
1 cinnamon stick
6 green cardamom pods, bruised
4 whole black peppercorns
1 sugar cube
2 measures/3 tbsp unsweetened coconut milk
3 measures/4½ tbsp full-cream (whole) milk

Put the cloves, juniper berries, cinnamon, cardamom pods, peppercorns and sugar cube in a pan. Heat gently to release the aromas and flavours of the spices. Add 175ml/6fl oz water and bring to the boil over medium-high heat. Continue to boil for about ten minutes, or until reduced to 30–45ml/2–3 tbsp of spicy syrup. Remove from the heat and cool. Pour the syrup into a blender with the coconut milk and full-cream milk and process until smooth. Strain over cracked ice in a stemmed glass. Garnish with cinnamon sticks and a maraschino cherry.

St Clements

Oranges and lemons create a simple but thirst-quenching drink, which confirms that freshly squeezed fruit has a superior flavour to any of the ready-squeezed versions you can buy.

2 oranges
1 lemon
15ml/1 tbsp sugar, or to taste
75ml/5 tbsp water

Wash the oranges and lemons and then pare the rind off the fruit with a sharp knife, leaving the white pith behind. Remove the pith from the fruit and discard it. Put the orange and lemon rind in a pan with the sugar and water. Place over low heat and stir gently until the sugar has dissolved. Remove the pan from the heat and press the orange and lemon rind against the sides of the pan to release

Fennel Fusion

This hefty combination of raw vegetables and apples makes a surprisingly delicious juice. Cabbage has natural anti-bacterial properties, while apples and fennel can help to cleanse the system.

half a small red cabbage
half a fennel bulb
2 apples
⅔ measure/1 tbsp lemon juice

Roughly slice the cabbage and fennel and quarter the apples. Using a juice extractor, juice the vegetables and fruit. Add the lemon juice to the juice mixture and stir. Pour into a glass and serve.

all their oils. Cover the pan and let cool. Remove and discard the rind. Purée the oranges and lemon and sweeten the fruit pulp by pouring the cooled citrus syrup over it. Set aside for 2–3 hours to allow the flavours to infuse. Strain the fruit pulp, pressing the solids in the sieve to extract as much of the juice as possible. Pour into a tall glass filled with finely crushed ice, and decorate with slices of orange and lemon.

Summer Tonic

The many nutrients in lettuce include betacarotene, iron and folic acid. This is a particularly appetizing way of getting your share of them.

3 large vine-ripened tomatoes
half a Little Gem (Bibb) lettuce
5cm/2in piece cucumber
1 small garlic clove
small handful fresh parsley, stalks included
⅔ measure/1 tbsp lemon juice

Halve the tomatoes and lettuce. Peel and chop the cucumber. Juice all the ingredients together and serve in a tall glass.

Raspberry and Orange Smoothie

This exquisite blend combines the sharp taste of raspberries and oranges with the creaminess of yogurt. It takes minutes to prepare, making it perfect for breakfast. Serves two to three.

250g/9oz raspberries, chilled
200ml/7fl oz natural (plain) yogurt, chilled
300ml/½ pint orange juice, chilled

Place the raspberries and yogurt in a food processor or blender, and process for about a minute until smooth and creamy. Add the orange juice to the raspberry and yogurt mixture and process for about 30 seconds, or until thoroughly combined. Pour into tall glasses and serve immediately.

Avocado and Lime Smoothie

Inspired by guacamole, this wonderfully thick smoothie combines mild and spicy flavours perfectly. It serves four.

3 ripe avocados
juice of 1½ limes
1 garlic clove, crushed
handful of ice cubes
400ml/14fl oz vegetable stock, chilled
400ml/14fl oz full-cream (whole) milk, chilled
150ml/¼ pint sour cream, chilled
few drops Tabasco
salt and ground black pepper
extra virgin olive oil, to serve

For the salsa:
4 tomatoes, peeled, seeded and finely diced
2 spring onions (scallions), finely chopped
1 green chilli, seeded and finely chopped
15ml/1 tbsp chopped fresh coriander (cilantro)

juice of half a lime
salt and ground black pepper

Prepare the salsa first. Mix all the ingredients and season to taste with salt and pepper. Chill while you prepare the smoothie. Halve and stone the avocados. Scoop out the flesh and place in a blender. Add the lime juice, garlic, a handful of crushed ice and about 150ml/¼ pint of the vegetable stock, and process until smooth. Pour the mixture into a large pitcher, and stir in the remaining stock, milk, sour cream, Tabasco and seasoning. Pour the smoothie into glasses and spoon a little salsa on to each. Add a splash of olive oil to each portion and garnish with fresh coriander leaves. Serve immediately, with a spoon.

Georgia 'n' Ginger

This is named after the US state of Georgia, which is famous for its peaches. The recipe serves six.

1 can (450–500g/1–1¼lb) sliced peaches in syrup
750ml/1¼ pints strong coffee
120ml/4fl oz whipping cream
25ml/1½ tbsp brown sugar
1.5ml/¼ tsp ground cinnamon
generous pinch ground ginger

Drain the peaches, retaining the syrup. In a blender, process half of the coffee and the peaches for 1 minute. In a clean bowl, whip the cream. Put 250ml/8fl oz cold water, the sugar, cinnamon, ginger and peach syrup in a pan and bring to the boil over a medium heat, then reduce the heat and simmer for 1 minute. Add the blended peaches and the remaining coffee to the pan and stir well. Serve, topped with whipped cream and decorated with orange rind.

Strawberry Soother

Relax with this comforting strawberry blend, which is rich in vitamin C and healing phytochemicals.

225g/8oz strawberries
1 peach or nectarine

Hull the strawberries, then quarter the peach or nectarine and pull out the stone. Cut the flesh into rough slices or chunks. Juice the fruit, using a juicer, or process in a food processor or blender for a thicker juice, and serve immediately.

Citrus Shake

This refreshing juice is great for boosting the immune system. Citrus fruits are a rich source of vitamin C.

1 pink grapefruit
1 blood orange
30ml/2 tbsp lemon juice

Peel the grapefruit and orange and cut them into rough segments. Juice the fruit, then stir in the lemon juice.

Lemonade on Ice

Home-made lemonade may not be fizzy, but it has a fresh, tangy flavour, unmatched by bought drinks. The basic lemonade will keep well in the refrigerator for up to 2 weeks and makes a thirst-quenching drink at any time of day. This recipe serves six.

6 lemons
225g/8oz caster (superfine) sugar
1.75 litres/3 pints boiling water

For each iced drink:
4 scoops lemon sorbet
thin lemon and lime slices
3 ice cubes, crushed

Tropical Soother

This reviving juice helps keep the liver and kidneys good and healthy. Melon is an especially good kidney tonic.

1 papaya
half a Cantaloupe melon
90g/3½oz white grapes

Start by making the lemonade. Wash the lemons and dry them thoroughly. Pare all the lemons thinly, avoiding the bitter white pith, and put the rind in a large heatproof bowl. Add the sugar. Squeeze the lemons and set the juice aside. Pour the measured boiling water over the lemon rinds and sugar. Stir until the sugar dissolves. Leave to cool, then stir in the lemon juice. Strain the lemonade into a large jug and chill.

For each glass of iced lemonade, place four scoops of sorbet in a tall glass and tuck some lemon and lime slices down the sides. Add the crushed ice. Top up each glass with about 200ml/7fl oz of the lemonade. Garnish with mint sprigs and half-slices of lemon and lime.

Halve and skin the papaya, then remove the seeds with a spoon and cut into rough slices. Cut open the melon and remove the seeds with a spoon. Cut into quarters and slice the flesh away from the skin, then cut into rough chunks. Juice all the fruit.

Melon Pick-Me-Up

This spicy blend of melon, pear and fresh root ginger will revive your body, stimulate your circulation and fire you into action.

half a Canteloupe melon
2 pears
2.5cm/1in piece fresh root ginger

Quarter the melon, remove the seeds and slice the flesh away from the skin, then quarter the pears. Using a juice extractor, juice all the ingredients, pour into a tall glass and serve immediately.

Apple Shiner

Enjoy radiant skin and instant energy with this cleansing fusion of fresh fruits and lemon juice.

1 apple
half a Honeydew melon
90g/3½oz red grapes
⅔ measure/1 tbsp lemon juice

Quarter the apple and remove the core. Cut the melon into quarters, remove the seeds and slice the flesh away from the skin. Using a juice extractor, juice the fruit. Alternatively, process the fruit in a food processor or blender for 2–3 minutes until smooth. Pour the juice into a chilled glass, stir in the lemon juice and serve.

Green Leaves

This healthy juice is exceptionally rejuvenating. Grapes are one of the most effective detoxifiers, and are used for alleviating many kinds of skin, liver and kidney disorders.

1 apple
150g/5oz white grapes

small handful fresh coriander (cilantro)
30g/1oz watercress
⅔ measure/1 tbsp lime juice

Quarter the apple. Juice the fruit, coriander and watercress, then stir in the lime juice. If you find this mixture too sour, use less lime.

Humzinger

This tropical cleanser will help boost the digestive system and the kidneys, making your eyes sparkle, your hair shine and your skin glow.

half a pineapple, peeled
1 small mango, peeled and pitted
half a small papaya, seeded and peeled

Use a sharp knife to remove any "eyes" left in the pineapple, and cut all the fruit into rough chunks. Using a juice extractor, juice the fruit. Alternatively, use a food processor or blender and process for 2–3 minutes until very smooth. Pour into a glass and serve immediately.

Cranberry, Cinnamon and Ginger Spritzer

Partially freezing fruit juice gives it a wonderfully slushy texture that is very refreshing. The combination of cranberry and apple juice contributes a tart, clean flavour that's not too sweet. Serves four.

600ml/1 pint chilled cranberry juice
150ml/¼ pint clear apple juice
4 cinnamon sticks
about 400ml/14fl oz chilled ginger ale

Pour the cranberry juice into a shallow freezerproof container and freeze for about two hours, or until a thick layer of ice crystals has formed around the edges. Mash with a fork to break up the ice, then return the mixture to the freezer for a further 2–3 hours until almost solid. Pour the apple juice into a small pan, add two cinnamon sticks and bring to just below boiling point. Pour into a pitcher and leave to cool, then remove the cinnamon sticks and set them aside with the other cinnamon sticks. Chill the juice until very cold. Spoon the cranberry ice into a food processor. Add the apple juice and blend very briefly until slushy. Pile into cocktail glasses or flutes, top up with chilled ginger ale and garnish with fresh or frozen cranberries. Put a long cinnamon stick into each glass to use as a swizzle-stick.

Super Clean

This delicious drink will really kick-start your system. Carrots are a key detox vegetable: they cleanse, nourish and stimulate the body.

3 carrots
30g/1oz young spinach
115g/4oz cooked beetroot in natural juice
2 celery sticks

Top and tail the carrots. Process all the ingredients in a blender until smooth, then pour into a glass and serve.

Bartending know-how

Beetroot is another key vegetable in cleansing the system. Like carrot, it is exceptionally good for the liver. Always use fresh beetroot (not the sliced pickled stuff that comes in jars). Not only does it add rich, lustrous colour to a vegetable juice blend, but it also contributes a pronounced degree of natural sweetness to the drink.

Iced Mango Lassi

Based on a traditional Indian drink, this is excellent with spicy food, or as a welcome cooler at any time of day. The recipe serves three to four.

For the yogurt ice:
175g/6oz caster (superfine) sugar
150ml/¼ pint water
2 lemons
500ml/17fl oz Greek yogurt

For each drink:
4 measures/6 tbsp mango juice

To make the yogurt ice, put the sugar and water in a pan and heat gently, stirring occasionally, until the sugar has dissolved. Pour the syrup into a pitcher. Leave to cool, then chill until very cold. Grate the lemons and squeeze them. Add the rind and juice to the chilled syrup and stir well to mix.

By hand: Pour the syrup mixture into a container and freeze until thickened. Beat in the yogurt, and return to the freezer until thick enough to scoop.

If using an ice cream maker: Churn the mixture until it thickens. Stir in the yogurt and churn for 2 minutes more until well mixed. Transfer to a plastic tub or similar freezerproof container and freeze.

To make each lassi, briefly blend the mango juice with three small scoops of the yogurt ice in a food processor or blender until just smooth. Pour the mixture into a tall glass or tumbler and add a few ice cubes. Top each drink with another scoop of the yogurt ice and garnish with fresh mint sprigs and mango wedges. Serve at once.

Tropical Fruit Soda

For many children, scoops of vanilla ice cream served in a froth of lemonade would make the perfect treat. This more elaborate version, with its tropical fruit content, will appeal to adults too. It serves four.

10ml/2 tsp sugar
1 papaya
1 small ripe mango
2 passion fruit
8 large scoops vanilla ice cream
8 large scoops caramel or toffee ice cream
about 400ml/14fl oz chilled lemonade or
    soda water

Line a baking sheet with foil. Make four small mounds of sugar on the foil, using about 2.5ml/½ tsp each time and spacing them well apart. Place under a medium grill (broiler) for about two minutes until the sugar mounds have turned to a pale golden caramel. Immediately swirl each pool of caramel with the tip of a cocktail stick or skewer to give a slightly feathery finish. Leave to cool.

Cut the papaya in half. Scoop out and discard the seeds, then remove the skin and chop the flesh. Skin the mango, cut the flesh off the stone and chop it into bitesize chunks. Mix the papaya and mango in a bowl. Cut each passion fruit in half, and scoop the pulp into the bowl of fruit. Mix well, cover and chill until ready to serve.

Divide the chilled fruit mixture among four large tumblers. Add one scoop of each type of ice cream to each glass. Peel the caramel decorations carefully away from the foil and press gently into the ice cream. Top up with lemonade or soda water and serve.

Yellow Pepper Revitalizer

This vibrant fresh fruit and vegetable combination will help to rejuvenate and revitalize your body. It is rich in immune-boosting vitamin C, protective betacarotene and energizing natural fruit sugars. As well as these handy attributes, it also tastes sensational – zesty, crisp, fresh and naturally sweet.

3 carrots
1 apple
1 yellow pepper

Scrub and trim the carrots and quarter the apple. Roughly chop the pepper. Using a juice extractor, juice all the ingredients, pour into a glass and serve immediately.

Revitalizer

This classic combination will benefit those suffering from constipation and arthritis. Natural fruit sugars will provide a boost of energy.

3 carrots
1 apple
1 orange

Top and tail the carrots, then quarter the apple. Peel the orange and cut into rough segments. Juice the carrots and fruit.

Licuado de Melon

Among the most refreshing drinks Mexicans make are fruit extracts mixed with honey and chilled water. This recipe is enough for four.

1 watermelon
1 litre/1¾ pints chilled water
juice of 2 limes
honey

Cut the watermelon flesh into chunks, discarding the black seeds. Cover with chilled water and leave for 10 minutes. Tip the mixture into a large sieve set over a bowl. Using a wooden spoon, press the fruit to extract all the liquid. Stir in the lime juice and sweeten with honey. Pour into a pitcher, add ice cubes and stir. Serve in tumblers.

Strawberry Kiss

A new spin on strawberries and cream, this makes a superb opener to a summer lunch.

12 strawberries
1½ measure/2 tsp lemon juice
½ measure/2 tsp whipping cream
2.5ml/½ tsp caster (superfine) sugar

Liquidize all the ingredients with a handful of crushed ice, and turn out into a wine glass. Garnish with a whole small strawberry.

Citrus Agua Fresca

These refreshing fruit juices are sold from street stalls in towns all over Mexico. The recipe serves four.

12 limes
3 oranges
2 grapefruit
600ml/1 pint water
75g/6 tbsp caster (superfine) sugar

Squeeze the juice from the fruits. Some fruit pulp should be used, but discard the seeds. Pour the mixture into a large pitcher. Add the water and sugar and stir until all the sugar has dissolved. Chill for at least an hour before serving with ice and extra fruit wedges. The drink will keep for up to a week in a covered container in the refrigerator.

Tamarind Agua Fresca

Sometimes referred to as the Indian date, tamarind is native to Asia and North Africa, and has now travelled to Mexico. It is used medicinally and as an antiseptic. The fruit has a sweet-sour taste and makes a drink similar to lemonade. This recipe serves four.

1 litre/1¾ pints water
225g/8oz tamarind pods
25g/2 tbsp caster (superfine) sugar

Pour the water into a pan and heat until warm. Remove from the heat and pour into a bowl. Peel the tamarind pods and add the pulp to the warm water. Soak for at least four hours. Place a sieve over a clean bowl. Pour the tamarind pulp and water into the sieve, then press the pulp through the sieve with the back of a wooden spoon, leaving the black seeds behind. Discard the seeds. Add the sugar to the tamarind mixture and stir well until dissolved. Pour into a pitcher and chill thoroughly before serving in tumblers filled with ice.

Bartending know-how

Jars of tamarind pulp or paste are available for buying at Indian and Asian food stores.

Pineapple and Lime Agua Fresca

The vivid colours of this fresh fruit drink give some indication of its wonderful flavour. It makes a delicious midday refresher or pick-me-up at the end of a hard day. The recipe serves four.

2 pineapples
juice of 2 limes
475ml/16fl oz still mineral water
50g/2oz caster (superfine) sugar

Peel the pineapples and chop the flesh, removing the core and "eyes" (see below). You should have about 450g/1lb flesh. Put this in a food processor or blender, and add the lime juice and half the mineral water. Purée to a smooth pulp. Stop the machine and scrape the mixture from the side of the goblet once or twice during processing. Place a sieve over a large bowl. Tip the pineapple pulp into the sieve and press it through with a wooden spoon. Pour the sieved mixture into a large pitcher, cover and chill in the refrigerator for about an hour. Stir in the remaining mineral water and sugar to taste. Serve with ice.

Bartending know-how

Remove pineapple skin with a deep spiral action to cut out the "eyes".

Granita di Caffè

This is basically coffee ice, or slush. The recipe serves four.

200ml/7fl oz strong coffee (about five generous cups of espresso or filter/cafetière brewed coffee using 80g/14 tbsp coffee per 1 litre/1¾ pints water)
400ml/14fl oz water
140g/5oz sugar
2.5ml/½ tsp vanilla essence (extract)
1 egg white (optional)
120ml/4fl oz whipped cream

Pour the brewed coffee into a large bowl and set aside. Boil half the water with the sugar, stirring to dissolve. Refrigerate. When the sugar syrup is cold, add it, the remaining water, and the vanilla to the coffee. Stir until well blended. If using, whisk the egg white and fold it into the mixture. Pour the mixture into a shallow freezerproof tin, such as an ice-cube tray or baking sheet, and freeze. About every 30 minutes, break the mixture up with a fork to create the traditional, grainy, shaved-ice consistency. When it is well frozen, serve in individual cups, and top them with a little whipped cream.

Mexican Coffee

The Aztec Indians were the first known chocolate aficionados, and chocolate is an ingredient in many Mexican recipes. Combined with coffee, it makes a rich, smooth drink. This recipe does four.

30ml/2 tbsp chocolate syrup
120ml/4fl oz whipping cream
1.5ml/¼ tsp ground cinnamon
25g/2 tbsp brown sugar
pinch ground nutmeg
475ml/16fl oz strong black coffee
whipped cream

Whip together the chocolate syrup, cream, cinnamon, sugar and nutmeg. Pour the hot coffee into the mixture and stir, before dividing among four mugs. Top with a dollop of whipped cream and garnish with shavings of cinnamon.

Coffee-Chocolate Soda

This is a fun, refreshing drink that tastes as good as it looks. The combination of chocolate ice cream and coffee-flavoured fizz makes for an unusually textured but thoroughly exciting cocktail. The recipe serves two.

250ml/8fl oz strong cold coffee
60ml/4 tbsp double (heavy) cream, or 30ml/2 tbsp evaporated (unsweetened condensed) milk (optional)
250ml/8fl oz cold soda water
2 scoops chocolate ice cream
chocolate-covered coffee beans, roughly chopped, to garnish

Pour the coffee into tall glasses. Add the cream or evaporated milk, if using. Add the soda water and stir. Gently place a scoop of ice cream into the mixture. Garnish with some of the roughly chopped chocolate-covered coffee beans. Serve with a long spoon or a straw.

Variation

Try also chocolate mint, vanilla, hazelnut or banana ice cream and sprinkle with chocolate shavings, fruit slices or even a few roughly chopped pieces of hazelnut.

Chilled Coffee Caribbean

Use coffee that is not too strong. Filter coffee gives a clean, clear texture. Serves two.

600ml/1 pint strong filter coffee, cooled for about 20 minutes
half an orange and half an lemon, thinly sliced
1 pineapple slice
sugar, to taste
1–2 drops Angostura bitters (optional)

Add the cooled coffee to the fruit slices in a large bowl. Stir and chill in the freezer for about an hour or until very cold. Remove from the freezer and stir again. Remove the fruit slices from the liquid. Add sugar to taste, and stir in the bitters, if using. Add three ice cubes per drink to tall glasses, or whisky tumblers, then pour over the chilled coffee drink. Garnish with half-slices of orange or lemon.

Cappuccino

There can be nothing more enjoyable than a steaming hot cup of coffee on a cold winter's day. This is the classic espresso and milk drink, to serve two.

160–250ml/5½–8fl oz very cold full-cream (whole) milk
about 15g/½oz dark-roast espresso coffee, finely ground

Pour very cold milk into a metal pitcher or frothing device, steam until a fine, smooth foam has formed, and set aside. Next, brew two cups of espresso, and pour into cappuccino or regular coffee cups. Pour the steamed milk over the coffee, holding back the froth with a spoon until last, when it can be spooned on to the surface.

The ideal cappuccino should be about one-third each espresso coffee, steamed milk and frothed milk. (After brewing the coffee you may need to re-steam the milk for just a moment if it has begun to "fall", or lose the froth.) Top with a sprinkle of chocolate or cocoa powder, if desired.

Caffè Latte

This is a very basic breakfast drink, as served in homes and bars throughout Italy and France. It can be made with only a manual espresso pot and a pan to heat the milk. Serves two.

2 parts espresso or very strong coffee
6 parts boiled milk
sugar (optional)
steamed, frothed milk for topping (optional)

Pour the brewed coffee into glasses or large French coffee bowls. Add the hot milk and sugar, if using, and stir well. Top each glass with a spoonful of steamed, frothed milk if desired.

Bartending know-how
If you are having a period of abstinence from caffeine, be assured that the decaffeinated versions of coffee are much improved these days. Carbonated water is now the only decaffeinating agent.

Café di Olla

This recipe is traditionally brewed in large quantities over a wood fire in a heavy earthenware Mexican cooking pot, called an *olla*. It serves four.

1 litre/1¾ pints water
150g/5oz dark brown sugar
5ml/1 tsp molasses
1 small cinnamon stick
50g/2oz dark-roast coffee, medium grind
aniseeds (optional)

Place the water, sugar, molasses, cinnamon and aniseeds, if using, in a pan and slowly bring to the boil. Stir thoroughly to dissolve the sugar and molasses. When the mixture reaches boiling point, stir in the dry coffee, remove from the heat, cover, and steep for 5 minutes. Strain into earthenware mugs and serve immediately. Add a few of the aniseeds, for that extra touch of spice.

Normandy Coffee

Like Washington State in the USA and England's West Country, Normandy is known for its apple orchards, and gives it name to many dishes made with apple juice or apple sauce. This recipe blends the flavour of apples with spices for a delicious, tangy coffee drink. It serves four.

475ml/16fl oz strong black coffee (espresso strength, or filter/cafetière brewed at 75g/ 13 tbsp coffee per 1 litre/1¾ pints water)
475ml/16fl oz apple juice
25g/2 tbsp brown sugar, to taste
3 oranges, thinly sliced
2 small cinnamon sticks
pinch ground allspice
pinch ground cloves

Bring all the ingredients to the boil over a medium heat, then reduce the heat and simmer for 10 minutes. Strain the liquid into a preheated flask or serving pitcher. Pour into cappuccino-style cups, adding a cinnamon stick to each, if you wish.

Bartending know-how
Use a French or Viennese roast coffee – dark but not as dark as for espresso, so that the spice and molasses aren't overwhelmed.

Café con Leche

Many Mexicans start the day with this spiced milky coffee, and those who have enjoyed a hearty midday meal will often opt for a cup of it with a pastry as the afternoon snack. This recipe serves four.

50g/2oz ground coffee
475ml/16fl oz boiling water
475ml/16fl oz full-cream (whole) milk
4 cinnamon sticks
sugar, to taste

Make up the coffee in a cafetière. Pour the milk into a heavy pan, add the cinnamon sticks and bring to the boil, stirring occasionally. Using a slotted spoon, lift out the cinnamon sticks and use a smaller spoon to press down on them to release any liquid they have absorbed. Set the cinnamon sticks aside for serving. Add the coffee to the hot milk, then pour into cups. Add a cinnamon stick to each cup. Drinkers should add sugar to taste.

Horchata

This delicious, aromatic rice drink tastes wonderfully creamy, yet does not contain a drop of milk. Mexicans swear by it as a means of settling stomach upsets or curing hangovers, and it is often served at breakfast. This recipe makes four.

450g/1lb long grain rice
750ml/1¼ pints water
150g/5oz blanched whole almonds
10ml/2 tsp ground cinnamon
finely grated rind of a lime
50g/2oz caster (superfine) sugar

Tip the rice into a sieve and rinse thoroughly under cold running water. Drain, tip into a large bowl and pour over the water. Cover and soak for at least two hours and preferably overnight. Drain the rice, reserving 600ml/1 pint of the soaking liquid. Spoon the rice into a food processor or blender and grind as finely as possible. Add the almonds to the processor or blender and continue to grind in the same way until finely ground. Add the cinnamon, grated lime rind and sugar to the ground rice and ground almonds. Add the reserved soaking water from the rice and mix until all the sugar has dissolved. Serve in tall glasses with ice cubes. Garnish with strips of lime rind.

Coffee Milkshake

This cold coffee drink does not require a blender. The recipe serves two.

200ml/7fl oz chilled strong coffee (four cups espresso, or filter/cafetière brewed using 70g/12 tbsps coffee per 1 litre/1¾ pints water)
2 eggs, well-beaten
450ml/¾ pint cold milk
100ml/3½fl oz single (light) or double (heavy) cream
15ml/1 tbsp sugar
pinch of salt
4 drops vanilla or almond essence (extract)

Mix the ingredients in a shaker. Serve at once, sprinkled with ginger cookies.

Atole

This drink, which is made from tehe white corn, *masa harina*, is traditionally flavoured with *piloncillo* (Mexican unrefined brown sugar) and ground cinnamon. It has the consistency of a thick milkshake. Fresh fruit purées are often added before serving and some recipes introduce ground almonds or milk. This one serves six.

200g/7oz white *masa harina*
1.2 litres/2 pints water
1 vanilla pod
50g/2oz *piloncillo*, or soft dark brown sugar
2.5ml/½ tsp ground cinnamon
115g/4oz fresh strawberries, chopped pineapple or orange segments (optional)

Put the *masa harina* in a heavy pan and gradually beat in the water to make a smooth paste. Place the pan over a medium heat, add the vanilla pod and bring the mixture to the boil, stirring constantly until it thickens. Beat in the sugar and ground cinnamon and continue to beat until the sugar has dissolved. Remove from the heat. If adding the fruit, purée it in a food processor or blender until smooth, and then press the purée through a sieve. Stir the purée into the corn mixture and return to the heat until warmed through. Remove the vanilla pod. Serve.

Champurrada

This popular version of Atole is made with Mexican chocolate. A special wooden whisk called a *molinollo* is traditionally used when making this frothy drink. The recipe serves six.

115g/4oz Mexican chocolate
1.2 litres/2 pints water or milk, or a mixture
200g/7oz white *masa harina*
25g/2 tbsp soft dark brown sugar

Put the chocolate in a mortar and grind with a pestle until it becomes a fine powder. Alternatively, grind the chocolate in a food processor. Put the liquid in a heavy pan and gradually stir in all the *masa harina* until a smooth paste is formed. Use a traditional wooden *molinollo* or a wire whisk for a frothier drink. Place the pan over a medium heat and bring the mixture to the boil, stirring all the time until the frothy drink thickens. Stir in the ground chocolate, then add the sugar. Serve immediately.

Mexican Hot Chocolate

This sumptuous version of hot chocolate relies on the beguiling flavours of almond, cloves and cinnamon for its sweetly spicy appeal. The recipe serves four.

1 litre/1¾ pints full-cream (whole) milk
1 cinnamon stick
2 whole cloves
115g/4oz plain dark chocolate, chopped into small pieces
2–3 drops almond essence (extract)

Heat the milk gently with the spices in a pan until almost boiling, then stir in the chocolate over a medium heat until melted. Strain into a blender, add the almond essence and whizz on high speed for about 30 seconds until frothy. Pour into warmed heatproof glasses and serve immediately.

Iced Mint and Chocolate Cooler

This makes a stimulating alternative to dessert, and is in a different class altogether to mint-choc-chip ice cream. The recipe serves four.

60ml/4 tbsp drinking chocolate
400ml/14fl oz full-cream (whole) milk
150ml/¼ pint natural (plain) yogurt
2.5ml/½ tsp peppermint essence (extract)
4 scoops chocolate ice cream

Place the drinking chocolate in a small pan and stir in about 120ml/4fl oz of the milk. Heat gently, stirring, until almost boiling, then remove the pan from the heat. Pour the hot chocolate milk into a heatproof bowl or large pitcher and whisk in the remaining milk. Add the yogurt and peppermint essence and whisk again. Pour the mixture into four tall glasses, filling them no more than three-quarters full. Top each drink with a scoop of ice cream. Garnish with mint leaves and chocolate shapes. Serve immediately.

Coffee Frappé

Similar to a milkshake, this frappé recipe is another long, cold coffee drink that is both refreshing and uplifting. The recipe serves two.

450ml/¾ pint cold strong coffee (brewed using about 80g/14 tbsp coffee per 1 litre/1¾ pints water)
8 drops vanilla essence (extract)
60ml/4 tbsp condensed milk
sugar, to taste

Add the cold brewed coffee to a large blender. Next, add the vanilla essence, a couple of handfuls of crushed ice and the condensed milk. Blend well until a smooth texture is obtained. Pour into tall, clear glasses, and stir in sugar to taste. Garnish with some whipped cream and banana slices, if you wish.

GLOSSARY

What follows is a list of the generic terms most frequently encountered in the cocktail world.

ABV: Stands for "alcohol by volume", and shows the total percentage within the drink that is accounted for by pure ethyl alcohol. All alcoholic products must, by law, give this information.

Aperitif: Any drink taken before eating as a stimulant to the appetite. Can be as simple as a glass of dry white wine, champagne or sherry. Can also be a dry or sour cocktail.

Cobbler: A long drink consisting of spirit with sugar and ice, served with plenty of fruit to garnish. American in origin, it is the forerunner of all lavishly garnished cocktails.

Chaser: A longer drink that is taken immediately after a small one, typically a glass of beer to follow a shot of neat spirit. It soothes the throat after the high alcohol of its predecessor.

*Below: Champagne is an excellent **aperitif** for whetting the appetite.*

*Above: A **cup** makes a refreshing, long drink as a party starter. They are generally lavishly garnished with fruit.*

Collins: A long drink originally called the Tom Collins after a particular variety of gin. A Collins is now any spirit mixed with lemon juice and sugar, and topped up with soda. It is basically a long version of the Sour.

Cooler: An indeterminate long drink that consists of any spirit with fruit juice (usually citrus), sugar and a sparkling topper (which may be soda, lemonade or ginger ale). Classically decorated with a spiral citrus twist.

Crusta: Any drink that comes in a glass with a frosted rim, usually of sugar (although the salt-rimmed Margarita is theoretically a Crusta too). Should also technically be served with a continuous twist of lemon rind lining the glass.

Cup: Essentially the cold version of Punch, a Cup is a mixture of wine or cider with spirits and fruit juices, served from a large bowl full of fruit garnishes and ice. Best served in summer.

Daisy: A soured spirit that also contains a measure of fruit syrup such as grenadine, topped up with soda.

Egg-nog: A long mixture of spirit or fortified wine with whole egg, sugar and milk, served cold and usually seasoned with nutmeg. Traditional as a Christmas drink in the USA.

Fix: Virtually the same thing as a Daisy. Consists of spirit, lemon juice, a fruit syrup and a sparkling topper, but with the Fix, it is essential to put the squeezed lemon rind into the drink.

Fizz: Almost any long drink topped up with soda, but classically just spirit, lemon juice, sugar and soda, perhaps with a drop of egg white to help the texture. Buck's Fizz, a champagne drink, marked a radical departure for the Fizz.

Flip: A short drink containing egg, sugar and either spirit or fortified wine, usually seasoned with nutmeg. Similar to an egg-nog, but without the milk.

Frappé: Any drink that is served over a snow of finely crushed ice.

*Below: A gin and lemon **fizz** topped with fruit and flower ice cubes.*

*Above: A tall glass can be used for fruity drinks served **on the rocks**.*

Highball: Simply spirit with ice, topped up with soda or some other sparkling mixer, but with no other ingredient.

Julep: A hot-weather American drink, served in a tall glass. Consists of spirit (classically bourbon) and plenty of crushed ice, on a base of mint leaves pressed with sugar. As the ice melts, it becomes a long drink.

Mulling: The technique of gently heating wine, beer or cider with spices, fruit and perhaps a shot of spirit. To be served hot during the British Christmas season.

Neat: Any spirit drunk on its own without ice or mixer. "As it comes" is the synonymous phrase.

On the rocks: Any drink served over ice cubes or cracked ice, usually in a tumbler or Old-Fashioned glass.

Pick-me-up: Any drink whose purpose is to revive the drinker, whether in mid-morning or to counteract the effects of over-indulgence. It is a bit of a loaded term, since it shouldn't be forgotten that all alcohol depresses the central nervous system, rather than "picks it up".

Pousse-café: A small cocktail in which two or more ingredients are poured slowly into the glass one by one to create a layered effect. Must be served without ice or garnishes.

Punch: An old British colonial drink consisting of spirits and wine, heated up with spices and fruit, and served from a large bowl. Similar to mulled wine, and likewise traditionally served at Christmas.

Rickey: A unsweetened measure of spirit with lime juice and ice, topped up with soda.

Sangaree: May be based on a spirit, but is usually fortified wine with sugar, soda and a nutmeg topping.

Shooter: A small, strong cocktail served in a shot glass, intended to be downed in one. Historically, any tot of neat spirit taken in the same way.

*Below: A **pousse-café** layered with Kahlúa, Bailey's Irish Cream and Grand Marnier.*

*Above: A **sour** made from gin, fresh lemon juice and a pinch of sugar.*

Shrub: A drink consisting of spirit (usually brandy or rum) bottled with fruit juices and loaf (or lump) sugar, and left to infuse for several weeks.

Sling: A long drink consisting of spirit with lemon juice, sugar and soda. Similar to a Collins, it now generally contains a shot of some liqueur as well.

Smash: An undersized version of the Julep, made with ground mint, sugar and spirit, but served in a small glass and with not as much ice.

Sour: Any spirit mixed with lemon juice and a pinch of sugar, sometimes taken with a small splash of soda, but always as a short drink.

Swizzle: Cocktail of Caribbean origin involving spirit, lime juice, bitters, sugar and ice, frothed up by being vigorously stirred with a swizzle-stick held between the palms of the hands. Must be served Antarctically cold.

Toddy: A cold-weather drink consisting of spirit, lemon juice and sugar (or perhaps honey), to which hot water is added. Implicitly believed in as a cold remedy by previous generations.

INDEX

Acknowledgements

The publisher would like to thank Danes Ltd (tel. 01273 674 022; www.danesltd.co.uk) for supplying Kikor, Poncino Livornese and Monasterium bottles for photography.

The publisher would also like to thank the following for the use of their pictures in the book (l=left, r=right, t=top, b=bottom). **AKG**: 6, 7t and b, 8t and b; **Album Archivo Fotográfico**: 111t; **Cephas**: 9b, 12b, 35t, 65t and b; **Tim Ellerby**: 9t, 12t, 13bl, 64tl and b.

TU VEUX EN SAVOIR PLUS SUR LES HABITUDES DE VIE LIÉES À UN MODE DE VIE SAIN ET ACTIF?

TU AIMERAIS FAIRE LE BILAN DE TES CONNAISSANCES?

RENDS-TOI SUR LE C̶ ̶ ̶ ̶ ̶B DE
LA COLLECTION ̶ ̶ ̶ ̶ ̶ ̶. L'ADRESSE

www.erpi.com/ ̶ ̶ ̶ ̶ctifs.cw

Tu y trouveras:

- ✓ **ton plan d'action virtuel que tu pourras compléter EN LIGNE**;

- ✓ **des informations variées et fiables sur les habitudes de vie (ex.: diagrammes, photographies, tableaux, textes, vidéos, etc.) qu'on t'invite à adopter ou à maintenir dans ton plan d'action**;

- ✓ **des suggestions de lectures, des adresses Internet et diverses ressources**;

- ✓ **des activités complémentaires à celles de ton cahier et des outils pratiques pour réaliser de courts projets**;

- ✓ **et plus encore...**

Comment avoir accès au **Compagnon Web**?

1. Va à l'adresse **www.erpi.com/sainsetactifs.cw**

2. Entre le nom d'utilisateur et le mot de passe ci-dessous:

Nom d'utilisateur

cw904118

Mot de passe

be48gf

3. Suis les instructions à l'écran

Assistance technique: tech@erpi.com

11105W

Sains et actifs

2e secondaire

ÉDUCATION PHYSIQUE ET À LA SANTÉ • CAHIER DE SAVOIRS ET D'ACTIVITÉS

Richard Chevalier

Stéphane Daviau

ERPi

ÉDITIONS DU RENOUVEAU PÉDAGOGIQUE INC.

5757, RUE CYPIHOT, SAINT-LAURENT (QUÉBEC) H4S 1R3
TÉLÉPHONE : 514 334-2690   TÉLÉCOPIEUR : 514 334-4720
erpidlm@erpi.com   w w w . e r p i . c o m

Directrice de l'édition
Diane Pageau

Chargées de projet
Valérie Lanctôt
Marie-Soleil Boivin
Sylvie Gagnon

Recherchistes (photos et droits)
Pierre-Richard Bernier
François Daneau
Marie-Chantal Masson

Réviseures linguistiques
Valérie Lanctôt
Nathalie Larose

Correctrice d'épreuves
Isabelle Rolland

Directrice artistique
Hélène Cousineau

Coordinatrice aux réalisations graphiques
Sylvie Piotte

Conception graphique
Benoit Pitre

Édition électronique
Interscript

Couverture
Benoit Pitre

Consultants scientifiques

- **Luc Denis,** directeur des programmes de Sports-Québec (responsable notamment du Programme des Jeux du Québec et du Programme national de certification des entraîneurs (P.N.C.E.) pour le Québec). Membre du conseil d'administration de l'Association canadienne des entraîneurs (depuis 2006).

- **Marielle Ledoux,** Dt.P., Ph. D., professeure titulaire du Département de nutrition de l'Université de Montréal. Coauteure de l'ouvrage *Nutrition, sport et performance,* conseillère des athlètes du Centre national multisport-Montréal et formatrice à l'Institut national de formation des entraîneurs.

- **Patrick Leduc,** joueur professionnel de soccer, entraîneur et directeur technique de soccer au Collège Français de Longueuil et à l'Association régionale de soccer de la Rive-Sud.

- **Michel Portmann,** Ph. D. (physiologie de l'effort), professeur titulaire retraité du Département de kinanthropologie de l'UQAM et entraîneur d'athlètes olympiques, dont Bruny Surin.

Consultants pédagogiques (enseignants en éducation physique et à la santé au secondaire)

Benoît Lavoie, École secondaire Camille-Lavoie, CS Lac-St-Jean.

Robert Richard, École Mitchell, CS Sherbrooke.

Patrick Robert, Collège Jean-de-Lamennais, Laprairie.

José-Antonio Tessier, École secondaire Les Compagnons de Cartier, CS des Découvreurs.

Johanne Tremblay, Polyvalente de La Baie, CS Rives-du-Saguenay.

Monique Trudeau, Lycée-Séminaire de Chicoutimi, Saguenay.

Remerciements

Les auteurs et l'éditeur remercient Frédérick Girard-Rannou et Marina Gagnon pour avoir accepté de livrer leur témoignage d'un parcours sain et actif, transmis dans la section RENCONTRE AVEC.

Ils remercient également les 35 enseignants et enseignantes en éducation physique et à la santé des régions de Montérégie, Sherbrooke, Québec et Saguenay-Lac-Saint-Jean pour avoir transmis leurs conseils judicieux lors de l'élaboration de cet ouvrage.

Ils tiennent également à remercier le Collège Français secondaire de Longueuil pour avoir gracieusement contribué à la séance de photographies des exercices illustrés dans la section BILAN DE TA CONDITION PHYSIQUE. Un merci tout spécial à Rubiela Amaya, Nathalie Gendron, Pierre Giguère et Christine Lemieux.

Dépôt légal – Bibliothèque et Archives nationales du Québec, 2009
Dépôt légal – Bibliothèque et Archives Canada, 2009

Imprimé au Canada   1234567890 SO 14 13 12 11 10 09
ISBN 978-2-7613-2992-7   11105   ABCD   ENV94

Par souci d'environnement, ce cahier est imprimé sur le papier contenant 100 % de fibres recyclées postconsommation, fabriqué au Québec, certifié Éco-Logo, traité avec un procédé sans chlore et fabriqué à partir d'énergie biogaz.

Table des matières

RENCONTRE AVEC

Frédérick Girard-Rannou,
joueur de football 28

Marina Gagnon, patineuse artistique 62

ZOOM SUR…

Andrei Kostitsyn : vedette du hockey
et épileptique 14

Ana Ivanovic : championne de tennis
à l'adolescence difficile 75

Le petit déjeuner de **Michael Phelps** 79

Vue d'ensemble
de ton cahier

La collection **Sains et actifs** accompagne les élèves du secondaire dans le développement de la compétence 3 du programme de formation en éducation physique et à la santé : *Adopter un mode de vie sain et actif.*

Le contenu se présente sous une forme dynamique et colorée, appuyée par de nombreuses photographies et rubriques. Au-delà de l'attrait visuel, ces éléments jouent un rôle important dans les savoirs liés aux habitudes de vie et aux paramètres d'une vie saine et active. Les activités proposées te permettront de faire le point sur tes connaissances et de t'interroger sur les causes et les conséquences de certains choix dans un mode de vie pour en tirer tes propres conclusions.

Nous t'invitons à mieux comprendre ce qu'on entend par *adopter un mode de vie sain et actif* et à te questionner sur les divers aspects de tes habitudes de vie : activité physique, alimentation, sommeil, hygiène personnelle et dépendances nuisibles pour ta santé.

Adopter un mode de vie sain et actif... une compétence pleine de bon sens !

Fais le point,
Tout bien réfléchi ! et
Bilan de ta condition physique

Des activités diverses te permettent de vérifier ta compréhension, d'interpréter les informations et t'invitent à réfléchir sur les aspects liés à l'importance d'adopter un mode de vie sain et actif. Une section spécifique où tu pourras faire le bilan de ta condition physique actuelle pour t'aider à fixer tes objectifs personnels à intégrer à ton plan d'action.

RENCONTRE AVEC
Marina Gagnon,
patineuse artistique

RENCONTRE AVEC
Frédérick Girard-Rannou,
joueur de football

Frédérick étudie en 3e secondaire et pratique le football au niveau Bantam comme receveur éloigné.

RENCONTRE AVEC te présente des adolescents actifs qui
accordent de l'importance à un mode de vie sain et actif.
L'activité physique prend une grande place dans leur
horaire et ils y trouvent des sources de valorisation, de
motivation, de développement personnel et de plaisir.

ZOOM SUR…

ANDREI KOSTITSYN :
et épileptique

Andrei Kostitsyn est né le 23
Biélorussie. Il a été recruté
dans la LNH en 2003 par le
pu être choisi encore plus
hésité à le faire en raison
d'épilepsie chez lui. Les
comme étant le joueur le
à repêcher.
Andrei Kostitsyn a ma
LNH le 13 décembre
à leur gardien Curtis
Andrei, qui a joué sa
Il connaît alors un dé
son frère Sergei se
pour la majeure pa
Alexei Kovalev, qu

Andrei Kostitsyn,
joueur des Canadiens de Montréal.

ZOOM SUR… te fait
connaître des personnalités
dont le profil est lié aux
thèmes traités dans la
section où elles apparaissent.

En rafale

Les bonnes raisons pour ne pas suivre une di

On entend beaucoup parler de diètes et les médias font la
produits susceptibles de faciliter la perte de poids. Attention !
plus à ton âge, de bien s'informer sur la question.

**Est-ce vrai que suivre une diète peut présenter des risques
pour ma santé ?**

La plupart des diètes engendrent des carences en vitamines,
en minéraux ou en énergie, ou encore divers effets secondaires tels qu'une déshydratation, une grande fatigue, de la
difficulté à se concentrer, des troubles digestifs, des perturbations hormonales, etc. Or, ton corps en pleine croissance
a besoin de l'énergie, des vitamines et des minéraux fournis
par les aliments pour bien fonctionner. En le privant de nourriture, tu t'exposes à plusieurs problèmes de santé.

Les diètes peuvent-ell
équilibre mental ?

Dans un style dynamique
et concis, prenant
l'allure d'un blogue,
EN RAFALE te présente
des questions et des
réponses portant sur
des sujets importants
liés à la santé et à
l'activité physique.

Diabète

Le diabète est une maladie liée
à une trop grande présence de
sucre dans le sang. Le diabète
de type 1 est causé par un problème d'origine génétique tandis
que le diabète de type 2 est en
lien, la plupart du temps, avec un
surplus de masse grasse dans le
poids corporel et l'insuffisance
d'activités physiques. Ce type de
diabète peut être aggravé par une
mauvaise alimentation.

Des textes en encadré
complètent chacune des
sections par des données
provenant d'études,
d'enquêtes ou d'organismes
qui sont des références
précieuses pour parfaire
ta compréhension des
thèmes développés.

Des rubriques ajoutent, aux endroits appropriés,
de l'information pertinente au thème traité dans
chaque section du cahier.

PENSE-BÊTE !
Stratégie d'adoption d'un
mode de vie sain et actif

1. Connaître l'effet de tes habitudes de vie actuelles
sur ta santé et ton bien-être.
2. Évaluer la qualité de tes habitudes de vie actuelles.
3. Élaborer un plan d'action personnel visant à modifier certaines de tes habitudes de vie actuelles et à inclure la pratique
régulière d'au moins une activité physique dans ton agenda
à raison d'au moins trois fois par semaine.
4. Mettre en pratique ton plan d'action en lien avec tes objectifs personnels sur une période de huit semaines.
5. Faire le bilan de ton expérience et mesurer
tes résultats.

PENSE-BÊTE ! résume
les renseignements
importants à retenir
pour ta réflexion sur
ton plan d'action.

Les mots clés, qui sont surlignés en vert, sont
définis pour t'aider à mieux comprendre le
sujet traité. Ces mots clés sont repris dans
le glossaire à la fin du cahier.

Coordination motrice
Capacité à réaliser un mouvement
avec précision.

Référence au **COMPAGNON**
WEB de la collection, où tu
trouveras des renseignements
complémentaires, des idées
de projets et des activités
supplémentaires. Tu y trouveras
aussi un canevas qui te permettra
de créer ton portfolio personnel et
ton plan d'action virtuel.

Suggestions de publications,
de sites Web, d'organismes
de soutien ou de
référence en lien
avec le thème abordé.

POUR EN
SAVOIR PLUS
Consulte l'avis scientifique
émis par Kino-Québec en 2000,
« L'activité physique, déterminant
de la santé des jeunes »,
ou visite leur site Internet,
www.kino-quebec.qc.ca

À l'âge de 12 ans, la majorité des jeunes présentent au moins un facteur de risque de développer une maladie cardiovasculaire, principalement en raison de leur obésité, de leur pression artérielle, de leur consommation de tabac ou de leur sédentarité.

POUR EN SAVOIR PLUS

Consulte l'avis scientifique émis par Kino-Québec en 2000, « L'activité physique, déterminant de la santé des jeunes », ou visite leur site Internet, www.kino-quebec.qc.ca

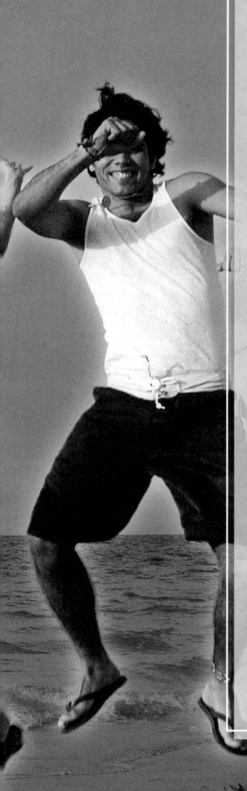

Une vie saine et active

Une année s'est écoulée depuis ton arrivée au secondaire. Tout est moins nouveau maintenant et plus familier, sans doute. Tu as eu le temps aussi d'apprivoiser la nouvelle compétence en éducation physique et à la santé, *Adopter un mode de vie sain et actif.*

L'année dernière, tu as même conçu et appliqué un plan d'action qui visait la pratique régulière d'au moins une activité physique et l'amélioration de certaines de tes habitudes de vie. Cette année, tu feras un pas de plus vers une vie saine et active. En effet, tout au long de l'année, tu auras l'occasion d'approfondir ta réflexion sur tes habitudes de vie et d'ajuster ton plan d'action en fonction de ce que tu vis maintenant et de ce que tu deviens.

Souviens-toi de ceci : cet exercice de réflexion te fournit une occasion unique de faire le point et d'améliorer ton bien-être physique et mental et, par là, ta santé pour toute ta vie.

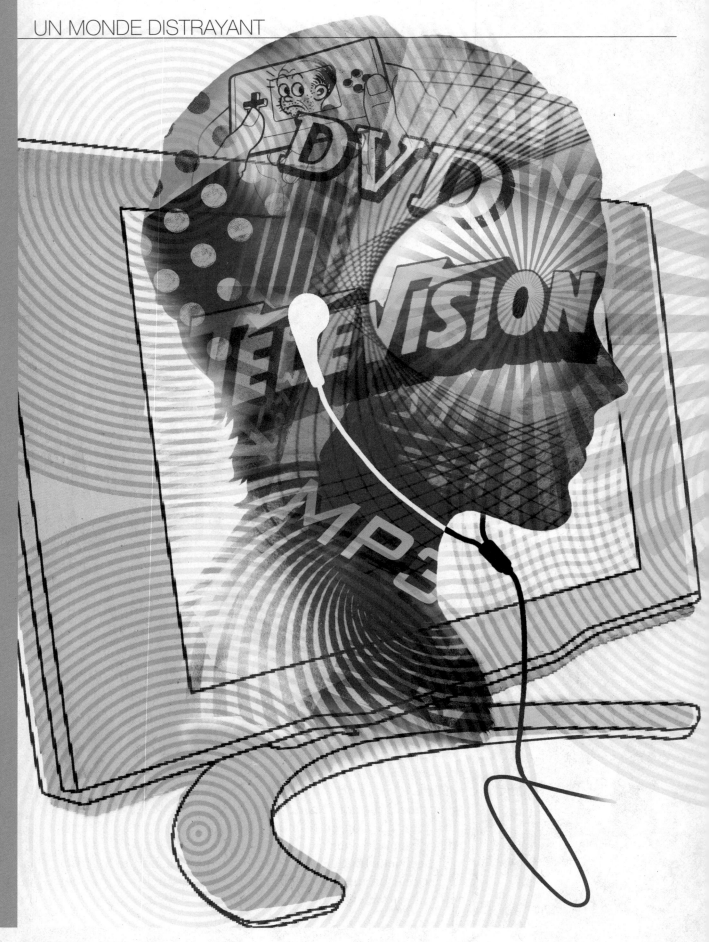

❶ Un monde distrayant

Ton environnement extérieur n'arrête jamais de stimuler tes sens par les sons, les images et les objets. Le monde virtuel qui t'attire et la publicité omniprésente qui te sollicite sans relâche y contribuent pour beaucoup. À lui seul, le monde virtuel accapare de plus en plus ton temps de loisir.

Il arrive même que des jeunes de ton âge deviennent accros au monde virtuel ; c'est la cyberdépendance. Lis à ce propos la rubrique Tout bien réfléchi !, «La cyberdépendance, nouvelle drogue des temps modernes ?», à la page 8.

Quant à la publicité, on la voit et on l'entend partout : télévision, radio, journaux, magazines, métro, autobus, panneaux publicitaires géants, Internet, etc. Cette publicité t'est en bonne partie adressée. Qu'il s'agisse d'un nouveau modèle de jeans, de rouge à lèvres, de lecteur MP3, de cellulaire, de console vidéo, de chaussure de sport, ou d'un nouveau type de hamburger, le message qu'on te transmet, c'est qu'en adoptant le produit annoncé, tu seras *cool* et au goût du jour.

En fait, les jeunes de ton âge sont exposés à une multitude de publicités… par jour !

Le monde qui t'entoure est de plus en plus distrayant. C'est un beau défi pour toi de faire abstraction des sirènes de la distraction pour te concentrer sur tes études et adopter de saines habitudes de vie.

Le monde virtuel accapare de plus en plus ton temps de loisirs

Le monde qui t'entoure est de plus en plus distrayant

De 40 à 50 heures par semaine ! C'est le temps que passent désormais les jeunes de 10 à 16 ans devant les innombrables écrans auxquels ils sont exposés (télévision, ordinateur, console de jeux, MP3 et cellulaire dit *intelligent*). Le monde dans lequel tu vis serait-il devenu trop virtuel ?

1.1 Du jeu à la consommation excessive

À partir de combien d'heures de consommation d'Internet ou de jeu par jour ou par semaine peut-on parler de consommation excessive ?

> Généralement, la personne cyber-dépendante essaie de fuir ou d'exprimer un besoin ou un malaise intérieur

La frontière entre le raisonnable et le déraisonnable est difficile à fixer. Tu peux être souvent devant ton ordinateur pour des raisons *utilitaires* : travaux scolaires ou recherches particulières sur un sujet qui t'intéresse, etc. Parfois, les excès sont passagers si tu découvres, par exemple, un nouveau jeu vidéo ou que tu participes à des forums de discussion passionnants sur Internet. Tu vas alors y consacrer plusieurs soirées entières, mais le retour à tes autres activités et à ton entourage se fera naturellement. Il ne s'agit pas là de dépendance mais de passions passagères.

Cependant, passer, jour après jour, plusieurs heures à surfer sur Internet ou à jouer à des jeux vidéo, surtout si on le fait seul ou seule, peut commencer à ressembler à une dépendance au monde virtuel. C'est au moment où il n'y a plus d'échanges avec les autres qu'il faut commencer à se poser des questions.

Quand la cyberdépendance prend le contrôle de ta vie, tes activités s'organisent autour du jeu ou du clavier, et ton fonctionnement social, intellectuel et affectif s'en trouve affecté. Généralement, la personne cyberdépendante essaie de fuir ou d'exprimer un besoin ou un malaise intérieur. De nombreuses personnes qui ont un problème avec le jeu compulsif jouent dans le but de fuir des émotions douloureuses. Par exemple, les joueurs dépressifs peuvent ressentir un regain d'énergie ou une libération d'endorphine en jouant. Il s'agit essentiellement d'une dépendance psychique qui se traduit par un constant désir de jouer ou de surfer sur Internet.

1.2 Un monde où règne la loi du moindre effort physique

Le monde qui t'entoure présente une autre particularité : la facilité physique. Les innovations technologiques qui sont apparues depuis quelques décennies ont constamment réduit la nécessité de fournir un effort physique significatif dans la vie de tous les jours.

Résultat : tu te retrouves dans un environnement où les seuls muscles qui travaillent sont souvent ceux des doigts pianotant sur un clavier ou une console de jeux. Voilà un autre défi pour toi : bouger davantage ! Cette habitude de vie est importante parce qu'elle vient épauler la formidable poussée de croissance de ton corps.

Tu te retrouves dans un environnement où les seuls muscles qui travaillent sont souvent ceux des doigts pianotant sur un clavier ou une console de jeux

Tout bien réfléchi !

Lis le texte ci-dessous et souligne les conséquences de la cyberdépendance.

La cyberdépendance, nouvelle drogue des temps modernes?

Quand l'ordinateur occupe de plus en plus de place dans la vie, il peut devenir un véritable objet de dépendance. Omniprésent, il entraîne de nombreux comportements compulsifs irrépressibles. Les cyberdépendants vérifient leur boîte de messagerie électronique toutes les 10 minutes, ils visitent et revisitent inlassablement les mêmes sites Internet ou passent d'innombrables heures à jouer en réseau. Même en vacances, en auto, en bus ou en train, ils ne peuvent pas se séparer de leur objet préféré et l'emportent partout où ils vont.

La cyberdépendance est une forme de toxicomanie moderne. Lorsqu'on s'accroche de façon exagérée à son écran, il arrive même qu'on en oublie de manger. Toxique pour la santé quand elle devient incontrôlable, la consommation du clavier nous fait perdre notre énergie.

Véritable aspirateur de vie sociale, la cyberdépendance nous isole des autres, exactement comme opèrent, de manière lancinante, toutes les autres drogues. Engloutis dans l'univers virtuel, les cyberdépendants perdent le contact avec les autres et avec le *monde réel*. Le désinvestissement par rapport à leurs engagements familiaux et scolaires engendre des tensions tant à la maison qu'à l'école.

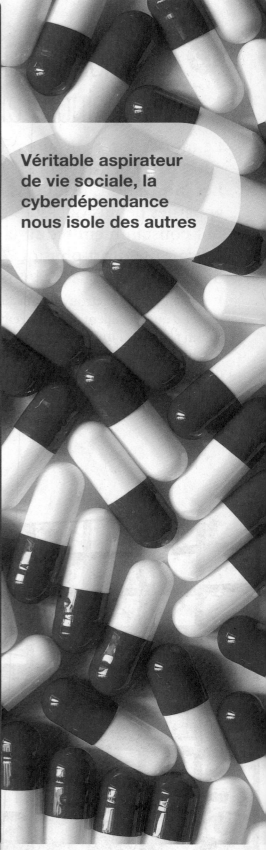

Véritable aspirateur de vie sociale, la cyberdépendance nous isole des autres

Fais le point

Et toi, éprouves-tu une cyberdépendance ?

Le tableau qui suit présente les principaux symptômes psychologiques et physiologiques qui permettent de détecter si tu es susceptible de développer une cyberdépendance. Après avoir lu les énoncés, inscris un ✔ sous la colonne qui correspond à la fréquence à laquelle tu ressens ce symptôme.

Les symptômes psychologiques que tu peux ressentir	Jamais	Rarement	Souvent	Toujours
Éprouver une sensation de bien-être, voire d'euphorie devant l'ordinateur.	☐	☐	☐	☐
Avoir de la difficulté à arrêter une activité à l'ordinateur et même en être incapable.	☐	☐	☐	☐
Négliger ta famille ou tes amis.	☐	☐	☐	☐
Ressentir un vide, une déprime, une irritabilité quand tu n'es pas devant l'ordinateur.	☐	☐	☐	☐
Mentir à tes enseignants ou à ta famille sur tes activités virtuelles.	☐	☐	☐	☐
Avoir des problèmes à l'école parce que tu passes trop de temps devant ton écran pour t'amuser.	☐	☐	☐	☐
Les symptômes physiologiques qui peuvent t'affecter	Jamais	Rarement	Souvent	Toujours
Souffrir du syndrome du canal carpien (douleurs dans les poignets).	☐	☐	☐	☐
Avoir les yeux secs.	☐	☐	☐	☐
Souffrir de migraines.	☐	☐	☐	☐
Avoir des douleurs au dos et dans la nuque.	☐	☐	☐	☐
Adopter de mauvaises habitudes alimentaires en mangeant de façon irrégulière et en sautant des repas.	☐	☐	☐	☐
Négliger ton hygiène personnelle.	☐	☐	☐	☐
Éprouver des troubles de sommeil et modifier ton cycle de sommeil : avoir des difficultés à t'endormir ; te réveiller la nuit ; avoir l'impression de ne pas avoir assez dormi au réveil ; etc.	☐	☐	☐	☐

Prends maintenant le temps d'analyser tes résultats selon les symptômes que tu as indiqué ressentir et leur fréquence. À la lumière de cette analyse, tu pourras déterminer les solutions à mettre en place pour t'éviter de développer un réel problème, qui aurait de graves répercussions sur ta santé physique et mentale. À toi d'y voir !

flexion   extension

② Un corps et un esprit en mutation

Tu la vois et tu la sens, la formidable poussée de croissance de ton corps ? Elle se poursuit de plus belle depuis ton entrée au secondaire. Tu as probablement gagné en taille et en poids durant l'été. As-tu une photo de l'année dernière pour le constater ?

Ces changements corporels modifient le rapport entre ta taille et ton poids et ont une influence sur ta **coordination motrice**, voire sur ta force physique. Il peut arriver que tes mouvements soient moins précis et d'une amplitude exagérée, exécutés avec maladresse. Du point de vue musculaire, tu peux remarquer une baisse de vigueur lorsque tu pratiques certaines activités physiques. Le phénomène est normal et, heureusement, passager.

Ton corps est en train de s'ajuster à tes nouvelles dimensions, c'est-à-dire à ton poids, à ta taille et à ta composition corporelle, soit le rapport entre la masse maigre (essentiellement les muscles) et la masse grasse qui est essentielle et normale en période de croissance.

Sous l'influence de la poussée hormonale qui survient à la puberté, la masse grasse a tendance à augmenter chez les filles. Chez les gars, c'est plutôt la masse maigre (les muscles) qui augmente.

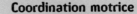

Coordination motrice
Capacité à réaliser un mouvement avec précision.

2.1 Un esprit qui mûrit

Il n'y a pas que ton corps qui change, ton esprit aussi

Tu as définitivement quitté l'enfance et tu es en route vers le passage au monde adulte

Il n'y a pas que ton corps qui change, ton esprit aussi. Tu gagnes en maturité ; les choses te semblent différentes de ce qu'elles étaient il y a un an, et très différentes de ce qu'elles étaient il y a deux ou trois ans. La **perception** que tu peux avoir des gens qui t'entourent (ex. : amis, camarades de classe, enseignants, parents, etc.) change petit à petit. Un vent d'autonomie et d'indépendance, principalement face aux figures d'autorité, souffle en toi. En même temps, tu ressens un besoin encore plus grand d'être accepté ou acceptée par tes pairs, et de faire partie de la *gang*. Tu as définitivement quitté l'enfance et tu es en route vers le passage au monde adulte. Au cours de l'adolescence, tu navigueras entre ces deux mondes et tu te poseras plusieurs questions tout en définissant ta propre identité.

Perception

Acte par lequel l'esprit et les sens saisissent les objets et les personnes, et les interprètent.

Ces changements d'ordre physique et psychologique peuvent faire passer au second plan ton besoin de réfléchir sur tes habitudes de vie. Tu te dis peut-être qu'il y a tellement de choses qui changent dans ton corps et dans ta tête que te questionner sur tes activités et sur ce que tu manges chaque jour est vraiment secondaire. Ce réflexe est bien normal. Cependant, tu dois au contraire te rappeler que tes habitudes de vie et les comportements qui y sont rattachés font de toi ce que tu es maintenant et ce que tu deviendras plus tard.

Comme la puberté débute presque deux ans plus tôt chez les filles que chez les gars, il est fréquent que celles-ci soient plus grandes et plus lourdes que les gars du même âge. Bien sûr, ces derniers se rattrapent par la suite !

La puberté est une étape vraiment importante : c'est le processus par lequel ton corps parvient à maturité et se prépare pour la reproduction. Les changements que ton corps subit à la puberté vont t'aider à profiter de l'âge adulte.

Œstrogène

Hormone sexuelle femelle, produite par les ovaires.

Progestérone

Hormone de la gestation, produite par les ovaires.

Testostérone

Hormone sexuelle mâle, sécrétée par les testicules.

PRINCIPAUX CHANGEMENTS SURVENANT AU COURS DE L'ADOLESCENCE	
CHANGEMENTS PHYSIOLOGIQUES	
GARÇONS vers l'âge de 11 ans	**FILLES** de 9 à 14 ans
Augmentation du volume des testicules Apparition des premiers poils pubiens Élargissement des épaules Changement dans l'apparence du pénis	Développement des seins Apparition des premiers poils pubiens Élargissement des hanches Augmentation marquée de la taille Début de la production d'**œstrogène** et de **progestérone** Début des menstruations
vers l'âge de 14 ans	
Mue de la voix Apparition des premiers poils au visage Augmentation marquée de la taille Début de la production de **testostérone** Début des éjaculations nocturnes	
GARÇONS ET FILLES vers l'âge de 12 ans	
CHANGEMENTS PSYCHOLOGIQUES	
Épanouissement de l'esprit Prise de conscience du monde extérieur Développement d'une vision personnelle du monde Acquisition du processus de prise de décision	
CHANGEMENTS SOCIAUX	
Transfert vers les amis de l'importance accordée aux parents Transformation des rapports aux autres Développement du réseau social Changement de centres d'intérêt	
CHANGEMENTS AFFECTIFS	
Augmentation des sautes d'humeur Apprentissage de la gestion des émotions Développement de l'image de soi	

ZOOM SUR...

Andrei Kostitsyn.
Joueur des Canadiens de Montréal.

Andrei Kostitsyn.
En pleine bataille pour la rondelle.

Andrei Kostitsyn.
Lance et compte !

ANDREI KOSTITSYN : vedette du hockey et épileptique

Andrei Kostitsyn est né le 23 février 1985 à Novopolotsk, en Biélorussie. Il a été recruté au 1er tour du repêchage d'entrée dans la LNH en 2003 par les Canadiens de Montréal. Il aurait pu être choisi encore plus tôt, mais les équipes ont longtemps hésité à le faire en raison de la découverte de forts symptômes d'épilepsie chez lui. Les recruteurs le décrivaient à l'époque comme étant le joueur le plus talentueux, voire le meilleur joueur à repêcher.

Andrei Kostitsyn a marqué son premier but en carrière dans la LNH le 13 décembre 2005, face aux Coyotes de Phoenix et à leur gardien Curtis Joseph. L'apprentissage a été long pour Andrei, qui a joué sa première vraie saison en 2007-2008.

Il connaît alors un début de saison plutôt lent, mais explose lorsque son frère Sergei se joint à l'équipe au mois de décembre. Il forme, pour la majeure partie de la saison, un trio avec Tomáš Plekanec et Alexei Kovalev, qui se révèle d'ailleurs le meilleur trio du Canadien pour cette saison. Il marque plusieurs buts spectaculaires et termine l'année avec une récolte respectable de 26 buts et 27 passes, pour un total de 53 points.

Sports et maladies

SPORTS ET DIABÈTE

L'activité physique est bonne pour la santé de tous, que l'on soit ou non diabétique. Tous les médecins encouragent la pratique d'un sport chez les diabétiques, car l'activité physique favorise un meilleur contrôle de cette maladie. Bien qu'il ne soit pas encore prouvé que les jeunes diabétiques pratiquant régulièrement un sport soient mieux équilibrés que leurs camarades sédentaires, on sait que le sport est un excellent moyen, pour eux, d'être bien dans leur tête et de ne pas se sentir différents des autres. Les jeunes diabétiques ne doivent plus être dispensés de sport à l'école. De même, ils doivent être intégrés dans tous les sports en dehors de l'école, sous réserve de certaines précautions, qui reposent sur quelques connaissances simples.

Deux sports posent néanmoins problème : la plongée sous-marine et la boxe. Celle-ci expose à des lésions des yeux et du cerveau, et, à ce titre, doit être formellement déconseillée aux diabétiques, même très bien équilibrés. En revanche, tous les arts martiaux (ex. : judo, karaté, etc.) peuvent être pratiqués sans problème.

SPORTS ET ÉPILEPSIE

Tu souffres d'épilepsie et tu hésites à pratiquer un sport ? Oublie ça ! Tu peux pratiquer toutes sortes de sports. Prends simplement quelques précautions avant de te lancer sur le terrain. Informe ton entraîneur ou ton entraîneuse, tes amis et tes coéquipiers de ton épilepsie de sorte qu'ils puissent te venir en aide en cas de crise.

Épilepsie

L'épilepsie est un trouble neurodégénératif caractérisé par des crises périodiques dont la gravité varie. Ces crises sont provoquées par des décharges électriques incontrôlables dans les neurones du cerveau.

Il existe deux types de crises généralisées : l'épilepsie tonico-chronique (*le grand mal*) et l'absence (*le petit mal*).

Dans la première, la plus spectaculaire, le corps est soumis à des mouvements incontrôlés des membres et du tronc, qui peuvent durer plusieurs minutes.

En revanche, durant une crise d'absence, qui affecte essentiellement les enfants, la personne perd soudainement contact avec le monde extérieur, sans toutefois perdre connaissance.

L'épilepsie, c'est comme un petit orage électrique dans la tête. Comme les vrais orages, ça n'arrive pas tous les jours et ce n'est pas si grave…

Le plus gros problème des personnes épileptiques, ce n'est pas l'épilepsie, mais plutôt… les préjugés.

PENSE-BÊTE!

Stratégie d'adoption d'un mode de vie sain et actif

1. Connaître l'effet de tes habitudes de vie actuelles sur ta santé et ton bien-être.
2. Évaluer la qualité de tes habitudes de vie actuelles.
3. Élaborer un plan d'action personnel visant à modifier certaines de tes habitudes de vie actuelles et à inclure la pratique régulière d'au moins une activité physique dans ton agenda à raison d'au moins trois fois par semaine.
4. Mettre en pratique ton plan d'action en lien avec tes objectifs personnels sur une période de huit semaines.
5. Faire le bilan de ton expérience et mesurer tes résultats.

Diabète

Le diabète est une maladie liée à une trop grande présence de sucre dans le sang. Le diabète de type 1 est causé par un problème d'origine génétique tandis que le diabète de type 2 est en lien, la plupart du temps, avec un surplus de masse grasse dans le poids corporel et l'insuffisance d'activités physiques. Ce type de diabète peut être aggravé par une mauvaise alimentation.

Tes habitudes de vie sous la loupe

Ton corps est comme une éponge qui absorbe tout ce que tu lui offres : ce que tu manges, ce que tu bois, ce que tu inhales, ta façon de dormir, de bouger, etc. Il absorbe tout, mais cela ne veut pas dire qu'il apprécie tout ce que tu fais. Parfois, il encaisse tes comportements contre son gré.
Il peut le faire pendant un bon bout de temps, mais un jour, il se rebiffe et te fait savoir, d'une manière ou d'une autre, qu'il en a assez.

Par exemple, si tu as manqué de sommeil pendant quelques jours, ton corps fera en sorte que tu somnoles, peut-être même en classe, parce qu'il a besoin de refaire ses forces. Il te fera perdre ta concentration et ta bonne humeur parce qu'il est épuisé. C'est sa manière à lui de te dire : « S'il te plaît, dors un peu plus, je n'en peux plus ! »

Autre exemple de rébellion, plus subtile celle-là, c'est lorsque ton corps est privé de mouvements depuis trop longtemps. Que fait-il alors pour te le faire savoir ? Eh bien, il te coupe le souffle, provoque chez toi des courbatures au moindre petit effort, rend tes muscles aussi souples qu'une barre d'acier et, bien souvent, t'alourdit de deux ou trois kilos dont tu te passerais bien !

Un dernier exemple ? Pourquoi pas ! Lors d'une fête chez des amis dont les parents étaient absents, tu as découvert la bière. Tu en as même pris un peu trop. Mais ton corps, ton foie surtout, incapable d'absorber une telle quantité d'alcool, s'est alors mis en mode *Arrêt* et te l'a fait savoir : étourdissements, maux de tête, nausées.

Par contre, si tu manges bien, dors bien et bouges bien, ton corps, trop heureux de tant d'attention de ta part, te le rend au centuple en te donnant énergie, vigueur et concentration.

Tes habitudes de vie, tes comportements de tous les jours en d'autres termes, influencent donc au plus haut point l'état de bien-être de ton corps.

> **Un jour, il se rebiffe et te fait savoir, d'une manière ou d'une autre, qu'il en a assez**

Comme tu es en pleine croissance, nous mettrons sous la loupe cinq habitudes de vie que tu connais déjà et qui sont directement liées à ce processus :

❶ l'activité physique ;
❷ l'alimentation ;
❸ le sommeil ;
❹ l'hygiène personnelle ; et
❺ des dépendances nuisibles pour la santé (alcool, cigarette et drogues).

Tout au long de l'année, tu auras l'occasion d'approfondir ta réflexion sur ces cinq habitudes de vie et les comportements qui y sont rattachés. Tu auras aussi à ajuster le plan d'action que tu as conçu et expérimenté l'année dernière. Le but visé, cette année, est de consolider tes acquis sur le plan des habitudes de vie et de la pratique régulière de l'activité physique. Maintenant, sors ta loupe : on commence par l'activité physique !

plan d'action   p. 95

❶ L'activité physique : un besoin essentiel

Les nombreux effets de la pratique régulière de l'activité physique sont là pour le confirmer

Si tu vises un seul bloc d'activité sans arrêt, assure-toi qu'il dure au moins de 30 à 45 minutes, que tu le répètes de 3 à 5 fois par semaine, et qu'il est d'une intensité modérée à élevée

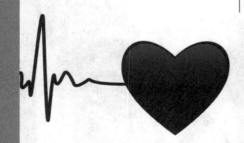

Bouger régulièrement, alors que ton corps se transforme pratiquement sous tes yeux, est essentiel pour que tu te sentes bien physiquement et mentalement. Les nombreux effets de la pratique régulière de l'activité physique sont là pour le confirmer. Rappelons-les brièvement.

Le plus extraordinaire, c'est que tu n'as pas à courir trois marathons par semaine pour profiter de ces bienfaits. Il te suffit d'accumuler, au total, au moins 60 minutes par jour d'activité physique d'intensité modérée à élevée.

Tu peux donc additionner les durées des différentes activités physiques que tu pratiques dans une journée. Tu peux même faire deux ou plusieurs blocs d'activité d'intensité modérée dans ta journée, en autant que chaque bloc dure au moins 10 minutes consécutives.

Si tu vises un seul bloc d'activité sans arrêt, assure-toi qu'il dure au moins de 30 à 45 minutes, que tu le répètes de 3 à 5 fois par semaine, et qu'il est d'une intensité modérée à élevée. Prends bien note que, dans ton plan d'action, on te demande une durée moindre d'activité physique, soit de 20 à 30 minutes consécutives d'intensité modérée à élevée.

plan d'action p. 95

C'est que, si tu ne pratiques pas d'activité physique d'intensité au moins modérée en dehors de ton cours d'éducation physique et à la santé, par exemple, il faut bien que tu commences quelque part. La durée des activités physiques prescrite dans ton plan d'action se veut un bon point de départ pour devenir plus actif ou plus active physiquement.

Et, même si cette durée est inférieure à celle recommandée par les experts, elle te procurera déjà certains bienfaits physiques et psychologiques.

DURÉE MINIMALE DE L'ACTIVITÉ PHYSIQUE À UNE INTENSITÉ MODÉRÉE À ÉLEVÉE	
MODE CONTINU (sans arrêt)	**MODE EFFORT-RÉCUPÉRATION** (avec arrêts)
de 30 à 45 minutes	60 minutes divisées en blocs de 10 minutes
DE 3 À 5 FOIS PAR SEMAINE	CHAQUE JOUR

Bien entendu, si tu en fais plus, les bénéfices seront encore plus marqués. Mais attention à ne pas en faire trop non plus, car fatigue et blessure peuvent être au rendez-vous.

Effort physique
Mobilisation de toutes les forces du corps en vue d'atteindre un but.

Poids-santé
Poids d'une personne auquel est associé le plus faible risque de développer certains problèmes de santé.

Flexibilité
Caractère de ce qui se courbe facilement.

Concentration
Capacité de maintenir une performance sur une longue période, qui dépend du maintien de la vigilance, de la capacité de détection du stimulus et de la résistance à la distraction, donc du contrôle de l'esprit.

PENSE-BÊTE !

Être actif ou active physiquement…

– Te donne plus de souffle et te fait récupérer plus vite après un effort physique.

– Améliore ta capacité à faire un effort physique et la réponse de ton corps aux situations d'urgence.

– T'aide à maintenir un **poids–santé** en assurant un équilibre entre l'absorption et la dépense de calories.

– Renforce tes muscles et tes os, un atout pendant la croissance.

– Améliore ton équilibre et ta **flexibilité** pendant que tu grandis.

– Améliore ta coordination motrice et ton efficacité dans l'**effort physique** au moment même où ta croissance perturbe ces qualités physiques.

– Favorise une meilleure qualité de sommeil (tu verras plus loin comment).

– Aide ta **concentration** en classe et contribue à améliorer ton rendement scolaire.

– Accroît ta confiance en soi (tu te sens mieux dans ta peau).

– Facilite la **détente mentale** et diminue l'anxiété.

– Aide à vaincre l'ennui (l'activité physique, ça occupe !).

– Améliore tes relations avec les autres parce que l'activité physique, ça se pratique souvent en groupe.

Détente mentale
Relâchement d'une tension intellectuelle, morale, nerveuse.

Un *état second* légal grâce aux endorphines !

Peut-être as-tu déjà remarqué le regard euphorique du coureur de fond (longue distance) qui en est à sa 100e minute d'exercice ? Après tant d'effort, il devrait grimacer de douleur, non ? Au contraire, on dirait qu'il est dans un état second ! Qu'est-ce qui explique son état ? C'est l'effet des **endorphines** dont la sécrétion a quintuplé (cinq fois plus élevée) depuis le début de sa séance d'exercice. Les endorphines sont sécrétées par le cerveau et appartiennent à la même famille biochimique que les opiacés (héroïne, morphine, opium). Ces hormones engourdissent la douleur et nous plongent dans un état second… tout à fait légal !

Pour qu'un effort te procure un effet euphorisant, celui-ci doit être d'une intensité modérée et de longue durée, habituellement plus de 45 minutes. L'effet euphorisant et son niveau d'intensité varient d'une personne à l'autre. C'est comme pour un médicament : la même dose n'aura pas le même effet chez tous les individus qui le prennent.

1.1 Mais... il y a un hic!

En fait, tu te doutes bien que bouger est bénéfique pour la santé. Si tu es toi-même une personne physiquement active, tu en es encore plus convaincu ou plus convaincue, sûrement.

Le hic, c'est que tu arrives à une période de la vie où les statistiques démontrent que les jeunes de ton âge commencent, en grand nombre, à délaisser l'activité physique. Le phénomène est encore plus accentué chez les filles (voir le texte «Pourquoi les filles deviennent-elles moins actives que les gars?» à la page 23). Selon les mêmes statistiques, vous serez encore plus nombreux à la fin du secondaire à ne pas bouger suffisamment. D'où vient ce désintérêt graduel envers l'activité physique alors que le corps, en pleine croissance, en a tant besoin?

Beaucoup d'experts ont tenté de répondre à cette question. Ils ont trouvé finalement trois raisons qui pourraient expliquer cette perte d'intérêt envers l'activité physique. Si tu deviens, ou te sens devenir, physiquement moins actif ou moins active depuis quelque temps, il est pertinent que tu connaisses ces raisons pour comprendre que ce désintérêt n'est pas un phénomène irréversible, bien au contraire.

> **D'où vient ce désintérêt graduel envers l'activité physique alors que le corps, en pleine croissance, en a tant besoin?**

Trois raisons qui pourraient expliquer cette perte d'intérêt envers l'activité physique

Savoir pourquoi tu risques de devenir de moins en moins actif ou de moins en moins active physiquement pendant ton secondaire pourra même t'aider à garder le cap sur l'activité physique.

Voici ces raisons.

★ La perte du plaisir

Le plaisir diminue, non pas à cause de l'activité elle-même, mais plutôt à cause du contexte, soit les conditions dans lesquelles tu la pratiques. Par exemple, tu fais partie d'une équipe de hockey ou de basketball, mais on te fait jouer moins souvent depuis quelque temps, te faisant ainsi sentir que tu es moins habile que d'autres. Peut-être que trop d'accent est mis sur la victoire ou que tu subis une pression de plus en plus forte de la part des entraîneurs, de tes coéquipiers ou de tes parents. Ou encore, tu as tout simplement moins de temps pour t'entraîner et t'améliorer.

Peu importe le motif qui explique la diminution du plaisir que te procure l'activité physique, tu auras la tentation d'abandonner si celle-ci n'a jamais été associée à des valeurs autres que le rendement et la performance, ou si tu ne la pratiquais pas par choix personnel.

★ Le match des intérêts

Quand tu étais plus jeune, tes parents, bien souvent, organisaient ton temps pendant tes périodes de loisir. Aujourd'hui, ce n'est plus le cas. Tu as probablement tendance à te détacher – un peu, du moins – du nid familial et à découvrir de nouveaux intérêts : la musique, les sorties en groupe, une relation amoureuse, etc. Cette situation t'amène à faire des choix inédits et peut entraîner un conflit d'intérêts avec la pratique d'une activité physique, parfois au détriment de toute pratique sportive.

Pourquoi certains bougent pour deux ?

Sur le plan individuel, les deux principales attitudes observées chez les jeunes qui pratiquent régulièrement des activités physiques sont les suivantes :

- Le plaisir est le motif principal qu'ils invoquent. Rire, s'amuser avec ses amis, relaxer, relever un défi personnel et ne pas chercher seulement à gagner sont autant d'éléments qu'ils associent au plaisir d'être actifs.

- Ils croient en leur capacité d'exécuter certaines activités physiques et de surmonter les difficultés associées à l'adoption et au maintien d'un mode de vie actif.

L'activité physique favorise la concentration en classe et peut contribuer à améliorer tes résultats scolaires

★ Les nouvelles responsabilités ou exigences de la vie

De nouvelles responsabilités ou exigences viennent généralement avec l'adolescence. Tu ressens peut-être cela comme une pression, ce qui t'incite à avoir un comportement plus adulte et moins enfantin. Dans ce contexte, la pratique régulière d'activités physiques est souvent perçue par les jeunes de ton âge comme étant inutile dans le processus de transition vers l'âge adulte, parce que certains l'associent aux *jeux* de l'enfance. À cette perception négative de l'activité physique s'en ajoute parfois une autre : la croyance que le temps consacré à l'activité physique nuit aux résultats scolaires. C'est dommage, car l'activité physique favorise la concentration en classe et peut contribuer à améliorer tes résultats scolaires.

Peut-être qu'aucune de ces raisons ne te concerne parce que tu es présentement physiquement actif ou active. Garde-les quand même à l'esprit parce que, d'ici la fin de ton secondaire, il se pourrait qu'une de ces raisons compromette ta pratique de l'activité physique.

L'activité physique améliore les résultats scolaires

Savais-tu que plusieurs études, dont certaines menées à Trois-Rivières, ont démontré que les résultats scolaires des élèves fréquentant une école qui fait une large place à l'éducation physique sont supérieurs à la moyenne ? Selon les chercheurs, après un cours d'éducation physique, l'attention et la concentration des élèves sont plus élevées. De plus, des données récentes corroborent aussi l'effet positif de l'activité physique sur le fonctionnement de l'**hippocampe**, une zone du cerveau essentielle à la mémoire et à l'apprentissage.

Hippocampe

Zone du cerveau essentielle à la mémoire et à l'apprentissage, située dans les hémisphères gauche et droit. C'est dans l'hippocampe que se déroule la phase d'enregistrement de la mémoire : un souvenir — une odeur, un poème, un visage, le chemin de l'école — doit être enregistré avant d'être stocké dans le cerveau.

Si, à la suite d'un accident, l'hippocampe est endommagé, on peut se souvenir des informations enregistrées avant l'accident, mais on aura beaucoup de mal à acquérir de nouveaux souvenirs.

1.2 Pourquoi les filles deviennent-elles moins actives que les gars ?

Entre le début et la fin du secondaire, presque deux fois plus de filles que de gars délaissent l'activité physique ou n'en font pas suffisamment.

Mais pourquoi donc les Amélie, Sandra, Tamishka et autres jeunes filles deviennent-elles moins actives que les Philippe, Vincent, Samir et autres jeunes garçons ? On peut penser que c'est parce que les gars, en pleine croissance, et donc en pleine production de testostérone, ont plus envie de se dépenser physiquement. Cette explication d'ordre biologique ne tient pas la route longtemps. En effet, avant la puberté, la masse musculaire des filles est comparable à celle des garçons et, après la puberté, les écarts en matière de performance motrice sont plus grands entre les personnes de même sexe qu'entre celles de sexe différent !

Les influences sociales expliqueraient davantage la différence entre les gars et les filles dans le domaine de l'activité physique.

POUR EN SAVOIR PLUS

Consulte le Rapport sur la problématique des jeunes filles et la pratique de l'activité physique, « Les filles c'est pas pareil », publié par Kino-Québec, ou visite le site Internet de l'organisme Bien dans sa tête, bien dans sa peau, www.biendanssapeau.ca

Les filles ont également moins de modèles pouvant les inciter à faire de l'activité physique et elles reçoivent moins d'appuis et d'encouragements de la part de leurs parents ou des adultes qui les entourent.

Autre conséquence de l'influence sociale : à capacité égale, les filles se perçoivent comme étant moins bonnes que les garçons. Ce phénomène fait son apparition dès l'âge de six ans et s'accroît au fil des ans. Il est même fréquent que cette perception les entraîne à choisir des activités traditionnellement réservées aux filles ou, pire, à abandonner complètement toute activité physique de peur de décevoir.

D'autres études soulignent que, comparativement aux adolescents, les adolescentes semblent avoir :

- Une vie sociale axée sur les relations interpersonnelles plutôt que sur la compétition.
- Une préoccupation plus grande de l'image qu'elles projettent.

À cet égard, la gêne entraînée chez certaines adolescentes par l'apparition de changements liés à la puberté (ex. : poils, seins, règles et augmentation du pourcentage de gras) et la crainte de compromettre leur féminité (par l'apparition de gros mollets ou de larges épaules à la suite d'une pratique soutenue) peuvent malheureusement les inciter à réduire ou à abandonner toute pratique d'activités physiques.

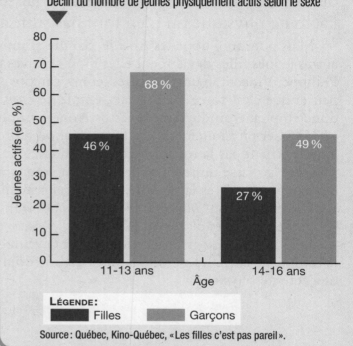

Ce que disent les statistiques !

Dès l'âge de 11 ans, les filles sont moins nombreuses à être actives que les garçons. En effet, 46 % des filles, comparativement à 68 % des garçons, sont actives. Au secondaire, les filles sont de moins en moins nombreuses à être actives et leur taux de participation de 27 % demeure bien en deçà de celui des garçons du même âge (14-16 ans), soit 49 %.

Déclin du nombre de jeunes physiquement actifs selon le sexe

Jeunes actifs (en %)

- 11-13 ans : Filles 46 %, Garçons 68 %
- 14-16 ans : Filles 27 %, Garçons 49 %

Âge

LÉGENDE : Filles — Garçons

Source : Québec, Kino-Québec, « Les filles c'est pas pareil ».

Les filles ont également moins de modèles pouvant les inciter à faire de l'activité physique et elles reçoivent moins d'appuis et d'encouragements de la part de leurs parents ou des adultes qui les entourent

Fais le point

1 À l'aide du tableau ci-dessous, compare l'activité physique que tu fais à celle que tu faisais l'année dernière.

Activités pratiquées	1re année du secondaire	2e année du secondaire
À L'ÉCOLE	_____ _____ Durée [_____] Nombre de fois par semaine [_____]	_____ _____ Durée [_____] Nombre de fois par semaine [_____]
APRÈS L'ÉCOLE	_____ _____ Durée [_____] Nombre de fois par semaine [_____]	_____ _____ Durée [_____] Nombre de fois par semaine [_____]
LA FIN DE SEMAINE	_____ _____ Durée [_____] Nombre de fois par semaine [_____]	_____ _____ Durée [_____] Nombre de fois par semaine [_____]

En analysant tes réponses, quelle conclusion peux-tu en tirer?

_____

_____

_____

_____

_____

2　**a)** Quelles sont les trois raisons qui amènent les personnes de ton âge à délaisser l'activité physique ?

_____

_____

_____

b) Parmi ces trois raisons, quelle est celle qui s'applique le mieux à toi actuellement ? Si tu es physiquement actif ou active, quelle est celle qui pourrait éventuellement t'amener à réduire ta pratique d'activités physiques ?

_____

_____

_____

_____

3　Quelle serait ta plus grande source de motivation pour recommencer ou continuer à être actif ou active de façon régulière ?

_____

_____

_____

_____

_____

_____

4　En observant les jeunes autour de toi (ex. : tes amis, ta famille, etc.), es-tu d'accord avec les statistiques qui disent que les filles sont moins actives que les garçons ? Justifie ta réponse.

_____

_____

_____

_____

_____

_____

_____

_____

5 Quelles sont les cinq habitudes de vie que tu dois respecter pour demeurer en santé ?

a) Inscris-les dans le tableau ci-dessous et indique par un ✔ jusqu'à quel point tu les respectes.

Les cinq habitudes à respecter	Jusqu'à quel point les respectes-tu ?			
	Tous les jours	Souvent	Parfois	Jamais

b) Pour chacune des habitudes de vie que tu respectes tous les jours ou souvent, donne un exemple montrant que tu y prêtes une attention particulière.

_____

_____

_____

c) Pour chacune des habitudes de vie que tu as de la difficulté à respecter (parfois ou jamais), explique comment tu pourrais remédier à la situation.

_____

_____

_____

6 Pendant combien de temps dois-tu faire de l'activité physique chaque jour pour t'assurer d'obtenir un bénéfice pour ta santé ? Encercle la lettre correspondant à la bonne réponse.

A. Soixante minutes d'activité physique modérée.

B. Six blocs de dix minutes d'activité physique modérée.

C. De trente à quarante-cinq minutes d'activité intense.

D. Toutes ces réponses.

E. Aucune de ces réponses.

7 Un des énoncés suivants est faux. Encercle la lettre correspondant à cet énoncé.

A. Le fait de bouger dans toutes sortes d'activités ou de sports t'aide à maintenir un poids-santé.

B. En mangeant santé, tu augmentes tes chances d'avoir de l'énergie et une bonne concentration pour les choses que tu as à faire durant la journée.

C. L'activité physique fait diminuer l'amplitude articulaire de tes muscles.

D. La pratique d'une activité physique permet d'augmenter la confiance en soi.

RENCONTRE AVEC

Frédérick Girard-Rannou, joueur de football

Frédérick étudie en 3e secondaire et pratique le football au niveau Bantam comme receveur éloigné.

Son rêve : Jouer un jour dans la Ligue canadienne de football et se rendre le plus loin possible dans ses études pour avoir un bon emploi après sa carrière de joueur de football, tel qu'ingénieur en hydroélectricité chez Hydro-Québec, comme son père. Pour ses études universitaires, il souhaite aller à l'Université Laval, où il pourrait joindre l'équipe de football du Rouge et Or.

Sains et **actifs :** *Quelle activité physique pratiques-tu de façon régulière ?*
F.G.-R. : Je joue au football depuis deux ans comme receveur éloigné parce que j'ai de bonnes mains pour attraper le ballon, je saute haut et je suis rapide.

Sains et **actifs :** *Qu'est-ce qui te fait tant aimer le football ?*
F.G.-R. : J'aime me défouler et dépenser mon énergie. Je suis hyperactif et le football me permet de dépenser cette énergie. J'aime courir, relever des défis, et j'aime le jeu, le travail, l'esprit d'équipe. C'est moi qui ai choisi ce sport. Avant de commencer à jouer au football, j'ai joué au soccer pendant sept ans. J'aime jouer au football parce qu'il s'agit du sport où le travail d'équipe est le plus développé. Si un joueur ne fait pas ce qu'il doit faire, c'est tout le jeu qui sera mal exécuté. C'est encore plus important qu'au soccer. On dépend toujours d'un autre joueur pour réussir un jeu correctement.

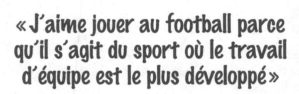

« J'aime jouer au football parce qu'il s'agit du sport où le travail d'équipe est le plus développé »

Sains et **actifs :** *En quoi la pratique de ton sport influence-t-elle ton mode de vie ?*
F.G.-R. : Il faut s'exercer, s'entraîner. Pour l'année prochaine, je dois m'entraîner pour être plus rapide, plus fort. Je dois bien manger, des légumes surtout. Pour tous les sports, c'est bon de manger des légumes. Faire du *cardio*, c'est important aussi. C'est mon entraîneur qui m'a dit d'en faire. Dans les séances d'entraînement, on fait souvent du *cardio* et notre entraîneur nous dit de manger des légumes pour avoir plus d'endurance sur le terrain. Pour ma part, je mangerais des pizzas et des choses comme ça, mais quand tu pratiques un sport, tu te dis : « Je vais faire ce qu'il faut pour être meilleur et plus performant. »

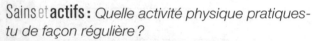

« Je suis hyperactif et le football me permet de dépenser cette énergie »

« Je vais faire ce qu'il faut pour être meilleur et plus performant »

FRÉDÉRICK GIRARD-RANNOU

Sains et actifs : *Dans ta vie, quelle place occupe la discipline ?*

F.G.-R. : C'est important d'étudier, de faire ses devoirs pour avoir de bonnes notes à l'école. Mes parents m'ont aidé à me discipliner. Dans mon agenda, j'inscris tout ce que je dois faire, comme mes devoirs, pour ne pas en oublier. Puisque les devoirs comptent pour le bulletin, il faut en faire le plus possible.

Quand j'embarque sur le terrain de football, je me mets dans ma bulle. Je me donne un but pour aller plus loin, comme me dire : « Ce ballon, je dois l'attraper. » J'essaie de me mettre moins de stress sur le dos parce que, si tu es trop stressé, ça peut te faire faire de mauvaises choses. J'enlève le stress en m'amusant le plus possible. Si tu prends ton sport trop au sérieux, si tu essaies de tout faire parfaitement, c'est certain que ça va te donner du stress et c'est là que tu vas manquer ton jeu. Il faut que tu te donnes des buts, mais il faut surtout que tu t'amuses. J'ai plusieurs amis qui jouent au football avec moi. On se tient ensemble. J'ai aussi d'autres amis, mais je ne suis pas obligé de les suivre. Il faut avoir du caractère pour savoir s'arrêter et ne pas faire des choses qui nous seraient nuisibles. Avant un match, je n'irai pas manger trois sacs de chips et une pizza. Le matin d'un match, je mange un bon repas.

> **« Il faut avoir du caractère pour savoir s'arrêter et ne pas faire des choses qui nous seraient nuisibles »**

La veille d'un match, c'est mauvais de me coucher à trois heures du matin parce que je vais être fatigué sur le terrain le lendemain, et que ma performance sera moins bonne que si je me couche à neuf heures. Là, je vais être en forme et bien correct.

Sains et actifs : *Quelle est ton opinion sur les substances nuisibles ?*

F.G.-R. : Des fois, il y a du monde avec qui on devrait éviter de se tenir. Ça peut être nuisible de se tenir avec des jeunes qui traînent dans les parcs parce qu'ils vont fumer. Je me tiens loin de ces gens-là parce que ça pourrait avoir un impact sur ma santé.

> **« Pour développer mes forces, l'été, je passe mes journées à vélo »**

Sains et actifs : *Quel plan d'action t'es-tu donné pour t'aider et t'améliorer ?*

F.G.-R. : À l'école, je suis inscrit dans l'option sport. J'ai six cours d'éducation physique par période de neuf jours. Quand je n'ai pas de séances d'entraînement de football, je prends ça *relax* et j'essaie de ne pas faire trop de conneries. J'ai trois entraînements de football par semaine et c'est là que je m'entraîne. Après ma saison de football, j'ai un mois de repos. Ensuite, je vais dans un camp d'entraînement pour recommencer à m'entraîner et pour développer mes habiletés, comme le *cardio*. C'est le *Speed Camp*, spécialement conçu pour les joueurs de football. Ceux qui y participent ont la chance de développer leur endurance cardiovasculaire. Après ça, on recommence le football. Pour développer mes forces, l'été, je passe mes journées à vélo, au moins cinq heures par jour. L'hiver, je suis toujours sur les monts en train de faire du *snowboard*, ou je vais au *Speed Camp* quand il y en a. Concernant mes faiblesses, avant, mon *cardio* était moins fort. Lorsque j'ai commencé à jouer au football, j'étais plus essoufflé parce que je n'étais pas habitué de courir toujours des *sprints* avec l'équipement sur le dos, surtout quand il faisait chaud. J'ai commencé à avoir un meilleur *cardio* avec le *Speed Camp*. Et, plus tu t'habitues, moins tu es essoufflé. Lors des entraînements de football, on court autour du terrain pour développer notre *cardio*. Et au début de l'année, c'est juste ça qu'on fait, du *cardio*.

« Mon passé va avoir de l'impact sur mon futur »

Sains et actifs : *Crois-tu que ton mode de vie actuel aura une influence sur tes projets d'avenir ?*
F.G.-R. : C'est certain que ça aura une influence. Si je commence à m'entraîner, plus tard, je vais être plus performant et je vais aller plus loin dans le football. Je commence aussi à avoir de meilleurs résultats dans mes notes, donc je vais aller plus loin. Mon passé va avoir de l'impact sur mon futur.

Sains et actifs : *Qu'est-ce que la pratique de ton sport t'a permis de découvrir et de comprendre sur toi ?*
F.G.-R. : Que j'avais beaucoup de talent, que j'étais bon dans les sports. Dans la plupart de ceux que je pratique, j'apprends vite. Puis, dans le football, j'ai vraiment appris vite. C'est seulement ma deuxième année et il y a des gens qui ne le croient pas. Plusieurs pensent que ça fait six ans que je joue au football. J'ai appris aussi que, si tu fais plus d'efforts, c'est meilleur pour ta performance. Les joueurs de football ont du cœur et plus de caractère. Ils veulent faire de bonnes performances. Un joueur de football va essayer d'aller plus loin dans les sports,

tandis qu'une autre personne va aller jouer au Nintendo chez elle.

Maintenant, aussi, j'ai compris l'importance d'avoir de meilleures notes et je travaille pour y arriver. Il faut avoir de bonnes notes pour être joueur de football plus tard parce que la plupart des gars qui jouent au football vont à l'université. Si tu n'as pas de bonnes notes, tu ne peux pas aller très loin dans le football. Je n'aimerais pas me rendre loin dans le football et qu'on me dise que je ne peux pas jouer dans l'équipe parce que mes notes ne sont pas assez bonnes. Je serais déçu. On ne peut pas revenir dans le passé pour corriger nos erreurs.

« Si tu n'as pas de bonnes notes, tu ne peux pas aller très loin dans le football »

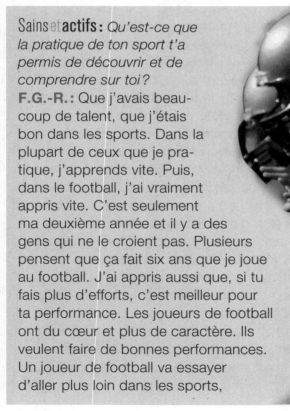

FRÉDÉRICK GIRARD-RANNOU

Sains et actifs : *Crois-tu que la société doit encourager l'adoption d'un mode de vie sain et actif ?*

F.G.-R. : C'est certain, mais ce n'est pas tout le monde qui peut devenir parfait. On ne peut pas dire au monde quoi faire. Puisque les médias ont de l'influence, il se pourrait qu'il y ait du monde qui comprenne. Il y aura toujours des gens qui ne feront rien. C'est comme les annonces sur la pollution. Il y en a encore qui vont jeter leurs déchets dehors et qui vont s'en foutre.

Sains et actifs : *Peux-tu me décrire comment les autres (ex. : ton meilleur ami, ton entraîneur) te perçoivent ?*

F.G.-R. : Comme un gars qui a de la volonté, beaucoup d'énergie, qui aime faire du sport, être dehors, bouger et qui se fait des amis facilement. Je suis sociable. Dans la plupart des sports, je réussis. Aussi, je suis généreux avec le monde. J'aime bien faire plaisir. Ils diraient aussi que je suis souvent en train de jouer au football. Mes amis acceptent mes décisions de ne pas aller avec eux à cause de mes séances d'entraînement. Des fois, je peux aller manger une pizza et faire des activités avec eux, mais j'essaie d'éviter de faire ça avant une partie.

> **« L'important, c'est de ne pas perdre les occasions qui se présentent et d'en profiter au maximum »**

Sains et actifs : *Qu'est-ce qui est le plus important pour toi dans la vie ?*

F.G.-R. : Ne pas penser juste à soi, aider les autres et avoir des buts dans la vie. Sans but, on n'ira jamais très loin.

Au football, nous étions dans les séries et on jouait contre une des meilleures équipes. Ça m'a incité à aller plus loin et à travailler plus fort. C'est comme ça que tu apprends. Je me suis donné à fond et c'est ça mon but. J'ai compris ce que je voulais et j'ai réussi. Il faut avoir la mentalité d'apprendre. C'est comme ça qu'on gagne.

J'aimerais dire que l'important, c'est de toujours se donner à fond, de toujours avoir un but, sinon tu vas le regretter plus tard et tu ne vas pas pouvoir revenir dans le passé pour changer ça. L'important, c'est de ne pas perdre les occasions qui se présentent et d'en profiter au maximum.

Sains et actifs : *Pourquoi est-il important d'avoir un mode de vie sain et actif ?*

F.G.-R. : Quand tu as une vie saine et active et que tu veux faire des sports, tu vas pouvoir en faire plus que quelqu'un qui reste chez lui. Si tu restes à la maison à ne rien faire, c'est là que tu vas manger plus, que tu vas grossir. Quand tu iras dehors, tu te diras : « Je ne suis plus comme avant et je peux moins faire d'efforts physiques. »

Je conseillerais aux jeunes d'essayer de se donner des buts, d'aller le plus loin possible. C'est comme ça qu'on avance. Plus tu te donnes et plus tu pratiques, plus tu avances.

Sains et actifs : *Qu'est-ce qui nuit à un mode de vie sain et actif ?*

F.G.-R. : Ce sont les mauvaises influences. Tu pourrais être moins sociable. Si quelqu'un te dit : « Viens, on va aller faire un mauvais coup ! », tu vas aller le faire. Les mauvaises influences peuvent te faire dévier du but que tu t'es fixé dans la vie.

1.3 Les accidents et les blessures liés au sport

Toute médaille a son revers. Le revers de l'activité physique, c'est le risque de blessures. Mais, bien souvent, ces blessures sportives peuvent être évitées.

Chaque année, en effet, il y a encore trop de jeunes de ton âge qui se blessent bêtement, pourrait-on dire, en pratiquant une activité physique, pour les raisons suivantes :

1. Ils portaient un équipement de protection inapproprié ou incomplet, peut-être même qu'ils n'en portaient pas du tout.
2. Ils n'étaient pas suffisamment préparés sur le plan de la condition physique (ex. : échauffement inapproprié).
3. Ils ne maîtrisaient pas suffisamment l'activité pratiquée.
4. Ils ont été téméraires.
5. Ils en ont tout simplement trop fait.
6. Les règles de sécurité n'ont pas été respectées.

Un point faible au niveau du squelette (ex. : pieds creux, jambes arquées, genoux tournés vers l'intérieur, inégalité de la longueur des jambes, etc.) peut aussi être la cause de blessures ou de douleurs. Heureusement, la plupart de ces blessures restent mineures et sans séquelles.

Il arrive, par contre, que certaines blessures nécessitent une hospitalisation et une intervention chirurgicale, sans compter le risque de séquelles à long terme associées aux blessures graves.

Les blessures

Une blessure est un dommage physique qui se produit lorsque le corps est appelé à fournir des doses d'énergie au-delà de ses capacités ou lorsqu'il est privé d'un élément vital, tel que l'air, l'eau ou la chaleur.

La différence entre les maladies et les blessures est que ces dernières se produisent parfois très soudainement. Une personne se porte parfaitement bien et, en quelques secondes, elle peut être blessée, handicapée à vie ou même mortellement blessée.

Les blessures sont souvent considérées comme des *accidents*, un terme qui induit en erreur, car il suggère que rien ne pouvait être fait. Mais, en réalité, on peut éviter certaines blessures avec des mesures de prévention et de protection adéquates.

Trop, c'est comme pas assez !

Comment savoir si tu t'entraînes trop ? À cause des différences physiques (taille et poids) parfois importantes qui existent entre des jeunes en pleine croissance, il est difficile d'établir la quantité maximale d'activité physique qu'une personne de ton âge peut faire. Par contre, un état de fatigue inhabituel, et qui ne serait pas lié à un changement dans tes habitudes de vie, est le premier signe tangible que tu t'entraînes peut-être trop, ou encore de la mauvaise façon en ne t'accordant pas assez de temps pour récupérer entre tes entraînements.

Par exemple, si tu te fatigues de plus en plus rapidement pendant les entraînements de soccer ou d'arts martiaux, ou que tu mets beaucoup de temps à récupérer après une séance d'entraînement, dis-toi que tu as sûrement besoin d'une période de repos.

Si, malgré les lumières qui s'allument, tu continues à te surentraîner, ton corps risque à coup sûr de s'épuiser et d'en donner des signes concrets (ex. : baisse de ton **système immunitaire** ; **anémie** ; etc.), en plus de se blesser sérieusement.

Blessure au niveau de la plaque de croissance

En cas de fracture, tu dois savoir qu'un os en croissance présente une capacité de réparation étonnante. En effet, les fractures guérissent plus vite et plus facilement chez les ados que les chez adultes. Toutefois, certaines fractures peuvent être plus sérieuses.

Pendant la croissance, les os des bras et des jambes s'allongent grâce à l'activité de cellules spécialisées situées aux extrémités des os, à un endroit appelé *plaque de croissance*, illustrée ci-dessous.

Heureusement, ces fractures sont très rares et surviennent surtout lorsqu'on ne porte pas d'équipement adéquat (ex. : des protège-tibias si on joue au soccer) ou qu'on abuse de la pratique d'activités physiques et qu'on accumule de la fatigue, ce qui augmente le risque de blessures et de fractures.

> **Au contraire, trop d'entraînement peut diminuer la force et l'endurance de tes muscles**

Système immunitaire
Ensemble des moyens de défense de l'organisme contre les agressions extérieures.

Anémie
Appauvrissement du sang en fer. Les principaux symptômes de l'anémie sont la pâleur et la faiblesse.

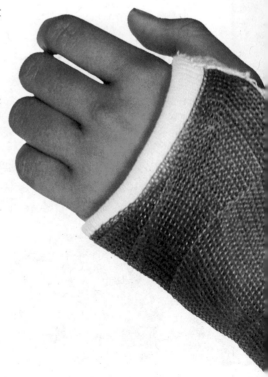

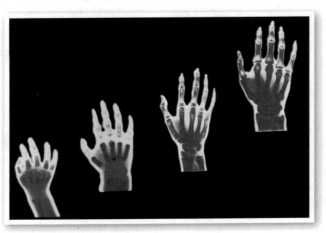

Savoir doser ton effort

Lorsque tu t'entraînes pour améliorer ta condition physique, tu dois apprendre à doser tes efforts afin de permettre à tes muscles de récupérer pendant et après les séances d'activité physique.

Entre les séances

Quand tes séances d'activité physique sont longues (plus de 60 minutes) et qu'elles comportent des périodes d'efforts intenses ou très intenses (pouls et essoufflement élevés), il vaut mieux te reposer une journée entre chacune.

Si tu t'entraînes tous les jours, tu dois suivre un programme planifié et alterner le niveau d'intensité de tes séances. Par exemple, le lundi, faire un entraînement vigoureux ; le mardi, un entraînement moins vigoureux ; et ainsi de suite.

Tu dois savoir que des recherches indiquent qu'un entraînement quotidien ou à raison de deux fois par jour ne favorise pas nécessairement une amélioration de la performance. Au contraire, trop d'entraînement peut diminuer la force et l'endurance de tes muscles, comme l'ont révélé les études sur les nageurs d'élite. Combien d'athlètes ayant un énorme potentiel ont ainsi abandonné leur entraînement parce qu'il était mal dosé ?

Pendant la séance

Ici, tout dépend de l'intensité et de la durée de ta séance d'activité physique. Si tu fais du *cardio* à une intensité modérée, tu peux le faire en continu, donc sans pause, de 20 à 30 minutes sans affecter ton rendement cardiovasculaire et musculaire.

Mais, si ta séance comporte des efforts intenses, ceux-ci doivent être suivis d'une période de récupération au moins équivalente en durée. Par exemple, si tu fais un effort intense qui dure une minute, il devrait être suivi d'une période de repos ou d'effort léger d'une minute.

Si l'effort est maximal, le temps de récupération avant d'enchaîner avec le prochain effort devrait être trois fois plus long. Par exemple, si tu fais un effort maximal pendant 30 secondes, tu devrais récupérer pendant environ 90 secondes.

En somme, il est important, lors de séances intenses, que tu t'accordes des périodes de récupération afin de permettre à tes muscles de récupérer et de refaire le plein d'énergie.

Permettre à tes muscles de récupérer et de refaire le plein d'énergie

1.4 Les règles de base : équipements et mouvements

Pour rendre ta pratique de l'activité physique sécuritaire et agréable, et diminuer le risque de blessures, d'**accidents** sportifs ou de fatigue liée au surentraînement, tu dois connaître et adopter certaines règles de base.

L'équipement

Accident
Événement malheureux qui cause des dégâts, des blessures, voire la mort.

> Tu dois connaître et adopter certaines règles de base

★ Porter un équipement de protection approprié

Si l'activité physique que tu pratiques présente un risque de chute ou de collision (avec un objet, des partenaires ou des adversaires), assure-toi de porter un équipement protecteur approprié respectant les normes canadiennes.

> Voici des exemples de pièces d'équipement protecteur de base :
> - Un casque pour le vélo, la planche à roulettes, le patin à roues alignées, le ski, la planche à neige et le hockey.
> - Des protège-poignets et des protège-coudes pour le patin à roues alignées.
> - Des protège-tibias pour le soccer et les arts martiaux, comme le taekwondo.
> - Des protège-genoux pour le volleyball.
> - Des lunettes de protection pour la pratique des sports de raquette sur petite surface (badminton, racquetball, squash).

★ Porter de bonnes chaussures

Ah ! Si les pieds pouvaient se plaindre, les « ouille ! » et les « aïe ! » fuse-raient de toutes parts dans les gymnases et sur les terrains de sport. C'est que beaucoup de jeunes de ton âge préfèrent l'allure déglin-guée de la chaussure de sport délacée plutôt que son confort pour les pieds. Penses-y un instant. Quand tu pratiques régulièrement une activité physique où tu dois supporter le poids de ton corps (ex. : marche, course à pied, *step*, tennis, danse aérobie, basketball, badminton, soccer, etc.), tes pieds encaissent des centaines de coups.

Les mauvais choix...

Les jeunes choisissent souvent une chaussure en fonction de la beauté, du style et de l'originalité plutôt qu'en fonction du confort et de la spécificité de l'activité qu'ils pratiquent.

Souvent, les mauvaises chaussures causent des problèmes au pied (ex. : une fasciite) en raison de l'absence de coussinets d'absorption dans la semelle.

Certaines autres chaussures n'offrent, quant à elles, aucun support pour la cheville, ce qui augmente le risque de se tourner le pied (foulure).

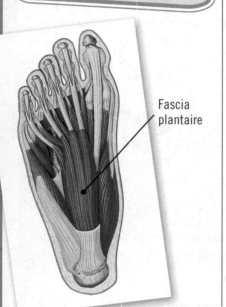

Fascia
plantaire

Par exemple, après 30 minutes de course, tes pieds auront martelé le sol des centaines de fois. Après une séance de *cardio* ou d'entraînement de basketball ou de soccer, tes pauvres pieds auront effectué des dizaines de déplacements latéraux, de pivots, de sauts, d'arrêts et de départs brusques !

Si tu portes des chaussures d'abord pour leur marque, et qu'elles ne sont pas conçues pour bouger sur une surface de gymnase ou un terrain extérieur, si elles sont mal lacées, usées à la corde, glissantes, trop petites ou trop grandes, tu risques de te retrouver avec des ampoules, des ongles noirs (surtout si les ongles d'orteils n'ont pas été coupés depuis un certain temps), de même qu'avec une tendinite, une fasciite (inflammation du **fascia plantaire** sous le pied) ou une entorse à la cheville.

Fascia plantaire

Large bande fibreuse qui court sous le pied, depuis le talon jusqu'à la base des orteils, et qui recouvre tendons et ligaments.

★ Le confort des pieds avant tout

Retiens donc ceci : une bonne chaussure de sport doit offrir suffisamment d'espace pour les orteils, comprendre une languette, un col et une semelle intérieure dotée de généreux coussinets, et être faite de matériaux de qualité. Elle doit aussi comporter une semelle extérieure antidérapante, résistante à l'abrasion, pas trop haute et pourvue d'une empeigne laissant échapper la chaleur.

Si tu pratiques plusieurs activités physiques, la chaussure multisport est un bon choix. Pourvue d'une bonne stabilité latérale et de coussinets plus que convenables au niveau du talon et de la plante des pieds, la chaussure multisport encaisse tant les sauts et les chocs répétés que les déplacements latéraux. Elle constitue un achat intéressant pour les sportifs indécis ou ceux qui aiment la variété. Tu peux les trouver dans n'importe quel magasin d'articles de sport.

PENSE-BÊTE !

Retiens ceci : une bonne chaussure de sport doit...

– Offrir suffisamment d'espace pour les orteils.

– Comprendre une languette, un col et une semelle intérieure dotée de généreux coussinets.

– Être faite de matériaux de qualité.

– Comporter une semelle extérieure antidérapante, résistante à l'abrasion et pas trop haute.

– Être pourvue d'une empeigne laissant échapper la chaleur.

★ S'habiller comme une pêche en été et un oignon en hiver

Les muscles en action sont, et de loin, les plus gros producteurs de chaleur. Voilà pourquoi tu as chaud quand tu bouges, et ce, même par un temps de −15 °C. Comment s'habiller alors pour faire de l'activité physique ? C'est simple : par temps chaud, on s'habille comme une pêche et par temps froid, comme un oignon.

La pêche a une seule pelure légère. L'été ou à l'intérieur, on s'habille donc légèrement afin de faciliter l'évacuation de la chaleur produite par les muscles. Un t-shirt et un short constituent une pelure de pêche idéale.

L'hiver, on s'habille comme un oignon, qui possède plusieurs pelures. Tu portes donc plusieurs couches de vêtements pour te permettre d'en enlever ou d'en ajouter si tu as chaud ou froid. Habituellement, on porte trois couches de vêtements qui jouent un rôle précis pour nous protéger tant du froid que de la surchauffe.

■ La **première couche** est en contact avec la peau et te garde au sec en absorbant l'humidité produite par la transpiration. Les sous-vêtements longs à séchage rapide, à base de polyester ou de polypropylène, sont idéals comme première couche. L'épaisseur du sous-vêtement est choisie en fonction de l'activité pratiquée. Pour des activités de nature aérobique, comme le ski de fond, le jogging d'hiver ou la raquette à neige, vive le sous-vêtement mince et léger ! Pour des activités à arrêts fréquents, comme l'escalade de glace, le patinage, la glissade ou le ski de fond en famille, choisis des sous-vêtements un peu plus épais. À éviter : les sous-vêtements de coton qui glacent la peau une fois mouillés.

Les muscles en action sont, et de loin, les plus gros producteurs de chaleur

Un t-shirt et un short constituent une pelure de pêche idéale

C'est simple : par temps chaud, on s'habille comme une pêche et par temps froid, comme un oignon

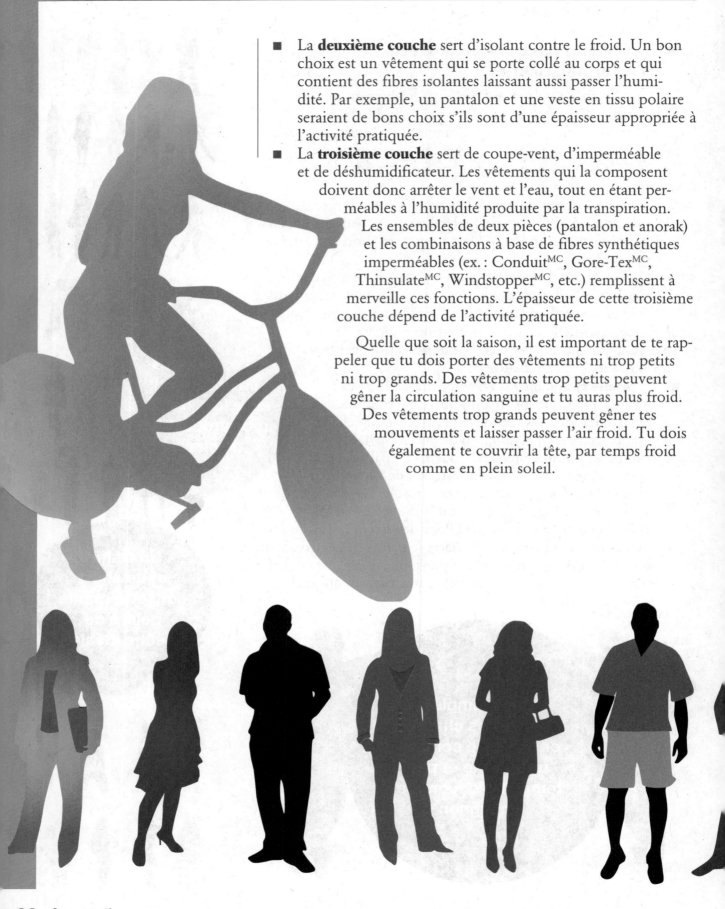

- La **deuxième couche** sert d'isolant contre le froid. Un bon choix est un vêtement qui se porte collé au corps et qui contient des fibres isolantes laissant aussi passer l'humidité. Par exemple, un pantalon et une veste en tissu polaire seraient de bons choix s'ils sont d'une épaisseur appropriée à l'activité pratiquée.

- La **troisième couche** sert de coupe-vent, d'imperméable et de déshumidificateur. Les vêtements qui la composent doivent donc arrêter le vent et l'eau, tout en étant perméables à l'humidité produite par la transpiration.

Les ensembles de deux pièces (pantalon et anorak) et les combinaisons à base de fibres synthétiques imperméables (ex. : Conduit^{MC}, Gore-Tex^{MC}, Thinsulate^{MC}, Windstopper^{MC}, etc.) remplissent à merveille ces fonctions. L'épaisseur de cette troisième couche dépend de l'activité pratiquée.

Quelle que soit la saison, il est important de te rappeler que tu dois porter des vêtements ni trop petits ni trop grands. Des vêtements trop petits peuvent gêner la circulation sanguine et tu auras plus froid. Des vêtements trop grands peuvent gêner tes mouvements et laisser passer l'air froid. Tu dois également te couvrir la tête, par temps froid comme en plein soleil.

★ Éviter les maux de dos avec un bon sac à dos

Savais-tu que ?

- Les maux de dos sont à la hausse chez les jeunes.
- Bien qu'il n'y ait pas une cause unique au mal de dos, l'inactivité, la posture, l'habitude de la télé et le sac à dos en sont les principales causes.
- «Au Québec, près de 35 % des jeunes de 9 ans rapportent des maux de dos et environ la moitié des jeunes de 13 et de 16 ans (42 % et 53 % respectivement) disent en éprouver au moins 1 fois par mois» (Santé Québec, ISQ, 2000).
- La moitié des jeunes porte un sac trop lourd pesant 20 % ou plus de leur poids, soit près de 9 kilos, en moyenne.

Le poids de l'ado reste la mesure de référence pour connaître le poids qu'il ou elle peut transporter :

Maximum 10 %	
Exemples des 10 % recommandés	
Poids de l'ado	Poids du sac
39 kilos	3,9 kilos
43 kilos	4,3 kilos
48 kilos	4,8 kilos
60 kilos	6,0 kilos

Si tu veux en savoir plus sur les **bonnes postures**, consulte le Compagnon Web.

Choisir

Le choix du bon sac d'école est aussi important que la manière de le porter.

Le sac à dos est recommandé parce que sa charge peut être répartie de façon équilibrée.

Le sac à dos... Un choix s'impose !

Bien porté, *dans le dos*, il permet d'utiliser les muscles forts du corps.

Alléger

Plus le sac est gros, plus les jeunes sont portés à le remplir. La charge maximale ne doit pas dépasser 10 % du poids de l'élève de 5 à 17 ans.

Adapter

Mettre les objets les plus lourds le plus près du corps, vers le centre de gravité.

Empêcher le sac de ballotter en attachant les sangles sur la poitrine et les hanches.

✘ Surtout ne pas le porter uniquement sur une épaule, en bandoulière ou dans une main.

S'asseoir

Avoir une bonne posture : assis ou assise au fond de la chaise, bien adossé ou bien adossée, les deux pieds au sol.

Bouger

Éviter de rester en position assise trop longtemps sans bouger.

Exécuter les bons mouvements

As-tu remarqué comment Patrick frappe sur le volant ? Il n'utilise que son bras. S'il continue ainsi, il risque de développer une tendinite à l'épaule. Cindy, quant à elle, ne semble pas très à l'aise sur ses skis de fond : elle marche, le corps tout crispé, au lieu de glisser, détendue, sur la neige. Fatigue précoce en vue et, donc, risque plus élevé de blessures en cas de chute et d'effort prolongé !

Ces exemples illustrent l'importance d'exécuter les bons mouvements quand on pratique une activité physique. Beaucoup de blessures sont liées à une mauvaise technique. Une bonne technique, au contraire, favorise la fluidité du mouvement, mais aussi, chose très importante, l'envie de poursuivre la pratique de cette activité. Qui a envie d'aller faire du patin à roues alignées sans jamais avoir appris à patiner et en se cabrant à chaque coup de patin de peur de tomber sur le dos ?

Pour acquérir une bonne technique, voici ce que tu dois faire.

A. Détendre tes muscles

Dès que les muscles deviennent tendus, les mouvements perdent de leur fluidité et, forcément, de leur précision. Donc, avant d'aller plus loin, habitue-toi à détendre tes muscles. Une suggestion : de temps en temps, fais des exercices où tu contractes fermement les muscles pour ensuite les relâcher complètement en te concentrant sur la sensation de détente qui s'ensuit.

B. Prendre conscience de ton corps en mouvement

Une mauvaise coordination vient souvent du fait qu'on a une faible conscience de son corps en mouvement. Si tu as l'impression d'habiter un corps étranger dont tu perçois mal les mouvements, effectue de temps à autre les exercices décrits ci-dessous.

Fatigue précoce en vue et, donc, risque plus élevé de blessures en cas de chute et d'effort prolongé !

Beaucoup de blessures sont liées à une mauvaise technique

Exercices 1 et 2 : Transfert de poids d'une jambe à l'autre

Debout, le corps détendu, les jambes légèrement écartées, transfère le poids de ton corps d'une jambe à l'autre en alternance (balancement de droite à gauche et vice-versa). Puis, comme deuxième exercice, place un pied devant l'autre en transférant le poids de ton corps de l'arrière vers l'avant (mouvement de va-et-vient). Pour chacun de ces exercices, réalise à quel point le pied qui supporte le poids du corps s'alourdit, tandis que l'autre s'allège.

Exercice 3 : Transmission du mouvement du centre du corps vers le bras

Lorsque tu fais un mouvement, tu dois sentir qu'il part du centre du corps et qu'il se termine en **périphérie** (bras). Par exemple, si tu lances une balle ou un ballon, le bon mouvement consiste à transférer ton poids de la jambe arrière vers la jambe avant en même temps que tu exécutes une rotation du bassin, puis des épaules et, finalement, de l'avant-bras. Ce faisant, tu transmets le mouvement depuis le centre du corps vers le bras lanceur.

Périphérie
Surface extérieure d'un volume.

Pour pratiquer cette manœuvre, refais les exercices de transfert de poids (voir les exercices 1 et 2 à la page 40) en ajoutant une rotation du bassin. Commence par transférer ton poids sur une jambe, puis tourne le bassin. Lorsque ce mouvement devient facile, ajoute un mouvement de lancer au-dessus de la tête. Fais l'exercice d'abord devant un miroir, puis sans miroir et, finalement, les yeux fermés.

Cette habileté à transmettre le mouvement du corps vers le bras est indispensable pour ménager tes articulations. Le stress de l'effort – dans ce cas-ci, le lancer d'une balle, est alors réparti sur plusieurs articulations, et non sur une seule – comme cela se produit lorsqu'on effectue un lancer ou une frappe seulement avec le bras.

C. Apprendre à faire des mouvements lents

La vitesse tue la précision. Par exemple, t'initier au coup droit au tennis en essayant de frapper la balle de toutes tes forces risque d'augmenter davantage ta frustration que ton habileté à bien frapper la balle. En faisant le même geste lentement, ton cerveau enregistre plus facilement les différentes séquences du mouvement. Un bon truc consiste à exécuter un nouveau mouvement au ralenti devant un miroir. Lorsque le geste devient plus coulant, tu peux augmenter ta vitesse d'exécution (fais-le d'abord en trois secondes, ensuite en deux secondes, puis en une seconde).

D. Connaître le bon mouvement et le répéter plusieurs fois

Pour améliorer l'exécution d'un mouvement, il faut apprendre à le faire correctement et, ensuite, s'y exercer. C'est pourquoi il est souvent préférable de suivre un cours. Tenter d'apprendre toi-même à pratiquer un nouveau sport risque de faire en sorte que tu n'exécutes pas les mouvements de la bonne manière, ce qui, à la longue, pourrait entraîner des blessures. Ton cours d'éducation physique et à la santé te permet justement d'apprendre les bons mouvements. Comme il s'agit, la plupart du temps, de mouvements appris, et non innés, la pratique répétitive est inévitable et nécessaire à la progression. N'abandonne pas, même si tes mouvements manquent de coordination au début : c'est normal. À force de le répéter, le mouvement va se raffiner et, bientôt, tu l'exécuteras sans même y penser.

E. Pratiquer l'imagerie mentale

Cette méthode consiste à visualiser de façon claire et précise, dans sa tête, le mouvement à exécuter. C'est ce que fait, par exemple, Alexandre Despatie quand il reste immobile sur la planche pendant quelques secondes avant d'exécuter son plongeon. Il repasse dans son cerveau le film du plongeon à exécuter. Il en imagine toutes les séquences jusqu'à son entrée dans l'eau.

Tu peux faire la même chose lorsque tu apprends un nouveau mouvement ou que tu veux te préparer à l'exécuter. Que ce soit le tir en suspension au basketball ou le smash au badminton, imagine que tu fais le mouvement dans ta tête en fermant les yeux et en recréant le plus précisément possible tous les gestes que tu feras. Tu verras : ton mouvement va devenir mieux coordonné et plus fluide. Tu te sentiras plus en confiance et tu seras mieux concentré ou mieux concentrée sur ton action le moment venu.

Visualiser de façon claire et précise, dans sa tête, le mouvement à exécuter

En rafale

Légendes urbaines sur le sport et les blessures

Légende. L'entraînement avec poids et haltères est une activité dangereuse qui peut engendrer des blessures chez les jeunes.

Réalité. L'entraînement avec poids et haltères est sécuritaire lorsqu'il est fait sous la supervision d'une personne compétente.

C'est pourquoi **la supervision par un entraîneur qualifié ou une entraîneuse qualifiée est nécessaire** afin d'assurer une évaluation des capacités de l'athlète, une bonne exécution des mouvements ainsi qu'une progression adéquate des charges et du volume d'entraînement.

Légende. Deux adolescents du même âge sont au même niveau de maturité.

Réalité. Il peut y avoir une différence de maturité biologique pouvant aller jusqu'à quatre ans entre deux individus du même âge. En effet, l'âge où les adolescents atteignent leur vitesse maximale de croissance diffère d'un individu à l'autre. Malgré ces variations, les experts estiment que la vitesse maximale de croissance est atteinte chez la majorité des adolescents vers l'âge de 15 ans.

Un sondage effectué auprès de jeunes de 13 à 16 ans dans des écoles britanniques rapporte que, pour 100 heures d'entraînement en musculation, 0,012 **blessure** est répertoriée, en comparaison avec 0,8 et 0,14 **blessure** pour 100 heures de pratique de rugby et de soccer, respectivement.

Ces résultats sont similaires à ceux d'une autre étude qui note une incidence de blessure de 0,9 % chez 551 adolescents réalisant un entraînement en force, comparativement à 2 % chez 681 joueurs de soccer de 6 à 17 ans et à 35 % chez 5128 joueurs de football de 8 à 15 ans. Comme ces études le démontrent, toute pratique sportive comporte son risque de blessure.

Fais le point

1 Réponds aux questions suivantes concernant les blessures qui peuvent se produire lorsqu'on fait des activités sportives ou d'autres types d'activités physiques (ex. : aller à vélo chez des amis, corder du bois au chalet, etc.).

a) À partir des lectures que tu viens de faire, explique ce qu'est une blessure.

_____

_____

_____

_____

_____

b) T'es-tu déjà fait une blessure lors de la pratique d'une activité sportive ou d'une autre activité physique ? Si oui, explique brièvement les circonstances de cet incident et comment tu aurais pu l'éviter.

_____

_____

_____

_____

_____

_____

_____

c) Comment peut-on éviter de se blesser lors de la pratique d'une activité physique ?

_____

_____

_____

_____

_____

_____

2 Fais-tu partie des adolescents qui s'entraînent dans le but d'atteindre des objectifs un peu trop élevés ou, au contraire, de ceux qui ne bougent pas assez ?

a) Remplis le tableau suivant en y indiquant toutes les activités physiques que tu pratiques dans une journée, la durée de chaque activité ainsi que ton évaluation de l'intensité de l'effort que tu fournis.

Jour	Activités	Durée 1 = 30 MIN OU MOINS 2 = 30 MIN À 60 MIN 3 = 1 H ET +	Intensité de l'effort fourni 1 = FAIBLE 2 = MODÉRÉE 3 = ÉLEVÉE
Lundi			
Mardi			
Mercredi			
Jeudi			
Vendredi			
Samedi			
Dimanche			

b) D'après tes réponses, lequel des énoncés suivants te décrit le mieux ?

Je ne suis pas assez actif ou active. ☐

Je suis physiquement actif ou active. ☐

Je suis en surentraînement. ☐

c) Que peux-tu faire pour remédier à la situation si tu te trouves dans la catégorie des personnes qui ne sont pas assez actives ou qui sont en situation de surentraînement ?

_____

_____

_____

_____

_____

3 Dans les pages précédentes, on t'explique que l'imagerie mentale peut t'aider à apprendre un nouveau mouvement ou un geste technique. As-tu déjà mis cette méthode en pratique ? Si oui, explique dans quelle situation tu l'as fait. Si non, décris une activité dans laquelle tu pourrais en tirer profit.

_____

_____

_____

_____

_____

_____

4 Remplis la grille de mots entrecroisés ci-dessous à partir des descriptions ou questions qui suivent.

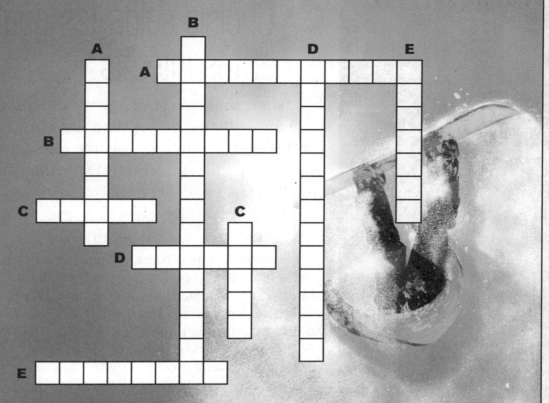

Verticalement

A. Je suis la partie de la chaussure qui laisse échapper la chaleur.

B. Une personne qui s'entraîne trop risque d'être en situation de…

C. Combien de couches de vêtements doit-on porter l'hiver pour s'assurer de ne pas avoir froid ou trop chaud ?

D. Quel type de matériel est le plus efficace pour la première couche de vêtements portés en hiver ?

E. Je suis une des causes des maux de dos chez les jeunes au Québec et ailleurs dans le monde.

Horizontalement

A. Quelles sont les chaussures recommandées dans les cours d'éducation physique ?

B. Comment nomme-t-on la blessure qui survient après avoir répété souvent le même geste ?

C. Quel est le sigle de l'association qui établit les normes de sécurité qu'un équipement doit respecter ?

D. Dans quelle partie du corps le mouvement doit-il être amorcé pour augmenter l'efficacité du geste moteur ?

E. Comment nomme-t-on l'inflammation du fascia plantaire ?

1.5 Choisis selon tes goûts et tes intérêts

Sébastien pratique le taekwondo depuis l'âge de 9 ans. Quand on lui demande pourquoi, sa réponse est spontanée : « Parce que j'aime ça ! » Alexandra, elle, a découvert le volleyball alors qu'elle était en 1re secondaire. Si on lui pose la même question, on obtient la même réponse : elle aime jouer au volleyball.

Ne cherche plus la toute première condition pour être physiquement actif ou active : il faut aimer l'activité qu'on pratique ; ce qui signifie avoir du plaisir, un plaisir qui nous transporte pendant une heure ou deux au-delà du train-train quotidien ! Dans ces conditions, il est certain que tu vas continuer à pratiquer cette activité.

Au contraire, si tu en es à pratiquer une activité juste parce qu'on t'a dit qu'il fallait que tu sois plus actif ou plus active, ou encore pour faire plaisir, disons, à tes parents, ça ne sera pas long avant que tu ne laisses tout tomber.

Si tu ne pratiques aucune activité physique

Demande-toi pourquoi. Peut-être te décourages-tu rapidement quand vient le temps d'apprendre un nouveau mouvement ? Peut-être as-tu déjà eu de mauvaises expériences en pratiquant un sport ou une activité physique (ex. : rejet par tes pairs, trop de compétitions, trop d'entraînement, etc.) ? Peut-être n'as-tu tout simplement pas d'intérêt pour l'activité physique ? C'est une bonne question, car si c'est le cas, il est certain que cela ne t'attirera pas. Se peut-il aussi que tu n'aies pas trouvé d'activité qui te plaise parce que tu ne sais pas encore très bien qui tu es ? Pour mieux connaître tes goûts, fais le test à la page 50. Ensuite, de deux choses l'une : ou tu comprendras encore mieux pourquoi tu aimes l'activité que tu pratiques, ou il te sera plus facile de choisir la bonne activité, celle qui collera à tes goûts et à tes intérêts.

Tout bien réfléchi !

Tu sais qu'il existe une grande variété d'activités physiques que tu pourrais pratiquer. Mais as-tu déjà réfléchi à celles qui te conviendraient le mieux selon ton caractère, tes traits de personnalité ou ton tempérament ?

1 Coche la case qui représente le mieux ta situation sur l'échelle de chacun des traits de caractère énumérés dans le tableau ci-dessous.

	Plus comme ceci ←	Entre les deux	Plus comme cela →	
Sociable	☐ ☐	☐	☐ ☐	**Solitaire**
J'aime être avec les gens, interagir et faire des choses avec les autres. Je n'aime pas faire les choses seul ou seule.				Je préfère faire les choses seul ou seule. J'aime la solitude. Les interactions sociales me fatiguent.
Spontané	☐ ☐	☐	☐ ☐	**Organisé**
J'adore faire les choses sous l'impulsion du moment. Je suis très spontané ou spontanée. Je me fatigue rapidement de la routine.				J'aime planifier et sentir que je maîtrise la situation. Je veux savoir ce qui vient ensuite. J'aime la routine et je n'aime pas les surprises.
Intrinsèquement motivé	☐ ☐	☐	☐ ☐	**Extrinsèquement motivé**
Je me motive entièrement moi-même. J'ai beaucoup de volonté. Je ne compte pas sur les autres pour m'encourager.				J'ai besoin d'aide pour faire des choses difficiles. Il faut que je me récompense et qu'on m'encourage pour persévérer.
Compétitif	☐ ☐	☐	☐ ☐	**Coopératif**
J'aime les jeux compétitifs. Ma performance est meilleure quand je suis en compétition. La compétition met du piquant dans le jeu.				J'évite les situations compétitives. La compétition me perturbe et nuit à ma performance. Je trouve rarement du plaisir dans la compétition.
Combatif	☐ ☐	☐	☐ ☐	**Doux**
Je suis une personne énergique et assurée. J'agis. J'écarte les obstacles. Je m'organise pour satisfaire mes besoins.				Je suis facile à vivre et détendu ou détendue, et je fais parfois peu d'efforts pour satisfaire mes besoins. Je déteste l'agressivité et j'évite les affrontements.
Concentré	☐ ☐	☐	☐ ☐	**Distrait**
Je me concentre facilement et longtemps sur une tâche. J'aime être absorbé ou absorbée par ce que je fais.				Je perds facilement ma concentration. Mon esprit vagabonde. Je préfère faire plusieurs choses en même temps. J'ai de la difficulté à me concentrer sur une seule tâche.
Amateur de risques	☐ ☐	☐	☐ ☐	**Prudent**
Je recherche les sensations fortes. J'aime l'aventure. Je suis prêt ou prête à prendre des risques pour faire des choses qui m'attirent.				J'évite de prendre des risques. Je préfère être en sécurité que de me retrouver dans une mauvaise situation, même si cela signifie que je ne ferai pas des choses qui m'attirent. Je suis une personne prudente.

Source : ©2004, James GAVIN, Ph. D., tiré de Richard CHEVALIER, *Kiné-Santé*, ERPI, vol. 6, n° 5, mars 2005.

2 Si tu reprends les traits de caractère qui te définissent le mieux et que tu observes le tableau suivant, tu verras les activités physiques qui pourraient le mieux te convenir.

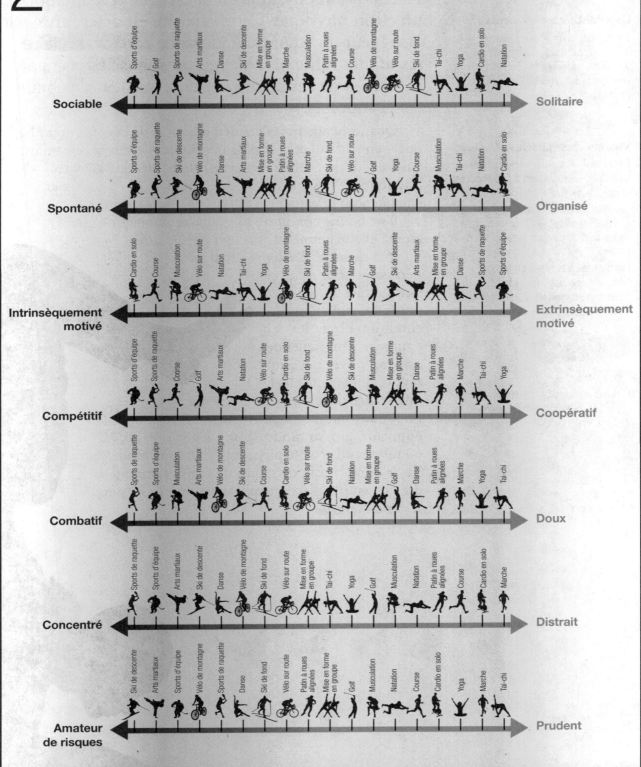

Endurance cardiovasculaire

Capacité du cœur et des poumons de fournir, pendant un certain temps, un effort modéré qui fait travailler l'ensemble des muscles de manière dynamique.

Vigueur des muscles

Capacité d'un muscle à être endurant ou fort, ou mieux encore, à être endurant et fort à la fois.

Les muscles travaillent en **endurance** lorsqu'ils répètent pendant un certain temps une contraction avec un effort modéré.

Les muscles travaillent en **force** lorsqu'ils développent une forte **tension** au moment d'une contraction maximale de courte durée.

Tension

État des muscles qui subissent un étirement ou un raccourcissement de leurs fibres.

1.6 Ta condition physique

La condition physique est la capacité d'adaptation à un effort physique. Cette capacité est déterminée par la vigueur du cœur ou **endurance cardiovasculaire** (as-tu du souffle?), la **vigueur des muscles** (as-tu de la force et de l'endurance?) ainsi que leur flexibilité (es-tu souple?).

Quand tu améliores ces déterminants de la condition physique – en particulier et le plus important, l'endurance cardiovasculaire – tu profites des nombreux bienfaits de l'activité physique sur la santé physique et mentale, et tu gagnes en énergie pour effectuer tes activités de tous les jours.

Une bonne condition physique te donne un autre atout: elle te permet d'effectuer plus rapidement la quantité d'activité physique nécessaire pour rester en santé. Voici pourquoi: une bonne condition physique t'autorise à pratiquer des activités physiques à un niveau d'intensité élevé. Or, une séance de 30 minutes d'activité physique pratiquée à une intensité élevée équivaut, grosso modo, à une séance de 50 à 60 minutes d'activité physique d'intensité modérée. Tu as donc besoin de moins de temps pour atteindre la quantité d'activité physique nécessaire pour rester en santé.

Tu peux déterminer le niveau d'intensité d'une activité physique en te basant sur certains signes physiques facilement observables, comme le pouls, la respiration et la chaleur dégagée par ton corps en mouvement.

Concrètement, une activité physique est pratiquée à une INTENSITÉ MODÉRÉE quand :

- Ton pouls est nettement plus élevé qu'au repos (au moins 60 battements de plus à la minute).
- Ta respiration est plus rapide.
- Tu commences à avoir chaud, voire à transpirer.

Une activité physique est pratiquée à une INTENSITÉ ÉLEVÉE quand :

- Ton pouls est beaucoup plus élevé qu'au repos (au moins 80 battements de plus à la minute).
- Ta respiration est très rapide.
- Tu as très chaud et tu transpires, peut-être même beaucoup.

Il y a une autre façon, sur laquelle nous reviendrons plus loin, de déterminer l'intensité d'une activité physique : en connaissant sa **zone d'entraînement cardiovasculaire**.

Zone d'entraînement cardiovasculaire

Zone qui correspond à une intensité modérée de l'effort, soit le niveau d'intensité nécessaire pour améliorer ou maintenir à un niveau satisfaisant son endurance cardiovasculaire lors de la pratique d'une activité physique ou d'un sport.

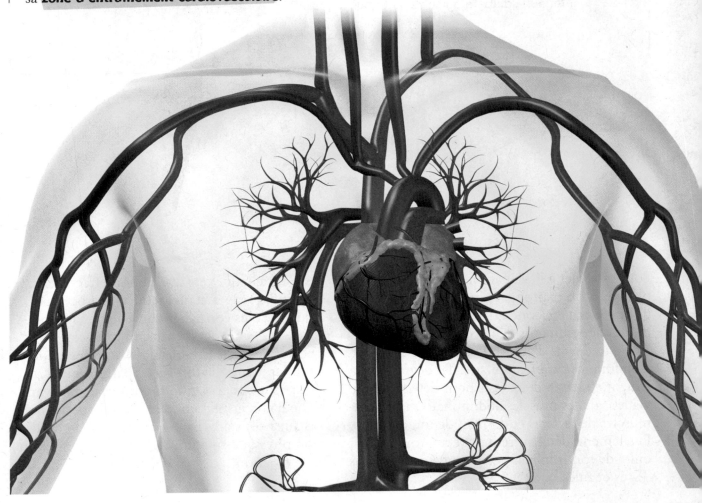

Bilan de ta condition physique

❶ Évalue ta condition physique.

Voici ta fiche de condition physique.

Ton poids : _____ kg   Âge : _____ ans

Ta taille : _____ cm   Fille ☐ Garçon ☐

As-tu une contre-indication médicale en rapport avec le test d'endurance (ex. : problèmes cardiaques, asthme sévère, étourdissements, handicap physique aux membres inférieurs, diabète ou autres) ? Si oui, laquelle ?

_____

(preuve médicale requise et signature du parent)

_____

Pour procéder à l'évaluation de ta condition physique, on te propose cinq tests. Chacun de ces tests a été conçu dans le but d'évaluer un des déterminants de la condition physique. Ainsi, tu devras d'abord te soumettre à un test d'endurance cardiovasculaire. Tu devras également effectuer deux tests pour déterminer la vigueur de tes muscles abdominaux et celle des muscles de tes bras et du haut de ton corps. Finalement, deux autres tests établiront la flexibilité de ton tronc en position assise, puis celle de tes épaules.

Pour chaque test que tu dois effectuer, on t'indique le matériel requis, la procédure à suivre et les consignes particulières à respecter, le cas échéant. De plus, tu trouveras pour chacun des tests le tableau des normes établies pour les jeunes de ton âge, à partir duquel tu pourras te situer. On te fournit également une fiche d'enregistrement de tes résultats. Tu pourras ainsi constater l'amélioration de ta condition physique au cours de l'application de ton plan d'action.

A Évalue ton endurance cardiovasculaire.

Il existe plusieurs tests pour évaluer ce déterminant important de la condition physique. Nous t'en présentons deux : le test des 12 minutes et le test navette. Ton enseignant ou ton enseignante te précisera celui que tu passeras. Il pourrait s'agir aussi d'un autre test, qui n'est pas décrit ici.

Le test des 12 minutes

CE QU'IL FAUT

- Un chronomètre ou une montre.
- Un parcours plat dont la longueur, en mètres, est connue (ex. : piste d'athlétisme, périmètre d'un gymnase, terrain de football ou tout autre circuit dont on a préalablement mesuré la longueur).

> Idéalement, afin de trouver le bon rythme de course et de te familiariser avec la distance que tu peux parcourir en 12 minutes, tu devrais d'abord faire un essai témoin quelques jours avant le vrai test.

CE QUE TU DOIS FAIRE

- Bien t'hydrater avant le test en prenant de petites quantités d'eau au moins 20 minutes avant de débuter l'activité.
- Parcourir en joggant (ou en marchant de temps à autre si tu ne peux pas garder le rythme du jogging tout au long du parcours) la plus grande distance possible en 12 minutes.

LES CONSIGNES À RESPECTER

- Arrêter le test si :
  - Tu te sens étourdi ou étourdie.
  - Tu es très essoufflé ou très essoufflée.
  - Tu ressens un malaise inhabituel.

CE QU'IL NE FAUT PAS FAIRE

- Boire en grande quantité juste avant le test.
- Prendre un gros repas moins de 90 minutes avant le test.
- Partir trop rapidement.
- Changer de rythme trop souvent : il faut essayer de garder une vitesse constante pendant les 12 minutes.
- Arrêter trop rapidement à la fin du test : il faut, au contraire, marcher lentement pendant une ou deux minutes.

TON RÉSULTAT

plan d'action p. 96

Une fois le test terminé, consulte le tableau ci-dessous pour déterminer ton niveau d'endurance cardiovasculaire en fonction de la distance parcourue. Indique ensuite ton résultat dans l'espace prévu plus bas, puis reporte-le dans ton plan d'action, le cas échéant.

Sexe et âge	Endurance cardiovasculaire			
	Très élevée	Élevée	Moyenne	Sous la moyenne
Garçons 12-14 ans	> 2700 m	2400 m - 2700 m	2200 m - 2399 m	< 2200 m
Filles 12-14 ans	> 2000 m	1900 m - 2000 m	1600 m - 1899 m	< 1600 m

Source : K. H. COOPER, *The Aerobics Program for Total Well-being: Exercise, Diet, Emotional Balance*, New York, Bantam Books, 1985.

Date du test 1
(année, mois et jour) :
20_____ / _____ / _____

Ton résultat : _____

Ton niveau d'endurance :
_____

Date du test 2
(année, mois et jour) :
20_____ / _____ / _____

Ton résultat : _____

Ton niveau d'endurance :
_____

Date du test 3
(année, mois et jour) :
20_____ / _____ / _____

Ton résultat : _____

Ton niveau d'endurance :
_____

Le test navette

CE QU'IL FAUT

- Système audio et extrait sonore pré-enregistré du test qui émet un bip déterminant la vitesse de la course.
- Deux lignes parallèles bien visibles et espacées de 20 mètres dans le gymnase.

CE QUE TU DOIS FAIRE

- Après une période d'échauffement, courir le plus longtemps possible en faisant des allers-retours entre les deux lignes. La vitesse, annoncée par le bip, augmente de 0,5 km/h toutes les minutes (une minute correspond à un palier), ce qui t'oblige à augmenter ta vitesse de course. Le test prend fin quand tu n'es plus capable de terminer le palier en cours ou de suivre le rythme imposé par les bips (retard de 1 m à 2 m que tu ne peux pas rattraper).

LES CONSIGNES À RESPECTER

- Arrêter le test si :
  - Tu te sens étourdi ou étourdie.
  - Tu es très essoufflé ou essoufflée.
  - Tu ressens un malaise inhabituel.

CE QU'IL NE FAUT PAS FAIRE

- Boire en grande quantité juste avant le test.
- Prendre un gros repas moins de 90 minutes avant le test.
- Arrêter trop rapidement à la fin du test : il faut, au contraire, marcher lentement pendant une ou deux minutes.

TON RÉSULTAT

- Une fois le test terminé, consulte le tableau ci-dessous pour déterminer ton niveau d'endurance cardiovasculaire en fonction du dernier palier atteint. Indique ensuite ton résultat dans l'espace prévu plus bas, puis reporte-le dans ton plan d'action, le cas échéant.

plan d'action p. 96

Endurance cardiovasculaire			
Garçons	**11-12 ans**	**13-14 ans**	**15-16 ans**
Très élevée	8 et plus*	9 et plus	10 et plus
Élevée	6,5-7,5	7,5-8,5	8,5-9,5
Moyenne	5-6	6-7	7-8
Sous la moyenne	4,5 et moins	5,5 et moins	6,5 et moins
Filles	**11-12 ans**	**13-14 ans**	**15-16 ans**
Très élevée	6 et plus	6,5 et plus	6,5 et plus
Élevée	5-5,5	5-6	5-6
Moyenne	4-4,5	4-4,5	4-4,5
Sous la moyenne	3,5 et moins	3,5 et moins	3,5 et moins

*Dernier palier atteint.

Source : Adapté de Olds T. TOMKINSON, G. LEGER, L. G. CAZORLA, « Worldwide Variation in the Performance of Children and Adolescents : An Analysis of 109 Studies of the 20-m Shuttle Run Test in 37 Countries », *J Sports Sci*, 2006, 24(10) : 1025 – 1038.

Date du test 1
(année, mois et jour) :

20_____/_____/_____

Ton résultat : _____

Ton niveau d'endurance :

_____

Date du test 2
(année, mois et jour) :

20_____/_____/_____

Ton résultat : _____

Ton niveau d'endurance :

_____

Date du test 3
(année, mois et jour) :

20_____/_____/_____

Ton résultat : _____

Ton niveau d'endurance :

_____

B Évalue la vigueur de tes muscles abdominaux.

CE QU'IL FAUT

- Un tapis d'exercice au sol.
- Un chronomètre ou une montre.

CE QUE TU DOIS FAIRE

- Exécuter en une minute le plus grand nombre de demi-redressements assis en suivant les directives ci-dessous, les pieds non tenus. Pour effectuer ce test :
  - Allonge-toi sur le dos, les bras le long du corps en déposant tes mains sur tes cuisses, les genoux pliés suffisamment pour avoir les pieds à plat au sol.
  - Pointe le menton vers la poitrine.

- Contracte tes abdominaux afin que le bas de ton dos colle au sol pendant le test, un peu comme si tu voulais créer une empreinte au sol.
- Redresse le tronc en faisant glisser les mains jusqu'aux genoux de façon que tes omoplates décollent du sol. Il est très important d'expirer pendant le lever du tronc.
- Reviens au sol, puis répète le mouvement.

- Tu peux ralentir la cadence ou t'arrêter quelques secondes si ton corps te le demande. Lorsque tu n'arrives plus à dé-coller complètement les omoplates du sol, le test est terminé.

TON RÉSULTAT

Une fois le test terminé, consulte le tableau ci-dessous pour déterminer la vigueur de tes muscles en fonction du nombre de demi-redressements effectués. Indique ensuite ton résultat dans l'espace prévu plus bas.

Vigueur des abdominaux				
Garçons	12 ans	13 ans	14 ans	15 ans
Très élevée	64	59	62	75
Élevée	54	51	54	67
Moyenne	32	39	40	45
Sous la moyenne	22	28	24	26
Filles	12 ans	13 ans	14 ans	15 ans
Très élevée	50	59	48	38
Élevée	43	50	41	35
Moyenne	30	40	30	26
Sous la moyenne	19	22	20	15

Source : Normes provenant du programme *Élèves en forme*, Association régionale du sport étudiant de Québec et Chaudière-Appalaches.

Date du test 1
(année, mois et jour) :
20_____ / _____ / _____

Ton résultat : _____

Ta vigueur musculaire :
_____

Date du test 2
(année, mois et jour) :
20_____ / _____ / _____

Ton résultat : _____

Ta vigueur musculaire :
_____

Date du test 3
(année, mois et jour) :
20_____ / _____ / _____

Ton résultat : _____

Ta vigueur musculaire :
_____

c Évalue la vigueur des muscles de tes bras et du haut de ton corps.

CE QU'IL FAUT

- Un tapis d'exercice au sol.
- Un chronomètre ou une montre.

CE QUE TU DOIS FAIRE

- Exécuter, sans limite de temps, le plus grand nombre de tractions (*push-ups*), c'est-à-dire des flexions et extensions complètes des bras avec le corps allongé. Le test prend fin quand tu n'es plus capable d'exécuter une traction complète sans que ton dos ne se courbe vers le sol.

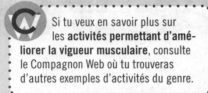
Si tu veux en savoir plus sur les **activités permettant d'améliorer la vigueur musculaire**, consulte le Compagnon Web où tu trouveras d'autres exemples d'activités du genre.

TON RÉSULTAT

Une fois le test terminé, consulte le tableau ci-dessous pour déterminer la vigueur de tes muscles en fonction du nombre de tractions complétées. Indique ensuite ton résultat dans l'espace prévu plus bas.

Vigueur des bras et du haut du corps				
Garçons	**12 ans**	**13 ans**	**14 ans**	**15 ans**
Très élevée	31	39	40	42
Élevée	28	36	32	37
Moyenne	18	24	24	30
Sous la moyenne	9	11	13	20
Filles	**12 ans**	**13 ans**	**14 ans**	**15 ans**
Très élevée	20	21	20	20
Élevée	17	17	16	20
Moyenne	10	11	10	15
Sous la moyenne	2	4	3	7

Source : Normes provenant du programme *Élèves en forme*, Association régionale du sport étudiant de Québec et Chaudière-Appalaches.

Date du test 1
(année, mois et jour) :
20 _____/_____/_____

Ton résultat : _____

Ta vigueur musculaire :
_____

Date du test 2
(année, mois et jour) :
20 _____/_____/_____

Ton résultat : _____

Ta vigueur musculaire :
_____

Date du test 3
(année, mois et jour) :
20 _____/_____/_____

Ton résultat : _____

Ta vigueur musculaire :
_____

D   Évalue la flexibilité de ton tronc en position assise.

CE QU'IL FAUT

- Un mur ou un meuble solide sur lequel tu peux appuyer tes pieds.

CE QUE TU DOIS FAIRE

- Te mettre en position assise avec les jambes tendues et les pieds espacés de 25 cm à 30 cm, appuyés contre un mur (ou un meuble).
- Pencher le tronc lentement vers l'avant, sans plier les genoux.

- Si tu ne peux pas toucher le mur du bout des doigts, c'est que tes mollets et tes muscles ischio-jambiers (situés à l'arrière des cuisses) sont plutôt raides.
- Si tu touches le mur du bout des doigts ou, mieux, avec les poings, alors Bravo ! Cela signifie que ton tronc est flexible quand tu te penches vers l'avant.

TON RÉSULTAT

Une fois le test terminé, consulte le tableau ci-contre pour déterminer la flexibilité de tes muscles en fonction de la position atteinte. Indique ensuite ton résultat dans l'espace prévu plus bas.

Position atteinte	Flexibilité
Les paumes des mains touchent le mur.	Très élevée
Les poings touchent le mur.	Élevée
Les bouts des doigts touchent le mur.	Moyenne
Les bouts des doigts ne touchent pas le mur.	Sous la moyenne

Date du test 1
(année, mois et jour) :
20_____ / _____ / _____

Ton résultat : _____

Ta flexibilité musculaire :
_____

Date du test 2
(année, mois et jour) :
20_____ / _____ / _____

Ton résultat : _____

Ta flexibilité musculaire :
_____

Date du test 3
(année, mois et jour) :
20_____ / _____ / _____

Ton résultat : _____

Ta flexibilité musculaire :
_____

E Évalue la flexibilité de tes épaules.

CE QU'IL FAUT

- Un bâton.

CE QUE TU DOIS FAIRE

- Te coucher sur le ventre, menton collé au sol, bras allongés devant toi, mains écartées à la largeur des épaules.

- Prendre le bâton et, **sans fléchir les poignets ou les coudes, ni décoller le menton du sol** (position de départ), lever le bâton le plus haut possible (position du test). Un ou une partenaire peut évaluer la hauteur à laquelle tu lèves le bâton.

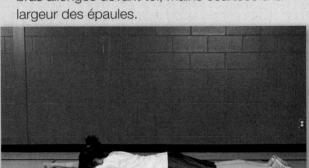

TON RÉSULTAT

Une fois le test terminé, consulte le tableau ci-contre pour déterminer la flexibilité de tes muscles en fonction de la position atteinte. Indique ensuite ton résultat dans l'espace prévu plus bas.

Position atteinte	Flexibilité
Bâton levé nettement au-dessus de la tête.	Très élevée
Bâton levé juste au-dessus de la tête.	Élevée
Bâton levé au niveau de la tête.	Moyenne
Bâton levé à peine au-dessus du sol.	Sous la moyenne

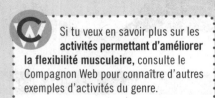

Si tu veux en savoir plus sur les **activités permettant d'améliorer la flexibilité musculaire,** consulte le Compagnon Web pour connaître d'autres exemples d'activités du genre.

Date du test 1
(année, mois et jour) :

20 _____ / _____ / _____

Ton résultat : _____

Ta flexibilité musculaire :

_____

Date du test 2
(année, mois et jour) :

20 _____ / _____ / _____

Ton résultat : _____

Ta flexibilité musculaire :

_____

Date du test 3
(année, mois et jour) :

20 _____ / _____ / _____

Ton résultat : _____

Ta flexibilité musculaire :

_____

❚❚ Fais le bilan de ta condition physique actuelle.

À la suite de la première évaluation de ta condition physique, indique par un ✔ tes points forts et tes points faibles.

	Endurance cardiovasculaire	Vigueur des abdominaux	Vigueur des bras et du haut du corps	Flexibilité des épaules	Flexibilité du tronc
Points forts					
Points faibles					

N'oublie pas de reporter ton niveau d'endurance car-diovasculaire à la première étape de ton plan d'action.

plan d'action   p. 96

Pour t'améliorer dans ces tests, n'hésite pas à t'exercer en les répétant souvent.

RENCONTRE AVEC

Marina Gagnon,
patineuse artistique

Marina étudie en 5e secondaire et elle pratique le patinage artistique depuis 8 ans. Elle est de niveau Junior Argent, catégorie Star. Elle enseigne également le patinage artistique aux jeunes de trois ans et plus, garçons et filles.

Son rêve : Pratiquer un métier en relation avec le patin ou le sport en général. Elle aimerait devenir entraîneuse de patinage artistique pour transmettre sa passion aux autres et, si possible, devenir physiothérapeute et suivre une équipe sportive dans ses déplacements.

Sains et actifs : *Quelle activité physique pratiques-tu de façon régulière ?*

M.G. : Je pratique le patinage artistique depuis huit ans.

Sains et actifs : *Qu'est-ce qui te fait tant aimer le patinage artistique ?*

M.G. : J'aime pratiquer ce sport parce que j'aime m'améliorer en le faisant. Ce n'est pas un sport d'équipe, donc je ne me sens en compétition avec personne. En même temps, ça me permet de dépenser l'énergie que j'ai en trop. Puisqu'on a beaucoup de devoirs en 5e secondaire, ce sport me permet de me détendre, de voir autre chose et de parler avec d'autres personnes.

> « Ce n'est pas un sport d'équipe, donc je ne me sens en compétition avec personne »

Sains et actifs : *En quoi la pratique de ton sport influence-t-elle ton mode de vie ?*

M.G. : Pour faire du patin, il faut que tu sois en santé et que tu fasses attention à toi. Mais, je pense que c'est un sport qui peut s'adresser à n'importe qui, vu que tu peux aller à ton rythme : il n'y a pas un poids fixe que tu es obligé d'avoir. Moi, je fais attention à mon poids, j'essaye de manger santé souvent. Je ne me verrais pas ne pas patiner présentement. Mais, c'est l'école qui passe en premier et, ensuite, le patin. Avec le patin, j'ai beaucoup d'entraînement, donc ça prend beaucoup de place dans ma vie. Avec mes amis, on ne pratique pas nécessairement le même sport. On parle du patin, mais on parle surtout du sport en général. Je suis capable de me passer du patin une semaine ou deux, mais après, je m'en ennuie. L'important, c'est d'avoir un bon équilibre entre les études, le patin et les rencontres avec mes amis.

Sains et actifs : *Dans ta vie, quelle place occupe la discipline ?*

M.G. : Il faut s'imposer un contrôle sur soi-même et ne pas se fâcher si on ne réussit pas un saut la première fois. Ça prend beaucoup de pratique et il ne faut pas se décourager. Ce n'est pas tout le monde qui évolue au même rythme. Pour ce qui est du stress lors des compétitions, c'est difficile à gérer parce qu'il y a beaucoup de gens qui te regardent. Tu as une seule chance : si tu ne l'as pas, tu ne l'as pas ; et si tu l'as, tu l'as.

On a environ huit compétitions par année, et il faut toujours essayer de performer. Pour contrôler son stress, on se dit qu'on a travaillé toute l'année pour cette compétition. Peu importe ce qui arrive, on veut donner notre 100 %. Si on tombe, on se dit : « Ce n'est pas grave, j'ai travaillé fort pour en arriver là et je ne veux pas gâcher tout le reste de mon programme pour une erreur. » Donc, on essaie de se concentrer encore plus sur les autres mouvements qui vont suivre.

Le patin nécessite beaucoup d'heures d'entraînement et puisque la 5e secondaire est exigeante, je commence à avoir plus de difficultés à gérer mon temps. Je veux étudier en sciences pures au collège. Je suis des cours de maths 536, de chimie et de physique. C'est beaucoup d'heures d'étude alors parfois, il faut que je mette de côté le patin, même si ça ne me fait pas plaisir. Pour réussir à gérer mon temps, j'essaie d'estimer le nombre d'heures qu'il me faudra pour faire mes devoirs. J'essaie de les faire le soir même. Puisque je ne veux pas couper le patinage, je me dis que je dois en faire un peu chaque soir. Si je suis vraiment fatiguée, je vais me lever un peu plus tôt le lendemain matin pour terminer ce que j'avais à faire.

« Peu importe ce qui arrive, on veut donner notre 100 % »

Sains et actifs : *Quelle est ton opinion sur les substances nuisibles ?*

M.G. : Moi, je me dis qu'une personne qui se donne à fond dans un sport, c'est parce que, d'une certaine façon, elle veut être en santé. Si tu prends des substances nuisibles pour la santé, tu ne t'aides pas. Tu pratiques un sport, mais, dans le fond, avec les substances, tu élimines l'action que tu viens de faire. Les personnes qui sont dopées lors d'une épreuve sportive, oui, elles vont performer plus que les autres qui ne le sont pas, mais jusqu'à un certain point.

RENCONTRE AVEC

Sains et actifs : *Quel plan d'action t'es-tu donné pour t'aider et t'améliorer ?*

M.G. : Je n'ai pas beaucoup d'entraînement à faire en dehors de la glace. Quand je suis sur la glace, c'est souvent pour une période de deux heures. Mon temps est divisé habituellement en deux : je vais faire des sauts et, ensuite, de la danse. Je ne fais pas d'entraînement en gymnase, en dehors de la glace. Habituellement, on commence avec les sauts plus faciles et on augmente la difficulté.

Avec mon entraîneur, on se donne des défis précis et on essaie de s'améliorer à chaque compétition. Parfois, les compétitions sont assez rapprochées, donc c'est difficile. À l'école, je me donne aussi des défis personnels pour mes notes et j'essaie de les atteindre. J'aime relever des défis.

Pour les obstacles, quand tu as des blessures, tu ne peux pas continuer à t'améliorer ou à travailler autant. Mais, on fait des exercices, puis on essaie de continuer quand même. Lorsque les défis sont trop grands ou que les obstacles se multiplient, ce qui pourrait décourager n'importe qui, la meilleure solution, pour moi, c'est d'en parler avec ma mère et mon entraîneur. Ça m'aide.

« J'aime relever des défis »

Sains et actifs : *Crois-tu que ton mode de vie actuel aura une influence sur tes projets d'avenir ?*

M.G. : Je pense que oui, parce que, pour faire le travail que j'ai à faire à l'école, puis le travail au patin, les heures d'entraînement, il faut que je sois vraiment organisée. Il faut que mon horaire soit prévu, minute par minute. À l'école, je ne vois pas de différence en comparaison avec les autres années où je m'entraînais moins, parce que je fournis toujours les mêmes heures d'étude, soit une vingtaine d'heures par semaine, incluant toute la journée du dimanche.

Sains et actifs : *Qu'est-ce que la pratique de ton sport t'a permis de découvrir et de comprendre sur toi ?*

M.G. : Que je suis une personne qui aime voir le résultat de ses efforts. Que je suis une personne organisée et que j'aime beaucoup aider les autres, surtout ceux à qui je donne des cours.

J'ai aussi compris qu'il y a des parents qui sont très exigeants envers leurs enfants. Parfois, un enfant peut être talentueux dans un sport et avoir plus de difficultés dans un autre, ce qui est normal. Mais, ce ne sont pas tous les parents qui vont le comprendre du premier coup. Tout le monde évolue à son rythme. Un jour, on peut être rendu au même niveau, mais deux ans après, on est complètement différent. Parfois, on a l'impression que l'enfant ne veut pas vraiment être là, qu'il ne se sent pas à sa place et que c'est plus le rêve du parent de le voir progresser là-dedans. On voit que c'est plus le but du parent que celui de l'enfant.

« Je suis une personne qui aime voir le résultat de ses efforts »

Sains et actifs : *Crois-tu que la société doit encourager l'adoption d'un mode de vie sain et actif ?*

M.G. : Oui, parce que pour être actif, il faut faire du sport. Il y a des études qui prouvent que, quand tu fais du sport, tu es plus concentré dans tes études et tes devoirs en classe, puis tu es moins énervé. J'aime l'expression *un esprit sain dans un corps sain*. Ça résume ce que je disais avant. Oui, il faut s'entraîner mais, oui, il faut faire attention à notre santé aussi. Il faut que ça passe avant. Je pense que tout le monde pourrait faire un sport juste pour s'amuser. Juste en bougeant pendant une ou deux heures par semaine, on serait déjà capable de voir une différence.

« Tout le monde pourrait faire un sport juste pour s'amuser »

Sains et actifs : *Peux-tu me décrire comment les autres (ex. : ta meilleure amie, ton entraîneur) te perçoivent ?*

M.G. : Comme une fille perfectionniste qui aime aider et donner son conseil aux autres pour les aider à réussir. Je suis une personne qui aime écouter. Quand une personne a des problèmes, j'aime être là pour elle, pour lui apporter mon soutien.
Il y en a qui trouvent que je travaille trop dans les sports et dans les devoirs, c'est certain. Puisque j'aime avoir de bonnes notes à l'école, je me donne à fond, même si j'ai plus confiance en moi dans le patin qu'à l'école. Il y en a aussi qui trouvent que je suis une fille trop sage. Moi, je ne trouve pas ça important, parce que je ne me prive pas réellement. Entre l'école et le patin, j'ai le temps de voir mes amis. Je ne trouve pas que j'ai un mode de vie si dur que ça. J'ai quand même du temps pour moi.

« J'ai besoin du soutien de mes parents pour évoluer »

Sains et actifs : *Qu'est-ce qui est le plus important pour toi dans la vie ?*

M.G. : Ma famille, parce que j'ai besoin du soutien de mes parents pour évoluer. J'aime être entourée de gens et ne pas me sentir seule. Puisque je suis enfant unique, ma famille, mes grands-parents, ma mère et mon père sont vraiment importants pour moi. Aussi, au patin, j'aime avoir le commentaire des gens qui ne connaissent pas le patin, juste pour voir ce qu'ils en pensent à première vue. Parfois, ça fait du bien d'avoir une opinion autre qu'une opinion professionnelle.

« Tout le monde évolue à son rythme »

Sains et actifs : *Pourquoi est-il important d'avoir un mode de vie sain et actif ?*

M.G. : Tu peux voir les résultats de tes entraînements, souvent. Ce n'est pas comme des notes à l'école. Quelqu'un, à l'école, va peut-être valoir 40 % dans un examen. Mais, qu'il pratique n'importe quel sport, s'il est bon dans ce sport, ça va le motiver à continuer et ça va lui donner un but. Dans un sport d'équipe, tu peux encourager les autres, tu peux te défouler, tu peux laisser sortir ton énergie.
Je me dis que, si tu es bien dans ta peau, que tu te couches le soir et que tu as encore de l'énergie pour bouger et faire n'importe quoi, pourquoi ne pas t'engager dans un sport ou une activité avec tes amis ?
Le seul effet négatif que je peux voir c'est d'avoir moins de temps pour voir mes amis. Ça apporte aussi de la persévérance.
Dans la vie, il ne faut jamais se décourager, peu importe que tu aies un échec au départ.

« Tu peux te défouler »

Tu as maintenant de nouveaux défis

Maintenant que tu as déterminé un ou plusieurs défis, que dirais-tu de t'améliorer ? Tu en as envie, mais tu ne sais pas comment t'y prendre ? Allons-y de façon méthodique en commençant par le déterminant le plus important : l'endurance cardiovasculaire.

★ Si tu veux améliorer ton endurance cardiovasculaire, tu dois…

- D'abord, choisir une ou plusieurs activités aérobiques, c'est-à-dire des activités qui activent de façon modérée les grandes masses musculaires des cuisses et du bassin (ex. : marche rapide, course à pied, ski de fond, patin à roues alignées, raquette à neige, vélo, natation, etc.).

- Pratiquer ces activités à une intensité modérée pendant un minimum de 20 minutes consécutives, au moins 3 fois par semaine.

- T'assurer que l'intensité de l'activité aérobique est au moins modérée, en vérifiant de temps en temps ta fréquence cardiaque à l'effort.

Celle-ci doit se situer dans la zone d'entraînement cardiovasculaire que permet d'établir la formule suivante :

$(220 - \text{âge}) \times 75\% = $ fréquence cardiaque cible minimale ;

$(220 - \text{âge}) \times 85\% = $ fréquence cardiaque cible maximale.

> Par exemple, si tu as 13 ans, l'application de la formule donne ceci :
>
> Fréquence cardiaque cible (FCC) : $220 - 13 = 207$
>
> FCC minimale : $207 \times 75\% = 155$
>
> FCC maximale : $207 \times 85\% = 176$
>
> Cela signifie que, pendant ton effort cardiovasculaire, ta fréquence cardiaque devrait se situer entre 155 et 176 battements à la minute, soit entre 39 et 44 battements aux 15 secondes.

★ Si tu veux améliorer ta vigueur musculaire, tu dois…

- Choisir un exercice qui sollicite la région musculaire dont tu souhaites améliorer la vigueur (ex. : les cuisses, le ventre, les bras). Par exemple, si tu te situes sous la moyenne en ce qui a trait à la vigueur des muscles abdominaux, tu peux tout simplement reprendre l'exercice proposé comme test d'endurance (demi-redressements assis) pour entraîner et renforcer tes abdominaux.
- Répéter cet exercice pendant une minute, au moins trois fois par semaine (idéalement cinq fois).

★ Si tu veux améliorer ta flexibilité, tu dois…

- Choisir un ou plusieurs exercices d'étirement. Tu peux reprendre les exercices proposés comme tests de flexibilité.
- Maintenir la position d'étirement pendant un minimum de 20 secondes, faire une pause, puis recommencer l'exercice une seconde fois, au moins 3 fois par semaine (idéalement tous les jours).

Si tu veux en savoir plus sur les **divers exercices que tu peux faire pour amé-liorer ta vigueur musculaire et ta flexibilité et les exercices à éviter**, consulte le Compagnon Web où tu trouveras un répertoire d'exercices et un **modèle** que tu pourras utiliser pour élaborer ton programme personnel.

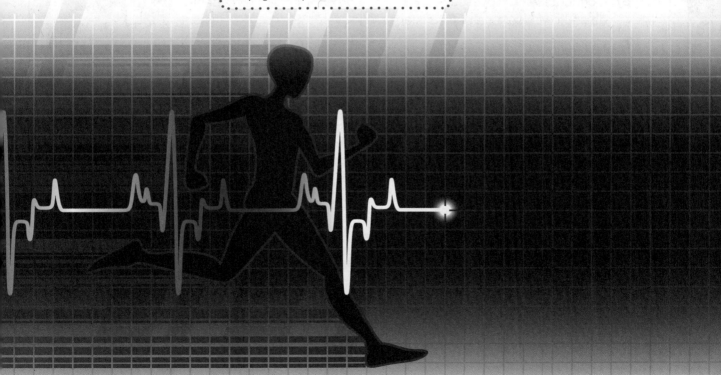

Fais le point

1   Selon toi, quel aspect dois-tu travailler en premier pour améliorer ta condition physique ? De quelle façon vas-tu t'y prendre ?

_____

_____

_____

_____

2   Indique si les énoncés suivants sont vrais ou faux en cochant les cases appropriées.

	VRAI	FAUX
a) Pour améliorer ta flexibilité, tu dois faire tes exercices au moins trois fois par semaine.	☐	☐
b) La meilleure position pour effectuer des redressements assis, c'est les mains derrière la nuque.	☐	☐
c) Pour améliorer ta vigueur musculaire, tu dois choisir des exercices qui font travailler des endroits précis.	☐	☐
d) L'endurance cardiovasculaire est le déterminant le moins important de la condition physique d'un individu.	☐	☐
e) L'endurance cardiovasculaire consiste à déterminer si tu es capable de courir vite sur une petite distance.	☐	☐
f) La flexibilité est le déterminant le plus important de la condition physique d'un individu.	☐	☐
g) La force musculaire se mesure par la capacité à effectuer des tâches de la vie quotidienne qui demandent d'exercer une certaine force.	☐	☐

3   Après avoir pratiqué une activité physique de façon soutenue, quels signes de bien-être physique et mental es-tu en mesure de constater dans ton organisme ? Énumères-en quelques-uns.

_____

_____

_____

_____

_____

Tout bien réfléchi !

Prends connaissance de ce que vit actuellement Jean-Luc et précise les conseils que tu lui donnerais.

Jean-Luc vient de passer les divers tests liés à sa condition physique. Il savait bien qu'il n'était pas la personne la plus en forme, mais il ne s'attendait pas à recevoir un tel diagnostic : il est en mauvaise condition physique. Il a décidé de se prendre en main et de faire 2 heures d'activité physique d'intensité élevée par jour, soit 30 minutes de vélo, 30 minutes de course à pied et 1 heure de natation. Les premiers jours, la motivation y était, mais vers la fin de la deuxième semaine, Jean-Luc a commencé à ressentir une grande fatigue. Il avait de la difficulté à accomplir les mêmes activités que la première semaine et, même après une bonne nuit de sommeil de huit heures, il se sentait fatigué en se levant le matin. Jean-Luc est en train d'aggraver sa condition physique plutôt que de l'améliorer.

_____
_____
_____
_____
_____
_____
_____
_____
_____
_____
_____
_____
_____
_____

② L'alimentation

Nutritionniste

Personne titulaire d'un diplôme universitaire en nutrition, qui se consacre à l'étude des aliments, de leur valeur nutritive, des réactions de l'organisme à la suite de leur ingestion, et des variations alimentaires chez les gens sains et les gens malades.

Pour en savoir plus sur la **façon d'établir le relevé de ce que tu manges**, tu peux consulter le Compagnon Web où tu trouveras un hyperlien te permettant d'accéder au site de Santé Canada.

Croissance oblige, la demande de ton corps en alimentation est très forte. Il se transforme et exige du carburant pour assurer ta croissance en taille et en poids. Il serait même possible que tu manges plus qu'un adulte pendant cette période : tu dois répondre à tes besoins en énergie, qui sont supérieurs.

Réponds-tu de façon adéquate aux demandes de ton corps ? Pour le savoir, tu dois d'abord connaître ce dont tu as besoin chaque jour. Le tableau qui suit t'indique les portions quotidiennes des aliments recommandées par les **nutritionnistes** de Santé Canada.

Un principe important à te rappeler dans tes choix alimentaires est de viser un bon équilibre et une bonne variété d'aliments.

Nombre de portions quotidiennes recommandées par Santé Canada pour des jeunes de ton âge

Légumes et fruits	6-7 portions	Lait et substituts	3-4 portions
Produits céréaliers	6 portions	Viandes et substituts	2 portions

Exemples de portions des différents groupes alimentaires

Carotte : 125 ml (1 grosse carotte)	Veau : 75 g
Banane : 1 banane moyenne	Poulet : 75 g
Céréales froides, grains entiers : 30 g	Poisson et fruits de mer, frais ou congelés : 75 g
Bagel, grains entiers : ½ bagel, 45 g	Houmous : 175 ml
Riz et pâtes alimentaires : 125 ml, cuits	Beurre d'arachide ou beurre de noix : 30 ml
Lait écrémé, 1 %, 2 % : 250 ml	Noix écalées : 60 ml
Fromage à pâte ferme (ex. : cheddar, Mozzarella, suisse, feta) : 50 g	Œufs : 2 œufs
Yogourt (nature ou aromatisé) : 175 g	

Source : Santé Canada, *Bien manger avec le Guide alimentaire canadien,* 2007.

Pour vérifier si tu nourris suffisamment ton corps, et surtout si tu le fais de la bonne façon, tu dois établir le relevé de ce que tu manges, grosso modo, chaque jour de la semaine, incluant la fin de semaine. Pour ce faire, tu peux utiliser le journal alimentaire proposé par Santé Canada, qu'on te présente ici.

		Légumes et fruits	Produits céréaliers	Laits et substituts	Viandes et substituts	Huile et autres matières grasses
Repas						
Déjeuner	=					
Dîner	=					
Souper	=					
Collations	=					
Somme du nombre de portions du Guide alimentaire	=					

Source : Santé Canada, *Bien manger avec le Guide alimentaire canadien*, 2007.

POUR EN SAVOIR PLUS

Pour savoir à quoi correspond une portion, consulte le site de Santé Canada : http://www.hc-sc.gc.ca

Pour obtenir une **copie de ce journal alimentaire**, consulte le Compagnon Web où tu pourras trouver une fiche reproductible te permettant de constituer ton journal alimentaire pour toute une semaine. Tu y trouveras aussi des exemples types de menus pour les adolescents.

2.1 Les nutriments

Tu sais maintenant que ton corps a besoin de plus de calories, de glucides, de lipides, de protéines, de vitamines et de minéraux.

Pour t'aider à bien comprendre la nécessité de chacun de ces éléments nutritifs, voyons comment ils s'organisent. Ils se regroupent en deux classes : les MACRONUTRIMENTS et les MICRO-NUTRIMENTS. Les macronutriments incluent les glucides, les lipides et les protéines, des *nutriments énergétiques*, et fournissent de l'énergie à l'organisme. Les micronutriments désignent les vitamines et les minéraux, et l'eau. Ce sont des *nutriments essentiels*. Ils ne produisent pas d'énergie, mais contribuent néanmoins au bon fonctionnement de l'organisme.

Lipides (gras)

À quoi ça sert ?
Entrent dans la constitution des membranes cellulaires et des fibres nerveuses. Fournissent jusqu'à 70 % de l'énergie du corps au repos. Facilitent l'absorption des vitamines liposolubles. Servent d'isolant contre le froid et de coussins protecteurs pour les organes.

Où en trouver ?
Bons gras (monoinsaturés et polyinsaturés, incluant oméga-3 et oméga-6) : huiles végétales (ex.: maïs, lin, tournesol, olive, etc.), graines et noix, poisson. Mauvais gras (lipides saturés et gras trans) : produits d'origine animale (viande et produits laitiers), huile de palme et de coco, huiles hydrogénées.

Macronutriments

Glucides (sucres)

À quoi ça sert ?
Alimentent en énergie les cellules nerveuses, les globules rouges et les muscles pendant l'effort physique.

Où en trouver ?
Glucides complexes : fruits, légumes, lait, grains entiers, légumes racines (pommes de terre), pâtes, pain, riz et foie des animaux.
Glucides simples : fruits, certains légumes, sucreries.

Protéines

À quoi ça sert ?
Constituent le matériau de base des cellules. Participent à la formation de l'hémoglobine, des anticorps, des enzymes et des hormones. Servent à la croissance, à la réparation et à la reconstitution des divers tissus.

Où en trouver ?
Produits d'origine animale (viande rouge, poisson, volaille, fruits de mer, œufs et produits laitiers), légumineuses, noix et fèves de soya.

Nutriments

Minéraux

À quoi ça sert ?
Renforcent certaines structures (dents, squelette). Contribuent au bon fonctionnement de l'organisme.

Où en trouver ?
En quantité variable dans presque tous les aliments.

Micronutriments

Eau

À quoi ça sert ?
Constitue de 50 % à 60 % du poids d'un adulte. Est le deuxième élément vital, après l'oxygène.

Où en trouver ?
Eau du robinet, jus, fruits, légumes, boissons de toutes sortes.

Vitamines

À quoi ça sert ?
Rendent possible l'utilisation des glucides, des lipides et des protéines par les cellules. Accélèrent les réactions chimiques.

Où en trouver ?
Fruits, légumes, grains entiers, poisson et produits d'origine animale.

Source : Adapté de Richard CHEVALIER, *À vos marques, prêt, santé !*, ERPI, 2006, page 53.

En rafale

Les bonnes raisons pour ne pas suivre une diète

On entend beaucoup parler de diètes et les médias font la promotion de divers produits susceptibles de faciliter la perte de poids. Attention ! Il est important, encore plus à ton âge, de bien s'informer sur la question.

Est-ce vrai que suivre une diète peut présenter des risques pour ma santé ?

La plupart des diètes engendrent des carences en vitamines, en minéraux ou en énergie, ou encore divers effets secondaires tels qu'une déshydratation, une grande fatigue, de la difficulté à se concentrer, des troubles digestifs, des perturbations hormonales, etc. Or, ton corps en pleine croissance a besoin de l'énergie, des vitamines et des minéraux fournis par les aliments pour bien fonctionner. En le privant de nourriture, tu t'exposes à plusieurs problèmes de santé.

Les diètes peuvent-elles avoir un impact sur mon équilibre mental ?

Le fait de te priver de manger, et ce, malgré la sensation de faim que tu éprouves, peut t'amener à développer une relation malsaine avec la nourriture et le plaisir qui y est associé. Pour certaines personnes, la nourriture devient une telle préoccupation qu'elle prend la forme d'une obsession, qui peut même les amener à développer des troubles de l'alimentation.

Est-ce vrai que les diètes peuvent mener à un gain de poids ?

En effet, bien que la majorité des personnes qui suivent des diètes réussissent à perdre du poids à court terme, elles finissent en général par reprendre le poids perdu, et même plus, à long terme. Le corps réagit à une diète de la même manière qu'à une famine : en réduisant sa consommation d'énergie. Lorsqu'on recommence à manger comme avant, ou plus qu'avant pour compenser la privation, le corps a tendance à entreposer les calories qu'il reçoit sous forme de graisses. C'est pourquoi, en l'absence d'un programme d'activité physique permettant de dépenser les surplus, on reprend le poids perdu, et souvent davantage.

POUR EN SAVOIR PLUS

Consulte l'étude, « 4 bonnes raisons pour ne pas suivre une diète », menée par Équilibre, Groupe d'action sur le poids, ou visite leur site Internet, www.equilibre.ca

2.2 Les troubles de l'alimentation

Notre comportement alimentaire est influencé à la fois par nos instincts et par nos habitudes. La recherche du plaisir y tient également une place importante. Il arrive à tout le monde de faire des excès, dans un sens comme dans l'autre. Mais, parfois, cela se transforme en un véritable problème de santé.

Les troubles de l'alimentation sont relativement fréquents à l'adolescence. Dans la très grande majorité des cas, ils touchent les filles. Ils vont du simple régime amaigrissant à la désorganisation totale du comportement alimentaire. Dans tous les cas, ces troubles tirent leur origine d'une défaillance de l'estime de soi liée à une perception négative de l'image corporelle.

Par image corporelle, on entend la «perception qu'une personne a de son corps». Cette perception peut être positive ou négative, selon le degré de satisfaction ressenti à l'égard de son corps. Ce sentiment de satisfaction est, quant à lui, largement influencé par le fait de percevoir ou non une différence entre une silhouette idéalisée et la représentation qu'on se fait de sa propre silhouette.

L'image corporelle est fortement touchée durant l'adolescence. Le corps change beaucoup au cours de cette période. C'est tout à fait normal. Ces changements de silhouette sont le résultat de l'action des hormones sur les organes et les tissus. Ces transformations physiques viennent cependant brouiller l'image que les jeunes se font d'eux-mêmes. Souvent, ils n'aiment pas leur nouvelle apparence et commencent à se préoccuper de leur poids, parfois même, de façon excessive. Il faut dire que les fabricants d'images et les gourous de l'ultra-minceur n'aident pas les choses en faisant la promotion, dans les magazines, du corps mince et parfait… retouché à l'ordinateur, bien sûr. Ainsi, la peur de développer un surplus de poids peut amener des personnes à se préoccuper de leur poids à un point tel que cela finit par porter atteinte à leur santé physique et mentale.

Il existe deux troubles majeurs de l'alimentation : l'**anorexie** et la **boulimie**. L'anorexie est une grève de l'appétit motivée par l'obsession de la minceur, qui repose sur une image corporelle négative, totalement imaginaire et déconnectée de la réelle apparence de la personne. Elle se manifeste par un amaigrissement important et la disparition des règles. L'anorexie s'accompagne souvent d'hyperactivité physique et d'un surinvestissement dans les activités scolaires et intellectuelles.

Défaillance de l'estime de soi liée à une perception négative de l'image corporelle

Le corps change beaucoup au cours de cette période. C'est tout à fait normal

Il faut dire que les fabricants d'images et les gourous de l'ultra-minceur n'aident pas les choses

Anorexie
Syndrome observé surtout chez les adolescentes et caractérisé par une restriction volontaire et souvent inavouée de l'alimentation, provoquant une aménorrhée (arrêt des règles) et un amaigrissement important.

Boulimie
Trouble de l'alimentation caractérisé par des accès irrésistibles de fringale, contraignant la personne à l'ingestion massive et ininterrompue de grandes quantités d'aliments, suivis de comportements compensatoires inappropriés (ex. : vomissements provoqués, laxatifs, jeûnes, séances d'activité physique excessives) ou d'endormissement.

Il s'agit d'une maladie grave et difficile à traiter, qui peut même entraîner la mort. Les rechutes sont nombreuses et la maladie peut devenir chronique.

La boulimie est caractérisée par une perte de contrôle momentanée du comportement alimentaire faisant place à une irrésistible envie de manger. La crise, qui peut durer une heure ou deux, se manifeste par des accès d'ingestion d'aliments en quantité excessive, suivis généralement d'épisodes de vomissements provoqués. La crise s'accomplit le plus souvent en cachette et peut être associée à d'autres symptômes comme des dépendances (ex. : alcool, drogue, etc.) ou des signes de dépression. La prise de poids est souvent inexistante, étant donné le rejet quasi immédiat des aliments. En général, les chances de guérison sont bonnes, mais les rechutes sont fréquentes.

Pour ces deux troubles de l'alimentation, un traitement médical le plus précoce possible est essentiel et s'accompagne le plus souvent d'une psychothérapie individuelle ou familiale.

L'anorexie est un problème lié à la perception de son image corporelle : on ne se voit pas tel qu'on est, mais tel qu'on s'imagine être.

ZOOM SUR...

ANA IVANOVIC : championne de tennis à l'adolescence difficile

Ce qu'a dit Ana Ivanovic, championne de tennis, sur sa période ado :

« Comme toutes les adolescentes, je n'aimais pas mon corps et je voulais perdre du poids », raconte-t-elle au journaliste de *La Presse,* Vincent Brousseau-Pouliot, le 28 juillet 2008. Ana poursuit ainsi : « Mon entraîneur plaisantait parfois, car j'étais une fille légèrement enrobée. À cet âge, vous n'êtes pas heureux dans votre peau… »

Ana a atteint les quarts de finale du Zurich Open 2008 avec un score impressionnant de 6-2, 6-4 sur la Française, Marion Bartoli. Elle a réussi 5 as sur le chemin de sa victoire remportée en 80 minutes. Elle a littéralement explosé lors du premier jeu en servant plusieurs coups de fond puissants à Bartoli qui en avait plein les bras. Ana a dominé lors de la première manche, qu'elle a conclue avec une avance plus que confortable.

Ana Ivanovic (1987-…).
Déterminée à remporter le prochain point.

2.3 Des besoins différents lorsque tu bouges

Si tu fais au moins 30 minutes d'activités physiques modérées par jour, ou encore de 2 à 3 heures d'activités physiques vigoureuses par semaine, on peut dire que tu es physiquement actif ou active.

Dans ce cas, tu dépenses plus de calories que la moyenne des gens, et parfois même beaucoup plus. Tes besoins en nutriments, vitamines et minéraux inclus, sont forcément plus grands aussi.

Mais, ne t'en fais pas. Si, au départ, ton alimentation est adéquate, tu n'as rien de spécial à faire, car ta dépense énergétique plus élevée te fera tout naturellement manger davantage. C'est un principe d'**autorégulation** du corps (voir la rubrique ZOOM SUR… Le petit déjeuner de Michael Phelps, à la page 79). Il n'est pas nécessaire non plus de manger plus d'aliments riches en protéines sous prétexte qu'on se fait du muscle.

Le fait de manger davantage augmente automatiquement l'apport en protéines, qui n'est déjà pas déficient dans les pays développés, comme c'est le cas ici. Lis à ce propos le témoignage de la championne de patinage de vitesse, Clara Hugues.

Toutefois, si tu es végétarien ou végétarienne et que tu consommes très peu de viande, de volaille ou de produits laitiers, ou si tu limites ton apport calorique quotidien, tu dois porter encore plus d'attention ton apport en protéines doit être ajusté.

Tu dois t'assurer de deux choses quand tu fais beaucoup d'activités physiques.

Témoignage. Clara Hugues, patineuse de vitesse, médaille d'or 5000 m aux Jeux olympiques d'hiver de Turin (2006)

« Bien des gens sont surpris d'apprendre que je n'ai pas de diète spéciale pour mon entraînement ou mes compétitions. Je m'alimente bien pour [obtenir] un bon niveau d'énergie dans mon corps et dans mon esprit. Mais, j'ai un faible pour les sucreries ; particulièrement le chocolat. Alors, si j'ai une envie irrésistible, j'en mange, mais une quantité raisonnable. »

Source : Marielle LEDOUX, Nathalie LACOMBE et Geneviève ST-MARTIN, *Nutrition, sport et performance*, Géo Plein Air, 2006, page 203.

 Si tu veux en savoir plus sur l'**apport quotidien recommandé en protéines**, consulte le Compagnon Web où tu trouveras des suggestions de repas pouvant contribuer à combler tes besoins en protéines.

Autorégulation
Régulation d'un processus physiologique par l'organisme lui-même, sans intervention extérieure.

★ Boire suffisamment d'eau pour éviter la déshydratation

■ Avant ton activité physique

Deux ou trois heures avant ta séance d'activité physique ou ton cours d'éducation physique et à la santé, tu dois boire l'équivalent d'un grand verre d'eau (300 ml à 400 ml). Ainsi, tu t'assures d'avoir assez de réserves d'eau pour que ton corps puisse bouger sans être en déséquilibre.

■ Pendant ton activité physique

Selon la durée et l'intensité de ta séance d'activité physique, tu dois boire plusieurs gorgées d'eau à la fontaine ou, si tu as une bouteille d'eau, l'équivalent d'un petit verre d'eau (150 ml à 250 ml) toutes les 15 à 20 minutes. En prenant ainsi de petites quantités d'eau, plutôt qu'une grosse quantité, tu aides ton organisme à assimiler l'eau que tu lui fournis.
Si l'activité vigoureuse dure depuis plus d'une heure, tu as intérêt à boire une eau légèrement sucrée et salée parce que tes muscles commencent à manquer de carburant (sucre) et que tu as sans doute perdu pas mal de sodium par la sueur. Une boisson réhydratante pour sportifs ou une préparation maison peuvent faire l'affaire parce qu'elles sont justement légèrement sucrées et salées.

■ Après ton activité physique

Si ta séance d'activité a duré plus d'une heure, et qu'elle était d'intensité moyenne à élevée, tu dois boire 1 ou 2 verres d'eau au cours des 30 minutes qui suivent la fin de ta séance.

BOISSON ÉNERGISANTE FACILE À PRÉPARER
• 5 ml de sel
• 1 L d'eau
• 60 ml de jus d'orange
• Jus de citron, au goût
• 45 ml à 90 ml de sucre blanc
Mélanger le tout et boire frais.

★ Manger suffisamment de glucides pour éviter la panne d'énergie

Les glucides (voir le schéma des nutriments à la page 72) sont la source d'énergie alimentaire la plus importante pour l'activité physique. Par conséquent, si tu prévois pratiquer une activité physique modérée ou vigoureuse pendant plus de 60 minutes, tes muscles auront besoin de plus de glucides pour pouvoir bien tenir le coup.

Dans ce cas, trois heures avant l'activité, prends un repas léger composé de deux à trois aliments riches en **glucides de digestion lente**. Ce repas fera monter graduellement ton taux de sucre dans le sang.

Si tu disposes de moins de deux heures avant ton activité, prends une collation riche en glucides de digestion rapide. Si tu es légèrement ou modérément actif ou active, le repas que tu prendras après ta séance d'activité physique n'a pas à être différent. Par contre, si tu pratiques des activités vigoureuses et prolongées presque tous les jours, tu peux aider tes muscles à refaire le plein d'énergie rapidement en consommant les aliments présentés dans le tableau ci-dessous après ton activité physique. Tu éviteras ainsi une fatigue musculaire précoce lors de ta prochaine séance.

COLLATIONS SUGGÉRÉES APRÈS UN ENTRAÎNEMENT OU UNE ACTIVITÉ PHYSIQUE VIGOUREUSE	
250 ml de lait au chocolat	1 boîte de raisins secs
1 portion d'amandes avec un fruit	2 fruits de grosseur moyenne
1 yogourt faible en gras avec un fruit	1 petit muffin
1 bagel	1 banane
2 tranches de pain	1 barre de céréales faible en gras
4 galettes de riz	1 bol de céréales à grains entiers avec un fruit

L'énergie dont on parle porte le nom de **glycogène**. Il s'agit d'un type de sucre formé de grosses molécules. En fait, ces molécules sont constituées dans le muscle même avec du glucose, et elles sont si grosses que le glycogène ne peut pas ressortir du muscle une fois qu'il y est créé. Comment accélérer le renouvellement de tes réserves de glycogène ? C'est simple : il te suffit de prendre une collation contenant quelque 50 g de glucides (1 g/kg de poids corporel). Il est aussi important de prendre ces glucides le plus tôt possible après l'activité physique (intervalle de 30 minutes) sous forme liquide pour favoriser leur absorption et la réhydratation en même temps.

Glucide de digestion lente

Sucre que l'organisme met un certain temps à digérer et, donc, à assimiler. Lorsqu'on mange ce type de sucre, le taux de sucre dans le sang augmente lentement, et non subitement, comme c'est le cas des sucres simples, tels que ceux contenus dans les sucreries. Les fruits, les légumes, le lait, les céréales à grains entiers, les pommes de terre, pour n'en nommer que quelques-uns, sont des aliments riches en sucres complexes.

Glycogène

Glucide emmagasiné principalement dans les muscles et le foie, et formé de grosses molécules de sucre. Ces grosses molécules font en sorte que, une fois le glycogène formé dans le muscle, il ne peut en ressortir. Le glycogène est une source d'énergie de premier plan pour les cellules musculaires.

ZOOM SUR...

Le petit déjeuner de **MICHAEL PHELPS**

- Michael Phelps, né en 1985, est sans conteste le meilleur nageur de toute l'histoire de la natation! Il est 14 fois champion olympique, dont 8 fois aux Jeux olympiques de Pékin en 2008.

- Très jeune, Michael Phelps apprend qu'il a un trouble déficitaire de l'attention. Hyperactif, il doit trouver un moyen de canaliser son énergie: la natation est sa solution.

- Ses enseignants lui découvrent un talent certain pour la natation et, à 10 ans, il bat déjà le record national de sa classe d'âge. Il se qualifie pour les Jeux olympiques de Sydney en 2000, où il devient le plus jeune participant depuis 1932 – il n'a que 15 ans. Depuis, il a accumulé de nombreux records mondiaux et titres. En 2008, il avait battu 26 records mondiaux en individuel et 6 records mondiaux en relais.

- Est-il surprenant qu'il lui faille de 12 000 à 14 000 calories pour satisfaire son métabolisme… chaque jour?

- On peut le comprendre, car Phelps dépense – au bas mot – plus de 6000 calories par jour lorsqu'il s'entraîne. Et il le fait souvent: six jours par semaine!

- Dans le but de combler tous ses besoins nutritionnels, Phelps peut en effet ingurgiter jusqu'à 14 000 calories par jour. En comparaison, un homme de taille moyenne et légèrement actif en consomme de 2400 à 2600 par jour… Phelps le dit lui-même: son alimentation compte parmi les facteurs les plus importants de sa réussite.

- À lui seul, son petit déjeuner lui fournit plus de 3000 calories. Il se présente comme suit. D'abord, trois sandwichs aux œufs, préparés avec du fromage, de la laitue, des tomates, des oignons frits – monsieur est un fin gourmet! –, sans oublier la mayonnaise. Suivent deux tasses de café et une grosse omelette (cinq œufs!) et, un peu plus tard, un bol de gruau, trois tranches de pain doré, saupoudrées de sucre, puis – n'oublions surtout pas le dessert! –, trois crêpes au chocolat. Peux-tu imaginer ses repas du midi et du soir? Rien de moins que gargantuesques!

Michael Phelps.
En route vers une autre victoire.

Michael Phelps.
En pleine préparation mentale.

Tout bien réfléchi !

Lis le texte sur Ana Carolina Reston et explique dans tes mots les raisons de sa mort et ce qu'on veut dire par *quand maigrir peut tuer*.

QUAND MAIGRIR PEUT TUER
Le cas d'Ana Carolina Reston

Ana Carolina Reston était un célèbre mannequin brésilien. Elle est morte d'anorexie à 21 ans, le 14 novembre 2006, à Sao Paulo, au Brésil. Le jour de sa mort, elle pesait 40 kg et mesurait 1,74 m. Dans les jours qui ont précédé sa fin tragique, elle ne mangeait plus que des pommes et des tomates. Mannequin depuis l'âge de 13 ans, Ana Carolina avait été hospitalisée 3 semaines avant son décès pour une infection urinaire qui a évolué en insuffisance rénale, puis en infection généralisée. «Elle n'avait aucune résistance, et les médicaments ne faisaient plus d'effet en raison de son extrême faiblesse», a déclaré la tante d'Ana Carolina à la presse brésilienne. La directrice de l'agence pour laquelle la jeune femme travaillait a indiqué qu'elle venait de participer au catalogue d'un grand couturier au Japon, mais qu'elle avait dû rentrer au Brésil, car elle était trop maigre et fatiguée.

POUR EN SAVOIR PLUS

Pour en savoir plus sur les troubles de l'alimentation, consulte le site suivant où tu pourras trouver une foule de renseignements utiles :
www.anebquebec.com

Le cas de ce mannequin n'est pas unique, hélas ! Les troubles de l'alimentation graves comme l'anorexie et la boulimie sont, en effet, en hausse au Canada depuis quelques années.

Ana Carolina Reston (1985-2006).
En des temps meilleurs.

Le tableau « Quelques exemples de collations contenant environ 50 g de glucides » te renseigne sur des choix pertinents à faire pour augmenter ton apport en glucides, selon tes besoins. En consommant ce genre de collation, tu feras alors rapidement le plein de glycogène.

2.4 Des choix alimentaires gagnants

Tu te demandes sûrement ce qu'est un choix alimentaire gagnant. Non, ce ne sont pas des aliments qui te feront gagner une course ou un match de tennis.

Ce sont plutôt des aliments riches en nutriments, mais pauvres en calories. C'est notamment le cas des fruits, des légumes, des produits céréaliers, des poissons, de la volaille et des viandes ainsi que des produits laitiers (lait, yogourt et fromage) à faible teneur en gras.

Choisir des aliments gagnants, c'est donc choisir de manger ces aliments en priorité et régulièrement. Ce qui n'exclut pas de consommer à l'occasion des aliments pauvres en nutriments mais riches en calories, comme les gâteaux, les pâtisseries, les charcuteries, le bacon, les boissons gazeuses, etc. C'est une question de dosage : de bons aliments la plupart du temps ; à l'occasion, quelques bouchées pour se sucrer ou se saler le bec.

Normalement, ton menu quotidien devrait être composé de ce qui suit :
- 50 % de glucides.
- 20 % de lipides.
- 30 % de protéines.

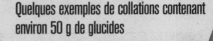

Quelques exemples de collations contenant environ 50 g de glucides

- 375 ml de jus de fruit (ex. : orange, pamplemousse, pomme, fruits mélangés)
- 250 ml de jus de raisin
- 625 ml de lait 1 % ou 2 %
- 3 ½ tranches de pain
- 2 pains pitas
- 125 ml de pouding au riz et aux raisins
- 500 ml de céréales de riz
- 375 ml de pâtes alimentaires cuites
- 250 ml de riz cuit
- 125 ml de raisins secs
- 2 grosses pommes
- 8 dattes
- 2 poires
- 6 pruneaux

Source : Richard CHEVALIER, *À vos marques, prêts, santé !*, 4e édition, ERPI, 2006, p. 75.

Quelques aliments riches en protéines et autres nutriments

Lait, yogourt, beurre d'arachide 100 % naturel, thon en conserve, poitrine de poulet, tofu (si tu aimes ça), saumon, œufs, etc.

Quelques aliments riches en glucides et autres nutriments

Fruits frais, légumes frais, jus de fruit naturels, céréales à déjeuner à grains entiers (très important !), riz à grain long, pâtes alimentaires, etc.

Quelques aliments riches en bon gras (lipides insaturés)

Huiles végétales (ex. : olive, lin, canola, tournesol), noix et graines, poisson, etc.

Fais le point

1 Indique dans la colonne de gauche du tableau tout ce que tu as mangé au cours de la journée d'hier en décrivant tes trois repas et tes collations. Puis, dans les colonnes de droite, inscris les quantités de macronutriments contenus dans les aliments que tu as mangés.

	Aliments consommés	Glucides (en g)	Lipides (en g)	Protéines (en g)
Déjeuner				
Collation				
Dîner				
Collation				
Souper				
Collation				
Total				

2 Ton menu quotidien devrait être composé de 50 % de glucides, de 20 % de lipides et de 30 % de protéines. Coche les cases qui décrivent le mieux les aliments que tu as consommés hier.

Ma consommation de glucides a été…   ☐ Excessive.   ☐ Suffisante.   ☐ Insuffisante.

Ma consommation de lipides a été…   ☐ Excessive.   ☐ Suffisante.   ☐ Insuffisante.

Ma consommation de protéines a été…   ☐ Excessive.   ☐ Suffisante.   ☐ Insuffisante.

Tout bien réfléchi !

Analyse le repas de Caroline et de Stéphane et indique lequel des deux a fait les meilleurs choix. Justifie ta réponse.

Caroline et son ami Stéphane viennent de terminer une randonnée à vélo dans la région de l'Estrie, plus précisément dans le coin de Granby, sur la piste de l'Estriade. Après la randonnée, ils décident d'aller souper dans un restaurant du coin. Ils doivent bien s'alimenter pour refaire leurs réserves énergétiques. De plus, en soirée, ils ont prévu aller au cinéma. Donc, ils doivent s'assurer de bien digérer et de ne pas avoir faim pendant la représentation. Voici les repas de Caroline et Stéphane.

Caroline	Stéphane
Entrée Petite salade César, petit pain et beurre	**Entrée** Soupe aux légumes avec craquelins
Boisson Grand verre d'eau	**Boisson** Grand verre d'eau
Mets principal Steak de surlonge saignant Pomme de terre au four avec beurre et crème sûre Légumes au beurre	**Mets principal** Poitrine de poulet grillée Riz vapeur Légumes vapeurs
Dessert Salade de fruits frais nappée de sauce au chocolat	**Dessert** Sorbet à la framboise

_____
_____
_____
_____
_____
_____
_____
_____
_____
_____
_____
_____

③ Le sommeil

«Il n'est rien qu'on doive tant recommander à la jeunesse que l'activité et la vigilance.»

Michel Eyquem de MONTAIGNE, *Les Essais*, chap. VI, «Du dormir», 1595.

Ces derniers temps, Vincent, 13 ans, a tendance à s'endormir pendant la journée. Il lui est même arrivé de cogner des clous durant un cours du matin. Son humeur aussi a changé : il est plus irritable et de mauvaise humeur.

Il faut dire que, depuis qu'il a un ordinateur dans sa chambre, il est pas mal occupé à clavarder et à surfer sur Internet, parfois même jusqu'à 23 h ou minuit. Il se couche donc plus tard maintenant, et pas toujours à la même heure. Mais la fin de semaine venue, il dort jusqu'à midi et plus !

De toute évidence, Vincent est une chouette au sommeil léger pendant la semaine et une marmotte au sommeil profond durant la fin de semaine.

Et toi, la nuit tombée, es-tu du genre *chouette* ou du genre *marmotte* ? Si tu t'endors sur les bancs de l'école, tu es probablement, comme Vincent, du genre *chouette*, ce qui n'est pas une bonne nouvelle puisque cela signifie que tu ne dors pas suffisamment.

Or, le manque de sommeil affecte la mémoire, la concentration en classe, le caractère, et, selon des études récentes, il favoriserait l'obésité et le diabète.

Le sommeil des adolescents : pas de tout repos !

De nombreuses recherches confirment que les troubles du sommeil constituent un facteur déterminant dans la performance scolaire des adolescents. Les études menées en 2000 par Roger Godbout, enseignant au Département de psychiatrie de la Faculté de médecine de l'Université de Montréal, démontrent que le sommeil est indispensable à la récupération de l'organisme et que l'assimilation des connaissances nouvelles est optimale lorsqu'elle est suivie d'une nuit complète.

Il existe en effet un lien fonctionnel entre l'apprentissage et l'activation du cerveau au cours du sommeil qu'on dit *paradoxal*. Cette phase du sommeil, où les rêves sont vifs et plus fréquents, permet de consolider les expériences nouvelles. Selon le Dr Godbout, les rêves optimisent nos capacités d'apprentissage et notre équilibre psychologique. La privation de sommeil, de son côté, altère de nombreuses tâches et affecte sérieusement la mémoire à court terme. À la suite d'une trop longue période de privation de sommeil, le cerveau s'en trouve affecté. On observe également des changements d'humeur, des problèmes de concentration et une diminution des performances cognitives.

Les adolescents ont besoin, en moyenne, d'au moins neuf heures de sommeil, mais la plupart en dorment moins de sept à cause des horaires de classe. On le sait, dans l'esprit des adolescents, se coucher tard est synonyme de *devenir grand*. À l'adolescence, dormir devient secondaire. Avec leur emploi du temps chargé (école, devoirs, travail, activités, responsabilités familiales, amis, etc.), certains sont même portés à réduire leur temps de sommeil pour arriver à tout faire. Aussi, la puberté est marquée par des changements importants de l'horloge biologique, entraînant une désorganisation du cycle veille-sommeil. Cela explique aussi pourquoi plusieurs adolescents ont du mal à s'endormir avant 23 h.

3.1 Six trucs pour bien dormir

Tu dois savoir que bien dormir n'est pas qu'une simple question de nombre d'heures de sommeil.

Certains individus ne dorment que six heures et s'en portent bien. D'autres ont besoin de neuf heures de sommeil, et les bébés, de seize heures ! Ce qui importe, c'est la *qualité du sommeil*.

Pour savoir si ton sommeil a été de qualité, tu n'as qu'à te demander dans quel état tu te réveilles le matin avant de partir pour l'école. Si tu es encore fatigué ou fatiguée quand tu te lèves, il est certain que la qualité de ton sommeil laisse à désirer. Quand on a un sommeil réparateur, on se réveille en pleine forme. On te présente ici les six trucs qui peuvent t'aider à améliorer la qualité de ton sommeil. Les appliques-tu déjà ?

Ce qui importe, c'est la qualité du sommeil

★1 Se coucher et se lever à des heures régulières

Selon la théorie de l'horloge interne, notre corps a besoin d'un horaire régulier pour bien dormir. Durant la semaine, essaie de te coucher à la même heure. Quand à l'heure de ton réveil, elle est déjà fixée par l'horaire de l'école. Bref, adopte un rythme sommeil-éveil et respecte-le le plus souvent possible.

★2 Faire de l'activité physique régulièrement, mais jamais tard le soir

L'activité physique favorise un sommeil réparateur. Les recherches montrent en effet que l'activité physique favorise le regroupement du sommeil en une seule période. Les chercheurs ignorent pourquoi l'activité physique nous aide à mieux dormir, mais les hypothèses abondent : l'activité physique engendre une fatigue physique et une détente mentale qui ne peuvent que favoriser un meilleur sommeil ; l'activité physique relaxe les muscles tendus par le stress de la journée (c'est l'équivalent d'un bain chaud) ; l'activité physique diminue l'anxiété.

★3 Passer au petit coin avant d'aller au lit

Imagine-toi que plusieurs oublient ce petit détail. Résultat : ils doivent se lever en pleine nuit pour y aller !

★4 Éviter de trop manger moins de deux heures avant d'aller au lit

Si tu as envie de grignoter au cours de la soirée, prends une collation légère ou un verre de lait. Le lait contient du tryptophane, un acide aminé qui facilite le sommeil.

★5 Dormir dans une chambre confortable

Ta chambre doit être tranquille, bien aérée, plutôt sombre, ni trop chaude ni trop froide.

★6 Enfin, ne pas se coucher trop tôt du jour au lendemain

Te coucher très tôt du jour au lendemain n'arrangera rien, car tu ne pourras pas t'endormir immédiatement : ton corps doit s'habituer à ce nouvel horaire. Commence progressivement à te coucher plus tôt, par exemple 15 à 20 minutes plus tôt durant la semaine, jusqu'à ce que tu atteignes une heure raisonnable en fonction de de ton horaire scolaire.

Savais-tu que 34 % des adolescents se plaignent de somnolence durant la journée et qu'un tiers de ces jeunes présentent même une tendance pathologique à s'endormir ? Un sondage réalisé en France apporte des renseignements intéressants sur les impacts négatifs de mauvaises habitudes de sommeil.

✔ Plus de la moitié des ados interrogés ressent de la somnolence durant la journée au moins une fois par semaine.

✔ 30 % ont une tendance pathologique à s'endormir durant la journée.

✔ Seulement 10 % en ont parlé à leur médecin.

✔ Les ados ne dorment pas suffisamment en semaine et récupèrent durant la fin de semaine.

✔ 70 % ont une carence en sommeil durant la semaine.

✔ Il existe un décalage important du lever et du coucher au cours de la fin de semaine (qui sont plus tardifs) par rapport à ceux la semaine : ce phénomène est un facteur qui perturbe le cycle veille-sommeil.

✔ 37 % souffrent de problèmes d'insomnie, particulièrement les filles.

✔ 34 % présentent des problèmes importants de stress, d'anxiété ou de dépression, particulièrement les filles.

✔ Enfin, 10 % prennent des médicaments pour lutter contre le stress et l'anxiété ou pour dormir.

3.2 Les bizarreries du sommeil

Les yeux grands ouverts, Annie, 14 ans, fixe encore le plafond de sa chambre. Pour la ixième fois, c'est devenu un réflexe, elle jette un coup d'œil sur le réveille-matin : 2 h 47. Encore une nuit interminable !

Finalement, vers 6 h, Annie réussit à s'endormir. Trop tard, hélas ! Dans 30 minutes, ce sera l'heure du réveil pour l'école !

Annie, on l'a compris, fait partie du club des **insomniaques**. Un gros club puisque 25 % des adultes Québécois en font partie.

Ils ne sont pas les seuls, cependant, à avoir des problèmes de sommeil. Certains, par exemple, dorment profondément, ron-flent même, mais cessent de respirer pendant quelques secondes, jusqu'à 400 fois par nuit (**apnée du sommeil**).

D'autres se retrouvent, toujours en plein sommeil, en pyjama dans la rue (**somnambulisme**), ou se réveillent en sursaut, le cœur battant, surpris d'avoir échappés à la bête (**terreur nocturne**).

D'autres encore, à peine couchés, sont assaillis par une envie incontrôlable de bouger les jambes (**syndrome des jambes sans repos**), et certains se mettent à parler (**somniloquie**) ou à grincer des dents (**bruxisme**) en dormant.

Comme tu peux le constater, le sommeil peut être perturbé de bien des façons, dont certaines sont hors de notre contrôle. Mais la grande majorité des jeunes de ton âge ne sont pas affec-tés par ces bizarreries du sommeil. Il n'empêche que plusieurs, dirait-on, semblent prendre tous les moyens pour ne pas dormir suffisamment.

Insomniaque
Personne qui a de la difficulté à s'endormir.

Apnée du sommeil
Suspension plus ou moins prolongée de la respiration durant le sommeil.

Somnambulisme
Automatisme inconscient se manifes-tant pendant le sommeil par des actes plus ou moins coordonnés (ex. : se lever, marcher, exécuter une tâche simple, etc.) dont il ne reste à la personne aucun souvenir au réveil.

Terreur nocturne
Cauchemar entraînant une peur aiguë.

Syndrome des jambes sans repos
Sensation désagréable et indéfinissable ressentie dans les membres inférieurs, déclenchée par l'immobilité, provoquant un irrépressible besoin de bouger les jambes en les agitant, en se levant ou en marchant.

Bruxisme
Fait de grincer des dents en dormant.

Somniloquie
Fait de parler en dormant.

POUR EN SAVOIR PLUS
Visite le site Internet de la Société canadienne de pédiatrie, sous la rubrique Santé des Ados, www.cps.ca

Fais le point

1 Pour ne pas ressentir de somnolence durant la journée, ton corps a besoin d'environ neuf heures de sommeil par nuit. Dors-tu suffisamment ? Pour le savoir, effectue les calculs suivants.

La semaine, je me couche en général vers _____ h.

Le matin, je me lève vers _____ h.

Donc, chaque nuit, je dors en moyenne _____ h.

2 Dresse ton bilan personnel au chapitre du sommeil en cochant, dans le tableau, les cases qui correspondent le mieux à ta situation, puis analyse tes résultats.

	SOUVENT	PARFOIS	JAMAIS
La semaine, je me couche après 22 heures.	☐	☐	☐
Même si je suis fatigué ou fatiguée, j'ai trop de choses à faire le soir pour me coucher tôt.	☐	☐	☐
Je fais parfois une sieste en revenant de l'école ou après le souper.	☐	☐	☐
Le soir, je m'endors devant la télévision dans le salon.	☐	☐	☐
Je mange toujours une collation avant d'aller au lit.	☐	☐	☐
Le samedi et le dimanche, je me lève après midi.	☐	☐	☐
Je fais des activités physiques exigeantes le soir avant de me coucher (ex. : hockey, natation, soccer, etc.).	☐	☐	☐
Je fais tout dans mon lit : mes devoirs, mes leçons, écouter la télévision, manger, parler au téléphone.	☐	☐	☐
Je bois et je mange des produits qui contiennent de la caféine après 15 h (ex. : boisson gazeuse, chocolat, thé glacé).	☐	☐	☐
Quand je me couche le soir, je mets beaucoup de temps à m'endormir.	☐	☐	☐
Total			

Si tu as plus de SIX CROCHETS sous la colonne…		
SOUVENT	Tu manques sûrement de sommeil et tu dois souvent ressentir de la somnolence durant la journée.	Tu devrais suivre les conseils qui te sont donnés dans le Compagnon Web.
PARFOIS	Il doit t'arriver certains jours de te sentir fatigué ou fatiguée et de trouver la journée longue.	Relève dans le CW les conseils que tu pourrais suivre pour remédier à la situation.
JAMAIS	Tu as adopté les comportements appropriés pour te sentir en forme tous les matins à ton réveil.	Relève dans le CW les conseils que tu pourrais suivre pour maintenir tes bonnes habitudes.

4 L'hygiène personnelle

> «Traite ton corps comme un temple, pas comme une cabane.»
>
> – Jim Rohn

La maxime de Jim Rohn résume bien l'utilité de l'hygiène personnelle : entretenir son corps avec tout le respect qu'il mérite.

Bien sûr, l'hygiène personnelle comporte ses pratiques de base comme se brosser les dents, utiliser la soie dentaire tous les jours, se laver le corps et se laver les cheveux deux à trois fois par semaine, se laver les mains fréquemment, se couper les ongles des doigts et des orteils régulièrement et dormir suffisamment. Mais, elle comporte aussi des pratiques particulières pour ceux qui font régulièrement des activités physiques ou un sport. Voici les huit éléments auxquels tu dois prêter une attention particulière.

Les vaccins

La **vaccination** est de mise selon ton choix d'activité physique.
- Activités aquatiques en plein air : vaccin contre l'hépatite A.
- Activités de plein air : rappels antitétaniques.
- Sports de contact : vaccin contre l'hépatite B.

Ton hydratation

Avant, pendant et après l'effort, une bonne **hydratation** est nécessaire. Afin d'éviter que ta gourde ne se transforme en réservoir à microorganismes, n'oublie pas de la rincer après chaque utilisation et même de la renouveler à l'occasion.

Ton hygiène corporelle

Après chaque activité physique, ton corps a besoin d'une bonne douche !

Ton hygiène vestimentaire

De préférence, les vêtements sont propres, suffisamment amples, ils protègent contre l'humidité et laissent échapper la transpiration.

Hygiène personnelle des gens qui font régulièrement des activités physiques

Ton hygiène bucco-dentaire

Étonnamment, l'activité physique a une incidence sur ton **hygiène bucco-dentaire**. Quand tu es en action, l'acidité buccale augmente, ce qui favorise le développement de caries. Il suffit donc de te brosser les dents après ton activité physique.

Tes pieds

Certains adeptes d'activités physiques développent des mycoses, ces champignons qui causent brûlures et démangeaisons aux **pieds**. Pour éviter la contamination, il est préférable de ne pas marcher pieds nus dans les vestiaires ou à la piscine.

Ton sommeil

Planifie un horaire de **sommeil** régulier en tenant compte du fait que tu dois prendre ton déjeuner trois heures avant une activité physique intense.

La pollution atmosphérique

Pendant une activité physique, tu t'exposes davantage à la **pollution atmosphérique**. Voici quelques astuces : pratique ton activité dans un espace vert, le matin, et évite les journées de canicule.

Fais le point

1   Afin de t'aider à savoir si tu respectes toutes les règles d'hygiène personnelle nécessaires lors de la pratique d'activités physiques, coche les comportements qui font partie de ta routine avant, pendant ou après une activité.

COMPORTEMENTS	Inscris un ✔ le cas échéant
LE SOMMEIL	
Je dors de sept à huit heures la nuit précédant une activité.	☐
Pour l'heure de mon réveil, je tiens compte du fait que je dois prendre mon déjeuner trois heures avant de pratiquer mon activité.	☐
L'HYGIÈNE CORPORELLE	
Je prends une douche en me savonnant bien avant mon activité.	☐
Je prends une douche en me savonnant bien après mon activité.	☐
L'HYGIÈNE VESTIMENTAIRE	
Je porte des vêtements secs et propres à chaque nouvelle activité.	☐
Mes vêtements sont suffisamment amples et ne comportent aucun point de compression.	☐
Mes vêtements me protègent contre l'humidité tout en laissant échapper la transpiration.	☐
Je ne porte pas de chaussures neuves lors d'une activité.	☐
Je cire mes chaussures si elles sont en cuir, pour éviter le durcissement et, si elles sont en tissu, je ne les lave pas à la machine ni ne les fais sécher sur un radiateur ou un calorifère.	☐
J'évite les chaussures qui comportent de grosses coutures internes.	☐
Je porte des chaussettes en fibres naturelles (coton ou laine).	☐
Je prévois plusieurs paires de chaussettes si mon activité dure toute une journée.	☐
L'HYGIÈNE BUCCO-DENTAIRE	
Mes dents sont en bon état : des dents en mauvais état peuvent favoriser l'apparition de dérèglements tendino-musculaires (ex. : claquages, infections virales chroniques, tendinites, etc.).	☐
Étant donné que l'effort augmente l'acidité buccale qui s'ajoute aux produits énergétiques sucrés, je me brosse les dents après la pratique d'une activité.	☐
L'HYDRATATION	
Je bois de l'eau avant, pendant et après une activité, en petites quantités répétées pour éviter de trop gonfler mon estomac.	☐
Je nettoie ma gourde ou ma bouteille après chaque activité.	☐
Je ne prête ma gourde ou ma bouteille à personne, car il s'agit d'un objet personnel.	☐

COMPORTEMENTS	Inscris un ✔ le cas échéant
LES PIEDS	
Je fais tout ce qu'il faut pour prévenir les lésions telles que les ampoules, les ongles noirs et les mycoses ; je porte de bonnes chaussures ; je ne marche pas pieds nus dans les vestiaires, à la piscine, etc. ; je me sèche bien les pieds et, plus particulièrement, entre les orteils après une douche, etc.	☐
Dans le cas de lésions, je les soigne : désinfection, pansement stérile, visite chez un spécialiste en cas d'hématome sous les ongles, traitement antifongique, etc.	☐
Je porte des chaussettes en coton, car elles sont plus absorbantes, ce qui permet d'éviter l'hypersudation.	☐
LA POLLUTION ATMOSPHÉRIQUE	
Je privilégie les espaces verts pour pratiquer une activité extérieure.	☐
J'évite les activités extérieures les journées de chaleur intense, de forte humidité ou d'absence de vent.	☐
Si je dois m'entraîner obligatoirement à l'extérieur, je le fais le matin quand l'air est un peu plus pur.	☐
LES VACCINS	
Je suis vacciné ou vaccinée contre le tétanos et je respecte les rappels antitétaniques, car je pratique un sport où les blessures cutanées sont fréquentes.	☐
Je suis vacciné ou vaccinée contre l'hépatite B, car je pratique un sport de contact.	☐
Je suis vacciné ou vaccinée contre l'hépatite A, car je pratique un sport aquatique ou parce que je dois souvent me rendre dans des pays où le risque d'attraper cette maladie est élevé.	☐

2 Quels sont les comportements liés à l'hygiène personnelle que tu aimerais améliorer ?

_____

_____

_____

_____

_____

_____

⑤ Des dépendances nuisibles pour ta santé

Substance illicite

Matière interdite par la loi.

Cannabis

Plante dont le principe actif responsable des effets psychotropes est le THC (tétrahydrocannabinol), une substance toxique inscrite sur la liste des drogues illégales. Sa concentration est très variable selon les préparations et la provenance du produit, mais elle est de plus en plus élevée grâce aux techniques de sélection et de manipulation génétique. Le cannabis est à la fois un psychostimulant et un psycho-dépresseur. Il agit comme une substance hallucinogène.

L'adolescence amène de gros changements, et pas seulement sur le plan physique ou hormonal. Pour plusieurs, les questions se bousculent au portillon du cerveau, des questions qui concernent la sexualité, les amours, la place de l'école dans la vie, les nouvelles attentes des parents (tu dois devenir plus autonome et plus responsable), le besoin de l'acceptation des pairs et de faire partie de la *gang*, etc.

Bref, on se cherche et on remet en question l'autorité des parents (dont on veut se distinguer) en usant parfois de provocation. Un tel contexte peut susciter en toi plusieurs envies : défier l'autorité parentale, provoquer les plus vieux, épater tes amis, avoir du plaisir pour combattre l'ennui ou ce que tu perçois comme étant la grisaille de l'école, vivre de nouvelles expériences et trouver tes limites.

La tentation est grande alors d'expérimenter les effets de certaines substances consommées par les plus vieux, comme l'alcool et la cigarette, ou encore des **substances illicites** tel le **cannabis**.

Le hic, c'est qu'en y goûtant une fois, on risque d'avoir envie d'y goûter une seconde fois, puis une troisième… jusqu'à ce qu'on perde le contrôle de sa consommation. Ce risque-là est bien réel puisque l'alcool, la cigarette et les substances illicites (certaines plus que d'autres) peuvent rapidement créer une **dépendance** physique ou psychologique, voire les deux à la fois. Lorsque ça arrive, la santé peut en pâtir, de même que le rendement à l'école et les relations avec les parents et les amis.

Dépendance

État résultant de la consommation répétée d'une substance toxique, qui se caractérise par le besoin de continuer la prise et d'augmenter les doses.

5.1 Mieux connaître les drogues

Des enquêtes indiquent que, parmi les jeunes de ton âge, un grand nombre ignorent le contenu de ce qu'ils consomment et les effets que cette consommation peut avoir sur leur santé, surtout lorsqu'il s'agit de substances illicites.

Si le contenu de drogues légales, comme l'alcool et le tabac, demeure sous le contrôle strict des agences gouvernementales, le contenu des substances illégales ne l'est pas du tout. C'est ce qui explique qu'il existe, par exemple, différentes qualités de cannabis.

Étant donné que ces substances sont illégales, si tu en consommes, tu ne sais jamais ce qu'elles contiennent. Ces substances sont vendues par des criminels qui cherchent à profiter de ta faiblesse et te font miroiter des plaisirs artificiels, nuisibles pour ta santé. C'est déjà un premier problème. Le pire est à venir lorsque la consommation devient une dépendance. À ce stade, en plus de ne pas contrôler le contenu de ce que tu consommes, tu ne te contrôles plus toi-même.

Évidemment, tu ne peux pas compter sur les revendeurs de drogue à l'école pour t'aider à te sortir de ce pétrin. D'ailleurs, la plupart du temps, ils ne savent même pas eux-mêmes de quoi leurs substances illégales se composent. Avant d'en arriver là, commence donc par te familiariser avec les drogues. Une personne avertie en vaut deux, pas vrai ? Et lorsqu'on est mieux informé, on y pense à deux fois avant de goûter aux fruits défendus !

Une drogue est une substance chimique qui agit sur le cerveau, c'est-à-dire qu'elle agit sur le psychisme de la personne qui en consomme. Une telle substance modifie le fonctionnement mental. Elle peut entraîner des changements dans les perceptions, l'humeur, la conscience, le comportement et diverses fonctions physiques et psychologiques. Certaines de ces drogues sont licites : elles sont permises par la loi (ex. : alcool, tabac, médicaments psychoactifs tels les antidépresseurs et les stabilisateurs de l'humeur). D'autres sont illicites, elles sont interdites par la loi. Par exemple, la cocaïne, l'ecstasy ou le *cristal meth* font partie des drogues illicites. Le cannabis est aussi une drogue illicite, mais sa consommation est parfois autorisée dans un cadre médical très précis.

Consulte le tableau de la page suivante. On t'y présente les principales drogues, licites et illicites, consommées de nos jours. Elles sont regroupées en quatre grandes catégories selon les effets les plus courants qu'on leur attribue.

POUR EN SAVOIR PLUS

Visite le site www.toxquebec.com ou rends-toi sur le Compagnon Web.

Sous chaque catégorie de drogue, des pictogrammes t'indiquent les types de dépendances qu'elles peuvent engendrer. Tu trouveras également leurs multiples appellations. Ainsi, la prochaine fois que tu entendras parler de ces substances, tu sauras de quoi il en retourne.

Produits	Les diverses appellations	Les effets
CANNABIS	**HASCHICH ET HUILE DE HASCHICH** (ex. : cube, *dime, bag, blast,* etc.) **MARIJUANA** (ex. : pot, mari, *skunk,* etc.)	• Désorientation • Euphorie • Détente • Réduction de l'anxiété • Troubles de l'humeur • Distorsion des perceptions, perte du sens du temps • Accélération du pouls
HALLUCINOGÈNES	**LSD, MDA, STP** (ex. : acide, bonbon, buvard, etc.) **CHAMPIGNONS** **MDMA** (ex. : ecstasy, *x, dove,* etc.) **2-CB, PCP, XÉTAMINE**	• Désorientation • Euphorie • Hallucinations • Humeur changeante • Déformation des perceptions (voir des sons, entendre des couleurs)
STIMULANTS MINEURS	**CAFÉINE** **NICOTINE**	• Excitation et stimulation • Réduction de la fatigue • Perte de poids • Augmentation de l'éveil et de la force musculaire
STIMULANTS MAJEURS	**AMPHÉTAMINES** (ex. : *speed, wake-up, pep pills,* etc.) **COCAÏNE** (ex. : *crack,* neige, *crystal, meth,* etc.) **MDMA** (aussi un hallucinogène) **MÉTHYLPHÉNIDATE** (Ritalin)	• Excitation et stimulation • Réduction de la faim et de la fatigue • Augmentation de l'éveil et de la force musculaire • Sensation de puissance • Idées de grandeur, euphorie

Source : Adapté de Québec, ministère de la Santé et des Services sociaux, *La drogue… Si on s'en parlait ?* [en ligne]. (Consulté le 1er décembre 2008.)

Dépendance psychologique : Besoin de consommer une substance donnée de plus en plus souvent pour être mieux dans sa peau, se détendre, se calmer, se stimuler, se donner du courage pour surmonter ses problèmes, etc.

Dépendance physique : Besoin physiologique créé par l'accoutumance du corps à l'action de la drogue engendrant une difficulté de s'en passer et provoquant, en état de manque, des réactions physiques plus ou moins fortes.

Ton plan d'action

« La différence entre la théorie et la pratique, c'est qu'en théorie, il n'y a pas de différence entre la théorie et la pratique, mais qu'en pratique, il y en a une. »

– Jan van de Sneptscheut

Cette maxime est encore plus pertinente quand on parle d'améliorer ses habitudes de vie : il ne faut pas seulement le dire, il faut le faire. C'est précisément ce que tu as fait en 1re secondaire et ce que nous t'invitons à poursuivre en 2e secondaire, mais un peu plus en détail.

Pour ce faire, tu dois concevoir, puis mettre en pratique, un plan d'action qui vise à améliorer certaines de tes habitudes de vie, dont la pratique régulière de l'activité physique. Au départ, ton plan doit donc inclure la pratique d'au moins une activité physique d'une intensité modérée à élevée pendant une durée minimale de 20 minutes sans arrêt, au moins 3 fois par semaine. Tu dois faire ton choix en pensant que tu t'engages à pratiquer cette activité pendant au moins huit semaines, soit l'équivalent d'une étape. Tu peux en faire plus… mais pas moins. Souviens-t'en et sois réaliste dans tes choix pour t'aider à réussir.

TON PLAN D'ACTION

ÉTAPE 1 ## Volet Activité physique

Ton objectif: Améliorer ou maintenir ton endurance cardiovasculaire.

Reporte ici le résultat obtenu lors de ton test d'endurance cardio-vasculaire (voir les pages 55 ou 56):

Nom du test _____ **Résultat** _____

Endurance cardiovasculaire en fonction de ce résultat:

TRÈS ÉLEVÉE ☐   MOYENNE ☐

ÉLEVÉE ☐   SOUS LA MOYENNE ☐

Précise si tu veux maintenir ton niveau d'endurance actuel parce que, selon le test, il est déjà élevé ou très élevé, ou encore si tu veux l'améliorer parce qu'il est moyen ou sous la moyenne.

LE MAINTENIR ☐   L'AMÉLIORER ☐

Activités choisies:

1. _____

2. _____

3. _____

Indique comment les activités que tu as choisies te permettront d'améliorer ton endurance cardiovasculaire.

_____

_____

_____

_____

_____

_____

_____

_____

_____

_____

_____

_____

Réaliseras-tu ce programme de mise en forme en solo ou en groupe ?

En solo ☐   En groupe ☐

Indique les personnes qui t'accompagneront.

Amis ☐   Camarades de classe ☐

Coéquipiers d'une équipe de sport ☐   Membres de la famille ☐

En tenant compte de ta disponibilité, des équipements auxquels tu as facilement accès et de ta condition physique, prends quelques minutes pour remplir le tableau ci-dessous. Il s'agit en quelque sorte de ton plan de match pour le volet Activité physique.

Modalité de pratique et horaire d'une semaine type

Activités	Fréquence/semaine	Durée/séance	Intensité/séance	Horaire type
1.	1 fois ☐	20 min ☐	Modérée ☐	**Lundi :** de ____ h à ____ h
	2 fois ☐	30 min ☐	Élevée ☐	**Mardi :** de ____ h à ____ h
	3 fois ☐	35 min ☐	Modérée et élevée ☐	**Mercredi :** de ____ h à ____ h
	4 fois ☐	40 min ☐	Calcul de ta Fcc* :	**Jeudi :** de ____ h à ____ h
	5 fois ☐	45 min ☐	Min _____	**Vendredi :** de ____ h à ____ h
	6 fois ☐	50 min ☐	Max _____	**Samedi :** de ____ h à ____ h
	7 fois ☐	60 min ☐		**Dimanche :** de ____ h à ____ h
		_____ min		

* Calcul de la fréquence cardiaque cible (FCC) : 220 — âge
Par exemple, si tu as 13 ans, voici le calcul :
FCC : 220 — 13 = 207
FCC minimale : 207 × 75 % = 155 battements/min
FCC maximale : 207 × 85 % = 176 battements/min
Ta FCC devra donc se situer entre 155 et 176 battements/min pendant ton effort cardiovasculaire.

TON PLAN D'ACTION

Activités	Fréquence/semaine	Durée/séance	Intensité/séance	Horaire type
2.	1 FOIS ☐ 2 FOIS ☐ 3 FOIS ☐ 4 FOIS ☐ 5 FOIS ☐ 6 FOIS ☐ 7 FOIS ☐	20 min ☐ 30 min ☐ 35 min ☐ 40 min ☐ 45 min ☐ 50 min ☐ 60 min ☐ _____ min	MODÉRÉE ☐ ÉLEVÉE ☐ MODÉRÉE ET ÉLEVÉE ☐ CALCUL DE TA FCC* : MIN _____ MAX _____	**Lundi :** de _____ h à _____ h **Mardi :** de _____ h à _____ h **Mercredi :** de _____ h à _____ h **Jeudi :** de _____ h à _____ h **Vendredi :** de _____ h à _____ h **Samedi :** de _____ h à _____ h **Dimanche :** de _____ h à _____ h
3.	1 FOIS ☐ 2 FOIS ☐ 3 FOIS ☐ 4 FOIS ☐ 5 FOIS ☐ 6 FOIS ☐ 7 FOIS ☐	20 min ☐ 30 min ☐ 35 min ☐ 40 min ☐ 45 min ☐ 50 min ☐ 60 min ☐ _____ min	MODÉRÉE ☐ ÉLEVÉE ☐ MODÉRÉE ET ÉLEVÉE ☐ CALCUL DE TA FCC* : MIN _____ MAX _____	**Lundi :** de _____ h à _____ h **Mardi :** de _____ h à _____ h **Mercredi :** de _____ h à _____ h **Jeudi :** de _____ h à _____ h **Vendredi :** de _____ h à _____ h **Samedi :** de _____ h à _____ h **Dimanche :** de _____ h à _____ h

* Calcul de la fréquence cardiaque cible (FCC) : 220 — âge

Par exemple, si tu as 13 ans, voici le calcul :

FCC : 220 — 13 = 207

FCC minimale : 207 × 75 % = 155 battements/min

FCC maximale : 207 × 85 % = 176 battements/min

Ta FCC devra donc se situer entre 155 et 176 battements / min pendant ton effort cardiovasculaire.

ÉTAPE 2 — Volet Habitudes de vie

Ton objectif : Améliorer trois comportements liés aux habitudes de vie, *autres que la pratique régulière de l'activité physique.*

Dans le tableau ci-dessous, on te présente une liste de comportements à adopter en matière d'alimentation, de sommeil et d'hygiène personnelle. Tu peux effectuer tes choix parmi ceux-ci ou en choisir d'autres de ton cru.

Habitudes en matière d'alimentation	Habitudes en matière de sommeil	Habitudes en matière d'hygiène personnelle
Déjeuner tous les matins.	Essayer de me coucher à la même heure le plus souvent possible.	Me brosser les dents chaque jour.
Manger plus de fruits et de légumes.	Éviter d'avoir des pensées négatives au moment d'aller au lit.	Passer la soie dentaire au moins une fois par jour.
Manger des céréales riches en grains entiers.	Éviter de faire des activités physiques vigoureuses deux heures avant de me coucher.	Me laver les mains avant de manger ou après un passage aux toilettes.
Consommer tous les jours du lait ou des substituts du lait (ex. : fromage, yogourt, boisson de soya).	Respecter le nombre d'heures de sommeil dont j'ai besoin (surtout la semaine).	Me laver les cheveux régulièrement.
Éviter de grignoter en regardant la télé ou en surfant sur Internet.	Éviter de consommer des produits contenant de la caféine le soir.	Prendre ma douche après mon cours d'éducation physique et à la santé.
Modérer ma consommation d'aliments riches en gras, en sucre raffiné et en sel (ex. : pâtisseries, beignes, frites, crous-tilles, crème glacée, boissons gazeuses).		Porter des vêtements appropriés et utiliser des équipements adéquats quand je pratique une activité physique.
Éviter de manger juste avant d'aller au lit.		Prendre les moyens nécessaires pour mieux dormir.
Prendre une collation santé l'avant-midi et l'après-midi (ex. : un fruit, un jus de fruit naturel, des noix, du fromage, etc.).		
Boire suffisamment d'eau quand je suis physiquement actif ou active.		

Indique trois comportements liés à tes habitudes de vie que tu souhaites modifier. Par exemple : manger au moins quatre portions de fruits et légumes par jour ; te coucher à des heures régulières ; ne pas fumer ; etc.

Comportement 1	
Comportement 2	
Comportement 3	

Justifie chacun de tes choix.

_____

_____

_____

TON PLAN D'ACTION

ÉTAPE 3 ## Ton journal de bord

Tiens ton journal de bord à jour pendant les huit semaines d'application de ton plan d'action

	Volet Activité physique			Volet Habitudes de vie
	ACTIVITÉS	**DURÉE TOTALE**	**INTENSITÉ MOYENNE** MODÉRÉE (M) ÉLEVÉE (E) MODÉRÉE ET ÉLEVÉE (ME)	**COMPORTEMENTS À MODIFIER** J'Y PARVIENS TOUJOURS (A) J'Y PARVIENS DE TEMPS À AUTRE (B) J'Y PARVIENS RAREMENT (C)
Semaine 1 _____ au _____ du _____	1. _____	_____	INTENSITÉ ____ FCC ENREGISTRÉE : ____	**Comportement 1** ___
	2. _____	_____	INTENSITÉ ____ FCC ENREGISTRÉE : ____	**Comportement 2** ___
	3. _____	_____	INTENSITÉ ____ FCC ENREGISTRÉE : ____	**Comportement 3** ___
Semaine 2 _____ au _____ du _____	1. _____	_____	INTENSITÉ ____ FCC ENREGISTRÉE : ____	**Comportement 1** ___
	2. _____	_____	INTENSITÉ ____ FCC ENREGISTRÉE : ____	**Comportement 2** ___
	3. _____	_____	INTENSITÉ ____ FCC ENREGISTRÉE : ____	**Comportement 3** ___

AJUSTEMENTS À APPORTER, SI NÉCESSAIRE, APRÈS CES DEUX SEMAINES

Tu expérimentes ton plan d'action depuis maintenant deux semaines. Note, s'il y a lieu, les difficultés que tu as éprouvées.

_____

_____

_____

Crois-tu pouvoir surmonter ces difficultés ?   OUI ☐   NON ☐

Si oui, comment ?

_____

_____

_____

Si non, as-tu apporté des changements à ton plan ? Lesquels ?

_____

_____

	Volet Activité physique			Volet Habitudes de vie
	ACTIVITÉS	**DURÉE TOTALE**	**INTENSITÉ MOYENNE** MODÉRÉE (M) ÉLEVÉE (E) MODÉRÉE ET ÉLEVÉE (ME)	**COMPORTEMENTS À MODIFIER** J'Y PARVIENS TOUJOURS (A) J'Y PARVIENS DE TEMPS À AUTRE (B) J'Y PARVIENS RAREMENT (C)
Semaine 3 du ____ au ____	1. _____	_____	INTENSITÉ ____ FCC ENREGISTRÉE : ____	**Comportement 1** ___
	2. _____	_____	INTENSITÉ ____ FCC ENREGISTRÉE : ____	**Comportement 2** ___
	3. _____	_____	INTENSITÉ ____ FCC ENREGISTRÉE : ____	**Comportement 3** ___
Semaine 4 du ____ au ____	1. _____	_____	INTENSITÉ ____ FCC ENREGISTRÉE : ____	**Comportement 1** ___
	2. _____	_____	INTENSITÉ ____ FCC ENREGISTRÉE : ____	**Comportement 2** ___
	3. _____	_____	INTENSITÉ ____ FCC ENREGISTRÉE : ____	**Comportement 3** ___

AJUSTEMENTS À APPORTER, SI NÉCESSAIRE, APRÈS CES DEUX SEMAINES

Tu expérimentes ton plan d'action depuis maintenant quatre semaines. Note, s'il y a lieu, les difficultés que tu as éprouvées.

_____

_____

_____

Crois-tu pouvoir surmonter ces difficultés ?   OUI ☐   NON ☐

Si oui, comment ?

_____

_____

_____

Si non, as-tu apporté des changements à ton plan ? Lesquels ?

_____

_____

_____

TON PLAN D'ACTION

	Activités	Durée totale	Intensité moyenne Modérée (M) Élevée (E) Modérée et élevée (ME)	Comportements à modifier J'y parviens toujours (A) J'y parviens de temps à autre (B) J'y parviens rarement (C)
Volet Activité physique				**Volet Habitudes de vie**
Semaine 5 du ___ au ___	1. _____ ___		Intensité ____ Fcc enregistrée : ____	**Comportement 1** ___
	2. _____		Intensité ____ Fcc enregistrée : ____	**Comportement 2** ___
	3. _____		Intensité ____ Fcc enregistrée : ____	**Comportement 3** ___
Semaine 6 du ___ au ___	1. _____ ___		Intensité ____ Fcc enregistrée : ____	**Comportement 1** ___
	2. _____		Intensité ____ Fcc enregistrée : ____	**Comportement 2** ___
	3. _____ ___		Intensité ____ Fcc enregistrée : ____	**Comportement 3** ___

AJUSTEMENTS À APPORTER, SI NÉCESSAIRE, APRÈS CES DEUX SEMAINES

Tu expérimentes ton plan d'action depuis maintenant six semaines. Note, s'il y a lieu, les difficultés que tu as éprouvées.

_____

_____

_____

Crois-tu pouvoir surmonter ces difficultés?   OUI ☐   NON ☐

Si oui, comment?

_____

_____

_____

Si non, as-tu apporté des changements à ton plan? Lesquels?

_____

_____

_____

	Volet Activité physique			Volet Habitudes de vie
	ACTIVITÉS	**DURÉE TOTALE**	**INTENSITÉ MOYENNE** MODÉRÉE (M) ÉLEVÉE (E) MODÉRÉE ET ÉLEVÉE (ME)	**COMPORTEMENTS À MODIFIER** J'Y PARVIENS TOUJOURS (A) J'Y PARVIENS DE TEMPS À AUTRE (B) J'Y PARVIENS RAREMENT (C)
Semaine 7 du ____ au ____	1. _____	_____	INTENSITÉ ____ FCC ENREGISTRÉE: ____	**Comportement 1** ___
	2. _____	_____	INTENSITÉ ____ FCC ENREGISTRÉE: ____	**Comportement 2** ___
	3. _____	_____	INTENSITÉ ____ FCC ENREGISTRÉE: ____	**Comportement 3** ___
Semaine 8 du ____ au ____	1. _____	_____	INTENSITÉ ____ FCC ENREGISTRÉE: ____	**Comportement 1** ___
	2. _____	_____	INTENSITÉ ____ FCC ENREGISTRÉE: ____	**Comportement 2** ___
	3. _____	_____	INTENSITÉ ____ FCC ENREGISTRÉE: ____	**Comportement 3** ___

AJUSTEMENTS À APPORTER, SI NÉCESSAIRE, APRÈS CES DEUX SEMAINES

Tu expérimentes ton plan d'action depuis maintenant huit semaines. Note, s'il y a lieu, les difficultés que tu as éprouvées.

_____

_____

_____

Crois-tu pouvoir surmonter ces difficultés ?   OUI ☐   NON ☐

Si oui, comment ?

_____

_____

_____

Si non, as-tu apporté des changements à ton plan ? Lesquels ?

_____

_____

_____

_____

TON PLAN D'ACTION

ÉTAPE 4   ## Ton bilan

Te voilà enfin au fil d'arrivée après huit semaines d'application de ton plan d'action.

A. As-tu atteint ton objectif en ce qui concerne ton endurance cardiovasculaire ?

Oui ☐   Non ☐

Si oui, démontre-le en reportant ici les résultats des évaluations de ton endurance cardiovasculaire.

Nom du test	Test 1 Date : _____	Test 2 Date : _____	Test 3 Date : _____
_____	Résultat : _____ Niveau : _____	Résultat : _____ Niveau : _____	Résultat : _____ Niveau : _____

Si non, parmi les raisons suivantes, coche celles qui pourraient expliquer que tu n'aies pas atteint ton objectif.

Manque de régularité ☐   Durée de l'effort insuffisante ☐

Intensité de l'effort trop faible ☐   Fréquence hebdomadaire insuffisante ☐

B. As-tu atteint ton objectif du volet Habitudes de vie en ce qui concerne l'amélioration de trois comportements ?

Oui, à 100 % ☐

Oui, en partie ☐

Non, pas du tout ☐

Indique le ou les comportements que tu n'as pas réussi à améliorer.

_____

_____

_____

_____

Pour quelles raisons, selon toi, n'as-tu pas atteint ton objectif à 100 % ?

_____

_____

_____

_____

_____

Nom: Groupe: Date:

C. Ce que tu retiens

D. Ce que tu comprends

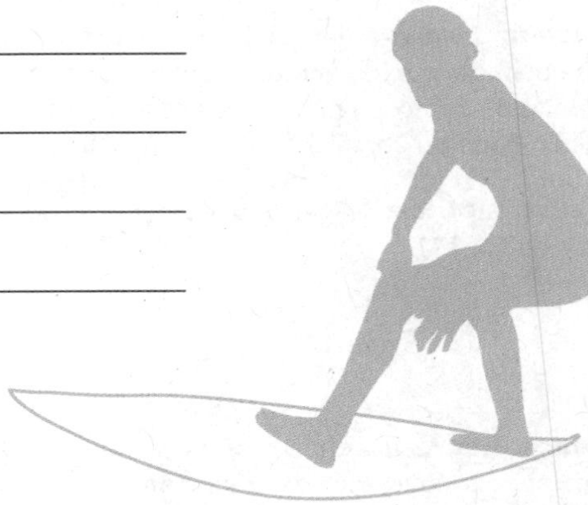

Glossaire

A

Accident : Événement malheureux qui cause des dégâts, des blessures, voire la mort **(p. 35)**.

Anémie : Appauvrissement du sang en fer. Les principaux symptômes de l'anémie sont la pâleur et la faiblesse **(p. 33)**.

Anorexie : Syndrome observé surtout chez les adolescentes et caractérisé par une restriction volontaire et souvent ina-vouée de l'alimentation, provoquant une aménorrhée (arrêt des règles) et un amaigrissement important **(p. 74)**.

Apnée du sommeil : Suspension plus ou moins prolongée de la respiration durant le sommeil **(p. 87)**.

Autorégulation : Régulation d'un processus physiologique par l'organisme lui-même, sans intervention extérieure **(p. 76)**.

B

Boulimie : Trouble de l'alimentation caractérisé par des accès irrésistibles de fringale, contraignant la personne à l'in-gestion massive et ininterrompue de grandes quantités d'ali-ments, suivis de comportements compensatoires inappropriés (ex. : vomissements provoqués, laxatifs, jeûnes, séances d'acti-vité physique excessives) ou d'endormissement **(p. 74)**.

Bruxisme : Fait de grincer des dents en dormant **(p. 87)**.

C

Cannabis : Plante dont le principe actif responsable des effets psychotropes est le THC (tétrahydrocannabinol), une substance toxique inscrite sur la liste des drogues illégales. Sa concentration est très variable selon les préparations et la pro-venance du produit, mais elle est de plus en plus élevée grâce aux techniques de sélection et de manipulation génétique. Le cannabis est à la fois un psychostimulant et un psychodé-presseur. Il agit comme une substance hallucinogène **(p. 92)**.

Concentration : Capacité de maintenir une performance sur une longue période, qui dépend du maintien de la vigilance, de la capacité de détection du stimulus et de la résistance à la distraction, donc du contrôle de l'esprit **(p. 19)**.

Coordination motrice : Capacité à réaliser un mouvement avec précision **(p. 11)**.

D

Dépendance : État résultant de la consommation répétée d'une substance toxique, qui se caractérise par le besoin de continuer la prise et d'augmenter les doses **(p. 92)**.

Détente mentale : Relâchement d'une tension intellectuelle, morale, nerveuse **(p. 19)**.

E

Effort physique : Mobilisation de toutes les forces du corps en vue d'atteindre un but **(p. 19)**.

Endurance cardiovasculaire : Capacité du cœur et des poumons de fournir, pendant un certain temps, un effort modéré qui fait travailler l'ensemble des muscles de manière dynamique **(p. 52)**.

F

Fascia plantaire : Large bande fibreuse qui court sous le pied, depuis le talon jusqu'à la base des orteils, et qui recouvre tendons et ligaments **(p. 36)**.

Flexibilité : Caractère de ce qui se courbe facilement **(p. 19)**.

G

Glucide de digestion lente : Sucre que l'organisme met un certain temps à digérer et, donc, à assimiler. Lorsqu'on mange ce type de sucre, le taux de sucre dans le sang augmente lentement, et non subitement, comme c'est le cas des sucres simples, tels que ceux contenus dans les sucreries. Les fruits, les légumes, le lait, les céréales à grains entiers, les pommes de terre, pour n'en nommer que quelques-uns, sont des ali-ments riches en sucres complexes **(p. 78)**.

Glycogène : Glucide emmagasiné principalement dans les muscles et le foie, et formé de grosses molécules de sucre. Ces grosses molécules font en sorte que, une fois le glycogène formé dans le muscle, il ne peut en ressortir. Le glycogène est une source d'énergie de premier plan pour les cellules musculaires **(p. 78)**.

H

Hippocampe : Zone du cerveau essentielle à la mémoire et à l'apprentissage, située dans les hémisphères gauche et droit. C'est dans l'hippocampe que se déroule la phase d'enregis-trement de la mémoire : un souvenir – une odeur, un poème, un visage, le chemin de l'école – doit être enregistré avant d'être stocké dans le cerveau.

Si, à la suite d'un accident, l'hippocampe est endommagé, on peut se souvenir des informations enregistrées avant l'accident, mais on aura beaucoup de mal à acquérir de nouveaux souvenirs **(p. 22)**.

I

Insomniaque : Personne qui a de la difficulté à s'endormir **(p. 87)**.

N

Nutritionniste : Personne titulaire d'un diplôme universitaire en nutrition, qui se consacre à l'étude des aliments, de leur valeur nutritive, des réactions de l'organisme à la suite de leur ingestion, et des variations alimentaires chez les gens sains et les gens malades **(p. 70)**.

O

Œstrogène : Hormone sexuelle femelle, produite par les ovaires **(p. 13)**.

P

Perception : Acte par lequel l'esprit et les sens saisissent les objets et les personnes, et les interprètent **(p. 12)**.

Périphérie : Surface extérieure d'un volume **(p. 41)**.

Poids-santé : Poids d'une personne auquel est associé le plus faible risque de développer certains problèmes de santé **(p. 19)**.

Progestérone : Hormone de la gestation, produite par les ovaires **(p. 13)**.

S

Somnambulisme : Automatisme inconscient se manifestant pendant le sommeil par des actes plus ou moins coordonnés (ex. : se lever, marcher, exécuter une tâche simple, etc.) dont il ne reste à la personne aucun souvenir au réveil **(p. 87)**.

Somniloquie : Fait de parler en dormant **(p. 87)**.

Substance illicite : Matière interdite par la loi **(p. 92)**.

Syndrome des jambes sans repos : Sensation désagréable et indéfinissable ressentie dans les membres inférieurs, déclenchée par l'immobilité, provoquant un irrépressible besoin de bouger les jambes en les agitant, en se levant ou en marchant **(p. 87)**.

Système immunitaire : Ensemble des moyens de défense de l'organisme contre les agressions extérieures **(p. 33)**.

T

Tension : État des muscles qui subissent un étirement ou un raccourcissement de leurs fibres **(p. 52)**.

Terreur nocturne : Cauchemar entraînant une peur aiguë **(p. 87)**.

Testostérone : Hormone sexuelle mâle, sécrétée par les testicules **(p. 13)**.

V

Vigueur des muscles : Capacité d'un muscle à être endurant ou fort, ou mieux encore, à être endurant et fort à la fois.

Les muscles travaillent en endurance lorsqu'ils répètent pendant un certain temps une contraction avec un effort modéré.

Les muscles travaillent en force lorsqu'ils développent une forte tension au moment d'une contraction maximale de courte durée **(p. 52)**.

Z

Zone d'entraînement cardiovasculaire : Zone qui correspond à une intensité modérée de l'effort, soit le niveau d'intensité nécessaire pour améliorer ou maintenir à un niveau satisfaisant son endurance cardiovasculaire lors de la pratique d'une activité physique ou d'un sport **(p. 53)**.

Sources iconographiques

Photographies

CORBIS
p. 20 : Juice Images
p. 24 : K. Dodge
p. 46 : P. Barret
p. 75 (haut)
p. 79 (gauche) : Reix – Liewig/For Picture
p. 79 (droite) : F. Maohua/Xinhua Press

CP IMAGES
Couverture 1 (gauche) : AP Photo/
E. Verdugo
Couverture 1 (haut) : Ableimages
p. 14 (haut) : A. Wyld
p. 14 (centre) : AP Photo/T. Avelar
p. 14 (bas) : S. Kilpatrick
p. 75 (bas) : AP Photo/ M. Villagran
p. 80 : AP Photo/E. Savio

PHOTOTHÈQUE ERPI
p. 28 à 31
p. 62 à 65

PUBLIPHOTO/SCIENCE PHOTO LIBRARY
p. 33 (bas)

SHUTTERSTOCK
Couverture 1 (bas) : R. Becker-
Leckrome
Couverture 1 (centre) : K. Nichols
Couverture 1 (droite) : F. Pfluegl
p. 2-3 : Rgbspace
p. 6 : N. Lukiyanova/frenta
p. 7 (haut) : A. Kalina
p. 7 (bas) : IKO
p. 8 (gauche) : B. Nowak
p. 8 (droite) : Ackab Photography
p. 12-13 : G. Andrushko
p. 15 : J.-P. Kervinen
p. 15 (bas) : W. Cole
p. 16-17 : R. Becker-Leckrone
p. 17 (1) : S. Kovalev
p. 17 (2) : K. Nichols
p. 17 (3) : D. Shironosov
p. 17 (4) : J. Salcedo
p. 17 (5) : M. Krasnorutskaya
p. 18 (haut) : L. Medina
p. 18 (bas) : Gordan
p. 19 : Yobidaba
p. 21 : Kudryashka
p. 22 (haut) : Creations
p. 22 (bas) : T. Oliveira
p. 23 : K. A. Valerevich

p. 25 : K. Sekulic
p. 26 : M. Godbehear
p. 32 (bas) : E. Cote
p. 33 (haut) : S. Barnett
p. 34 : J. Moucka
p. 35 (haut) : Ulga
p. 35 (bas) : S. D. Kizil
p. 36 (bas) : stkobi
p. 37-38 : B. Maya
p. 39 (haut) : kozvic49
p. 40 : AlArt
p. 41-42 : Designus
p. 42 (droite) : J. Collingwood
p. 44 : R. Sumners
p. 47 : Roca
p. 48 : Ighost
p. 49 : G. Andrushko
p. 51
p. 52 : D. Shironosov
p. 53 : S. Kaulitzki
p. 54 : prism_68
p. 61 : S. Strathdee
p. 66 : Palto
p. 66-67 : B. Mazur
p. 69 : Roca
p. 71 : Morgan Lane Photography
p. 71 (haut, droite) : C. Baldini
p. 72 : K. A. Valerevich
p. 76 : D. Gilbey
p. 78 : D. Kappa
p. 77 (haut) : K. Sekulic
p. 77 (bas) : V. Polyakov
p. 81 (haut, droite) : K. Chagin
p. 81 (centre, droite) : Constant
p. 81 (bas) : K. Ioannhs
p. 83 : S. Coburn
p. 84 : Ustyujanin
p. 85 et 86 : K. D. French
p. 87 : M. Taylor
p. 89 : A. E. Knost
p. 91 : marylooo
p. 92 : Maxx-Studio
p. 93 : D. Zidar
p. 95 : Ighost
Couverture 4

TANGO PHOTOGRAPHIE
p. 39 (bas)
p. 57 à 60

TORTORA, G.J., DERICKSON, B., PRINCIPLES OF ANATOMY & PHYSIOLOGY, 11TH EDITION, JOHN WYLEY AND SONS, Inc.
p. 36 (gauche) : L. Dank

Documents écrits

UNE VIE SAINE ET ACTIVE
p. 6, 8 et 9 : Dimitri HAIKIN, psychologue, psychothérapeute et directeur du site Internet www.psy.be, « La cyberdépendance, nouvelle drogue des temps modernes ? », *Psy.be* [en ligne]. (Consulté le 5 février 2009.)

L'ACTIVITÉ PHYSIQUE
p. 24 : Québec, Kino-Québec, *Les jeunes et l'activité physique, situation préoccupante ou alarmante ?* [en ligne, pages 16-17]. (Consulté le 4 février 2009.)
p. 32 (bas) : Canada, Santé Canada, *Vie saine : sécurité et blessures* [en ligne]. (Consulté le 4 février 2009.)
p. 39 : Adapté de Québec, Régie régionale de la santé et des services sociaux Montérégie-Lanaudière, *Plein le dos… sans gros maux* [en ligne]. (Consulté le 26 novembre 2008.)
p. 43 : Conseil de médecine du sport du Québec, *L'entraînement en force chez les jeunes : mythes, réalités et recommandations* [en ligne]. (Consulté le 5 février 2009.)

L'ALIMENTATION
p. 73 : Adapté d'Équilibre, Groupe d'action sur le poids, *4 bonnes raisons de ne pas suivre une diète* [en ligne]. (Consulté le 5 février 2009.)
p. 74-75 (haut) : Adapté de Doctissimo, *Les troubles du comportement alimentaire : anorexie et boulimie* [en ligne]. (Consulté le 22 janvier 2009.)
p. 80 : LCI Monde, *Brésil – Un mannequin de 18 ans meurt d'anorexie* [en ligne]. (Consulté le 4 mars 2009.)

LE SOMMEIL
p. 86 (bas) : e-santé, *Les ados manquent de sommeil…* [en ligne]. (Consulté le 5 février 2009.)